John Hamilton was born ... ern Australia with his family ... ter serving in the Royal Austr ... er-man, establishing himself i ... ed as a reporter and foreign co ... eer took him to Washington, where he worked as White House correspondent, and to London, where he was chief correspondent and European editor for the Herald and Weekly Times group of newspapers.

His interest in Gallipoli began in 2000 when he was assigned by the *Herald Sun* to go to Turkey to cover the 85th anniversary of the landing at Anzac Cove. Since then he has returned to the peninsula six more times with the Australian War Memorial, writing feature articles and the bestselling books *Goodbye Cobber, God Bless You* and *Gallipoli Sniper*.

In 2011 he was awarded the Melbourne Press Club's Quill Lifetime Achievement Award, the latest in a list of honours that includes winning Australia's top award for journalism, the Walkley, two years in succession as well as the National Press Club Canadian Award of Journalistic Merit, for his international reporting. He was also nominated twice for the Graham Perkin Award for the Australian Journalist of the Year, for which he received a High Commendation.

John is a lifetime Australia Day Ambassador, holder of the Shrine of Remembrance Medal and is currently Adjunct Professor of Journalism Leadership at Swinburne University. Married to Charlotte Kay Ballard, he has two sons, James and Matthew.

Also by John Hamilton

Goodbye Cobber, God Bless You
Gallipoli Sniper

The PRICE of VALOUR

The PRICE of VALOUR

JOHN HAMILTON

PAN
Pan Macmillan Australia

First published 2012 in Macmillan by Pan Macmillan Australia Pty Limited
This Pan edition published in 2013 by Pan Macmillan Australia Pty Limited
1 Market Street, Sydney

National Library of Australia
Cataloguing-in-Publication data:

Hamilton, John, 1940–.

The price of valour: the triumph and tragedy of a Gallipoli hero, Hugo Throssell, VC / John Hamilton.

ISBN: 9781742613369 (pbk.)

Throssell, Hugo, 1884–1933.
Soldiers—Australia—Biography.
World War, 1914–1918—Campaigns—Turkey—Gallipoli Peninsula—Biography.
World War, 1914–1918—Campaigns—Palestine—Biography.
Victoria Cross—Biography.

940.426092

Typeset in 12/15 Sabon by Midland Typesetters, Australia
Printed in Australia by McPherson's Printing Group
Cartographic art by Laurie Whiddon, Map Illustrations

To Hugo Vivian Hope Throssell

To you, all these wild weeds
And wind flowers of my life,
I bring, my lord,
And lay them at your feet;
They are not frankincense
Or myrrh,
But you were Krishna, Christ and Dionysos
In your beauty, tenderness and strength.

– Katharine Susannah Prichard

Contents

Anzac positions on the Gallipoli peninsula, 1915

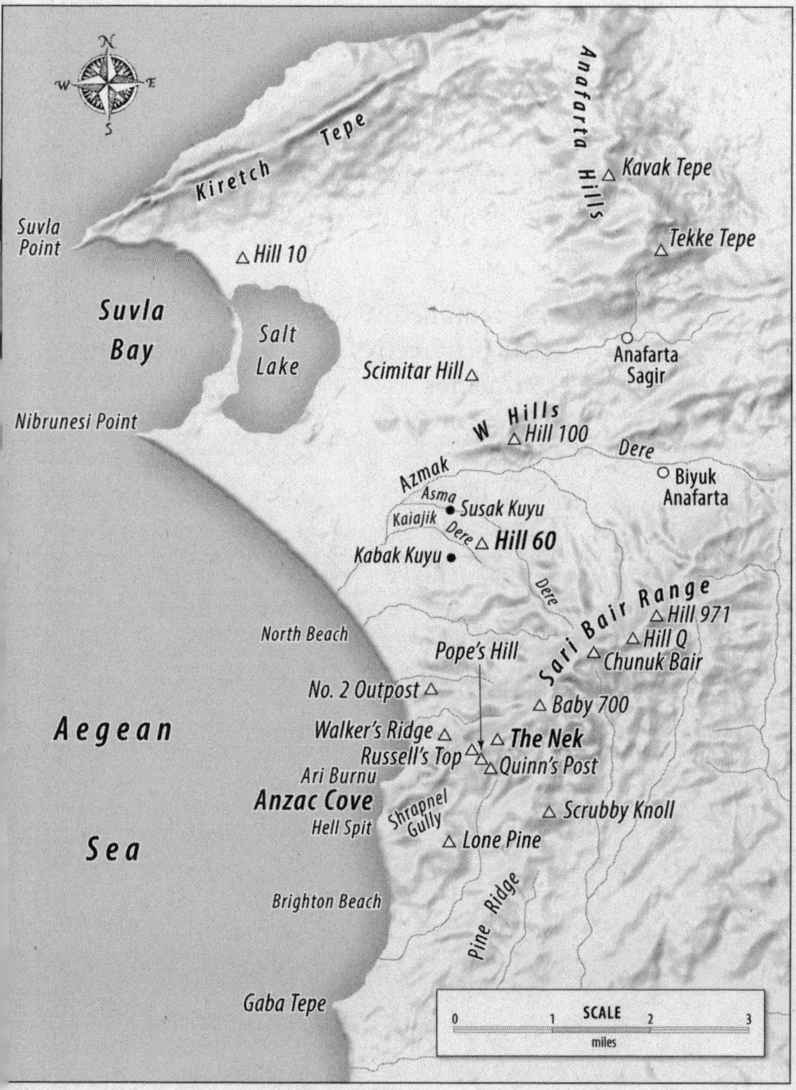

Author's note

The imperial system of measurements has been used throughout the book, reflecting its use in the source material. A quick conversion guide to the metric system is below, rounded to two decimal places.

1 inch	=	2.54 centimetres
1 foot	=	30.48 centimetres
1 yard	=	0.91 metres
1 mile	=	1.61 kilometres
1 ounce	=	28.35 grams
1 pennyweight	=	1.56 grams
1 pound	=	0.45 kilograms
1 ton	=	1.02 tonnes
1 acre	=	0.40 hectares
1 gallon	=	4.55 litres

Sterling currency symbols

£ = pound
s = shilling
d = pence

Introduction: Bomba Tepe

IN THE RECORDS OF THE First World War, the Suvla campaign on Gallipoli has come to mean failure, the well-tended war cemeteries, with their row upon row of flat markers, reminders of Allied disasters. Not many visitors come to this great plain now, with its gentle foothills climbing through thick, thorny, bush-covered spurs to the commanding heights of Sari Bair. Not many come to its war cemeteries, either. The flowers are tended and the grass is mown between the rows of headstones by Turkish workers employed by the Commonwealth War Graves Commission, but there are no worn footpaths here as there are at Anzac, marking the annual passage of thousands of Australian and New Zealand pilgrims. Few of these visitors bother to travel northwards on and up to Hill 60.

In winter Suvla is a forbidding place, bleak, windswept and very cold. In summer the great salt lake by the sea shimmers white in the heat, the fields are parched and brown with stubble, the scrub is thorny and impassable, and there is heat, more heat, and plagues of flies. That is when Hugo Throssell and the foreigners fought here, when the days were hot and the nights were often bitterly cold.

Yet springtime in Suvla is a warm, welcoming season when the plain and the foothills are green and beautiful, larks sing, the air hums with bees droning about their business, and wild crimson and dark, black-centred poppies sprinkle the landscape like drops of blood. It is springtime on Gallipoli when I visit; there has been a long, cold winter followed by heavy rains. The weather is still very changeable as the sap oozes white from fresh green shoots in the sunshine and the earth stirs for another season. It is cool and drizzly one day, warm and soft the next. Boot-clogging mud that drags your feet down dries out quickly and puffs up like dust as you walk along the same track twenty-four hours later.

The fields have been ploughed into thick brown furrows. Wheat is already vivid green, and other crops are being planted. When the weather settles more, black irrigation piping will be put into some fields, and the village women will be out, in their head coverings and baggy pants, stooping low as they plant tomato seedlings. In the little villages where they come from, like Biyuk Anafarta and Anafarta Sagir, the men will wait to take them home, sitting outside the town café in the shadow of the minaret, stirring lumps of sugar into their glasses of strong tea or cups of thick, sludgy coffee, talking as they always have of weather and crops, religion and politics. There may be the distant thunder of Turkish Air Force jet fighters on patrol overhead. The Dardanelles remains strategically important. Like the bees guarding their hives on the Suvla plain, the Turks are suspicious and alert, welcoming visitors but still wary. The red Turkish flag with its white crescent moon and star flaps proudly from many flagpoles. In every café, every business, every home, there is a plaque or portrait of Mustafa Kemal Atatürk, the first president and founder of modern secular Turkey, the wartime colonel with eyes like a hawk who once gazed down on Hill 60 and directed the battles against the invaders, the infidels, from the heights above.

We go for a walk on this April day in 2011, Kenan Çelik and I. Kenan is a historian and the pre-eminent guide to the battlefields of the Gallipoli peninsula. He leads the way up a track about 3 miles to the north of Anzac Cove. We have gone only 10 yards when he stoops and picks up a small green copper-coloured object. It is a spent bullet casing fired by a Turkish soldier from his Mauser rifle nearly 100 years ago.

Outside Biyuk Anafarta there is an overgrown local cemetery. Two graves stand alone, outside the boundary, in a place of honour beneath a carved stone pavilion. Kenan points out the names: Lieutenant Colonel Halit Bey of the 20th Infantry Regiment and Lieutenant Colonel Ziya Bey of the 21st Infantry Regiment. Their headstones say they were Martyrs, killed in the battle for Hill 60. They mark the only known graves of at least 576 Turkish soldiers killed on the hill.

The sign to Hill 60 is near the turn-off to Biyuk Anafarta. It sits on top of a rusting pole planted in a freshly ploughed paddock whose ridges and furrows, deep, brown and rich, contain soil that nearly a century ago became so well fertilised with human blood and bone that even now the crops seem to grow thicker and greener each springtime. The sign points along a track that meanders its way gently upwards to what the Australian war correspondent and official historian Charles Bean described as 'little more than a swelling in the plain'. Does this track really lead to a hill? Should it qualify even as a mound? To call it a hill seems far too grand, an exaggeration. We follow the sign and wander easily up the rutted road, which is only wide enough for a tractor, towards the mound and its grove of pine trees, where the wind sighs over the war cemetery with its flat grave markers and white memorials.

The Turks once called the swelling 'Kaiajic Aghyl' – 'Sheepfold of the Little Rock'. But as the generals studied the landmarks on their rough map of the Gallipoli peninsula after the first landings, on 25 April 1915, and as the gunners got to work on the map, simplifying names for the artillery, the Sheepfold of the Little Rock became 'Hill 60', as it lay within the 60-metre contour. The sea can be seen easily from the hill, which is really a long, slow rise on the seaward face, but sharper and steeper on the other sides. It is a spur in a branch of the more extensive Damakjelik Bair, a tangled network of hills and valleys that rise eastwards to the dark, brooding heights of Sari Bair.

Late in August 1915, Hill 60 became, briefly, a name symbolic of bloodshed and valour. Then it became a dim memory, overshadowed by the events of battles fought earlier in the same month. Hill 60 witnessed the Anzacs' forgotten fight.

We walk up the track. Ellis Ashmead-Bartlett, a British war correspondent here in 1915, wrote about a Gallipoli plains landscape of 'dark green, light green, and bright yellow . . . In a short ride across country you found yourself amid olive groves, Turkey oaks, witch elms, apricots and almonds, Scottish firs, and small tamarisks . . . You ride over fields and through gardens in which flowers abound in a reckless and beautiful profusion'. He also described the bird life: pigeons, kestrels, magpies, rollers, blackcaps, tits and red-throated warblers. We pass about thirty beehives set beside the track. A lone worker bee hovers, buzzing, like a suspicious sentinel, over purple irises that border a cemetery. In springtime Gallipoli hums and sings with life.

The Hill 60 cemetery is small and round, sited over some of the old Allied fire and communication trenches. At the end of the August battles, some were already filled with the dead. A British officer, Captain R Dudley Pendred, wrote: 'The sight of a dead hand sticking out from the wall of a trench with fingers and great long nails, as if in the act of scratching, was most revolting; as was that of a half decomposed scalp hanging over the parados'.

Today the only smell is the sweet fragrance of fresh pine from the grove to the side. The cemetery contains 754 burials. Only the graves of seventeen New Zealand, fourteen Australian and eleven British soldiers are known. There are also special memorials to another sixteen Australians, sixteen British and two New Zealanders either known or believed to have been buried somewhere here. The New Zealand Mounted Rifle Brigade sustained particularly heavy casualties in the battle for the hill and has its own memorial, a big cross in the centre of the cemetery recording the names of 182 officers and men who have no known graves. The main flat memorial stone in front of the cross provides a convenient table for compass and maps, to help you to get your bearings as you near the 'summit' of Hill 60.

Kenan leads the way out of the cemetery and heads onwards up the slight hill. Suddenly the evidence of war is everywhere. Lead shrapnel balls sit in furrows like round grey slugs, squares of rusty iron bomb fragments lie as neat as chocolate blocks, twisted scraps of spent green copper bullet casings pepper the soil, and short lengths of barbed wire sprout from the ridges. Then we see traces of a lost generation. A shirt button. The eyelet from a soldier's boot, still with a shred of leather attached. And then the human remains. Bone shards at first, some looking like pieces of white honeycomb, but brittle, and crumbly like aged cheese, others smooth, like creamy marble. And, in a deep furrow, unmistakably part of a femur.

The wind sighs again as Kenan leads me into a thick patch of pine forest. We push our way between branches that whip at our faces, our footsteps deadened by the thick brown carpet of pine needles. Kenan points. The forest floor is a maze of deep indentations: the trenches.

I try to imagine here, on this spot, Second Lieutenant Hugo Throssell in the immediate aftermath of the battle early on an August morning in 1915. Still in the trench he had charged, captured and held against the enemy in the darkness, now in the dawn, dazed, wounded and bloody, refusing to leave. A fellow officer, Captain Horace Robertson, described him:

> I gave him a cigarette and ordered him to the dressing station. He took the cigarette, but could do nothing with it. The wounds in his shoulders and arms had stiffened and his hands could not reach his mouth. He wore no jacket, but had badges on the shoulder straps of his shirt. The shirt was full of holes from pieces of bomb, and one of the 'Australias' was twisted and broken, and had been driven into his shoulder. I put the cigarette in his mouth and lighted it for him.

In August 1915, Hill 60 had become of increasing strategic importance for both sides. For the Allies, capturing the hill would mean that they held an unbroken line between Anzac and Suvla. From the hill's 'summit' the generals could keep an eye on what the Turks were up to around the two Anafarta villages. There were also two wells close to the hill, of vital importance during that hot, dry summer.

Today one of them is down the hill from an olive grove. The locals now call it Batarya Kuyusu. It is half hidden by weeds and stray clumps of wild wheat at the side of a creek bed.

Capturing it was 'worth anything', according to the British commander-in-chief at the time, Sir Ian Hamilton. Hundreds of men gave their lives for this well. Now it is a worthless small stone and mud-brick cone over a deep hole, with a tiny stone trough alongside to provide water to passing sheep and goats. It is seldom if ever used.

The wind is getting up. We walk on to the 'summit' of Hill 60, through the olive grove. It is not a long way. Ahead of us, across a gentle valley, a field of vigorously growing broad bean plants sweeps down and then up to another foothill. The Turks waited for the Allies where the broad beans grow today.

The fight for Hill 60 signalled the Allied commanders' last throw of the dice in the final disaster of the whole disastrous Gallipoli campaign. In eight days of battles for the Turkish trenches that made Hill 60 look like a chequerboard, there were at least 2500 Allied and just as many Turkish casualties. The hill became a reeking carrion hell of unburied bodies. There came a point in the battle when there were no fresh Allied troops left to fight. The generals had to cobble the remnants of units together. There was always the vain hope, in this one last chance, that something might go right.

Hugo Throssell and his 180 men, thrown into the attack at the end of Hill 60's battles, were the battered survivors of the Australian 10th Light Horse Regiment. They were on their last legs. The regiment had already suffered 138 casualties, including eighty dead, in an earlier battle. The remaining men had been stuck in the trenches within sight of but unable to reach their dead mates for three weeks before undergoing a forced night march to trenches overlooking Hill 60.

Before sunrise on 29 August 1915 – a roasting hot day – the Australian Light Horsemen stood in a thin strip of trench where the whispering pine grove is today, a trench already so choked with dead men that the first task was to throw bodies over the parapet to make space to fight. That early morning, Hugo Throssell, a tall, handsome Australian with dark eyes, a prominent nose and a firm jaw, led his desperate band of unmounted troopers into that last-ditch battle, for which he was later awarded the Victoria Cross (VC) in recognition of his leadership and gallantry.

The 'summit' of Hill 60 was never wrested from the Turks; they always held the heights. But they were so awed by the ferocity of the fighting at Hill 60 that they named it 'Bomba Tepe' – 'Bomb Hill'. They say they will remember this small mound by that name forever. Bomba Tepe is the name on the sign that today points the way to that 'swelling in the plain'.

✠

This is the story of Hugo Throssell and how he came to be awarded the VC. It is also a story about the tragedy and futility of war and how war claims victims long after the guns have fallen silent.

This is also a love story. War and fate threw Throssell together with a most unusual woman who changed his attitudes and his life. Hailed as one of Australia's greatest literary figures, Katharine Susannah Prichard was a progressive feminist and campaigner for women's rights well before her time. The war influenced her into becoming one of the founding members of the Communist Party of Australia.

The Captain and the Communist.

This is a story of his triumph and their tragedy.

Part 1
Triumph

1

The Lion of the Avon

Speaking for myself, having unbounded faith in the colony, our public debt is small; our colony is large; our resources are many and varied and our chief wants are population and capital and I verily believe that, under a wise and bold policy of public works, these wants will speedily be supplied.

Hon. George Throssell, Member for Northam, address in reply to the governor's opening speech of the first Western Australian Legislative Assembly, 20 January 1890

HUGO THROSSELL WAS BORN INTO A tough, resilient pioneering family on 26 October 1884. He was surrounded by older brothers and sisters in the family's low, rambling house, Fermoy, which was situated at the meeting place of two rivers – the meandering Avon, with its colony of white swans imported to remind the early settlers of their British homeland, and the Mortlock – close to the small town of Northam, Western Australia. In the 1880s, Northam was the jumping-off point for explorers, farmers and prospectors heading further east into the vast undeveloped frontier land. The town lay 60 miles from Perth, capital of the colony, which had been founded five decades earlier.

Hugo was the youngest son of George Throssell, known as the 'Lion of the Avon' and the 'Lord of Northam', and his wife, Annie, née Morrell.

Both the Throssell and the Morrell families had been among Western Australia's first settlers. George Throssell was born in Fermoy, County Cork, Ireland, the second son of Michael Throssell and his wife, Jane Ann Ledsam.

Michael worked as a soldier and a policeman before signing on in 1850 as a member of the British Enrolled Pensioner Force to act as a guard for convicts being transported to assist the free settlers in Western Australia as the latter struggled to establish the Swan River Colony. With his wife and three children Michael sailed from Britain aboard the 650-ton barque *Scindian*, which was carrying the first of its thirty-seven shipments of convicts to Australia. That first voyage lasted for eighty-nine days; the *Scindian* arrived at Fremantle on 1 June 1850 with seventy-five male convicts and 200 other passengers, including 163 pensioner guards and their families.

Michael received an immediate appointment as a gatekeeper of the convict establishment in Fremantle, for which he was paid £30 per year. By 1853, however, he was back in the police force, this time in Perth. But only a year later tragedy struck the Throssells when Michael's wife, Jane, died, aged only forty-four, followed one year later by Michael himself, aged forty-six, leaving four children. George, the eldest, was just about to turn fifteen.

Apparently undaunted, George sailed with his young sister, who had been born in Western Australia, and two brothers for Adelaide, where he arranged for his sister to be looked after by relatives in South Australia and for his brothers to live with other family members in New South Wales. Then, alone and short of money, George returned to Perth. There, as Donald Garden wrote in *Northam: An Avon Valley History*, 'the young teenager was thrown onto his own resources in the Colony; he was to prove more than equal to the challenge. In fact Throssell epitomises the nineteenth century ideals of the self-made man of humble origins who rose in the world by hard work and sober devotion to duty and self-improvement'.

George began by acquiring a job with W Padbury and Company, which exported agricultural products to Singapore, India and London and later ground the state's wheat through its Peerless Flour Mills. George also studied at night, at the Swan River Literary and Debating Society. At the age of twenty, he was promoted to manage the branch office of Padbury's at Guildford, the pioneer settlement upriver from Perth, in the fertile Swan Valley.

Annie Morrell's mother was known throughout the huge family as 'Big Grandma'. She was born Susannah Summerland in 1822 to a Quaker family in Lancashire, Britain. With her parents and eight brothers and sisters she arrived in the fledgling colony of Western Australia in May 1830 aboard a small sailing ship called the *James*.

Just over a year later the Morrell family also arrived, in another small sailing ship, the *Eliza*. John and Anne Morrell, and their eight children, aimed to be farmers, and, after two or three attempts on the coastal strip around Fremantle, they decided to go further inland.

There was an early tragedy when Anne died, about a year after they arrived, but John remarried two years later and pressed on with his plan. Eventually, he and his family arrived at the confluence of the Avon and Mortlock rivers and took up a land grant of 4600 acres.

By 1836, John Morrell had built Morby Cottage, a good-size house with framed and glazed windows and a snug fireplace, on the northern side of the present township of Northam. After clearing the scrub nearby, the family was soon ploughing rich river land.

Other settlers quickly followed, including the Summerlands. In 1839, Susannah Summerland and Richard Morrell married and moved to a new farm west of Northam, where they proceeded to raise another big family – eleven children altogether, including Annie.

George Throssell and Annie Morrell met in 1860. Later in the same year Richard Morrell, Annie's father, wrote, somewhat tersely, to his daughter's suitor:

> Dear Sir
> I received your note respecting your correspondence with Anne which of course I was aware of and have no objection to, for though I am but slightly acquainted with yourself yet I know you would not hold the good opinion of Mr Fannomer and others if your conduct and character was otherwise than what it should be, therefore I leave Anne to please herself in the matter.
> Yours etc etc
> Richard Morrell

And so, in June 1861, George Throssell, aged twenty-one, married nineteen-year-old Annie Morrell. Three months later they travelled over the hills from Perth to their new block of land in Northam. George established a general store and took the job of postmaster. The store, he said later, was started with nothing except 'hope, energy and a good wife'.

From this humble beginning George built a business that eventually dominated Northam and far beyond, and made a fortune. He gradually bought up blocks of land in the town and agricultural holdings nearby followed by land far beyond Northam. He was thus poised to profit from the huge pastoral growth to come. He later became a land developer, carrying out Northam's first subdivision; he named the new area Throssellton.

The store proved to be extraordinarily well placed when, in 1887, a major gold strike occurred at Golden Valley, 170 miles east of Northam. The town became a major train terminus: the railway was built from Perth to carry diggers through the hills to this jump-off point for the long trek through the wheatbelt and into the salmon gums and red, dusty desert country of the diggings. George seized the day. As one of his sons, Lionel, reminisced later:

> The sight at Northam station was exciting . . . as each train drew in with its hundreds of miners, prospectors, etc after the arrival of the steamers at Fremantle where, by judicious advertising and distribution of literature, they were advised to make their purchases at Northam . . . What trade this rush brought! Horses, pack and riding saddles, picks, shovels, sieves and general supplies, all of which were in tremendous demand.

George's farms produced the wheat that was ground into flour at his steam mill by the river and bagged for the diggers. He introduced new types of seed wheats from South Australia to increase yields from the harvest and imported large numbers of fruit trees to produce fresh fruit for the diggings.

Business pollinated business. George gave credit to small farmers, pocketed their interest and bought their produce. As a building contractor he erected the town's buildings. He pushed for manufacturing industry for Northam and shared in the production of ploughs and chaff cutters, strippers and tree pullers, and other agricultural machinery. He helped to establish blacksmiths and wheelwrights, turning out buggies, traps and wagons, and was behind the businesses in which horses were shod, harnesses made and carters engaged to shift the huge volumes of goods travelling out to the goldfields.

In 1890 a huge Throssell emporium was opened in Northam, with a celebration banquet for 200 people. George also established a branch at the goldfield itself; diggers either bought their supplies passing through Northam, or they stocked up at the other end of the journey. And, either way, George prospered.

The Lion of the Avon ruled his town and the district. If he wasn't doing business and making money he was busying himself in civic affairs and running practically everything in town. After joining local boards he helped to found the Northam Municipal

Council and became mayor of Northam, ruling from the solid red-brick town hall for seven years. Then he moved into state politics, elected to the new Legislative Assembly in 1890 and holding the seat for fourteen years, winning five elections and being opposed only once.

For a brief three months in 1901 he was also the premier of Western Australia.

Hugo Vivian Hope Throssell was the thirteenth of fourteen children born to George and Annie. His older sisters adored him as a mischievous little boy with a happy grin. These were times of big families and long strings of names soon contracted. Hugo was known by everyone in the family as 'Jim', while his elder brother Frank Eric Cottrell was called 'Ric'. This brother, two years older than Hugo, was Hugo's best friend, the closest person in his life both as he grew up and as an adult. Ric was Hugo's 'boon companion, protector and idol', according to the former's nephew. 'Hugo the brilliant, Eric the reliable,' summed up an army officer later. Another family member claimed that the brothers were like the biblical characters David and Jonathan, devoted to each other.

The Bible figured large in the life of the Throssells. 'My father and mother loved the Bible and read a chapter and had breakfast with the children all their lives', wrote their daughter Evelyn.

> He never discussed business on Sundays & let it be known that he didn't encourage visitors on that day, although mother & he would welcome anyone away from the home . . . All toys were gathered up on Saturday afternoon until Monday & we didn't think it a hardship. Now don't think our Sunday was a morbid one – my father used to say: 'Let it be a sunny day'.
>
> We always had all cooking done on Saturday so the maid could be free to go to church – and also when prayers were read each morning the maid came in and took her place.

For years George and Annie regularly hitched up a buggy and rode out a few miles from Northam to visit and read the Bible to an old couple who could neither read nor write themselves. The Throssells' devotion to their religion can be glimpsed today in the handsome memorials to them in the settlers' small St John's Anglican Church, built in 1890.

Hand in hand with this strict religious observance was a devotion to the temperance movement, which influenced the children enormously. Hugo was said later to have had his first ever nip of whisky the night before going into battle on Gallipoli. Before the war, the *Northam Advertiser* reported admiringly: 'Like the old lion, Jim prefers aqua purer [*sic*] or a drop of tea to any kind of microbe killer and so far it doesn't seem to have hurt him much'.

George had been converted to the temperance movement in the 1870s, despite earlier being granted a gallon licence to sell 'colonial wine' from his store and holding in part the licence for a pub.

But Northam by the end of the 1860s had gained a reputation as a hard-living town and, as one resident wrote, 'In summertime it is well known there is no district over the Hills . . . [in which] there more drinking than in our little Town'. There were other complaints that it was becoming almost impossible to find a sober labourer or tradesman in the place – fertile ground for those opposed to the demon drink.

In 1873 a prominent lecturer, the Reverend William Traylen, arrived in Northam and addressed a meeting in the Mechanics Institute on '"The Chemistry and Power of Alcohol" (With Illustrations)'. He tried to form the Hope of Northam Good Templars Lodge and enlist young men of the town to take the pledge along with George Throssell.

None was impressed until the Reverend Traylen again returned to the town to try again. This time, as Evelyn Throssell reported:

> Several young men apprentices and other lads were taking too much drink and Mr Traylen appealed to them to sign the pledge.

> One young man said to him: 'If you get Mr Throssell to sign we will' (six of them).
>
> After this had been told to Mr Throssell, he carefully weighed the matter and realizing his very grave responsibility he said 'For these young men on the threshold of life I'll sign and make one to form the I.U.G.T.'
>
> He gave up his licence there and then – not transferred it – and with his wife put their whole heart into the temperance movement and when thirteen people could be got to likewise (the number required) the Independent Order of Good Templars was established with the first meeting being held in the Throssell dining room.
>
> It must have been a great financial sacrifice for money was scarce in those days and there were six children at that stage to care for.
>
> However they took their stand on the side of temperance, total abstinence and never relinquished their interest (with) Mrs Throssell taking over the Band of Hope . . .

The Throssells stuck to their beliefs even when they moved into their grand new mansion on Northam's Nob Hill and began to entertain governors and their wives with receptions attended by 300 guests at a time. Evelyn wrote that they 'never offered anything intoxicating to the vice regal guests although it was thought by many it would not be possible to entertain their excellencies without wine. Then, after breakfast, the family prayers were read with the approval of the honoured guests who honoured their host for doing so'.

George had moved his huge family from the rambling single-storey house near the riverfront to a magnificent two-storey home again called Fermoy, after his birthplace in Ireland. The handsome building still stands on 5 acres, at the core of St Joseph's School, which has over 300 pupils. The ground floor is shaded by a colonnade supporting a series of arches. Sweeping steps lead to the upper floor, where there is a wide cast-iron-framed veranda. The family lived upstairs; the servants and the store rooms were below. Hand-carved marble fireplaces reflect the family's affluence, as do the hand-painted stained-glass panels with chaste Victorian maids depicting spring, summer and autumn, and an old man bent double with a bundle of firewood as winter.

Next door on a 17-acre site, George's successful merchant second son Lionel would build his own mansion, Uralia, which still exists. The huge single-storey Federation house with its wide veranda is where Hugo would also return to later.

As a young boy Hugo was first taught at the Fermoy mansion by the family governess, Miss Amy Carleton, and then attended a small state school in the town (which George had been contracted to build in 1878). It was an easy, carefree childhood, apart from the strict rulings of a stern yet indulgent Victorian father. Hugo had his own horse to ride down the hill and across the river flats from the stables behind the mansion. He also had a dog, and even a pet monkey, which abruptly disappeared after biting its owner while being fed. As Hugo's son wrote, Hugo 'survived his father's indulgence, the pampering of a gentle and loving mother and a household of sisters without being spoiled, saved perhaps by his generous good nature and an innate sense of adventure'.

Attendance at school also saved him from harm when an alarming intrusion at the Throssell home caused a major sensation in Northam and beyond on 5 May 1894. His mother and sister were at Fermoy when an obviously demented man called at the mansion looking for a job. Hugo's mother hailed a passing policeman for help, whereupon the man pulled out a revolver and fired it twice. The first shot hit the policeman in the knee; the second, aimed at his heart, was luckily deflected when it struck his pocket watch. The man then chased the Throssells inside, where they hid in a bedroom before he turned the gun on himself and committed suicide.

Hugo grew up in a remote part of the British Empire on the eve of Federation, and not long before the Boer War.

In 1896, the year in which Hugo was sent away to boarding school in Adelaide, in Melbourne the Reverend WH Fitchett was preparing to publish a book that became a sensation throughout the English-speaking world. *Deeds That Won the Empire* was a collection of tales about important events in British history and great heroes like Nelson and Wellington. A sixpenny edition sold 100,000 copies outright, and by the time Hugo left school the book had gone to fifteen editions and was almost compulsory reading for any teenager. In his preface, Fitchett predicted what was to come. It was almost a call to arms, an invitation to future heroes to step forwards:

> War belongs, no doubt, to an imperfect stage of society; it has a side of pure brutality. But it is not all brutal. Wordsworth's daring line about 'God's most perfect instrument' has a great truth behind it. What examples are to be found in the tales here retold, not merely of heroic daring, but of even finer qualities – of heroic fortitude; of loyalty to duty stronger than the love of life; of the temper which dreads dishonour more than it fears death; of the patriotism which makes love of the Fatherland a passion.

Hugo was going off to a boarding school at which these values would be reinforced. He was to attend a Methodist college named after a son of the old queen herself: Prince Alfred, Duke of Edinburgh. Hugo would learn such heroic values as loyalty, duty and patriotism, and would develop the mindset of a hero, embracing valour, honour and selflessness before death.

2
Leaving the Den

Australia! Australia! Of Southern Seas the Queen
In Nature's rich regalia none fairer can be seen.
The cross's silver tracing gleams o'er thy golden land,
And three seas, thee embracing, softly kiss thine opal strand.

AJN Tremearne, 'Australia, an Empire Hymn', c. 1910

EVERYONE AROUND HUGO CALLED HIM JIM by the time he went to boarding school. It was a Throssell family habit that persists to this day – ignoring names given at birth and instead using nick-names or familiar names with obscure or, in Hugo's case, forgotten origins. Hugo was going off to school as a privileged member of a new landed class, one of the 'flower of the youth of Western Australia, the sons of the old pioneering families', as Charles Bean later called the leaders and men of the 10th Light Horse Regiment who, like Hugo, found themselves on Gallipoli. The flowers were tied into a tight bunch by breeding, background and wealth, and, perhaps even more significantly, by the bonds formed by attending public schools together, often as boarders.

When Hugo, aged eleven, and Ric, thirteen, sailed for school in South Australia in 1896, most of the Western Australian public schools were still in the process of formation. The Anglican Hale School, the oldest, had been founded in 1858 but closed for a period in the 1890s when its future appeared uncertain due to competition from government-funded schools. Christian Brothers College, later Aquinas, which was Catholic, had been founded in 1894, while Scotch College, another great school, which catered for Presbyterian boys, opened three years later.

At Guildford on the Swan River in 1896, Charles Harper was teaching his sons, Gresley and Wilfred, along with boys from surrounding landed families in the living room of his gracious home Woodbridge, as he laid the foundations of the influential, and staunchly Anglican, Guildford Grammar School. When the First World War began, twenty-five old Guildfordians joined the 10th Light Horse Regiment. After they landed on Gallipoli they fought alongside men they had known as boys – team rivals on the cricket oval and the football field. Hale School, for example, would lose eleven old boys who had joined the 10th, two of them who would be fighting alongside Hugo Throssell on Bomba Tepe.

Because of the newness of the western schools, and since he could afford it, George Throssell had decided to send his boys to an older and more established school, Prince Alfred College in Adelaide. At that time the school motto came from the Bible's Proverbs 19:2: '*Ubi non est scientia animae, non est bonum*' (That the soul be without knowledge, it is not good). Significantly, this cumbersome phrase was replaced after the First World War with '*Fac fortia et patere*' (Do brave deeds and endure). It reflected doing one's duty on the battlefield and the fact that of the 870 Prince Alfred scholars who enlisted, 117 had been killed. But as the two young Throssells arrived at the brick school buildings in Adelaide, a world war was unthinkable. For George, a solid Christian education married with achievement on the sporting field was all that mattered. This would provide the boys with the foundation for a steady career, probably contributing to the family business.

Although the Throssells were Anglicans, the school they sent their sons to was firmly Methodist. It was founded in 1865 when a group of Wesleyan Methodists, with a benefactor, bought a site opposite Adelaide's parkland to establish a school that would match the Anglicans' prestigious St Peter's College.

The colony of South Australia had a population of only 172,000 at the time, and Adelaide was still a small town. But both the embryonic city and its new school project received a fillip with the arrival in 1867 of Prince Alfred, second son of the reigning monarch, Queen Victoria, on the first royal tour of the empire's far-flung Australian colonies. Adelaide was the Prince's first stop, and the whole population turned out to greet him. On 5 November the royal carriage made a brief stop at the site of the new school. After a hymn was sung, psalms read and a prayer offered, His Royal Highness laid a foundation stone with a golden trowel delicately engraved with fern leaves and a Sturt pea. Two years later the school named in his honour was open for business.

By 1896, pupils included the sons of Adelaide's business and church families as well as boys from the bush – from South Australia's Murray River district and from Broken Hill and Wilcannia, beyond the eastern border. A significant number also came from Western Australia: out of the ninety-eight boys enrolled at the college that year, ten travelled there from Perth.

There were two other brothers, Ross and Lindsay Chipper, from the west. They became firm friends with the Throssell brothers at Prince Alfred's. Like Hugo and Ric, they were extremely close to each other. Also like the Throssells, the Chippers went on to be farmers and to join up within days of each other in the same regiment – the 10th Light Horse.

The school historian, RM Gibbs, recorded in *A History of Prince Alfred College*:

> These Western Australian boys were a distinctive group. The cost and slowness of travel back to their homes meant they could not return there in mid-year holidays. They were rescued from a seemingly permanent incarceration in the school when Adelaide and country families asked them to stay for occasional weekends and holidays. This led to friendships long outlasting schooldays. Later, perhaps with distance lending

enchantment, the Western Australian old scholars were to prove sturdily loyal to the school.

On their way to Gallipoli in 1915, for example, twenty-five old boys, including Hugo Throssell, gathered at the Heliopolis Palace Hotel in Cairo to celebrate Old Scholars' Week, wearing the school colours of red and white.

Hugo spent seven years at Prince Alfred's, an unusually long stay for a student at the time, and the experience had a significant bearing on his life. He grew into a strikingly handsome young man, eventually levelling out at 5 foot 10 inches tall; he was broad chested, brown eyed and brown haired, and had a ready grin. From the beginning he made his name in sport, especially football. In 1901 he was playing at half-back for the Red and Whites. He was known as 'a splendid mark, a good kick and the worst man in the team to bump against'. In 1902 he was captain of football and was congratulated on the way he had managed his team during the season. He was also an excellent hurdler and a renowned gymnast, winning medals in six successive years and being team captain in his final year, when he also won the College Cup.

Hugo Throssell was the school hero. 'He was the idol of Prince Alfred's in his day and his manly traits were intertwined with romping boyishness', remembered one schoolmate.

While he was remembered and celebrated as a sportsman, he was also reasonably gifted scholastically. School records show that he gained prizes for general proficiency in his first years and passed well in examinations.

There is no record that he suffered from homesickness, and he always had Ric there for companionship. The closeness between the two brothers increased as they shared in the strict regimes of the boarding school. Even the boys' possessions were monitored. 'Every Entire Boarder should have a supply of articles similar to the following, each to be distinctly marked, and a list attached inside the trunk or portmanteau', said the school prospectus. There followed a list of over twenty items, beginning with 'One

Suit of Best Clothes' and ending with 'One Bible'. The instructions went on: 'All boys attending the School are desired to wear either the College cap or the College ribbon. Money for travelling or for pocket money can be forwarded by parents or supplied by the Head Master and charged to the account. It is desired that the pocket money should not exceed one shilling a week'.

The headmaster was Frederick Chapple. 'Like Queen Victoria, Frederick Chapple became a personal institution in his own realm', notes the school history. 'Though not so long in office as the Queen, Chapple served as the head of Prince Alfred College for thirty-eight years.' Strongly religious and fiercely energetic, Chapple believed that boys should be kept busy and that 'idleness, especially the lack of occupation in leisure hours, was the mother of all evil'. At the back of his own Bible was a quotation by Theodore Roosevelt: 'Far and away the best prize that life offers is the chance to work hard at work worth doing'.

In the schoolroom and on the playing field, Chapple's boys worked hard. For the boarders there was even a pre-breakfast gymnastics class to keep them busy. At night there was school by gaslight. They slept in a dormitory divided into cubicles and separated by wooden partitions about 2 yards high. The bathroom floor was covered in lead.

Discipline was strict and corporal punishment quite common. Hugo was once summoned to the English master's office after failing a grammar test on the distinction between the active and passive tense. His son later recreated the scene:

> 'You seem to be having difficulty in understanding the simple rules of English grammar, Throssell.'
>
> 'Yes, sir.'
>
> 'Allow me to illustrate. Remove your trousers and bend over.'
>
> 'Yes, sir.'
>
> 'I strike the boy.'
>
> The cane descended on his bare behind.
>
> 'I, subject; strike, verb active; the boy, object. Do you understand?'

'Yes, sir.'

'The boy is struck by me.'

Again the cane came down on his bottom with stinging effect.

'The boy, subject; is struck, verb passive; by me, predicate. Do you understand?'

'No, sir.'

The lesson was repeated.

For the Western Australians and other boarders from far away the midwinter holidays were sometimes hard to endure. In 1902 there were fourteen boarders left at the school as the other boys 'tore away to the railway station'. Chapple gave them two rules, according to the school history: 'to be in on time for meals, and not to go out after tea without his permission'. He also lent them his bagatelle board and croquet set, and his daughters arranged ping-pong and tennis tournaments, a party and a picnic. Gertie Chapple invited nice young ladies to join the entertainments and arranged a picnic to National Park in a five horse drag (Mrs Chapple and another daughter went along by train)'.

The breaks allowed the Throssell boys to visit South Australian country friends and to enjoy some hunting, shooting and fishing. They were friends with brothers Elliott and Robert Brummitt and went camping with them near the old copper town of Burra, in the mid north of South Australia. The Brummitts' mother reported: 'They enjoyed themselves thoroughly and counted as spoil eight wallabies, 100 rabbits and a great many crayfish. It is remarkable what delight boys take in killing things'. During another holiday she wrote: 'How many rabbits have been slain I should be afraid to say, 100 the first day. There is quite a menagerie of young birds to be taken to town tomorrow as trophies, 7 young magpies, 2 crows, 2 hawks and 3 parrots, all young birds'. Some parrots were taken back to Prince Alfred's by the boarders for eating.

But in October 1899 shooting of another kind grabbed the boys' attention. War broke out in South Africa, and across the world Britain's colonies rallied to the empire's call. As South

Australia sent its second contingent of Mounted Rifles overseas to fight, Chapple made a speech farewelling some of the old scholars who had joined up. He told them that the best thing to do for the colony's defence was to aid the empire in its hour of need, so that help would if necessary be ungrudgingly returned in the future.

Some of the old boys who had volunteered for the war addressed the school assembly. Trooper WJ Cowan distinguished himself by requesting a half-holiday for the boys. When the headmaster granted this there was wild cheering, and Chapple's daughters served refreshments and handed out cigars to the men.

The war lasted until June 1902. When the end was declared, Chapple allowed the boys another half-holiday so that they could hear the state governor read the British colonial secretary's telegram announcing the news from the steps of Adelaide's Parliament House. Altogether, more than sixty old boys served in South Africa. Two were killed, and a few others were decorated for conspicuous gallantry.

Chapple was a staunch patriot and constantly stressed pride of race and love of country to his boys. The Boer War prompted the formation of an army cadet corps at Prince Alfred's in February 1900, and Hugo Throssell immediately volunteered, spending two years in this part-time military training led by some old boys returned from South Africa. Martini-Henry carbines were issued and uniforms bought. The boys looked sartorially grand in their felt hats with fine cocks' feathers. Parading, route marches and shooting began. The school history comments that 'patriotism, it was believed, was the original motive for joining and the corps would contribute to physical development, discipline, self-control and self-reliance'. However, at the proclamation of Federation, in 1901, the country's defence was handed over to the Commonwealth, and state cadet bodies faded away for a while. By the time Hugo left school, a year later, cadet activities had dwindled to target shooting.

Hugo had by then developed a schoolboy crush on Henrietta

Watson, a visiting actress from Britain, apparently during a school cultural excursion to the theatre. He told a friend that she was the 'champion of champions' on the stage. Henrietta remained in his thoughts after he left school and had a dreamily romantic influence on his life later on.

Henrietta Watson was born in Dundee, Scotland, in March 1873, into a theatrical family, the daughter of actors J Boles-Watson and Madge Johnstone. She made her first stage appearance at the age of fifteen, as Little Willie in the play *East Lynne*, a huge success of the time. When she eventually died, aged ninety-one, in 1964, she had been on the stage and in British films for more than sixty years.

A strikingly handsome woman with fine features and deep-set dark eyes, she visited Australia a number of times in the 1890s, touring the states with different companies and making appearances in over a dozen plays.

It seems it was Henrietta, playing Milady de Winter, the wicked seductress, secret felon, murderess and arch villain in the tale of *The Three Musketeers* that made such a deep impression on young Hugo Throssell on his school excursion.

Back home in Northam after leaving school, Hugo Throssell, young, handsome and extroverted, took to the stage himself, perhaps because he was easily bored in the small dusty town, perhaps because it gave him the opportunity to meet some girls. He became a star with the Northam Dramatic Society, even going on tour with the company through neighbouring bush towns. 'The latest London success and cheered to the echo by Northam, York, Newcastle and Katanning,' began a review in the local paper, 'the brilliant three act comedy *My Little Husband* . . . starring Mr Hugo Throssell as Dr Candy Ild and Miss Maude Leeming as Nancy Roach'. Miss Leeming was 'very sweet with a tendency to flirt on the slightest provocation', while Mr Throssell was 'well suited and played the part of the comfortable old pedagogue to a tee'. In another play, *Niobe*, produced by the Northam Dramatic Society, he was described as being 'in love with himself'. Hugo kept the notices pasted in a large red scrapbook, along with other mementos of his life post-school.

Hugo once claimed that he had returned to Northam without having learnt a 'single solitary thing' that would help him to earn a living. He didn't exactly have to, however: he was well off, spoilt and back in Northam, the town owned by his family. He worked sporadically for his elder brother Lionel, who managed the family store and the flour mill that their father had built in nearby Newcastle (later renamed Toodyay). Lionel was old enough to be Hugo's father and disapproved of the young man's irresponsibility and pranks.

Hugo once disguised himself as a bushranger and bailed up Tommy, an old family retainer who carried papers between the Throssells' Northam and Newcastle offices. Tommy found himself tied back-to-front on his horse and sent back to Newcastle, asking 'What for? What for?' The culprit was never found, but the mail was still delivered, untouched. Everyone in Northam knew it must be Hugo.

Once again, he threw himself into sport. From 1903 to 1912 he kept records of the 'Running Performances of Hugo V Throssell'. They stretched over nearly two pages carefully divided into headings: 'Date. Sports. Race. My Mark. Scratch man, his mark. Winner and his mark. If beaten in heat or semi, by whom and his mark. My place. Remarks'. He ran in races in towns throughout the nearby countryside and in Perth; he was reported to have 'an attractive style of running'.

He also played football, captaining the local district team, the Federals, known as the 'old navy blue and reds' and the 'Feddies'. He did some wrestling, appearing as a support act when the Town Hall Pictures announced it would be showing the Edison Pictures productions of *Ben Hur* and *Little Bessie*: 'Mr Hugo Throssell v Ben Hur. In both contests Ben Hur undertakes to throw his opponent within 15 minutes'. He also boxed seriously, sparring with his coach in town and on the family property with an Aboriginal yardman called Nimble Jack. 'Throssell is a good cut of an athlete', began a report of the final of the local 11-stone amateur competition.

> Throssell won in the fifth round. After close in fighting in the centre Parsons went to the boards from a right cross to the head and in as many seconds was three times dropped with the same swing, the last blow proved his counting out being a light one to the side of the head followed by a cross on the point.
>
> In declaring Throssell the 11 Stone Amateur Champion of Northam and District the referee complimented both men and said for amateurs it was probably the best five rounds that could be witnessed in the State.

Soon after returning home from school, Hugo also joined the fine body of militiamen known as the Jennacubbine Mounted Rifles, one of the troops that made up the 4th Squadron of the 18th Australian Light Horse Regiment. They met in their uniforms outside the long, low Jennacubbine pub, an easy ride over the 15 miles of flat land from Northam, including long stretches for a dashing gallop or relaxed canter. The men provided their own horses, a simple matter for Hugo, as by that time he and Ric had begun dealing in the animals. Hugo's scrapbook shows that his mare Kent was a winner of the Regimental Cup.

While it was a colony, Western Australia always had mounted troops, which appeared and disappeared according to the degree of local interest. One of the earliest troops was the Pinjarra Mounted Volunteers, raised in 1862, while the Guildford Mounted Infantry had appeared in 1887 and a mounted detachment of the Bunbury Rifles in 1899. All of these areas became districts for the Western Australian Mounted Infantry following Federation and military organisation.

Major General Edward Hutton was the first commander of the Australian Army. In 1894, while commanding the New South Wales Military Forces, he presided over an intercolonial committee that prepared the *Manual of Drill for Mounted Troops of Australia*, which ran to 458 pages of detailed instructions. In the preface, Hutton wrote:

> In no country in the world will a mounted force be found more necessary for military operations than in Australia. Distances are so great, transport away from the great lines of rail is so difficult, that, as in America at the commencement of the great war of Secession 1862–65, so in Australia would success be to that force which had the best and most completely equipped mounted force.
>
> Success will be to that army which can best turn to account the splendid inherent resources which the Colonies of Australia possess in the supply of horsemen, who, while hardy and of an independent character, have all those British characteristics which have made and are now making an Empire and a race without parallel in the world.

In 1902, Hutton produced another manual for mounted troops, and in 1909 the federal government passed legislation providing for compulsory military training. Lord Kitchener visited Australia in 1910 to review the situation and made recommendations including that the forces be brought up to 80,000. From 1911, boys aged twelve had to join the junior cadets, which were mainly school based and did not include a uniform. From fourteen to eighteen years they were members of the uniformed school cadets, and from eighteen to twenty-six members of the citizens' military forces; the latter meant sixteen days' paid training each year until they turned twenty, after which they had to attend an annual muster.

The 1902 mounted service manual said:

> Each troop should be composed of men raised in the same locality, or, if detachments from existing corps, of men belonging to the same regiment or battalion. The permanent sections similarly should be made up by men who live in the same vicinity in civil life, or who will have some association in common.

> It will be found that the permanent section or comrade system, if carefully and intelligently adhered to in principle no less than in letter, will produce the highest form of discipline.
>
> Men will naturally fight better and with more confidence among those whom they know and trust rather than among strangers.

And so, in places like tiny Jennacubbine, local farmers, school friends and sporting team players rode and drilled together, and afterwards drank together. A foundation was being laid called 'mateship'. By 1914, when war broke out once again, there were already twenty-three light horse regiments in Australia.

✠

On 19 May 1906 tragedy came to the large Throssell family when the children's mother, Annie, died aged sixty-four. Perhaps simply worn out, she had been ill for five weeks, and George had been summoned home from a trip to the eastern states to be at her bedside. She expired of heart failure at six o'clock in the morning. 'The deceased lady leaves behind her a circle of almost un-numbered relatives', said the *Northam Advertiser*. There were, for a start, twelve surviving children and twenty-nine grandchildren.

> For the past forty-four years the deceased lady has been intimately associated with the religious and social life of the town and district of Northam. She has at all times taken a prominent part in every project designed to advance the well-being of the community and her efforts in the cause of temperance have been fruitful of great results.
>
> In past years the hospitality of 'Old Fermoy' was proverbial and more recently at 'New Fermoy' the deceased lady has been always in the habit of entertaining largely and liberally. Whether in local or State affairs she laboured constantly to advance the beneficent designs of her distinguished husband and her death will leave a blank in the life of the community which can never be filled.

The funeral, on 22 May, was the largest ever held in Northam: 'one of the largest indeed that has been witnessed in Western Australia'. The procession was a mile long, with 130 vehicles and a large number of horsemen. Annie was buried in the town cemetery. 'In deference to the special wish of the Hon. Geo. Throssell, the funeral was simply conducted. There were no plumes or black cloths, these being replaced by a profusion of flowers. Following the hearse was a coach laden with wreaths and flowers forwarded by sympathising friends.'

Free of their mother's stern influence, four of the Throssell boys, including Hugo and Ric, were soon in trouble. They were among eight 'Northam sportsmen' who were charged on summons that 'on the 15th and 16th day of August 1906 at Tammin they did kill and disturb kangaroos within a prohibited area'. The young men pleaded not guilty.

Constable Johns gave evidence that he had come upon the eight men in a prohibited area and that 'the party was dismounted from their horses and standing in a group. On the saddle of the first horse was a dead kangaroo. There were another three on the ground and there were four kangaroo dogs'. But their lawyer successfully argued that no one had actually seen the men kill the kangaroos, and so the charges were dismissed. Hugo stuck the lawyer's bill for 12 guineas – and costs of £1 11s 6d – in his scrapbook with a note: 'Not Guilty – but don't do it again'. It had been an expensive lesson. The next scrapbook entry, headed 'Jim's First Purchase!', was an invoice from an auctioneer who had bought a calf for him for 9 shillings.

✠

Hugo kept at his job with Lionel sporadically for six years, but his heart wasn't in the family business. He was a good horseman, keen on farming and animals, even breeding pedigree English setters. He made up his mind to go on the land, initially setting out to be a stockman in the outback: the harshest school of all.

Just before Christmas 1909, Hugo climbed aboard a steam train for the lurching ride that carried him nearly 500 miles north-east of Perth, to Meekatharra, a gold rush town with corrugated-iron roofs that shimmered in the heat. From there it was another ride, this time by horseback: 240 miles along a bush track that crossed a flat red sun-blasted plain to a station on the banks of the dry bed of the Ashburton River.

Ashburton Downs Station had around 770,000 acres. The land had been taken up originally in the 1880s by a group from Northam including the Lion himself, George Throssell. No doubt it was George who got Hugo the job, although he took no part in the running of the station, having sold his interest in 1892 to John Frederick Hancock and his three boys, Robert, John and George, who took turns to manage the station.

Before Hugo left Northam, his father had given him a letter that he kept for the rest of his life, folded and refolded so many times that eventually it barely held together.

> My dear Lad,
>
> While I feel it is wise that you launch out on your own and win that experience so necessary to success I still naturally feel some anxiety in you going so far from us at this time of year. Yet for years you and Ric were away from home. Keep us well advised of your movement and I hope to hold regular correspondence with you. I have written a letter to Hancock which will do no harm . . .
>
> Now my dear boy, farewell. May your Mother's God be with you and her precious memory be a protection and shield you.
>
> With my heart felt love
> Believe me
> Ever your
> Affectionate father
> George Throssell

There followed a touching postscript:

> I would get a pair of coloured glasses about 1/6 in case you feel the necessity of them. Mr Bull has rigged you out with medicines I see. Very kind of him. God be with you lad until we meet again.
> Dad

Sadly, father and son never did meet again.

Life as a stockman, a real bushman, working with horses, mending fences – and toughening up – was lonely. Hugo rode long distances by himself on the flat red emptiness of the plains, checking bores and wells wherever subterranean water could be found, clearing troughs of slime and rubbish so the stock could drink. Mustering days meant companionship, however, with the Hancock boys and the Aboriginal stockmen who worked for their food and tobacco. After the drafting and branding, contract drovers rode in to collect the mob from the station and take it along the dusty stock route to the port of Onslow.

Whenever Hugo called in at the homestead he picked up weeks-old mail and out-of-date newspapers and magazines. They gave him something to read by the light of the kerosene lamp at night in the bunkhouse. One evening he was turning the pages of a year-old *Spectator* magazine from London. Among the photographs of the high society of the day attending race meetings and garden parties, the men in their top hats and tails and the ladies in their sweeping lace gowns and enormous feathered hats, he found a familiar face: a winsome portrait of his boyhood crush, the actress Henrietta Watson, and a review of her latest success on the West End.

On a romantic impulse, Hugo tore a couple of pages from a lined exercise book and in his neat hand wrote her a fan letter, telling her how he had seen her performance all those years ago and still remembered it. The lonely stockman promised that one day he would travel to London. He finished with a flourish: 'I'll find a gold mine or a bird's nest, and we'll live happily ever after'. Never imagining that such a meeting would actually occur, he signed his letter

'Northam Jim'. He had no idea of her address, so he wrote on the envelope 'Miss Henrietta Watson, Actress, London'.

Extraordinarily, the letter reached her. Perhaps touched by the young man's compliments and bravado, Henrietta decided to reply.

Three months later, when the team from the coast called at Ashburton Downs with mail and supplies, there was a letter addressed to 'Northam Jim'. Henrietta had written: 'Perhaps it is destined we shall meet some day'.

Five years later the famous actress was showing Hugo, by that time a famous war hero, around London.

On the night of 26 August 1910, George Throssell fell down the stairs of his grand mansion, Fermoy. Four days later he was dead. Northam legend has it that he was on his way to a late-night assignation with a female servant when he tripped and fell. Some locals also say that Fermoy is haunted as a result of what happened there. Hugo, boundary riding on the fringes of the desert, did not hear of his father's death until it was too late to travel back for the funeral. He had to rely on the *Northam Advertiser* for the full account of what had happened. He kept the newspaper clipping with him afterwards, along with his father's last letter to him.

> A most painful sensation was occasioned in Northam on Saturday morning when it was reported that the Hon. Geo. Throssell had met with a terrible accident late on the previous evening, and that his life was consequently despaired of.
>
> Mr Throssell, who had been in excellent health for some time past, visited the city on Thursday returning by the express on Friday evening. He brought back one of his young grandsons (Master Hope) to spend a few days at 'Fermoy'.
>
> He drove home and after spending an hour or two with his two daughters (Miss Throssell and Mrs Callaghan) the family retired a little before eleven.

Mr Throssell was last to go to bed, and after switching off all the lights in the hall he went into the room where his young grandson was sleeping to see that he was all right for the night. After switching off the light in that room he started for his own bedroom. Walking along the side passage he came to what he thought was the pillar at the corner of the main hall. Instead it was the pillar at the head of a rather steep flight of steps leading down to the basement and billiard room.

Turning, to proceed as he thought along the main hall, Mr Throssell fell headlong down these stairs.

On the side on which he fell there is no banister, merely the bare wall, and he fell about eleven feet, striking his head on the side of the wall and inflicting a terrible wound which bled profusely.

His daughters, hearing the fall, rushed immediately to his assistance. He was quite conscious but had no feeling and was entirely helpless.

Being a very heavy man they were unable to move him but messages were despatched to 'Uralia' and for the doctor and Messrs G.L. and H. Throssell and Dr Rockett were quickly on the scene.

The serious nature of Mr Throssell's injuries was at once recognised. He was removed to his bed and everything possible was done for his comfort. A close examination revealed that the fall had occasioned concussion of the spine, causing complete paralysis of the arms and legs.

From the first the case was regarded as hopeless and the patient himself was one of the first to realise the absence of feeling in his limbs.

Throughout the day he conversed with members of his family but was unable to move.

At 10 o'clock on Sunday morning he partook of Holy Communion at the hands of the Rector, the Rev. R.H. Moore.

Mr Throssell spoke with the greatest cheerfulness, and the most profound resignation of his approaching end, and enquired closely into the affairs of the parish.

On Sunday night and during Monday he continued in the same condition. The whole of the members of the family – with the exception of Mr Hugo Throssell who is on the Ashburton Downs station – had been summoned to the house and Mr Throssell was able to converse with them all, and made many efforts to cheer them with jokes and witticisms, clearly indicating the brightness of mind and lightness of heart with which he approached the end of a long life of well-doing.

He frequently expressed some regret at the manner of his taking off, but this notwithstanding, his cheerfulness and resignation continued to the end.

On Tuesday morning there was a marked change for the worse, and his medical adviser and members of the family realised that the end was near.

At ten minutes after noon he passed peacefully away in the midst of his family, having suffered little pain and being conscious almost to the end.

The funeral was held the following afternoon. Despite the short notice, it eclipsed in numbers the attendance at Annie's farewell, four years before. Flags flew at half-mast for the former premier, tributes filled newspaper columns, and a special train from Perth carried scores of official mourners to the town. The Lion of Northam was buried alongside his Annie, the funeral procession 'being so long that the ceremony at the grave was almost concluded before the last of the long string of vehicles had arrived at the ceremony'. Sir John Forrest, the state's first premier, put it succinctly: 'Western Australia has lost one of its most able and patriotic sons and we have lost a dear kind friend'.

George Throssell left £50,829, a fortune in those days. There were also some debts. Before his father had died, businessman son Lionel had borrowed heavily to keep the company afloat. A slump the following year meant that many farmers were unable to pay for machinery they had bought from the firm, and Lionel was forced in time to pull back and earn his living from running a much smaller agency.

But George had made some canny investments, in land away from Northam. In 1903 the completion of the hugely ambitious

Coolgardie water scheme meant not only that water was now delivered by pipeline from the hills of Perth to miners working on the inland goldfields but also that there was a water supply for a new generation of pioneering farmers establishing a wheatbelt between the coast and the fringes of the gold country. Seven years after the water flowed, in one of his last speeches to parliament, George Throssell had noted that another 1.65 million acres of land had been allotted for farms. 'This means, if it means anything, that in a few short years we must be regarded as the chief wheat-producing centre of the Commonwealth.' George had thought ahead, as usual. He had already purchased two prime blocks for wheatbelt development.

3

Answering the Call

Crowned by radiant sun and sea
Dowered with golden liberty,
All our hopes are prayers for thee –
Westralia!

Land of promise proudly won
From the kingdom of the sun,
Now thy glory has begun –
Westralia!

Brightest land in all the world,
Rosy dawned and moon-impearled,
With the flag of faith unfurled –
Westralia!

Alfred T Chandler, 'Westralia', c. 1907

After a year at Ashburton Downs, Hugo returned to Fermoy in Northam for a family Christmas. He sat down with his closest friend and older brother Ric to persuade him that it was time for them to leave Northam and become pioneer farmers together on the 1000 acres of virgin bush that their father had acquired. The property was situated at a dot on the map, a flyspeck called Cowcowing, lying between two large salt lakes and dry clay pans, 60 miles north-east of their home town. Ric needed little convincing that this was the perfect spot in which to pursue their dreams.

Today, Cowcowing remains a railway siding with a silo in fringe wheatbelt country with a 12-inch annual rainfall – in a good year. A good year is when there is a harvest. In other years promising crops that sprout a verdant green in springtime are soon burnt brown when no more rain falls. The land is flat, seemingly limitless, stretching to a vast and distant horizon. It shimmers in the summer heat, shivers with icy winds in winter. There are occasional clumps of gimlet trees, so called because their branches seem to curl upwards, useful for building sheds and cattle yards. Vivid-green parrots banded with yellow and black flash among salmon and white gums – good for fence posts because the wood is too hard for white ants to devour. It is a tough land that breeds tough people.

Not much changes here. The two 500-acre blocks once farmed by Hugo and Ric Throssell near Lake Wallambin are today farmed by John Martin. His grandfather Joseph Chester Martin came here in 1907 and initially lived next door to the Throssells when they arrived, in 1910. Outside the Martins' homestead are the grey, weathered remains of an old white gum wheat wagon. Five horses would have pulled it, piled with ninety bags of wheat, to the nearest railhead. It would have taken two days to reach Dowerin, about 40 miles to the south-west.

Dowerin sprang into being when the railway arrived, in 1906. There were high hopes that the line would almost immediately continue on to Cowcowing to 'tap the splendid country there'. James Mitchell, a colleague of George Throssell who also succeeded him as premier of Western Australia, told parliament that the line would open up the best country in Australasia. 'The type of settler we need is one who will go out with his family, take hold of the right end of an axe and get going. The land is easily cleared and when the block is cleared he can extend his holding. If a settler has no capital, he must pay his price for his opportunities and that price is work.'

Local historians Eva Braid and Elizabeth Forbes wrote about the Cowcowing pioneer's in their book *From Afar a People Drifted*:

> The new settlers took the train to Dowerin, others drove, rode or walked. From Dowerin they took tracks northeast gaining advice from Agricultural Bank Inspectors, surveyors, rabbit inspectors, engine drivers, guards, travellers on railways or anyone else they saw. They read the *Journal of Agriculture* and the country pages of newspapers. They set off with whatever means they had, which sometimes was walking and feeling lucky if someone could show them the way and let them toss a few stores and clothes on a cart. The women took what they thought were the essentials. They were limited by space in the vehicles which were so loaded up most of the adults and older children had to walk part of the way at least. As the old hands of Cowcowing told stories of the older days it was often of meetings 'on the track'. Some went out in cavalcades of drays and carts, some made their lonely way with one vehicle and one horse, some went on bicycles, the treasured 'tin horse' that ate no feed and drank no water.
>
> Money was lent by the Agricultural Bank for fencing, clearing and dam construction, buildings and later for seed and super. Thus a man could select a block and start clearing. He could live on advances from the Bank against the clearing.
>
> The Lands Department appointed inspectors and published books and pamphlets to attract new settlers from the Goldfields and the United Kingdom, as well as instructing on farm methods.
>
> Most of the increase in the state's population from 1903 onwards came from the United Kingdom through the state's vigorous policy of immigration accompanied by assisted passages and the Government's 'Land of Opportunities' publicity.

The Cowcowing pioneers had also arrived from Europe.

When Jack Vladic, who came from an island off the Dalmatian coast, sent home for his wife, Tomica, she arrived by train at Dowerin two days after arriving by ship at Fremantle.

At Dowerin the sun was high and it was very hot. The couple waited until sundown, when Jack tied a parcel of groceries on top of Tomica's tin trunk, hoisted the lot on his shoulder and said it was time to walk to the farm.

They set out on the road to Cowcowing to the northeast. Every time Tomica asked how much further there was to go, Jack replied, 'Just a little bit more'. He repeated the phrase many times during the long night, and repeated it again the next morning when the sun came up and they were still walking through the bush.

Eventually they reached their new home, a little hessian hut at a place the locals would later dub 'Austrians Corner' after Jack's brother and sister-in-law joined them. Tomica and Jack would go on to prosper and have nine children.

The rush to take up land around Cowcowing did not, however, result in a township, despite many predictions, high hopes, political rows and bitter divisions. When the main railway line was extended eastwards, in 1911, it took in Wyalkatchem, just a few miles to the north, which grew into the main town centre, with another settlement established at Korrelocking, another siding to the east.

Hugo and Ric Throssell rode the 60 miles from Northam to Cowcowing with a team of horses, some food supplies and tools to clear the land. They arrived at their blocks late in 1910 in conditions that amounted to a mirage. It had been a perfect year for those established on farms around them. The rains had come and the crops were tall, full grained and ripening, waving in the breeze. The harvest would be bountiful. The settlers around Buckley's Tank – the name given to a freshwater soak nearby – decided to celebrate by holding an annual picnic and sports day, almost like an American Thanksgiving, remembered for years afterwards as the Cowcowing Picnic. The Throssell brothers and other bachelors were soon roped in to the organising committee.

> The ground was swept with tea-tree brooms, bough sheds erected, seats provided, tracks laid out for pedestrian sports for all ages and a race track.

> The women cooked for days before. Best clothes were got out and refurbished. Cases of sweets and fruit came out from Dowerin for the children. Prizes were found for all events, some taken from the tin trunks of treasures most women seemed to have, their small elegancies waiting for the day when a house was built.
>
> Over three hundred people from all around the lake, from Jirimbi to Mount Marshall, from Dowerin to Korrelocking, came by horseback and every sort of horse-drawn vehicle, by bicycle or on foot.

They posed for a photograph in their best clothes, the women swathed in gossamer veiling to keep out the bush flies, which swarmed in black clouds.

Today, near where they picnicked there is a fenced-off patch of dry red earth and a sign: 'Cowcowing Pioneers Cemetery'. There are only three marked graves.

✠

The Throssell brothers camped on their land at first then made a rough shack to live in with gimlet saplings as frames and clay rammed between wire netting as walls. There was a corrugated-iron roof and an improvised chimney stuck end-on at the side of the building. Mixed with water, the earth from ant hills set like cement for the floor, with scattered wheat sacks as rugs.

The brothers grew even closer as they set to work clearing their land. They chopped down the trees, grubbed out the stumps with pick and shovel, and harnessed up their team of heavy Clydesdales to pull an improvised scrub roller made from solid tree trunks chained together. They also borrowed a team of horses from their neighbours, the Martins, and with the two teams dragging scoops managed to scrape out a 12-foot-deep dam of around 80 feet by 40 feet in the hard, dry clay, to be thatched with brush in time for the spring rains. The outline of the dip from where the dam used to be can still be discerned today, but there is nothing left of the Throssells' homestead except for small bits of broken plates.

They had to cart water to drink, some from the soak at Buckley's Tank, some from primitive condensers that the pioneers built to distil water from the surrounding salt lakes. Most condensers were square 200-gallon tanks set on stones above a fire, with about 60 feet of 2-inch piping leading to a 100-gallon receiver tank. It might take twenty-four hours of boiling to produce 75 or 100 gallons of smelly water with a horrible flavour. Lacking minerals, it often caused dry retching and stomach trouble.

As they worked in separate sections of the property, the brothers devised, blowing hard and using index and little fingers at the corners of their mouths, a series of piercing whistles to signal with each other and indicate where they were and what they intended doing. The Throssells had a couple of hundred acres ready for ploughing when the first sowing season came around.

But the vision of a promised land did not last long. The glorious rains of 1910 were followed by months of pitiless heat and no thunderstorms to break the drought. It became a long, frustrating battle for survival. One farmer remarked bravely that, 'it was not a drought, just a lack of moisture' that plagued the district.

The drought of 1911 seemed to set a pattern. In the following years there would be some early rain, and the farmers would sow their wheat seed. The crop would grow to about 6 inches, but there would be no follow-up rainfall, and so the crop would never make heads. Instead, it was raked and put into wire-netting bins to be mixed with molasses for horse feed.

The settlers battled on. The fourth annual Cowcowing Picnic was planned for 13 September 1913, to be attended by Premier John Scaddan, popularly known as 'Happy Jack', who was being lobbied heavily to extend the railway to the settlement and build more government dams. Braid and Forbes described what happened:

> The young bachelors W.J. Boyne, Arthur Thomas, Will Boyce, Hugo and Eric Throssell worked hard over this event. The ground had been swept for acres around and the bough sheds and amenities could not

> have been neater. The women made a special effort with their best white tablecloths and pieces of china and silver. Such an array of large hats and gossamer veils there was that day at Cowcowing. Every sort of racing and sporting event had been arranged, all the fiddles and accordions, trumpets and cornets around the district were assembled, everyone ready to do their bit to prove the area deserved a railway. However it rained torrents during the afternoon and stopped all the festivities.

Frustration again. The official party then had to cancel more meetings with the settlers because the roads were impassable. Three times the minister for Lands visited Cowcowing to see the dry area and twice was bogged. He never saw the dams anything but full. When the flat rich-red land of Cowcowing was wet and the crops were growing green it did indeed look good enough to eat, as the old settlers would say. The government promised to extend the railway when it had the money.

The harvest of 1913 seemed to have been truly sent by God. It was a record, the most spectacular in Western Australia's history to that date – nearly 13.5 million bushels. For the people of Cowcowing it was the first chance of a holiday in years, for many since they had first arrived on their blocks. Many headed for Perth and the coast.

Optimism soared at Cowcowing. There was time now for some fun. Weatherboard and iron halls went up at nearby settlements. Dances were held and bands came up from Goomalling, Northam and sometimes even Perth to play. The local girls took out party dresses from their glory boxes and marked the names of eligible young men in their dance programs. Balls would open with the 'Grand March'. 'Mums, fathers, sisters, brothers, widows and orphans, all joined the March. Round the hall in couples, up the centre in fours, then sixes, then eights, finally breaking off into what is now known as the Circular Waltz.' There were picnic race meetings and house parties. The sporting clubs flourished.

Hugo was still playing football now with the Korrelocking Association, which took in young men playing for the Benjaberring, Korrelocking, Yorkrakine and Wyalkatchem football clubs.

To Hugo and Ric, it seemed worth sticking it out on the farm, clearing more scrub, ploughing at least a couple of hundred acres and producing some wheat, enough to sell and pull in some money at last to satisfy the demands of the Agricultural Bank.

Then came 1914, and everything turned once again to dust. The rains didn't come as summer passed to autumn at Cowcowing, and the wheat had to be planted in dry soil. It did sprout green after a little rain in June, but by the end of that month it was wilting. Reports came in that all of Australia was dry: the whole nation was in drought.

Some light showers in July kept hopes alive in the Western Australian wheatbelt, but by the next month the crops were shrivelled and brown after twenty-two consecutive nights of frost. Hugo and Ric shivered in their tin-roofed humpy. Dishes of water left standing overnight were solid with ice until late morning.

By August, chaff and hay had skyrocketed in price and were virtually unobtainable. Suppliers and storekeepers were refusing credit, and elsewhere in the state there were signs of general unrest, with eighteen major industrial disputes and mounting unemployment. Premier Scaddan complained to parliament that the poor were coming to his office and home every day asking for help because they did not have a roof over their heads or did not know where they could find their next meal. A deputation of unemployed people to the parliament said that they were stranded and needed work. Timber cutters were thrown out of their jobs after the government withheld licences to cut timber on Crown land. Well-meaning citizens formed the National Council of Women's Distressed Farmers Clothing Committee.

But, suddenly, news arrived from Britain signalling – though the people of Western Australia might not immediately have grasped it – that worse was to come. Their world was about to change forever, as the country was catapulted into the most disastrous tragedy in its history.

Although communication between Australia and the rest of the world was by cable or ship, Australians took a keen interest in overseas news, particularly from 'home'. The population of Western Australia was overwhelmingly British or Irish of origin. As Charles Bean wrote:

> Concerning the daily events of the world Australians were as well informed as most Anglo-Saxon people. The newspapers the city folk received with their breakfast and country ones up to a week later according to distance from the capitals on the coast – set forth in their 'cable pages' a gleaning of the world's news sent by their common agencies in London and Vancouver. The news was wide if rather thin; but among grown citizens and even children the facts of the Kaiser's recent expansion of his navy, of the race of the British 'Dreadnought' building to meet it, and of the German sabre-rattling in Morocco and the Balkan wars, were at least as well known as among their cousins in Great Britain.

On 28 June 1914 the assassination of an obscure archduke and his wife in a remote city in Europe filled escalating columns of newsprint as an enveloping crisis flared across the continent. Two days after the murders, the trains brought newspapers from Perth to the remote towns of the wheatbelt of Western Australia. The *West Australian* carried a report under six decks of headlines:

AUSTRIAN TRAGEDY.
ROYALTY ASSASSINATED.
STUDENTS' DASTARDLY CRIMES.
TWO ATTEMPTS IN SUCCESSION.
OUTRAGES IN BOSNIA.
ROYAL HEIR AND HIS WIFE KILLED.

London, June 29.
The details now to hand of the latest tragedy in the Royal House of Austria-Hungary show that the assassination of the Archduke Francis Joseph and his wife, at Sarajevo, the capital of Bosnia, was premeditated, and one of the most determined outrages on Royalty perpetrated in modern times. The Archduke, in spite of warning against dangers at Sarajevo, went thither in his capacity as Inspector-General of the Forces. The Archduke and the Duchess were motoring from the barracks to the Town Hall on Saturday, when a youth threw a bomb at the car. Owing to the fairly good pace at which the procession was travelling the bomb missed its mark but exploded under the following car, in which were members of the Royal suite. Colonel Merizzo, one of the occupants of the second motor, was injured, as well as about 20 other people in the crowd. The procession was continued by the Royal heir's orders, despite the outrage, and in his speech acknowledging an address of welcome, the Archduke gave expression to his joy that he and the Duchess had escaped the bomb obviously intended to kill them. When the civic function was over the Archduke, though pale and agitated, gave orders to be immediately taken to the hospital where were those injured by the bomb explosion. On the way a youth rushed out at a narrow street corner and fired two shots from a revolver at the Archduke and the Duchess. The first struck the Duchess, and the second the Archduke, and neither lived long enough to reach the hospital. Both the criminals were Servian young students, and after their dastardly work they were seized by the crowd, which sought to lynch them for their appalling crimes. The outrage is thought in Vienna to be due to pan-Servian agitation.

Soon the crisis was raging like an out-of-control bushfire as nations pushed and rushed each other into alliances. A month after the assassination, cables told amazed readers in Australia that Austria-Hungary had declared war on Serbia and that Russia was mobilising to help the Serbs. Then Germany issued a grim warning to Russia to not go any further.

If Germany declared war on Russia, the latter would call upon its ally France for help. And if France entered the conflict, Britain would probably enter, because there was an informal agreement between the two countries to support each other if attacked.

On 29 July the British government sent to Australia and the other Dominion countries coded telegrams warning that war was imminent. A second cable, to the Scottish-born governor-general of Australia, Sir Ronald Craufurd Munro-Ferguson, which arrived the next day, advised that it was time for the Australian government – if it thought fit – to bring into force the 'preliminary stage' of a secret defence scheme: the mobilisation of Australian men for the armed forces.

Australia was in the throes of a federal election campaign at the time. Prime Minister Joseph Cook, leader of the Conservatives, was in Victoria campaigning against Labor's Andrew Fisher, leader of the opposition. On the night of 31 July, Fisher, who went on to win the election and become prime minister on 5 September, stood in a cold hall in Colac, surrounded by dairy farmers, and famously declared: 'Should the worst happen, after everything has been done that honour will permit, Australia will stand by the mother country to our last man and our last shilling'. The next night, Prime Minister Cook followed Fisher onto the same platform. The *West Australian* report captured the mounting fervour:

> Speaking at Colac yesterday, the Prime Minister (Mr. Cook), referring to the situation in Europe said: 'I hope that the negotiations going on will result in peace, but if it is to be war, if the Armageddon is to come, you and I shall be in it. (Loud applause.) It is of no use to blink at our obligations. If the old country is at war so are we. (Loud applause.) It is not even a matter of choice, but of international law. The consent of Parliament is of course a very proper thing to have when the time is opportune, and if Parliament is sitting our self-government must extend of course to the complete control of our army and navy; but in times like this our resources must be placed where they are needed to be ready at once if the necessity arises. I hope that there will be no need for our brave men to leave our shores, but I am perfectly certain that if the need arises we shall see a response as spontaneous and complete as at any time in

> our history. (Tumultuous applause.) There will be no lack of volunteers, and the impression is that if war breaks out the trouble will be to get our men to stay at home. (Applause.) Good luck to the spirit that prompts them. (Applause.) Whatever obligations are necessary for the maintenance of the Empire in peace or war must be placed at the disposal of the responsible authorities when and wherever they are needed. We are ready to do our very best with and for the rest of the Empire in defending our interests in any part of the world. (Long and loud applause.)

War was declared on the night of 4 August in London. That same day the Western Australian Council of Churches had organised a day of prayer in Perth for the political situation in Europe. People gathered to worship at the Congregational Church in St Georges Terrace, which was near to the *West Australian* offices and many stayed milling around until midnight hoping for fresh news. But the declaration of war didn't trickle out until the next day, and they had to wait for accounts to be printed and posted on big white boards hastily erected outside the newspaper offices.

Country readers of the *West Australian* had to wait until 6 August to receive a report of what had happened – not on the front page but well back in the paper after the advertisements and under five decks of headlines:

> AUSTRALIA'S POSITION.
> OFFICIAL ANNOUNCEMENTS.
> THE OFFER OF NAVY AND TROOPS.
> MESSAGE FROM THE KING.
> PREPARATIONS FOR WAR.
>
> Melbourne, Aug. 5.
> The Prime Minister (Mr. Cook) to-day officially announced an outbreak of war between England and Germany. He added: 'Australia is now at war.'
>
> The following telegram has been received by the Governor-General from the Secretary of State for the Colonies: 'Referring to your telegram of August 3, His Majesty's Government greatly appreciate the

prompt readiness of your Government to place the naval forces of the Commonwealth at the disposal of the Admiralty, and your generous offer to equip and maintain an expeditionary force.'

The Throssell brothers had to ride 11 miles into Wyalkatchem to pick up the paper and read this report. Across the state one phrase stirred men's hearts and sounded like a trumpet call: 'an expeditionary force'! And then they read how Perth had reacted to the news:

Naturally enough yesterday's official news of the declaration of war excited an immense amount of interest in the city. The message conveying this momentous information filtered through a few minutes after midday, and an hour or so later, so intense was the interest awakened, that the matter was public property throughout the whole of the metropolitan area. The crowds which for the past few days have thronged about the newspaper bulletin boards in St. George's-terrace from midday began to grow in proportion, and eagerly devoured every titbit of information posted. During the day, while there was not wanting evidence that the gravity of the situation was appreciated by the community, there was little observable in the way of outward manifestation.

Of demonstration there was nothing during the day beyond occasional salvos of cheering at the bulletin boards or at the street corners where newsboys were doing a wonderful trade with their newspapers. As the day wore on a demand for rosettes of the national colours set in at the various business houses, and trading house managers gave instructions for the hoisting of the Union Jack on the flagpoles of their establishments. The latest news from the front formed the only topic of conversation, all other themes being forgotten.

Throughout the city in a thousand different quarters knots of more or less excited citizens were to be encountered speculating on what the future had in store . . . A few minutes before 10 o'clock a number of excited youths created a stir at the National Mutual Assurance buildings, St. George's-terrace. Here are situated the offices of the Austrian Consulate, on the entrance wall being fixed a plate bearing

> the Austrian coat of arms. A number of bricks were first thrown at the plate by some individual, one of the missiles, it is said, narrowly missing the wife of the caretaker who was at the moment standing near the entrance viewing the crowd. The plate was shortly afterwards removed by the caretaker and the incident closed.

The next day the paper reported: 'Everywhere was order and self-control and a quiet, tense yearning for news of some decisive battle'. Australia simply couldn't wait to go to war.

A special meeting of the federal Cabinet initially decided to put the ships of the Royal Australian Navy under the control of the British Admiralty and to dispatch an expeditionary force of 20,000 men to help the 'old country'. The force would comprise a full division of 18,000 men and a brigade of the Light Horse. The first light horse offer was for 2226 men and 2315 horses.

The reputation of the Australian Light Horsemen had been forged during the Boer War, with one British general writing: 'The Australian Light Horseman combines with a splendid physique, a restless activity of mind . . . on every variety of ground – mountain, plain, desert, swamp or jungle – the Australian Light Horseman has proved himself equal to the best'. Lord Kitchener, when he visited Australia in 1909 to review the Commonwealth's military forces, pronounced the Light Horse the 'pick of the bunch', adding that they were 'real thrusters'.

Kitchener's 1910 report had recommended compulsory military training in Australia, so by 1914 there were twenty-three light horse militia regiments throughout the country, comprising 456 officers and 6508 men of other ranks. Most were from the country, owning or breeding the horses on which they did their few weeks of annual training.

But in 1914 nearly half of the militia were aged only between nineteen and twenty-one. Australia could not send a boys' army overseas, however willing, so the new commanding officer, General William Throsby Bridges, decided on the formation of an entirely new army. The country's expeditionary force, he said, should have 'a name that will sound well when they call us by our initials. That is how they will speak of us'. It became the Australian Imperial Force: the AIF.

Half of the force was composed of youngsters already serving in the militia, with the other half of men not currently in the forces but who had once been in the militia or served in the Boer or other wars. Units were connected within the different states and, to encourage mateship, closeness and support, were local and territorial. Many friends, workmates and family members, including brothers, joined up together, often in the same outfit.

Initially, Western Australia had just one mounted regiment, with a machine-gun section attached, now known as the 25th Light Horse. But there was bitter disappointment after the recruiting halls opened and on the first day 4444 Western Australians rushed forwards to join the new AIF and share in what they called the 'Great Adventure' when it became known that no mounted troops were being asked for from the West. Many immediately enlisted in one of the infantry battalions, rather than miss out. Others held firm, believing that, sooner or later, Western Australia would be asked to supply mounted men. Several officers of the 25th even volunteered to resign their commissions and go in as rankers if necessary.

Meanwhile, conditions on the land were going from bad to worse. The *Western Mail* of 25 September 1914 reported: 'Crops a complete failure'. Everyone had done their best, but many would not produce even a pennyworth of wheat.

Many of the country football teams had already joined up. The first recruiters were accepting only the fittest men available. Country boys were coming forwards to join up for the Great Adventure – and to get paid. For many the offer of six shillings a day and an overseas trip was too good to miss.

Ric and Hugo Throssell at Cowcowing also decided to pack it in. They rode back to Northam, after selling off their team of Clydesdales, hiding their tools in an empty tank and turning their drought-stricken property over to their neighbour to look after.

On 29 September they both went before Dr H St John Mitchell in Northam and passed the medical examination. By 5 October, Hugo had been accepted by the army, and Ric signed on the next day.

By this time, almost grudgingly, the new army's leaders had at last bowed to pressure and agreed to accept the offer of a squadron of Light Horsemen from Western Australia, on the condition that the men supplied their own horses. The belated approval did little to calm the ruffled pride of the original militiamen. Western Australia had twice been overlooked after two major formations of the new Light Horse. The 1st Light Horse Brigade had been made up of four regiments – one each from New South Wales, Queensland and Victoria, and a combined regiment from South Australia and Tasmania. The rush of enthusiastic horsemen had continued, so the 2nd Light Horse Brigade was formed with one regiment from Queensland and two from New South Wales. Approval had now been given for the Western Australians to tack on a squadron to the 7th Light Horse Regiment from New South Wales. 'And what an assortment of Australian manhood that Squadron was!' exalted its historian, Arthur Olden. The first men rode into camp at Guildford in October 1914. 'Could any assemblage of well under 200 souls possibly be more cosmopolitan? Here were gentlemen of independent means, professional men, University graduates, commercial men, farmers, labourers, all shaken down together and actuated only by that splendid spirit which Western Australia showed from the beginning and from which, in the brightest and darkest days of the War till the last shot was fired, she never looked back.' Optimism was unbounded.

Within a month, after intense lobbying, the authorities gave more ground. The 3rd Light Horse Brigade was now raised, consisting of three regiments: the 8th from Victoria, the 9th from South Australia and a Western Australian regiment: the 10th Light Horse. Their leader was beside himself with delight. 'Tied myself down tight', he wrote, 'lest the strings on the cask of my soda water bottle should burst!'

4

Onward, Christian Soldiers

From grander clouds in our 'peaceful skies' than ever were there before
I tell you the Star of the South shall rise – in the lurid clouds of war.
It ever must be while blood is warm and the sons of men increase;
For ever the nations rose in storm, to rot in a deadly peace.
There comes a point that we will not yield, no matter if right or wrong,
And man will fight on the battle-field while passion and pride are strong . . .

Henry Lawson, 'The Star of Australasia', 1895.

Noel Murray Brazier prided himself on being the 'father of the regiment' and its chief recruiter. He seemed to know every well-connected family in Western Australia and many of its future troopers. He had met a good number of them before the war, as he travelled vast distances visiting farms and stations in his occupation as a surveyor. In 1894, for example, he had led a surveying party from Coolgardie in the eastern goldfields to the sheep and cattle station country in the mid-western Murchison region. He reported to the Lands minister that he had carried out over 330 miles of traversing, and 'independent of this we did about 600 miles of horseback work besides traveling over 1,000 miles with the horses from the time they left Perth until they returned'.

Brazier was born in Victoria, the fifth child of eight of the Reverend Amos Brazier and his wife, Jessie. His mother died young, so he was brought up by an elder sister. He started work in a newspaper office, but by working hard he qualified as a surveyor, a profession much in demand in Western Australia, with new land being opened up to the farmer settlers in the wake of the gold rushes. Brazier did well and bought his own acreage in the Upper Capel area, just west of the town of Kirrup. He called his homestead Capeldene and set out to make it a showpiece property where he could raise cattle and thoroughbred horses. He also married well: his wife, Maud, was the daughter of the Swan Brewery's general manager, an influential figure in the small social circle of isolated Perth. Maud and Noel had brought nine children into the world before he decided to ride away to war.

Brazier was a peppery character with a short fuse and strong opinions. He had a good knowledge of the Bible, which he often used in vigorous debate. He was intolerant of outsiders and was deeply protective of his own regiment, which soon became known as the 'Old Tenth'. Brazier himself was known as 'Colonel', even by his family, for all of his life. He had been a keen militiaman before the war and had been promoted to lieutenant colonel in 1913. Sometimes local troopers from the 25th Light Horse paraded before their proud leader on his property as he sat squarely on his horse and took the salute.

Now there was a real war, and, on 22 September 1914, Brazier noted in his diary: 'Went to Perth and reported for duty'. Four days later he attended a parade of the first contingent of Western Australians to leave the state. 'Fine looking men', he wrote. 'March discipline only fair. Lump in my throat all the same.'

After another four days Brazier was riding out into the countryside, contacting old friends, recruiting friends' sons and seeking out the men he had met as a surveyor on their farmlands. He was also selecting donated horses, or buying them, for his regiment.

In some ways it was like setting out on a crusade. The clergyman's son was going to lead a Christian regiment of mostly country boys in a righteous cause. A random study of 500 men who enlisted during the war with the 10th showed that 62 per cent registered in the country, with 88 per cent professing a religious denomination. Over half entered 'Anglican', as did Hugo and Ric Throssell, on their enlistment papers.

'Left for Beverley at 7 am', Brazier wrote in his diary on 30 September, as he rode off into the wheatbelt. 'Crops look rotten and feed scarce. Outlook very gloomy. Very hot. One horse only at Beverley. Got 16 men at Narrogin. Seven horses given.' The following day, at Wagin, he signed up fourteen men, four with horses; the next day, at Katanning, '15 men with horses, another 16 men without'.

Some were barely men. Hubert Howden Brockman, a blue-eyed, brown-haired farmhand from Beverley, enlisted on 19 September, putting his age as nineteen years and six months on his enrolment form. This was obviously later queried by the authorities, forcing his parents to write laboriously on lined notepaper: 'This to certify that our son Hubert Howden has our consent to join the Light Horse Squadron for service when required'. Just under a year later, Amy Brockman was writing to the office in charge of base records in Melbourne, seeking the death certificate of her son.

But there was, of course, no hint of any disaster ahead as the men walked and rode and caught trains from all over the state to join up. They came from a wide range of backgrounds and professions. Harry Corker, like nearly 20 per cent of the troopers, had been born in Britain. He was from Liverpool and had trained as a fellmonger. Now he was twenty-six years old, a lean, tanned, fair-haired stockman. He rode nearly 1000 miles to Perth from Muccau Station near Marble Bar to enlist in the 10th. Perhaps he was keen to get away from summer temperatures of 105 degrees Fahrenheit.

At the other end of the social scale was Alexander Phipps Turnbull, a 26-year-old Rhodes scholar and Perth solicitor who insisted on enlisting as a trooper. On one side of his family were the Lee Steeres, among the most prominent Western Australian pastoral families, and they worshipped regularly, sitting in the front pews of St George's Cathedral. The first Anglican Bishop of Perth, Dr Matthew Hale, had founded a school which today bears his name. Ten of Turnbull's fellow scholars from what was then called simply 'The High School' joined up with him.

George Arthur Leake was twenty-eight and also practised as a solicitor. His father had succeeded Hugo Throssell's father as premier of Western Australia. Part of his education had been at Uppingham, a prestigious British boarding school founded in 1584. Now he was back in Western Australia and with two friends had become partner in a property near Kellerberrin called Utopia. When the war came, they all rode off with the 10th – George, Guy Sholl and Leo Roskams, who had been born in Bristol and had already served six years with the Royal Engineers.

Guildford Grammar School's twenty-five old boys joining the 10th included the Harper brothers, sons of the school's founder. Gresley was a barrister and had won the languages prize in 1901; Wilfred was a farmer who had won seven prizes, ranging from mathematics to French. Both had played in the first XI cricket team and the first XVIII football team, and Wilfred was known as a champion sprinter. Another brother, Prescott, who joined up later in the war, was also a Rhodes scholar.

The 10th also contained many brothers, like the Throssells, going off to war together. There were the Harpers, the Chippers, the Gillams, the Coonans and the Bains.

Lance Corporal Lindsay Chipper and his older brother Trooper Ross Chipper were both farmers. Like the Throssells, they came from a wealthy background and had become firm friends with Hugo and Ric as boarders at Prince Alfred College. There was also another family of Chippers in the regiment: Trooper Henry Chipper, a Perth fireman, and his brother Arthur Chipper, a fair-haired stockman from further out in the country who was a horse driver in the 10th.

Troopers Syd Gillam and younger brother Hubert came from near Albany, and both had worked as surveyors' assistants. Marcus John, William Michael and Michael Joseph Coonan, all joined up on the same day. They were millhands from the state's south-west, where their parents, Michael and Ellen, owned the local pub. Duncan and Evan Bain came from a family of eight children born to Scottish parents, who had carved out a farm from the bush in 1903 near Katanning, south of Perth. It had been pioneering at its most primitive. Even the younger children, aged eight and ten, had been put to work on the property, wielding axes and dragging piles of brush and branches to be burnt. The family had initially lived in a three-room house made out of wheat bags sewn together, which they called Horisdale, but had graduated to a house made from mud bricks by the time that Duncan and Evan rode off together to join up in Perth.

Hugo and Ric Throssell made a bit of a show of it after they signed up in Northam. Gerry Throssell, a nephew, remembered that

> Uncle Ric and Jim stayed at our place . . . The next morning I asked Dad if I could go to the drill hall with them, instead of going to school. Dad said no. On the way to school I met Uncle Ric and Jim. Uncle Jim asked me to hold their horses while they signed up. I was sitting on one horse and holding the other when the headmaster came over and saw me and added my name to the list of boys AWL.

The Throssells waited in Northam until the entire Wyalkatchem football team, all eighteen of them, arrived. Hugo had been the team captain, so he led the new volunteers in a march down the main thoroughfare to the Northam railway station, where they joined the Kalgoorlie-to-Perth steam express.

Hugo's pep talk before a football game was said to go: 'We don't want to kill them, fellas, but a bit of maiming will be needed'. It was spoken in jest. But by the end of this war seven of the football team that rode through Northam would be dead, and others would come home maimed.

The new regiment was divided into A, B and C squadrons, and the clearing house for the newest recruits was set up at the Royal

Agricultural Society's showground at Claremont in Perth, where the men were assigned after they had passed riding tests. Captain Tom Todd was in charge, a handsome 46-year-old veteran born in New Zealand, who had won a Distinguished Service Order (DSO) and had been mentioned in dispatches in the Boer War. A former All Black, he had moved to Western Australia to join his brothers in a building contracting business and had been running a brickyard when the war began. 'There is no hurry,' he told his new soldiers reassuringly, 'this war will last for years'. A popular officer, he 'held his opinions strongly and expressed them in the most unequivocal language, but his breezy personality disarmed resentment and, as far as he was concerned, the hardiest fight left no sting of bitterness behind'.

Todd put recruits aboard a tall chestnut called Doctor Mac to see if they could ride. On one occasion, after a youth had fallen off three times, Todd intervened. 'My boy, what made you think you could ride?'

'I don't, sir.'

'Have you ever been on a horse in your life?'

'No, sir.'

'Well, what the hell did you come here for?'

'I didn't say I could ride, but I don't mind having a try, and I want to join the Regiment.'

'That's the way to talk', said Captain Todd. 'Well, go away for a week and practice riding and I'll give you another chance.'

'Thank you, sir.'

The boy was given another chance and, having passed the riding test, was sent on to Guildford, where the work had really begun. The squadron that had been originally formed as the nucleus of the 10th was now A Squadron. The men of B and C squadrons decided to march the 16 miles from Claremont to Guildford to join their comrades, rather than catch the train, 'just to try themselves out'. They were cheered into camp, where they quickly set up bell tents in which they slept at night, packed in eight or ten to a tent, their feet facing the centre pole. Their horses spent the nights tethered by head and heel ropes between long picket lines guarded by sentries.

The troopers' day began at dawn, when a trumpeter (two to a regiment) sounded the reveille to attend to 'stables' – cleaning the horse lines and feeding and watering the horses – before sitting down to breakfast themselves. There followed an intense day of training both in and out of the saddle. A journalist writing with the by-line 'Observer' sent an admirably full report on progress to the *West Australian*:

> On the banks of the Helena River just about half a mile to the eastward of the bridge over which Guildford is approached, the first regiment of Light Horse, which is being sent to the war from Western Australia, is being trained. The grounds are those which have been hitherto used as a remount depot for the Military Forces. They are very suitable for the purpose, being on comparatively hard soil, the tents being pitched on a partial slope, and the parade areas being on the grassy flats bordering the river . . . Most of the members of this squadron were men who had undergone some training at annual encampments. They entered into the task of preparing for active service with much enthusiasm, and most of them provided their own horses and general equipment . . .
>
> So great has been the demand for places in the ranks that there are now under canvas to-day over 50 men more than makes the complement. A visitor to the encampment is at once impressed with two things – the fine athletic appearance of the men, and the enthusiasm and earnestness of their work. At the invitation of Lt.-Col. Brazier I spent a full day in camp this week. From 6 o'clock in the morning until well after sundown, both officers and men were drilling or carrying out the work that is necessary and incidental to the preparation of a regiment for service abroad. In the ranks of which the various drilling companies were formed, one recognised men who few weeks ago were seen on the Terrace and in other business parts of the city. Professional and business men are among them. A barrister, fortunate in that he only practises his profession for the pleasure of it, having caught the war fever, was seen in the horse lines, bronzed and happy. A well-known stock auctioneer paced side

by side with a young solicitor and a young farmer owning wide tracks of wheat country in the Eastern areas. Men from the Nor'-West and from the timber ranges, men from the mines and the pearling grounds, worked side by side with the city fellows who have joined the ranks. And men from towns and distant parts are still coming in, eager to join and disappointed when told in kindly terms by the officers that the ranks are already too full. The extra men who have been enrolled will form the nucleus for a further contingent, or will be sent forward to fill the ranks as vacancies occur.

With the continual working of men and horses on the grounds near to the pitched rows of tents the sand is being worked up, and in the heat of Monday the men had to suffer the inconveniences of a considerable quantity of dust. In order that this discomfort might not, as work proceeds, be accentuated, Captain J. T. Todd took a party of mounted men through the bush in the direction of Kalamunda and discovering an area of 100 acres or so carrying only stunted scrub decided upon the point as a maneuvering ground when the time comes for the men to be trained in mounted drill. So far the drilling has been confined to foot work, though the men have been busily engaged at times in riding exercises and in training their horses. In the hospital, which is controlled by Dr. Haynes, there are at present three men who are suffering from injuries received through falls when exercising their horses. One man has a broken collarbone, another a dislocated collarbone, and the third is suffering from a broken wrist. These hurts were sustained on Sunday when, in the presence of several hundred people, the men were jumping low hurdles in sections of fours, and showing their skill or want of skill at tent pegging. Out on the new grounds, which will be used for mounted drill, several squads of men have done a lot of clearing, and when the commanding officer went out on Monday to inspect the place selected by Captain Todd, he expressed himself as very pleased with it, and also with the excellent preparatory work the men had done.

Up to the present matters are only in an embryonic stage. The men have not been supplied with the regulation kits, nor have more than a small proportion of them received their uniforms. On the paddocks adjacent to the drilling grounds there are turned loose several hundreds of horses, which have been brought from various districts south of Geraldton, and which have been purchased at what seems to be cheap prices by specially appointed expert buyers. Some hundred or so of horses are in the lines, which are kept remarkably clean. Saddles, bridles, and general equipment are being got ready at the buildings near to the camp and it is anticipated that very shortly every man will be provided with his own horse and gear. Then the work of mounted drill will be gone into in earnest. Long marches through towns and country will be made, but in the meantime the preparatory work is confined mostly to strenuous labour on foot. Sergeant Love, who saw a lot of active service in South Africa, and who is a noted horseman, has a small squad of rough riders who are engaged in the handling of those horses which have not been properly broken. Sections of men are instructed in signalling, in heliographic work, and in machine-gun work.

There is no lack of discipline. It redounds to the honour of the men and to the credit of the officers that not yet has there been started an offence list. Not one man has absented himself without leave and not one man has disgraced his uniform by becoming intoxicated. There seems to be a general idea of the necessity of holding up the good fame of the regiment, of which every man and every officer is so proud.

Brazier had insisted on having his friend Major Alan Love, a Perth accountant, promoted as his second-in-command, riding over the objections of military headquarters in Perth, which was typical of the pushy, pugnacious commander. It was his regiment, and even if he had been a militiaman he was now a regular soldier who had waited a long time for this chance to be part of the new AIF.

Along with a sprinkling of Boer War veterans like Todd, there were only two regular army officers in the regiment. One was the adjutant, Captain RE Jackson, a member of the prewar administrative and instructional staff. The other was just twenty years old, one of the first graduates of the 1912 class of the new Royal Military College, Duntroon. Horace Clement Hugh Robertson came from western Victoria and was the son of a state schoolteacher. He became known as 'Red Robbie' and went on to become one of Australia's most colourful and controversial generals. For now, he was attached to the 10th as the officer in charge of machine-guns.

Seven young officers of the Duntroon class of 1912 had found themselves posted to the three regiments that formed the 3rd Light Horse Brigade, of which the 10th was one.

The other regiments in the brigade were the 8th Light Horse, now being raised in Victoria, and the 9th, which was made up of two squadrons from South Australia and one other from Victoria.

Here command was split between youth and experience. Lieutenant Colonel Alexander Henry White, a charming and dashing militiaman aged thirty-two who hailed from Ballarat, where his family malted barley for Foster's beer, was put in command of the 8th. Major James O'Brien, a 52-year-old Boer War veteran, who had also served in the British Army in India, was nominated as his number two.

Over in Adelaide, the positions were reversed as the 9th was formed. A 44-year-old Boer War veteran, Lieutenant Colonel Albert Miell, described as 'an energetic and capable officer of long standing', was put in charge of the regiment while Major Carew Reynell, a tall, 32-year-old vigneron, was second in charge.

The command of the 3rd Light Horse Brigade, of which the 10th Regiment formed a part, was troubled from the start. Disintegrating personal relationships at the top went on to have disastrous consequences on Gallipoli.

The brigade commander was Brigadier General Frederic Godfrey Hughes, a portly, moustachioed and blimpish 56-year-old businessman from Melbourne who had never seen a shot fired in anger. His military career had begun when he was seventeen, when he joined the St Kilda Artillery Battery as a horse driver, wearing a flashy uniform with 'SK' on the shoulders. In Bean's withering description he was an 'elderly citizen officer belonging to leading social circles'. Long before the war he had graduated to an officer in the Victorian Horse Artillery. He led a contingent to London, all in blue uniforms with gold braid, highly polished riding boots and white helmets, to take part in a military tournament. Hughes liked uniforms, and he had added more gold braid to his when he became aide-de-camp to the governor-general, in 1907. Marrying Ada Eva Snodgrass, a lady with impeccable conservative connections and links to the Victorian squatocracy, had helped him. Hughes had even worn a fur-trimmed robe and gold chain, as mayor of St Kilda, for two terms. His transition into a red-tabbed general's uniform was easy.

He was born in 1858 and grew up in the shadow of the Crimean War and the Charge of the Light Brigade. As events later proved, his thinking had not progressed much since. He soon boldly exhibited that he was a stickler for doing things by the army manual, even if it was out of date. 'In time of war, as in peace, our Brigadier's idea of soldiering was to salute smartly, roll a greatcoat correctly, and note the march discipline', wrote an officer. Nepotism played a role in his organisation: he later used his influence to have his son Arthur and nephew Wilfred join his staff as commissioned officers, cocooning himself in his own personal comfort zone.

As second-in-command of the brigade, the army appointed a complete opposite. The new brigade major was Lieutenant Colonel John 'Jack' Macquarie Antill, widely known as 'Bull' Antill or simply the 'Bullant'. He was forty-eight, a tough square-jawed professional soldier, hugely experienced, but also a martinet and a bully. Born in Picton, New South Wales, he was descended from a long line of British Army officers. He had been a surveyor after leaving school and had joined the local militia when he was twenty-one.

Antill's military career proper began with a posting to India in 1893, where he was attached to the Devonshire Regiment and the 2nd Dragoon Guards of the British Army. Following that he returned home and was commissioned as an officer in the new

Commonwealth army. Five years later he was promoted to major in command of a squadron of the New South Wales Mounted Rifles, leading them off to the Boer War. He took part in a number of major actions, and his commanding officer noted that 'on two occasions he led his regiment at the gallop against positions held by the enemy, proving him to be a fearless and valuable leader in the field. He has shown great capacity in command of his regiment'. Antill returned a minor hero, with seven clasps on his service medal, having twice been mentioned in dispatches. He was appointed a Commander of the Order of the Bath, promoted to brevet lieutenant colonel and became chief instructor for the Australian Light Horse in New South Wales.

But then the nasty side of Antill's character began to emerge, and the Bullant began to bite. Appointed to the army's inspection staff, on one occasion he went overboard by visiting a militia camp and condemning 'the lack of discipline, the control and proficiency of the officers, the supervision, filthy lines, poor rifle exercises, bad marching, dirty band instruments and the appearance of the men'. His comments about a brother officer with whom he had served in South Africa were described as 'grossly unfair' by a court of enquiry called to look into the report. The court heard that the Bullant was harsh and tactless, and that parts of his report were 'unjust, unfair, misleading and not supported by evidence'.

Antill's career then stalled. Others were promoted over him. He was a rigid and uncompromising man. Orders were orders to be obeyed at all times without question. When the war came, the Bullant seized on his new opportunity when an election board in Sydney decided on his appointment interstate as brigade major for the 3rd Light Horse Brigade, headquartered in Melbourne.

Antill, the toughened war veteran, must have been shocked to find himself second-in-command to Frederic Hughes, the elderly martial clothes horse, and dismayed to discover that two of his regimental commanders, Lieutenant Colonels Alexander Henry White of the 8th and Noel Murray Brazier of the 10th, were also peacetime soldiers who had never seen active service. The Bullant decided he was going to let everyone know who he was. He started off by travelling to Adelaide, looking the 9th Regiment over and giving it such a tongue-lashing that the non-commissioned officers (NCOs) asked to be discharged and the officers protested directly to the commander, Lieutenant Colonel Albert Miell. The lieutenant colonel must have intervened sternly with his Boer War colleague: before Antill returned to Melbourne he diplomatically described the troops in public as 'a fine type of men'.

Hughes, meanwhile, went to Western Australia to meet Brazier and his men, telling the *Argus* on his return to Melbourne that he had found them to be 'very hardy and tough'.

By 10 December 1914, Brazier, who was forging ahead with training and equipping his regiment, had secured 501 riding horses, fifty light transport horses and thirty-three packhorses. The smell of burnt flesh and hair mingled with the choking dust of Guildford as Captain Edward Weston, the veterinary officer, supervised the selection and branding of the horses.

The composition of and equipment issued to a Light Horse regiment was now carefully defined and detailed. A regiment at the outbreak of the war had an establishment figure of twenty-five officers and 497 troopers. These were broken down into three squadrons – A, B and C – often with a four-man machine-gun section attached. Each squadron was divided into six troops consisting of approximately thirty-two men and their horses, and troops were further broken down into sections of four men. It was a remarkably close organisation, highly mobile, flexible and adaptable.

The equipment carried by a Light Horseman and his horse was exactly detailed and its weight estimated to a fraction of an ounce. The trooper was fitted out with everything from field cap to cord breeches, braces, flannel shirt, ankle boots, puttees and jack spurs. He had a haversack, water bottle, clasp knife and lanyard, and a leather bandolier, waist belt and attachment that held 100 rounds of .303 ammunition. Finally, there was his rifle, with sling, pull-through, cleaning rod and full oil bottle, bayonet and scabbard, another waist belt and frog. The total weight carried by each trooper was 39 pounds 8¼ ounces.

The horse carried everything from saddle to shoe case containing one fore and one hind shoe and nails, as well as a hoof pick, forage net, picketing gear and surcingle pad, and the trooper's greatcoat, mess tin and packed wallets containing everything from an emergency ration to the trooper's knife, fork and spoon, shaving brush and razor. The equipment weight carried by the horse was 76 pounds 5¼ ounces. With the addition of the rider, the total weight carried by the horse was 255 pounds 13½ ounces.

It was hot and dusty in the camp. The Swan River itself was cool and inviting for a swim, but bathers had to be wary of underwater tangles of old tree limbs and roots. Market gardeners grew luscious red tomatoes and sweet-fleshed melons, and a makeshift row of shanties sprang up near the camp to sell local produce. There was no beer in or around the camp, by order, so some stalls sold squashes and ices to the thirsty troopers at the end of the day's drilling. The area was dubbed by the troopers 'Hay Street', perhaps to remind them of the long street in Perth that was one part shopping area, the other part red-light district. But they didn't have much longer to wait in the camp.

On 18 December the 10th Light Horse moved out from Guildford, mounted and fully equipped on their fine horses, a long column of bronzed men with emu plumes in their slouch hats riding into the cool afternoon sea breeze and along Perth's streets, packed with a cheering crowd. They returned to Claremont, where the men and their horses were now to be billeted. The next day was 'devoted to military sports and the people of the metropolis witnessed a fine exhibition of horsemanship in the beautiful show ring'.

On 21 December, Brazier signed, with a flourish, the Certificate of Commanding Officer on the Throssell brothers' enlistment papers, appointing them both to A Squadron.

Initially, Hugo was an acting sergeant, Ric an acting corporal. Their enlistment papers show that Hugo, at 5 foot 10 inches, was one inch shorter than Ric, and at 161 pounds, five pounds lighter, too. Apart from that they were almost identical in looks – both described as having dark complexions, brown eyes and dark brown hair.

But as the men of the 10th galloped beside the Swan River, the reality of a modern war and what might lie ahead was only just beginning to dawn on Australia. Charles Bean observed at this time the attention of the whole people had become concentrated 'on the shocking initial disasters of the war in Europe, the retreat from Mons, the heartening recovery – by a bare margin – on the Marne, the horrors in Belgium, the swift advance and then stoppage of the Russian "steam roller", the first struggle at Ypres. And Australians were still rushing to enlist . . .'

The troopers under training were straining at the bit to be in action, fearful it all might end too soon. They had no doubt that the Allies would win.

'In remarkably short time', wrote Ian Jones in *The Australian Light Horse*,

> the light-horsemen emerged as the elite of the AIF – easily picked out by their leather bandoliers, leather belts, leather leggings, and spurs, moving with the swagger of natural-born winners and already the best disciplined branch of the army. They were eager to match themselves against British cavalry on the Western Front, shielded as they were by a propagandist press from ugly truths that were already evident. Cavalry – British, French, Belgian and German – were being slaughtered in their hundreds. But British senior officers with hunt club mentalities were staunch in their belief that cavalry could still triumph. They were eager to hurl the Australian Light Horse into the hellholes of France and Flanders.

5
Marching as to War

Brave sons of West Australia
Who are going to cross the main
To help uphold old England
Just independence to retain;
To fight for King and Empire
With steady heart and hand,
Doing your job manfully,
Cheerfully bowing to each command.

Margaretta Dore, 'Lines to Our Brave Volunteers', Broadsheet, Fremantle, 1914

IT WAS CHRISTMAS TIME, AND AS it was known that overseas embarkation for the 10th would not take place before the new year, general leave was granted for most of the officers and men of the regiment. Hugo and Ric Throssell went home to Northam and posed for photographs in their new uniforms outside the family mansion.

Meanwhile, officers like Horace Robertson, with no family ties, were sent with the horses to Rockingham, a sandy wasteland about 20 miles south of Fremantle, where a new camp had been established. Chaos soon reigned. Robertson wrote:

> The CO decided to turn our horses out in a paddock close to the camp . . . you can't suddenly turn 600 horses loose from lines where they

> have been tethered for months and expect the unusual freedom not to go to their heads. It did go to their heads and the party who were trying to control the horses were glad enough to escape with their lives when a mad stampede started.
>
> I did not see the start of the rush, but I was told that a black horse, answering the description of my own charger, led it, and he, together with about 50 other horses, ended in Fremantle, but the other 550 were scattered singly and in groups all over the countryside. Then things began to happen, for all the telegraph and telephone lines ran hot recalling all members of the regiment from leave, and most of us spent a very tiring, hungry Xmas scouring the sandy belt while the thermometer topped the century. However, all's well that ends well, and we eventually collected the whole 600 – some rather damaged – but to this day we have never quite lived down the title of 10th 'Lost' Horse.

On 2 January the regiment marched out from its old base at the showgrounds in Claremont and caught the steam ferry *Zephyr* down the Swan River, through the port of Fremantle and south to Rockingham, which the men soon detested as the dustiest and dirtiest place on earth. They trained for almost a month on sandy stretches, in fierce heat, bombarded by persistent bush flies. The only relief was a daily swim in the ocean. Each Sunday steamers arrived laden with relatives and friends bringing picnic hampers, who knew that the time for departure could not be far off.

One day a Mrs P Law-Smith arrived to present the regiment with a hand-embroidered standard emblazoned with a black swan on a yellow background, with the motto '*Percute et percute velociter*' (Strike and strike swiftly). Archbishop Riley, chaplain general of the forces, blessed the standard, then the regimental sergeant major marched forwards to receive it.

Everyone, it seemed, wanted to help the 10th in some way. Brazier wrote a letter to the editor of the *West Australian*:

> May we through your columns express our thanks to the many friends of the regiment who have contributed to our funds or in other ways helped

> us. We should have liked to have published a statement of receipts and expenditure, but, unfortunately, there is not time now . . . With the money placed at our disposal we have purchased instruments for the band, which we hope to form while on the trooper, two motor cycles for dispatch riders, and games, writing materials etc., for the use of the men.

At the beginning of February the regiment was moved back to Claremont, and word spread quickly that at last the Light Horse would be sailing. But for where? 'There was much speculation as to the destination', wrote Olden, 'but very little doubt existed that it would be Egypt. The Infantry and Artillery, and indeed the greater portion of the Light Horse were known to be already there, and there was small reason to suppose that the Third Light Horse Brigade, consisting of the 8th, 9th and 10th Regiments, should be switched at this juncture'.

The departure date was fixed as 8 February. A few days beforehand, Hugo Throssell received disappointing news: he would have to wait behind in Australia, because there wasn't enough room for the whole regiment and their horses on the first Light Horse troop ship. He and Ric would have to part.

Hugo received the order with a 'restless, almost rebellious spirit'. He was a man who always led from the front, the captain of school and country sporting teams, and he was hugely disappointed to be put on the backbench as his brother and his mates sailed away.

Before leaving, Ric wrote a letter to Hugo setting out some matters he wanted attended to in the event of his death. Hugo folded the letter away with the rest of his belongings, unread.

Hugo was at the Fremantle wharf to see Ric and the other troopers climb aboard the converted British India steamer *Mashobra* of 8236 tons, capable of 13 knots on a good day. 'The horses were the first got aboard', wrote Olden, 'and for the most part behaved wonderfully well, considering it was their maiden embarkation, the sling being brought into requisition in one or two cases only. The troops followed and were soon shaken down in their respective troop decks'.

Also leaving were two of Hugo's new friends, Phil Fry and Tom Kidd. Captain Henry Philip Fry was described later as Hugo's 'greatest chum'. He was also one of the most popular officers in the 10th.

Born in England – 35 per cent of the Anzacs overall were British-born – Phil Fry had connections to the Quaker family of Frys that included the famous Elizabeth Fry who, in 19th-century England had set herself the task of improving conditions for prisoners in the overcrowded jails. Many Quakers invested in the Western Australian Company, which was set up in 1840 to establish a model British colony on the south-west corner of Australia.

Phil Fry's family had arrived in 1894 and settled at Crendon Downs, a handsome property in hilly country 6 miles from Donnybrook in the State's south-west. The Frys had soon become friends with other families in this broad area, including the Braziers. It was little wonder that the then Lieutenant Phil Fry became another enthusiastic member of the militia before the war, often having his troops to stay at Crendon, where they could practise their drilling and shooting on a nearby rifle range.

Phil wrote to one relative during this time: 'I spent a long day yesterday, a troop parade on the Rifle Range. I started the day by going to early church. Left home at 7 am and returned at 10 pm'.

He was noted for his piety and generosity. When out riding, the family had the habit of unselfconsciously stopping by the roadside in the bush to say some prayers together, and 'Phil always knelt so simply', wrote an aunt.

Hugo once told a family member that Fry was 'a most popular officer and always the same to everybody. He always shared his parcels, and he got many, with Lt Throssell, and Phil always used to say his prayers. Lt Throssell never saw a fellow do it before (and he didn't) but he used to tell Phil to put in a word for him'.

Major Thomas Anderson Kidd was a ramrod-straight 6 footer, a natural and already experienced soldier, cool, calm and collected, with piercing blue eyes, a trim moustache and an uncanny ability for survival. His men later called him the 'Bomb-Proof Kidd' or the 'Bullet-Proof Kidd'. He would be a key comrade fighting alongside Hugo in battle and would come to recommend Hugo for the Victoria Cross.

Tom Kidd had been born in Victoria in 1879, the third son of six brothers and two sisters. Tom was part of another huge family – his mother, Emma Nankivell, was one of twenty-one children born to Robert Rogers Nankivell, a surveyor, architect, and builder and mining engineer. Tom's father – also Thomas Anderson Kidd – had been a bank manager with the London Chartered Bank on the Victorian goldfields, but after the great bank crash in Melbourne in the 1890s, the Kidd family moved to Western Australia. There they set up a forwarding business using drays and teams of horses from the ports of Albany and Geraldton via the railheads to mining camps and outback stations.

They settled in Geraldton, where young Tom and brothers Jim and Jack joined the militia and the splendidly uniformed Geraldton Mounted Rifles. Tom loved sport, playing tennis and also rowing with the local club, where they made him a life member before he sailed off for the First World War. But he was already a veteran.

When the Boer War came before the turn of the century, his family history has it that he tried to enlist by travelling to Melbourne, but was refused because he looked too young. So he then worked his passage on a ship to South Africa and enlisted there. A paper survives to show that Trooper T.A. Kidd enlisted with the Border Horse Regiment (Colonial Division) at Durban on 17 February 1900 and served until 31 October of the same year. He was only twenty when he joined up.

After seeing plenty of action on the veldt he returned to Australia to be selected as one of the Western Australian officers who were sent to Melbourne to represent the state at the opening of the first Commonwealth Parliament in 1901.

Tom Kidd then went home to Geraldton where he practised as an accountant and also bought a small farm at Eradu. He married

Mary (May) in 1905 and by the time he enlisted again for war they had three young children, Ena, Tom and John (known as Jacky), all less than seven years old.

Kidd was thirty-five years old when he signed up again in 1915. He saw his duty clearly before him. The remarkable journal that he kept on Gallipoli shows again and again his coolness under fire.

There was no secrecy about the *Mashobra*'s departure; after all, the cruiser *Sydney*, which had escorted the first convoy to depart Australia, on 1 November 1914, had broken off to engage and cripple the German raider *Emden* in the Battle of Cocos, and no further danger was currently anticipated in the Indian Ocean. There was no need, then, for a fresh convoy. As a result the six transports carrying the 3rd Light Horse Brigade left independently, and for several weeks they were strung out across the oceans between Australia and Suez. The 10th Light Horse Regiment's A and B squadrons were the first to sail. Olden described their send-off:

> It is doubtful if ever such a large and representative assemblage of Western Australian people had previously been seen at Fremantle to compare with that which gathered together on the wharf that day to bid adieu to their one mounted unit. A spirit of boisterous enthusiasm prevailed, both among the troops and their friends on shore. Doubtless much of it was assumed in order to conceal the deeper heart-feelings of wife and sister or husband and brother. But it was a spirit proper to the occasion. Western Australia was giving of its best for King and Country.
>
> At five o'clock in the afternoon the *Mashobra* drew slowly away from the wharf to the accompaniment of cheer upon cheer, the National Anthem, and the many battle cries, now so familiar to everyone. A final waving of hats and handkerchiefs, a last long called 'good-bye' as the steamer passed the Mole, and the 10th Regiment had gone!

While still lyrical about the departure, Olden was moved to write that it was 'a happy family aboard the *Mashobra*', but it was soon far from happy. The Bullant was aboard. Olden glossed over any unpleasantness by saying merely that: 'Lieut-Colonel J.M. Antill, the first Brigade-Major of the 3rd Light Horse Brigade, was in command of the troops, and, whilst enforcing a rigid discipline throughout the voyage did everything possible to ensure the comfort and well-being of the men'.

Antill had arrived in Perth well before the regiment sailed. At the dusty training ground at Rockingham he had set out to show everyone that as a professional soldier and Boer War veteran – the officer selected to balance Hughes, the elderly and inexperienced brigade commander – he, Antill, was the real boss. A clash with Brazier, the gentleman farmer and militiaman who had almost single-handedly raised the regiment from among his friends and contacts throughout Western Australia, was inevitable. The Western Australians had always been independently minded, and Brazier was a long-time supporter of the always-simmering secession movement. He saw Antill as an upstart, a wise man from the East, come to tell him what to do and order him and his men about. At the back of a notebook, Brazier began to write furiously, in pencil, a litany of what he called 'episodes' of the 'treatment' he received from Antill. The notebook is in the archives of the Australian War Memorial, and its words sizzle to this day. The first two entries give a typical example:

> 1. During the BM's visit to Rockingham he was the essence of oiliness and wired to Brigadier [Hughes] that 10 Regt was easily the best. The other COs eventually told us that owing to the continual buttering up of the 10th they got to hate us.
>
> 2. The *Mashobra* left Fremantle at 5 pm on Wednesday February 8 and 15 minutes from casting off, while all hands were waving, the BM came round near me and yelled out 'This is the worst disciplined regiment I have ever seen'. He was CO troops although I am his senior.
>
> I said nothing but felt a lot.
>
> Later on he came near me and made nasty remarks and I told him there were two adjutants on the ship capable of doing their duties and

> if he expected me to chase them around continually and worry them he was mistaken. He shut up and two days later got very oily again.

And so it goes on, for page after page. The relationship was doomed and grew steadily worse.

✠

Two weeks after the *Mashobra* sailed, the newly commissioned Second Lieutenant Hugo Throssell and his men were also sent off to war. Hugo had to be treated with a new respect as a commissioned officer and 'Northam Jim' was now to be officially addressed as Hugo Throssell. The new officer and his men climbed aboard a much smaller and slower vessel than the *Mashobra*, a converted cargo ship called the *Itonus*, which had started life as a cable layer. Theirs was the third ship off the rank, leaving after C Squadron sailed, on 17 February aboard the *Surada*. The war eventually caught up with all three ships. The *Itonus* was torpedoed off Malta in December 1916, the *Mashobra* sank less than five months later, after being shelled by an Austrian submarine, and the *Surada* was sent to the bottom by a German U-boat in 1918.

Third off the rank. Hugo swallowed his pride and commenced his official war diary in Fremantle, aboard the *Itonus*. '22/2/15 Fremantle, Noon: Embarked SS *Itonus* (Troopship 50) with 1 Sgt, 1 Cpl & 50 men – comprising 2nd Reinforcements 10th L.H. Regiment'. His next entries, about the voyage, are equally terse:

> 13/3/15 Aden 9.30 p.m. Arrived at Aden.
>
> 14/3/15 Aden 12 noon. Sailed from Aden to Suez.
>
> 20/3/15 Suez. Arrived and entrained for Cairo at 2 pm. Abbassia. 11.40 pm Arrived Abbassia Detail Camp five miles from Cairo.

The voyage for Ric and most of the regiment aboard the *Mashobra* had been much more lively. The ship's paper, the *Mashroba Bully Tin* carried this verse:

Well! At last we have got fairly going
And a few hundred miles out to sea,
And we're heading Nor' West without knowing
What our mission in future may be.
But whatever the job is, they'll find us
No less eager to start – nor sincere;
Still, we cannot forget that behind us
Is the Girl on the Fremantle Pier!

We've a good many things in our favour
Our troopship is comfy and new,
And the tucker possesses a flavour
Unlike the old Rockingham stew.
We are done with the dust for a season,
We've a chance to envelop a beer,
Still we miss – and not without reason
That Girl on the Fremantle Pier.

When the *Mashobra* reached the equator, Brazier entered the Crossing the Line ceremony with considerable gusto, noting that it was 'the funniest thing I ever saw. Much laughter'. Olden wrote: 'The introduction of the Regiment to Father Neptune was headed by Colonel Brazier, attired in a feather head-dress, a lot of red paint, and a battle axe – to represent a wild Cherokee Chief, "Kirrup of Kapeldene, King of the Cygnets, at the mention of whose great name no dingo dareth bark". And the Colonel was supported in his act by Doctor "Jim" Bentley as a prehistoric Medicine Man'.

James Bentley was from a horse-loving Irish family. As a boy he rode a horse to school and as he grew up trained jumpers and rode as a huntsman in Clare and County Limerick. His love of horses never left him. Late in his life (he died in 1962, aged eighty-two) he was a familiar tall figure on the Perth racecourse, dressed in a white suit and pith helmet, moving through the betting ring. He never missed a Saturday race meeting and in the evenings he was also a fanatical bridge player, becoming president of the Western Australian bridge club.

After attending school in Ireland, Bentley attended the University of Edinburgh, where he studied medicine and also played in the rugby team. For two years he was house surgeon at the Royal Infirmary at Preston in England before taking a job as medical officer aboard the liner *Oronsay*. In 1908 James Bentley moved to Western Australia to join the staff of the Claremont Hospital for the Insane, an isolated asylum built out of sight in the sand hills of Perth and reached by means of a two-horse cab driven 1½ miles over a rough track through the scrub from the township of Claremont. He was paid £300 a year, a salary described as 'hardly enough to pay for the officer's golf sticks', but became a dedicated psychiatrist.

At 6 feet 1 inch and a horseman he was ideal material for the Light Horse, and Brazier had quickly signed him up as the medical officer for the 10th, with the rank of captain, when he had turned up to enlist in December 1914.

The ships, with their cargoes of over 1000 men, hundreds of horses, stores and saddles, ammunition and equipment, dipped, rolled and churned their way across the Indian Ocean, belching black smoke from their coal-fired steam engines.

Cleaning crowded stalls below decks and exercising the horses, morning and afternoon, within the tight spaces available were the constant labours of the troopers. They practised rifle and bayonet drill, shot at targets bobbing in their ship's wake and learnt how to use semaphore flags. The men slept on the open decks in the tropics and swung in rows of creaking hammocks below deck when the weather was bad.

Boxing matches, concerts and well-meaning lectures on venereal disease ('Lieut Williams gave lecture on "Protection"', wrote Trooper Hubert Gillam) were some of the highlights of the voyages. Gillam also wrote about time spent playing rubbers of bridge. Somehow, alcohol had been obtained, and a trooper called Snowy had managed to get 'shicko' before being 'placed in clink at 12 noon'. He was later released under open arrest.

The ships carrying the 10th Light Horse arrived in Alexandria between 9 March and 4 April. Men, horses and equipment were loaded onto trains for the long trip to Cairo. From there the men had to lead their horses, many lame and with tender feet after the long voyage, through the night to a huge tented camp at Mena.

Hugo arrived on 6 March: '9am Left For Mena Camp', he noted from the transit stop at Abbassia. Others recorded more details about their experiences. Hubert Gillam wrote in his diary:

> We didn't get much of a chance to see much of Suez. We got well acquainted with the Arabs who were selling there [*sic*] wares. They are cute dealers and no doubt they did well at our expense. Arrived at Cairo at 3 am in morning and unloaded our horses and kits. Lined up on the road. Then every second man marched off to take tram to Mena. Found tram and also found it wouldn't hold us so marched back and got a horse each and set out for the camp on foot leading horses. Done the 8 miles by daybreak just getting to the camp as Reveille was sounded.

Trooper Donald Hassell sent a letter to his father in Albany from 'the edge of the desert' and told him that 'there are about 300 acres covered by tents and there must be close on 16,000 horses'.

Hugo had no idea where to find his brother Ric when he arrived at the camp. The first squadrons of the 10th were already out in the desert on training and exercises. He missed them when they rode in at dusk. Eventually, Hugo walked up and down the lines whistling the call that they had used to signal to each other in the paddocks of their farm at Cowcowing. Hugo's son later recounted their meeting:

> Ric was writing a letter home with a graphed army notebook perched on his knee when he heard. He flung back the tent flap.
>
> There was a figure at the end of the lines silhouetted against the light from the YMCA comforts tent. He whistled back. Jim came striding over grinning with pleasure.
>
> 'Ric, old man! Is that you? How are you? It's great to see you,' he said, thumping him on the shoulder.

But boredom soon set in for the Australians. There had been a last-minute decision to hold and train them in Egypt after troops from the Canadian Expeditionary Force, sent to train in England, had become stuck in 'archipelagoes of tents in a knee-deep sea of mud' on Salisbury Plain. The Egyptian desert therefore seemed to be a much better alternative before sending the troops on to the European front. Oliver Hogue, a New South Wales journalist, in camp with the 2nd Light Horse Brigade, wrote home bitterly: 'Yes, we were biding our time and I am telling no secrets when I say that the Australians swore terribly . . . We had left our happy homes in order to take part in the war and here we were burning our heels on the Egyptian sand – day after day, week after week'. Sergeant Alexander Phipps Turnbull, the solicitor and Rhodes scholar, sent a much fuller, if sometimes guarded, description to his grandmother in Perth of his arrival in Egypt as the 10th settled down to a new monotonous life:

> My dear Grannie:
>
> Well here we are encamped at the foot of the Pyramids and the rest of the Australian troops and Egypt was our destination as we thought. We arrived in Alexandria last Monday morning and disembarked that day; we were going hard till two o'clock putting all our horses and gear on the tracks and had everything on the train by four o'clock when we left Alexandria reaching Cairo about ten that night. It was a very interesting time in the train, the country is perfectly flat but every inch of it is cultivated and heavily irrigated and here and there dotted with native villages. Crops of every kind appear to be growing and they do their field work with cows, donkeys and camels and there seems to be hundreds of them. I was quite sorry to leave the boat in a way though it was getting a little monotonous with the same work and routine day after day but one could at least keep clean and we miss the nice baths and comparatively good living now. We were going hard all the first night; detrained in Cairo and then the majority of the men had a tramp of eleven miles landing the horses and did not reach the camp till close on daylight. The remainder had to unload and load baggage and came

out on the wagon and teams. The camp was not prepared in any way for us and all this week we have been very hard worked getting things into shape and the first few days one felt it, I can tell you, after coming off board ship. We thought we were in a sandy spot at Rockingham but this place beats any I have seen. We are right on the edge of the desert and can see nothing but a sandy waste as far as the eye can see on one side; there is not the vestige of growth or tree of any kind growing on it and when the wind blows from the desert quarter it is hard to see for drifting sand and it makes one's eyes very sore . . . We are right at the foot of two of the pyramids and they make the most imposing spectacle. I have not been up them yet nor had a look through the tombs, so I will be able to tell you about them later . . .

Most of the men here any time are pretty sick of it and are all anxious to get away and I think they may be going at any time now, probably to the Dardanelles. There are thousands and thousands of horses here. We got through with the loss of only three . . . my own horse unfortunately got badly kicked in the trucks coming from Alexandria and has to go into the horse hospital for treatment and none of our horses can be worked for another week when our further training can begin in earnest.

The encampment resembles a township in a way with roads through it and shops here and there and each regiment has its own canteen and stores. There are no restrictions as regards to drinks and there are also picture shows and music halls going every night and some of the turns at the latter are really very good, most of the artists are French or Italian so we cannot understand what they are singing. We are well treated in the way of leave, it being a camp regulation that men shall get at least one day a week, 50 per cent on Saturday and 50 per cent on Sunday.

I was in Cairo yesterday and had my first look around; a tram runs in and out from Mena in about three quarters of an hour and the fare is only one piasta or 2½ pence. It is a huge city and full of places of interest but of course I could not see much in half a day. It appears to be full of all nationalities and like all places where there are natives dirty and smelly in their quarters and full of vice. It is full of life and the streets are a seething mass of people against whom the military are well represented.

> Shepherds Hotel is one of the finest hotels I have seen and is a huge place; it is generally full of officers but the men here seem to have as much money to spend as the Officers if not more in most cases. It is a place that goes all night and just begins to get going about ten when we have to be in camp by eleven. Still it is just as well as it will keep us out of mischief . . .

But mischief was already abroad. Some troops had been repatriated to Australia for serious misbehaviour. Bean summed up the temptations: 'Proprietors of the lower cafés, chiefly Greeks, pressed upon the newcomers drinks amounting to poison, and natives along the roads sold them stuff of unheard-of vileness. Touts led them to "amusements" descending to any degree of filth'. Many soldiers came to regret not paying more attention to the shipboard lectures on 'protection'.

Events came to a head in the infamous 'Battle of the Wazza' in Cairo, when brothels were ransacked by Australian and New Zealand troops tired of being sold bad drinks in low bars and of being ripped off by pimps and madams while catching venereal disease from their girls. Hubert Gillam wrote in a circumspect way to his mother:

> We have been off on leave a couple of times and had a look over Cairo. It is an eye opener in some respects but is frightfully dirty. And the natives are the lousiest looking beggars I have ever set eyes on. When you are in town you can't walk two yards without they are chasing you with something to sell or to blacken your boots. Oh! They are hustlers at bargaining.

He noted in his diary on 2 April: 'Went into Cairo. Fight in the street at 3 pm. Row continued till about 7 pm and culminated in a riot. Several men shot. Militia called out and fight still in progress when we left . . . Intense excitement among troops and all leave stopped'.

On the same day, the infantry of the 1st Division began moving out of Mena. The word was that an offensive was looming, though nobody was sure exactly where. The Light Horse would not be needed for now. So for the men of the 3rd Light Horse Brigade the long days and hard work of camp life continued, with Hughes and the Bullant piling on the pressure, and the three regimental commanding officers irritable and increasingly resenting their interference. There were surprise turnouts, sometimes before dawn, with an alarm sounded and the troopers required to scramble for an instant muster and inspection by Hughes and Antill. The regimental commanders, however, felt that their men were being worked hard enough.

Reveille was normally at six o'clock, with rollcall ten minutes later. A third of each troop was then sent off to water the horses, three at a time, from a trough a mile away, while the others cleaned the lines and mixed horse feed. The horses had to be back, groomed and fed by seven-thirty, when the men marched onto the parade ground to receive their orders for the day before being dismissed for breakfast.

After breakfast the horses were exercised, walking 6 or 7 miles through the sand, before being watered and fed again. The men then had lunch. In the afternoon there was more work with the horses or foot drill. Again, the horses had to be fed and watered before two-thirds of each troop was dismissed for the night and the other third posted as sentries or guards after dinner.

Some of the brigade orders read as if preparations were being made for the Battle of Waterloo. Take, for example, 'Training', from Hughes's brigade order for 6 May:

> BUGLE CALLS: It is necessary that Officers and NCO's be familiar with all bugle and trumpet calls, such instructions to be arranged for.
>
> For the purpose of accustoming their commands to take part in Brigade drill, Officers Commanding Units will practice the Squadrons and Regiments of their command to manoeuvre by bugle call. The following particularly to be practiced:
>
> Attention; march at ease; walk march; trot; gallop; halt; sections right; sections left; troops half right; troops right wheel; troops half left; troops left wheel; sections about; mount and dismount, etc.

> TRUMPETERS: The trumpeters of the Brigade will be instructed under the senior Trumpeter Sergeant in Field Calls. It was noticed on Brigade parade yesterday that they knew little or nothing about these calls. The trumpeters are very backward and every attention is to be paid till they are perfect in sounding the calls, not only at the halt, but on the move mounted.
>
> The trumpeters will be inspected and tested by the Brigade Major early in the coming week.

The trumpeting by this time was taking place at Heliopolis. Within weeks of assembling, the 3rd Light Horse Brigade had moved 13 miles from Mena to a much more healthy and congenial camp on Heliopolis's racecourse, away from the fetid waterholes of the desert, which were blamed for sickness, including cases of pneumonia. 'The town near here is called Heliopolis and is where most of the whites live', Hubert Gillam wrote to his mother. 'It has some magnificent buildings but there doesn't seem much doing. The camp is very dusty and the surrounding country is bare. Locusts come over in millions at times. They eat everything before them. They are about twice as big as the Australian Grasshopper.'

Heliopolis proved a splendid new base, despite the locusts. There was a grand hotel only five minutes away, a Luna Park entertainment centre with a switchback railway next door and a racecourse grandstand where Hughes and his officers could enjoy comfortable quarters.

Relations between the officers were less than comfortable, however. It was about this time that Brazier's silent war with Antill exploded into the open. Brazier wrote in the back of his notebook of another 'episode', in which he said the Bullant had been pulling faces at him while he was having a discussion with Hughes: 'Lt-Col Antill with his eyes covered by the peak of his cap, contorted his mouth in all shapes'. A full-scale row then occurred between Brazier and Hughes himself, after the brigadier general publicly reprimanded the 10th's commandeer for having his second-in-command, Major Alan Love, drill the regiment instead of doing it himself. Brazier recorded that Hughes had sent him away 'like a whipped boy'. Matters could only get worse, and they did so after Brazier demanded to have the whole affair referred to Lieutenant General Sir John Maxwell, commander of all the forces in Egypt. Maxwell apparently decided to take no direct action in such a minor matter but Brazier's insistence had embarrassed Hughes.

✠

The Gallipoli campaign of 1915 was the idea of the War Council of the British Cabinet, developed as a strategy for breaking the deadlock of the trench warfare on the European Western Front, where the Germans and Allies faced each other along 470 miles of defences stretching from the Swiss border to the English Channel. The idea was to knock Germany's ally Turkey quickly out of the war and to open a new front in the east. Seizing the Dardanelles strait, which was guarded by forts on both sides, would allow the Allies to take control of the vital waterway linking the Mediterranean to the Black Sea, thereby creating a safe warm-water sea route to Russia.

The Turks, it was felt, would simply run away when the Royal Navy sailed through the strait and across the Sea of Marmara, anchoring off Constantinople – today's Istanbul. But when a naval assault on the Dardanelles failed miserably in March, an ill-conceived military expedition was mounted the following month to seize the Gallipoli peninsula, the land on the European side of the strait.

On 25 April, as part of the military operations, 16,000 Australian and New Zealand troops who had been training in Egypt while on the way to fight a war in Europe were instead landed on a narrow, high-banked, shingly cove barely 600 yards long and 20 yards wide on a peninsula in Turkey. Enie Bain and his brother Duncan, both of the 10th Light Horse Regiment, were at Heliopolis when they heard what was happening. Enie remembered:

> Rumours of war were continuous and about 26th April we heard of the Anzac landing. At that time it would be hard to estimate how many thousands of troops of all units were tearing their hair out and wasting time on training in Egypt. This was all useless once we got to Gallipoli.
>
> Had all those troops – who had been 'tearing their hair out' – been landed on Gallipoli by the 1st of May, the Anzac story could have been a glorious victory instead of a gallant defeat.

The rumours were soon confirmed as hard facts. Over 2000 Australians had been killed or wounded on the first day alone. The casualty rate was horrendous and the evacuation of the wounded a shambles. Transport ships ferried them back to Egypt, where hospital trains laden with 200 at a time took them to Heliopolis. They were then loaded into primitive motor ambulances, which ferried them to the great Heliopolis Palace Hotel, which had been hastily converted into the 3000-bed 1st Australian General Hospital. The Light Horse regiments' doctors, who were camped only five minutes' walk away, were soon pressed into service.

'Friends were sought out at the Hospital and varying stories of the Landing and opinions listed too', wrote Olden. 'But as day after day passed, bringing its stream of wounded into Heliopolis, until all the Hospitals and Auxiliary Hospitals gradually were filled, it became evident that our gallant comrades in Gallipoli were being hard pressed and that speedy reinforcement was necessary.'

The 1st Australian Division had lost about half of its infantry in the first week of desperate fighting. There were more than three brigades of mounted troops available in Egypt, but the Gallipoli peninsula's rugged terrain was no place for horses. Would they be prepared to leave the horses behind and go as dismounted infantrymen? No brigade was to be broken up, so each regiment was paraded and asked formally if it would go under these conditions. 'Colonel Brazier, addressing the Regiment placed the situation before officers and men and the idea met with such a burst of enthusiasm that he was in the proud position of being able to report to the Brigadier (General Hughes) that the Tenth had volunteered "to a man" ', wrote Olden. The 8th and 9th followed suit.

Events began to move quickly. The first unit to go from the 10th was the machine-gun section, under the young Duntroon graduate Horace Robertson. They left with the machine-gunners from the other two regiments on 8 May, to cheers from a parade assembled and addressed by the brigadier.

On 11 May, Hughes was ordered to prepare his brigade to move out for the front and to nominate those men who would have to stay behind with the horses. The following day he issued a special brigade order signed by Antill as his brigade major. It contained devastating news for Noel Brazier and Hugo Throssell. Major Alan Love, the 10th's second-in-command, would be leading the regiment to Gallipoli, and the prickly, argumentative Brazier would stay behind. The Order read: 'Lieut Col N.M. Brazier will take up the duties of Camp Commandant and will superintend the instruction of the details remaining in Camp and the care of the horses when the Brigade moves out'. Then the other officers who would remain in Egypt were listed. Hugo, together with Edward Weston, the veterinary officer, would stay – 'left in charge of 150 men and 550 horses', as Hugo tersely noted in his diary. The choice was probably made because he was such an excellent horseman.

'Talk about disappointment! It was no name for it. We nearly went mad', one trooper said about staying behind. 'The day that order came he [Hugo] spent rushing about the camp offering big money to anybody who would exchange with him and let him go, but of course nobody would and Hugo was the most disgusted man in Egypt.' Olden recalled that 'naturally a lot of heart-burning was caused, but the position was reluctantly accepted by the officers and men detailed for this work when the great importance of keeping the horses fit was impressed upon them'. Brazier unburdened himself in his diary: 'Oh Lord. How rotten are things in general. Nothing looks right. Some men have left but should not. We are all short of officers and the muddle is awful'.

The special brigade order had noted that 'all trumpets and bugles will be withdrawn, carefully packed and handed over to the Camp Commandant' and that 'rifles, bayonets and bandoliers will be drawn and issued to all Trumpeters'. There seemed to be some glimmer of recognition at the top that the nature of warfare had changed and that they were not going off to the Crimean War after all.

Numerous reports of snipers on Gallipoli had filtered back, so there were further hasty instructions. Officers' Sam Browne belts and swords were not to be taken to the front; all officers were to wear regular belts and bandoliers. They should dress almost the same as the men themselves, so that they would not be easily distinguished as officers, making them special targets for the snipers. However, they were to carry revolvers and ammunition. And there was to be no more shining of buttons or cleaning of brass: 'All bright work is to be dulled immediately'. The bright Gallipoli sun would quickly make polished metal into shining targets.

Corporal Henry Foss of the 10th described the regiment's departure, on 14 May:

> After stacking all our saddlery etc. and being issued the despised puttees instead of leggings, we were marched out of the parade ground with our packs up. There we piled our packs, rifles etc., which were placed under guard, and we were free to wander round for an hour or two.
>
> Immediately after tea we again fell in, and after being addressed by Major Love, and giving three cheers for old 'Go Alone' who was staying as Camp Commandant, we marched to the rear of the other regiments; cheering, laughing, singing and joking.
>
> We made our way to the railway station, cracking jokes as we passed the Skating Rink Hospital with the wounded who lined the streets and windows.
>
> The carriages proved to be of the old third class cattle variety . . . within an hour or so all impedimenta were aboard and the train moved out for Alexandria.
>
> Sleep was almost impossible but we did the best we could. Men were sleeping in every conceivable position, bar on their heads, or trying to do

so, and all were glad when we pulled up beside the wharf in Alexandria, just after daylight.

Then came a wait for half a day sitting on our packs, waiting for orders. In the meantime some half dozen stowaways being detected and placed under guard to return shortly to Cairo.

About three o'clock embarkation took place, our vessel being the ex-German passenger vessel, the *Lutzow*.

The 10th Light Horse Regiment of Western Australia, minus trumpets and horses, was off to war.

✠

The *Lutzow* had become shabby from ferrying so many men to Gallipoli. She was crammed to the gunwales for this latest voyage, with the 10th Regiment together with the entire 2nd Light Horse Brigade and a squadron of the 4th Regiment. Altogether, there were 106 officers and 2250 men aboard, as well as the ship's company – 'jammed as tight as sardines', wrote Foss, 'the tucker being of the roughest'. Tom Kidd, one of Hugo's close friends in the regiment, described the ship in his journal:

She is one of a number of steamers captured from the enemy and unmistakably German. At the time of our voyage she was manned by Greeks who evidently did not understand her.

On board everything was in a state of chaos and she was dirty from stem to stern. The few boats she had were leaky looking, not fitted up in accordance with the rules of the British Board of Trade.

As the *Lutzow* headed north into the Aegean, a new sound could be heard. Olden remembered that small rotary grindstones appeared in every nook and cranny of the ship.

The men utilised them for sharpening their bayonets and they were unceasing in motion from early morning till late at night. Many were the arguments round each wheel as to the best method of sharpening a bayonet, and each man put on the edge that he considered the most serviceable.

Before going ashore a church service was held, to which, of course, only a portion of the troops could gain access, but the bayonet sharpening was continued by the remainder, and the old hymn 'Oh God, Our Help in Ages Past' was thus accompanied by the hiss of revolving grindstones.

Kidd continued his description of the voyage:

We sighted and arrived at Cape Helles, Gallipoli, on the night of May 18th and anchored well out of range of the Turkish guns. The scene as we dropped anchor was to our minds at the time awesome indeed.

The land for several miles seemed to be lit up with rockets and star shells. A heavy rifle and gunfire continued furiously and the warships were pouring in regular broadsides. It meant that the Turks were making one of those big attacks usual at that time to drive our troops back into the sea from whence they came.

We remained at anchor throughout the day of May 18th and the rifle fire had almost died away but the enemy continued shelling the Allied forces and also the camp close to the beach.

With the aid of glasses we could distinguish a number of aeroplanes 'parked' close to the beach. Presently several of them rose in the air for the purpose of 'aerial reconnaissance' and very shortly afterwards they were under fire of the enemy's anti-aircraft guns. However we were shortly to become very much accustomed to this sort of thing.

We lay there awaiting orders and until the following day – it seemed evident we were quite unexpected.

While moving to a fresh anchorage we rubbed sides against a French steamer's bow and a bit more than paint was rubbed from the old *Lutzow*'s side.

During the afternoon of the 19th of May the *Lutzow* steamed for ANZAC Cove distant from 12 to 14 miles from Helles. We had an escort of two British destroyers and arrived off Gaba Tepe before dusk, anchoring well out from shore. Three or four battleships and cruisers including a quantity of destroyers were firing at the Turkish positions as we arrived.

There were no orders for our disembarkation, the Brigadier with the two other Regiments of the 3rd Light Horse Brigade had not turned up, we had the mortification of witnessing other units going ashore whilst we had to remain on board. A Turkish gun located among the hillocks of what is generally known as the Chocolate Hills shelled all landing parties and she treated the above troops in the usual manner.

The *Lutzow* also discharged a quantity of Japanese trench mortars and bombs for use of our troops in the trenches . . .

Directly darkness fell the Turks made their famous 19th/20th attack. They were repulsed and lost heavily. We witnessed the whole panorama from the steamer's deck (quite safe of course). Enemy guns had been bombarding throughout the day but at night the assault was launched. The old Battleship *Triumph* anchored alongside us and belched forth throughout the night.

Destroyers crawled up and down the coast using their searchlights especially on the flanks of our position. It was an awe-inspiring sight, the roar of guns, and crackle of musketry and noise of bombs. The night was beautifully calm and clear, which enabled us to hear everything.

As one never knows what the morrow may bring I retired to my cabin and slept well although the *Triumph*'s guns were shaking the *Lutzow* from stem to stern.

As Kidd slept there were the most frightful scenes of carnage ashore. Between five and nine-thirty in the morning, in a major attempt to repel the invaders, 42,000 Turkish troops in wave after wave charged at about 12,500 Anzacs manning the trenches on the heights. The Turks blew bugles, sounded martial music, shouted 'Allah! Allah!', and died. They were given no covering fire, no artillery support, and as soon as the Anzacs realised this they climbed out of their trenches and onto the parapets to get a better shot at the grey-uniformed enemy. They did so much shooting that the barrels of their rifles grew too hot to touch.

One soldier said it was better than a wallaby hunt back home. The Allied hunters on Anzac fired a total of 948,000 bullets from rifles and machine-guns that day.

By noon, Bean reported, 10,000 of the enemy had been killed or wounded. The Anzacs had lost only 160 killed and 468 wounded. The war correspondents were appalled by what they saw. Bean wrote:

> Any disused trench or pothole in No Man's Land was crowded with survivors, mostly wounded. Here and there in the scrub some staunch veteran continued to fire at the Anzac line throughout the day.
>
> But while some thus survived between the opposing trenches, the dead and wounded lay everywhere in hundreds. Many of those nearest to the Anzac line had been shattered by the terrible wounds inflicted by modern bullets at short range.
>
> No sound came from that dreadful space but here or there some wounded or dying man, silently lying without help or any hope of it under the sun which glared from a pitiless sky, turned painfully from one side to the other, or silently raised an arm towards heaven.

Ellis Ashmead-Bartlett described the scene a little later on, as he went for a tour of the front lines with the Anzacs' chipper and popular commander-in-chief, General Sir William Birdwood, in his pressed uniform and pith helmet:

> The ground presents an extraordinary sight when viewed through the trench periscopes. Two hundred yards away and even closer in places are the Turkish trenches and between them and our lines the dead lie in hundreds. There are groups of twenty or thirty massed together, as if for mutual protection, some lying on their faces, some killed in the act of firing; others hung up on the barbed wire. In one place a small group actually reached our parapet, and now lie dead upon it, shot at point blank range or bayoneted. Hundreds of others lie just outside their own trenches, where they were caught by rifles and shrapnel fire when trying to regain them.
>
> The men were resting after their exertions, lying in their bombproofs,

consuming large quantities of tinned meat, biscuits, jam – of which they are extremely fond – and tea.

In reply to the question of the general, 'How many did you kill?' the answer came 'That I can't say general; but look out here, and there are eight acres of them lying around.'

Flies were swarming in black clouds among the dead, and already the Anzac battlefield was beginning to stink like the open grave that it was. The stench could be smelt way out at sea.

The 10th waited offshore until the afternoon of 20 May, when the rest of the 3rd Light Horse Brigade arrived, aboard two destroyers from Lemnos. 'They came rushing up at a very high speed, reported to the Flagship (HMS *Albion*) then steamed shorewards', wrote Kidd.

Our turn came next; HMTB Destroyer *Silicia* ranging alongside accommodated us packed. We then made for the landing place. However, snipers got our range. Trooper Dave Doran who was sitting alongside myself had his forearm pierced with a bullet (he returned to the transport).

Steam pinnaces towed large lighters out to meet the Destroyer and we scrambled aboard as well as possible.

The sea was rather on the rough side, the barges were unwieldy, the pinnaces too light for the work, barges were packed to suffocation point and the snipers had our range, a nice combination indeed. However we eventually reached the landing stage.

Ashore near the stage we met quite a number of old friends.

After landing we took possession of an old Turkish trench overlooking the Anzac beach. We threw up some extra cover from snipers on the left flank who seemingly had positions near the beach.

A trooper of C Squadron was hit that night whilst lying on his blanket but was not seriously hurt. From then until daylight a hot fire was kept going by the enemy on the spot where we had bivouacked.

On the following day (the 21st May) we crossed to the hill facing the sea, made terraces and dug in sleeping places. Beachy Bill [the Anzacs' slang for a Turkish gun that shelled the cove in harassing fire] challenged us for the right of possession but apparently owing to some obstruction perhaps to the conformity of the ground to his front he could not place his shell close enough to our camp to do us any damage. However, he killed and wounded some of the crew of the NZ howitzer emplaced in country close to the beach. The lads behave splendidly in their baptism of fire.

6

Brother Lead and Sister Steel

We must be prepared to suffer hardships, privations, thirst and heavy losses by bullets, by shells, by mines, by drowning. But if each man feels, as it is true, that on him individually, however small or however great his task, rests the success or failure of the Expedition, and therefore the honour of the Empire and the welfare of his own folk at home, we are certain to win through to glorious victory.

Major General Aylmer Hunter-Weston, message to the British 29th Division before Gallipoli landing, 1915

THANKS TO THE REPORTS BEING PUBLISHED in the Australian newspapers, it is quite conceivable that the people at home knew more about conditions on Gallipoli than the troopers of the 10th Light Horse Regiment when the Western Australians arrived on the peninsula. The Light Horsemen would not have seen the newspapers, and most would have heard only incomplete accounts about the landing from the wounded hospitalised at Heliopolis.

The fighting after the landing had been savage and continuous. In the first nine days the Australian and New Zealand Army Corps (Anzacs) had suffered about 8000 casualties, of which 2300 had been killed. There was an urgent – and constant – need for reinforcements, and the 10th had been sailed in to meet part of that need.

The Turkish losses had been even heavier, estimated at around

14,000 for the first few days, but, despite this, the Turkish commander Mustafa Kemal had repeatedly thrown his men into the task of repelling the invaders. 'There is no going back a single step', he had ordered. 'It is our duty to save our country, and we must acquit ourselves honourably and nobly.' Time and again the Anzacs had counterattacked. They had dug in and would not be moved. Their aim was still to go on to capture Constantinople.

The 10th arrived onshore to find the armies settled in to a new kind of warfare on the small battlefield that had been called Anzac. Barely 400 acres in total, it measured only 1½ miles in length from north to south. The front line was just 1000 yards from the sea. There were three main ridges with the landscape in between a chaotic mixture of precipitous hills, jagged summits, plunging ravines and twisted gulleys.

The initial Anzac landing had taken place in early springtime. Now it was nearing the end of May, and it was getting hot. With the heat came the flies: the normal summer epidemic soon grew to a pestilential plague. The flies fed not only on the putrefying, swollen, grey-black corpses that lay everywhere on Gallipoli but also on the liquid faeces that filled the open latrines where men sat on wooden slats or poles, side by side, often groaning, with diarrhoea and dysentery. British historian Peter Hart wrote in his book *Gallipoli* that no fewer than 500 flies could breed from a single deposit of human excrement and that the latrines were fertile breeding grounds for fly-borne disease. He said one medical handbook estimated that a female fly could be the originator of some 5.5 trillion adult flies in six months. The flies defeated attempts at good sanitation practice and the limited supplies of disinfectant. They spread the disease known as the 'enteric', a debilitating form of paratyphoid fever, which sent men off the peninsula almost more quickly than they were arriving.

Thousands of men faced each other across a no-man's-land that in places was only 5 yards wide. They were living in vast rabbit warrens of dugouts, communications, reserve and forward trenches and saps (temporary trenches often dug out into no-man's-land as a jumping-off-point for an attack). They were all shovelled and scraped out of the yellow dirt, which was crumbly and dusty in the heat but turned into thick and clogging clay when it rained. Bits of tin, canvas and hessian served as roofs and awnings for the dugouts.

Periscopes peered over the parapets of the trenches on the ridgelines, spotters' telescopes watched through loopholes, and snipers waited for any movement that would betray a target. The long stalemate had begun.

Ashmead-Bartlett described Anzac at the time as having 'the appearance of being a prosperous mining camp in full swing'. It was a noisy, restless mining camp inhabited by about 30,000 Allied men, which later grew to between 50,000 and 60,000. The troopers theoretically spent two weeks in the firing line and two weeks in the reserve trenches not far away. This was interrupted by the unceasing tasks of digging new trenches, saps and dugouts, and carrying food, water and ammunition up to their lines on the heights. Men in tattered and cut-down uniforms, dented caps, shapeless slouch hats and stained sun helmets toiled up and down tracks with supplies. Water was often carried in containers like milk churns. Food consisted mainly of bully beef, biscuits and jam. One soldier said that the biscuits were like paving stones and practically bulletproof. The men put them into a shell case and pounded them with the handle of an entrenching tool to make a rough porridge. Some of the tins of bully beef, he claimed, were dated 1901. They had originally been sent to the Boer War and returned to army stores afterwards. The jam was generally a watery, nasty yellow apricot, which became crusted black with flies as soon as a tin was opened. Another soldier recalled that it took three men to transfer jam from a tin onto a biscuit: one opened the tin, another whisked away the flies, and a third spread the jam quickly and tried to cover it up.

There was the constant crack of rifle fire, the droning whine of ricochets, the stutter of machine-guns and the thud of exploding bombs from the front lines. 'The noise was continuous at times and the soldiers endured it, not as a temporary pain, but as a natural condition of life', wrote Alan Moorehead in his book *Gallipoli*. It was as inevitable as the weather. 'You were hit or not hit. Eating, sleeping and waking, the long scream went on.' Shells burst overhead at random, sending out showers of small lead shrapnel balls like blasts from a giant shotgun, killing or maiming those caught in the open below. Men had to run in zigzags between piles of sandbag traverses across open ground in the valleys, to avoid being picked off by the snipers hiding in the thick brush of the hills.

Stretcher bearers and mules carried the wounded down to the beach, where they waited for evacuation surrounded by mountains of stores. Naval officers shouted orders through megaphones to the men aboard the constant stream of boats and barges, and there was smoke and a rhythmic thumping noise from the steam-driven pumping engine, sucking and driving the water supplies that had been carried in lighters from the River Nile into iron reservoirs that had also been hauled ashore.

Henry Nevinson, a British war correspondent reporting for the provincial press wrote:

> So here the Anzacs live, practising the whole art of war. Amid dust and innumerable flies, from the mouths of little caves cut in the face of the cliffs they look over miles of sea to the precipitous peaks of Samothrace and the grey mountains of Imbros. Up and down the steep and narrow paths, the Colonials assiduously toil, like ants which bear the burdens of their race. Uniforms are seldom of the regulation type. Usually they consist of bare skin dyed to a deep reddish copper by the sun, tattooed decorations (a girl, a ship, a dragon) and a covering that can hardly be described even as 'shorts', being much shorter. Every kind of store and arm has to be dragged or 'humped' up these anthills of cliff, and deposited in the proper hole or gallery. Food, water, cartridges, shells, building timber, guns, medical stores – up the tracks all must go, and down them the wounded come.
>
> So the practice of the simple life proceeds with greater simplicity than any Garden Suburb can boast, and the domestic virtues which constitute

> the whole art of war are exercised with a fortitude rarely maintained upon the domestic hearth.

Tom Kidd continued his account as he began to get his bearings:

> May 22 sees it raining. The dugouts became puddles and the paths, well one only wanted to make his way along them to do it on a sliding scale. We sleep between wet blankets.
>
> We remove camp on the morning of May 23rd to Shrapnel Valley. We do not have transport facilities on Gallipoli as all ranks carry everything on their backs. Officers dress similar to the troops carrying rucksacks (or packs) and wearing similar equipment but without rifles.
>
> By means of a large communications sap we pass across hills behind GOC Headquarters until we reach a long valley which commencing at the steep hill I know now as Baby 700 between Quinns and Walkers Top with Popes at the head and the head in the centre runs right down to the sea opening out onto the beach which is known as Brighton Beach.
>
> We only command part of the hills and the head commanding this valley, portions of which are known as Dead Man's Gully and Shrapnel Valley.
>
> The enemy hold positions on which I now know is called the Chess Board between Quinns and Walkers and are able to snipe right down the valley to the sea coast. Undoubtedly dangerous to people passing along the route.

The 10th dug in to a more permanent camp on a side of Shrapnel Valley. Signaller Brown recorded that in the first week three officers were wounded by shrapnel and that in one morning, on 25 May, thirty men were hit by snipers, 'one from our regiment killed (Dolly Gray)'.

Trooper Gerald Gray was the regiment's first man to be killed in action. A 29-year-old ruddy-faced stockman, he hailed originally from South Australia but had moved to Western Australia to farm with his brother. He had tried to enlist for the Boer War but had been turned down because he was underage. His nickname came from a song popular at the time of the Boer War, 'Goodbye Dolly Gray'.

The day before he was killed, Gray had taken part in the great armistice of 24 May, called so that the men could bury the dead from the Turkish charge less than a week before. Kidd wrote in his journal that: 'Unfortunately being orderly officer I had to remain in camp. The remainder of the officers donned white armlets and went up on top . . . some 3000 Turks were buried, or rather covered over with earth, with also about 500 of our own dead'. Later in the day he went up the valley to the front line: 'We were able during the armistice to search around the lower gullies or nullahs and everywhere we found Turkish dead in an advanced stage of decomposition. The atmosphere was heavily charged with the smell of rotting humans which until one became accustomed to it, inclined to rend you a bit bilious'.

Trooper Syd Livesey, who had once driven coach-horses for a living, sent a letter home that was reprinted in the *Albany Advertiser*:

> One of my mates (W. Blake) and myself went up to the firing line to see the dead buried. Both sides stopped firing at half-past seven in the morning, and they were not to start again until 4.30 p.m. At the said time both sides left their trenches with picks and shovels and small white flags, to carry out their grim task. It was a strange sight, to see the Australians and Turks mixed up. Some exchanged cigarettes with the Turks and talked with them quite friendly. The dead were lying very thick in some places, just as they fell, and there were stray Australians here and there who had been killed at the time of the landing nearly four weeks before. They were in a state of decay and the smell was not very nice. At 7 a.m. that day they would have killed each other at sight, and at 7.30 they were out together digging graves. It all seemed so strange. They dug long shallow graves and placed the dead in them side by side, clothes and all, just as they were killed. Well, this work went

> on without a hitch all day till about 4.20 p.m. Then both sides got back to their trenches. When time was up, they opened fire on each other's trenches, and it seemed as if both sides wanted to make up for the time they had lost.

Compton Mackenzie, a British staff officer, who later wrote in his *Gallipoli Memories* about that day, recalled being given a cigar to smoke by an Australian to try to mask the smell. At one point he looked down to see 'squelching up from the ground on either side of my boot like a rotten mangold the deliquescent green and black flesh of a Turk's head . . . I only know that nothing could cleanse the smell of death from the nostrils for a fortnight afterwards. There was no herb so aromatic but it reeked of carrion, not thyme nor lavender, not even rosemary'.

Meanwhile, Kidd got into trouble:

> A party consisting of Nicholas, Grimwood, Olden, Craig, Dave Jackson and myself were searching a watercourse high up on the side of a hill and forgot the passage of time. We were suddenly reminded that it was 4pm and [it] had come and gone by a sudden rush of shrapnel. We were evidently observed by the enemy climbing down the hill. We [had] some miraculous escapes. Olden received a bullet through his shoulder. All hands had a shot at record breaking to reach our dugouts. Olden is evacuated.

The awful scenes of death they had been witnessing centred on Quinn's Post, the most advanced position on the front line. It was the focus of incessant, bloody fighting. The Anzac and Turkish trenches were only 5 yards apart. Bean said that men witnessing bombs bursting up at Quinn's used to glance at the place 'as a man looks at a haunted house'.

It was to Quinn's that 100 men from the 10th Light Horse were sent on 27 May to begin digging a vital new communication trench. Two days later, at three-twenty in the morning, the Turks attacked, throwing bombs and shouting 'Allah! Allah!' For three and a half hours the troopers held off the attackers, before calling urgently for reinforcements. Soon almost the entire regiment was scrambling up the valley to join in the fray. With their supply of bombs dwindling, they rammed clip after clip of bullets into the magazines of their rifles and used their bayonets in bloody fighting as the Turks entered their trenches.

In a phrase later employed by the war poet Siegfried Sassoon, Brother Lead and Sister Steel won the day, and the attack was repulsed. Although no Australian was killed, six officers and nineteen troopers were wounded. It was the 10th's first real hand-to-hand fight.

Away from it all in Cairo, Hugo Throssell, together with the vet Edward Weston, the 150 men and the 550 horses that had been left behind, endured the 'dark weeks of Egypt' after the regiment sailed away and into action. It was an excruciating time for Hugo, with little to do for just over two months except to see that the men were kept under control and away from the temptations and stews of the Wazza and to ensure that the horses were properly fed, watered and exercised. 'No word of it and me getting away looks tho' I'm here for life', he wrote to his older brother Cecil in Northam.

Hugo and Ric each kept up a steady stream of postcards home, some of which have survived. One from Hugo to their niece Doreen said:

> How goes the music little Gingertop? Remember how I used to sing to you old girlie – well, you practice like anything and I'll promise to sing like *anythink* when I come home. Would you like me to bring you a little Arab slaveboy or a little donkey?
>
> Uncle Ric is well and I'm having a very easy time here in Egypt – the main hospitals are quite close to our camp and I've been across seeing some of the poor chaps this afternoon – they are all wonderfully *bright* and anxious to get back again to the front.

Ric, meanwhile, wrote from Gallipoli:

> Very hot here the last three weeks, about 100 every day. Heard an old cow bellowing the other night. Wouldn't mind putting her in the bail with or without rope.
>
> I'm getting Jim to forward me a tin of Nestlé's very best. He has sent me quite a lot of things lately, tobacco, matches, cocoa, Bovril – talk about 'Corn from Egypt' it's nothing to it. Tell Doc [one of the Throssell brothers] I think of him when I 'as my drappie of rum!!
>
> Love to all,
>
> Ric

Hugo was not the only soldier fed up with waiting. He sent home a postcard he'd received from a trooper which read:

> Dear Sir:
>
> Sorry I left you but could not stay behind and see my chums go away and was anxious for a scrap.

Hugo wrote across the front of the picture: 'This is a postcard from one of my chaps who took French leave and cleared off for the Dardanelles with an Infantry crowd. It's interesting if only to prove how keen the fellows are for a fight'. The next postcard home summed up his own frustrations: it was a photograph of him in full uniform feeding fish to a couple of pelicans.

The days of waiting did at least mean that Hugo made many firm friends among the troopers. Two of these were Sid Ferrier and Jack Macmillan. Both originated from Victoria.

Sutton Henry 'Sid' Ferrier had been born in 1879 and grew up in Carapook, a tiny hamlet between Coleraine and Casterton in the far west, close to Muntham Station where the pioneering Edward Henty first farmed in Victoria. Sid's grandparents James and Mary Ferrier had arrived from Scotland in 1852 and had nine children including Sid's father, John, who married Alicia Hanlon and proceeded to raise a 'cricket team' of eleven children.

They actually played cricket, too, and Sid grew up with a local reputation as a fine bowler and a fieldsman who could both catch and throw a ball with great accuracy.

Fate had taken Sid from Carapook to work as a farming contractor in Western Australia. Fair haired and blue eyed, he was thirty-five when he joined the 10th. His calm, sure manner on the battlefield later impressed everyone: 'as cool and quiet going about there as if he'd been walking in a stackyard loading wheat', wrote one eyewitness.

John Lachlan Macmillan, known as 'Jack', was 6 feet 4 inches, with a 44½ inch chest, but he seemed to everyone who met him to be much bigger. A British newspaper reporter wrote that 'from the tip of the emu plume in his slouch hat to the tip of his stout boots, there is little less than seven feet of him and the man is 220 pounds of lean muscle and hard bone. The men who fought alongside him say that his heart is the biggest part of him; "as big as a cabbage", observed one brawny bushman'.

Jack Macmillan was the son of John Macmillan, another Scottish immigrant who had become a wealthy grazier after settling at Hazelwood Station in today's Latrobe Valley. After the old man died in 1899, the station property was sub-divided and in 1910 Jack Macmillan married Maud Anderson, a widow from Toorak, and went to live at Metung on the Gippsland Lakes.

Macmillan was older than most. He put his age down as forty-one when he enlisted in Victoria in 1914 and his occupation as grazier, but it seems he was actually aged forty-five.

Being older, his initial appointment was as a horse driver in the 3rd Light Horse Brigade Train, and he sailed with them to Egypt, where he transferred to the 10th as he had a Western Australian connection, having at one stage of his life joined the rush to Kalgoorlie to prospect for alluvial gold.

When he finally set off for Gallipoli, Macmillan took along his most prized possessions, a wind-up gramophone and a selection of 78 rpm records, which he played in the trenches.

During this time, relations between the most senior officers of the brigade festered and grew worse. In Heliopolis the frustrated Brazier was not bothering to answer commands from the 3rd Brigade headquarters at Anzac and was insisting that he took orders only from the local commander in Egypt, General Sir John Maxwell. There was a fierce row when Antill, on Gallipoli, heard that Brazier was using one of the cars left behind when the brigade had sailed. He insisted that Brazier stop using the car, lock it up with the others and send him the keys at Anzac. Brazier simply appealed to the local commander, who ruled that he could keep the keys and the car.

Then Hughes became sick with pneumonia. He was sent back to Egypt for a rest and stayed one night with Brazier, who described him as 'a wreck'. Hughes tried to re-establish his authority over the lieutenant colonel by asking for the cars to accompany him into Cairo to pick up some comforts for the troops. Hughes dismissed the drivers and organised for the cars to be sent to a motor transport company. But Brazier, who had been tipped off, went again to General Maxwell, who rescinded the order. The cars went back to Brazier.

After Hughes returned to Gallipoli he had to be evacuated twice more to a hospital ship offshore. Antill became the man in charge.

But between them they decided that Brazier had to be brought to heel and that the best thing would be to send for him to take charge of his regiment on Gallipoli, where he could be closely supervised. Besides, they had also decided that they wanted to get rid of Alan Love, acting commander of the regiment on Gallipoli, who, like many others, had become physically ill and mentally exhausted. He had found himself to be an unpopular leader.

Love had written to Brazier saying that he wanted a break: 'I hope the end of our trench fighting will soon be over as it is most nerve wracking'. He almost pleaded that he wanted to get away 'from shells and bullets which lately has been a very difficult job as they have pelted them in at times like hail'. Later, he wrote again, and Brazier noted comments on the letter:

> I am informed by Brigade HQrs that you are expected here any day and the sooner the better for they are worrying the life out of me . . .
>
> I have been bad with diarrhoea for about 14 days and am just about played out and intended, as soon as you arrived, having a week's spell on the hospital ship or in Lemnos.
>
> You can imagine I have had a rough passage with so many officers knocked out and can appreciate the urgency of getting others appointed.
>
> Antill is as great a bully as ever and leads us a cat and dog life. [Brazier: 'Wait awhile'.] I understand there is a possibility of his getting command of the brigade if the Brigadier again breaks down. What ho then! [Brazier: 'Never'.]

At Quinn's Post, Tom Kidd had earnt himself the nickname 'Bomb-Proof Kidd'. He had volunteered to lead one of two parties of twenty-two men in an attack against the Turks who had constructed new positions in front of the Australian trenches. He had been far from optimistic, writing later that he had handed to the doctor, James Bentley, 'my paybook with money, binoculars and last but not least a letter to my wife before we lined up'.

When Kidd's party first attacked the enemy trench they found it occupied by only two Turks, the remainder having fled along a communication trench. The Turks fought hard, but after one was killed the other threw down his rifle and surrendered. Now twenty-three Australians and one Turk were squeezed into a trench so small that movement was impossible. The troopers had been given only sixteen bombs; the prisoner watched 'with great interest' as Kidd and his men picked up and hurled back bombs thrown at them in the subsequent counterattack. Kidd and his men had treated the prisoner kindly, handing him a cigarette, some biscuit and water. He offered his sourdough ration in return, and in the heat of the furious battle they all became friends.

Inevitably, two bombs got through, burying themselves under the debris, and when they could not be found in time, they exploded, wounding many in the trench. By five in the afternoon – four hours after the fight began, Kidd and every man with him had been wounded, some severely. Few could handle a rifle any longer, so when the Turks suddenly leapt out and attempted to surround them, the Light Horsemen made a dash back to Quinn's Post. Every man reached safety, but they were so 'dazed and overstrained' that they couldn't at first give a coherent description of what had happened.

Of the forty-six men of the 10th who had taken part in the action only fourteen had come out unscathed, and three had been killed. When the time had come for the Australians to withdraw, a Turk of the counterattacking party had rushed at a wounded trooper with bayonet fixed, but the Turkish prisoner, amazingly, had saved the Australian's life by picking up a rifle and shooting two fellow Turks dead. Kidd wrote in his notebook: 'I don't know what became of our friend – I only hope he was killed outright and not captured'. The official history recorded that he was immediately killed by his own side.

After this action Kidd reported: 'Found my limb full of bomb splinters. Joe Scott picks them out with a knife. My left eye blackens, partially closed, left side of face all bruised. Go for a swim, collapse on platform just as good old Doc Bentley predicted would happen'.

Soon afterwards the 10th was moved away from Quinn's, nominally in reserve but with men constantly detailed for jobs on the front line, along the beach and at Russell's Top. They were rejoining the other two regiments of the 3rd Light Horse Brigade and coming under the overall command of Hughes and Antill for the first time since they had left Egypt. The regiments had been separated on arrival at Anzac for experience under other commanders.

While the brigadier had been forced to take time away ill, his brigade major, Antill, seemed to relish the Gallipoli conditions.

The Bullant dressed to impress those under him with his authority. He wore a shirt and tightly knotted tie as he strode about among the men in their ragged uniforms. His flat cap was pulled down to his eyebrows, shirt sleeves rolled correctly to the elbow, shorts worn down to the knee and tightly wound puttees from his calves to his boots. He used a long fly-whisk, grasped in his right hand, to emphasise his orders. Afterwards, he crowed that he was the only officer in the entire brigade who had managed to remain on Gallipoli for the duration of the campaign without being forced to leave the peninsula either sick or wounded.

As June and July passed the weather grew hotter. The wastage of men continued to grow because of sickness, and the troopers grumbled that there was 'not even a decent fight to show for it'.

Phipps Turnbull wrote to his Aunt Bertha in Perth: 'It is a terribly monotonous game this trench fighting, just farming yard by yard, one side trying to wear out the other'. He was by this time Sergeant Turnbull and was about to be commissioned as a second lieutenant.

So many officers were leaving, sick or wounded, with no official information as to how long they would be away, or indeed if they would return to duty at all, that special promotions on the battlefield were being made to fill the gaps. Ric Throssell was one of those elevated, becoming a sergeant. Enie Bain, who was ill at one stage with a 'bad headache, pain all over body, severe cough', summed up the reasons for the low numbers: 'Lack of water, shortage of tucker, men getting killed every day and more going away sick'.

Phil Fry, Hugo Throssell's 'greatest chum', was one of the officers sent away by Doctor Bentley. He left with severe influenza at the end of May and did not return until the beginning of August. He wrote home from hospital in Egypt, where conditions were poor and recoveries slow: 'It is very hot here and the mosquitos are very bad at night. I left my toes out last night and they are all over little red spots today'.

The heat at Gallipoli was also causing distress. 'It is getting very hot here and the small flies very bad though I am glad to say no blow flies', wrote Turnbull.

> One redeeming feature is the sea bathing and what we would do without it I don't know as the trenches are alive with lice and it is impossible to keep free from them, no matter how clean you are; you would be amused to see everyone sitting down having a good old louse hunt after we return from the trenches. We are getting very thin on it but are otherwise hard and healthy on it, the lack of nourishing food is bound to make one thin and our diet is the same from one day to the other; I am sure we will all make beasts of ourselves when we get to some decent living again but we deserve something good when all this is over.

Food and water supplies to the peninsula were inadequate. Diarrhoea and dysentery were increasing at such an alarming rate that by 14 July one medical return showed that a quarter of the 10th was down with either one or the other. Often it was hard to distinguish between them, and figures varied. The regimental diary for that day reads: 'No fresh meat yet issued. Sickness still prevalent. 2 officers and 93 men in hospital sick – 7 sick in bivouac and increasing daily'. Two days later it reported: 'Fitness of all ranks fully 30 per cent reduced'. And two weeks after that, a report showed that 421 men were away in hospital – 21 per cent of those who had landed towards the end of May and only 25 per cent less than the number of killed or wounded.

Reinforcements were arriving, but they were not keeping pace with the losses. More were needed. Hugo Throssell and his men were sent for at last.

Meanwhile, Hubert Gillam captured the monotonous existence of an ordinary soldier in three typically laconic diary entries:

> Monday: Nothing much doing during last night. Came out of the trenches at 11 am. Fairly warm day. Went round to the Base and had a swim and got some water. Water rations reduced by half last couple of days. Turks pumping in some shells from close range.

> Tuesday: Put in an hour on the Road Fatigue from 9am till 10am. Then went down and had a swim. Little firing during the night from towards the Salt Lake. Went into the trenches at 11 am. Very hot. Destroyer fired a lot into Turkish trenches about four in the morning.
>
> Wednesday: Came off duty at 11 am. Orderly for one and a half hours. Had dinner and went down and had a swim. Very hot day. Sea was lovely. Few shells falling over the camp. Five New Zealanders were hit yesterday with shrapnel. Bread issue but no lime juice as was stated on orders.

'There was no change of scene in the burnished sky,' wrote Bean, 'the hillsides worn into hundreds of little paths, the figures of men constantly tramping with water-tins or other burdens through the glaring white dust, the mule lines, and the all too obviously frequented latrines. There was no change in the smell from the distant corpses of the dead, and from the burning metal and fat of "bully-beef" tins in the nearest incinerator'.

Shortly after sunrise on 30 July a new figure arrived at Anzac Cove, helped from a lighter before scrunching up the beach and threading his way through the piles of stores. 'Lt Col Brazier arrived at 6 am looking as fat as a whale and fit as a fiddle', wrote Gillam in his diary. The commanding officer of the 10th Light Horse Regiment had arrived just in time for one of the greatest disasters in Australian military history.

On the heights, Hughes, waited with the Bullant and his fly-whisk for their old adversary to climb, panting, up the track carved into the side of Walker's Ridge. Brazier climbed as quickly as he could, sweating and gasping, to the top. At long last he was back with his regiment, the one he had formed and founded. He was welcomed home by his Light Horsemen. Gillam said that Brazier made himself appear a 'better man' than his predecessor, Love, by getting to the trenches as soon as he could and 'generally conversing with the men'.

At almost the same time as Brazier was being reunited with his regiment, Hugo Throssell and eighty of his men were sailing from Alexandria. Hugo had his photograph taken before they sailed – dashing, confident and keen looking in his uniform, bag over his shoulder, holstered revolver on his belt by his side.

'Our turn came at last', wrote one of Hugo's companions. 'Word came for us to embark and we fairly romped into the boats. We little knew what we were in for but I don't suppose it would have made much difference if we had. We knew we had a sporting chance, and no good man will ask for more.'

7
Plans and Plums

> The day so longed for is very near now. O that it had come at the period of our victories! But there is time enough still, and the first moves of the plan are now working like oiled machinery.
>
> General Sir Ian Hamilton, diary, 5 August 1915

THE ENTRY FOR 1 AUGUST 1915 in the war diary of the 3rd Light Horse Brigade is brief and to the point. 'Brig Gen Skeen, GSO1, attended and held conference with BG and BM. The attack on NEK. Orders prepared.'

Brigadier General Andrew Skeen was the hand-picked right-hand man of Lieutenant General Sir William Birdwood, overall commander of the Anzacs, a tough but popular British Army veteran who had served in the Indian frontier campaigns and the war against the Boers. Skeen was the architect of the original landing on Gallipoli. He was described as a 'quiet Scotsman with a scholastic air' by historian Sir Robert Rhodes James, while a contemporary officer, Sir Brudenall White, said he was 'at no time anything but the complete optimist'. The BG and BM we have already met – Brigadier General Frederic Hughes, the elderly peacetime soldier who liked bright uniforms and disciplined men marching in columns and who had found himself sick and out of his depth on Gallipoli, and Brigade Major Jack Antill, the Boer

War veteran and martinet bristling with an aggressive desire to take up the fight with anyone who came his way.

The Nek is a narrow land bridge on the northern Anzac heights measuring 33 by 25 yards, with sheer drops on either side, and with a most beautiful view, particularly towards the sweeping coastline that lies far beneath and on to the giant salt lake on the edge of the Suvla plain. In 1915 the land bridge itself was a no-man's-land and directly overlooked by the scrub-covered hill called Baby 700 – the strongest Turkish position in the heights above Anzac, with rows of trenches filled with soldiers. The end of the land bridge that was closest to Baby 700 was held by the Turks with two lines of trenches and a further maze of trenches behind them. On either flank were spurs from which Turkish machine-guns could sweep back and forth across the no-man's-land. The Allies held the other end, with another close network of trenches and saps.

On the night of 29 June the Turks had tried to attack the 8th and 9th Light Horse regiments, which were holding these lines at the time. The Turks had been soundly defeated. At daybreak, the men of the 8th had counted 255 corpses in its trenches and parapets, while an equal number of dead and wounded had lain across the bridge in front of them.

Now, on 1 August, orders were given for the Australians of the 3rd Light Horse Brigade to attack The Nek in the opposite direction. They would pit themselves against rifle and machine-gun fire not only from the trenches in front of them, as the Turks had done, but also from Baby 700 above them and from the spurs on either side of them. As Bean observed, 'to attempt a frontal assault upon this position was like endeavouring to attack an inverted frying-pan from the direction of its handle'. Even the planners had conceded in July that 'these trenches and convergences of communication trenches . . . require considerable strength of force. The narrow Nek to be crossed . . . [to] make an unaided attack in this direction almost hopeless'.

But this attack, said Skeen and the other planners, would be different from the Turks' failed attempt. This attack would be such a surprise – and would be so well supported – that it would succeed. The action was to be one small piece of a giant interlocking offensive, an interdependent scheme to break out of the stalemate in which they had been locked with the Turks since the landings in April. The scheme became known as the August Offensive.

Planning had begun as early as May on a surprise movement from the Anzacs' position against the Turks on the heights of the Sari Bair range. The key positions to be taken were Chunuk Bair and, further along, overlooking Suvla, Hill Q and the highest point of all, Hill 971. The Nek was a crucial position on the ridge on the way up to Chunuk Bair, which was going to be attacked during the night preceding the Nek offensive, and from another direction. As Skeen explained to Hughes and Antill at their meeting on 1 August, a New Zealand force would climb up an almost sheer ridge where it was reckoned the Turks were few and charge the enemy on the top, where and when they least expected it. The New Zealanders would then move on to Baby 700, and, from there to the back of the Turkish trenches at The Nek, creating a converging attack with the Light Horse. The idea was that while the Turks were fully occupied with the New Zealanders approaching from Chunuk Bair, the men of the 3rd Light Horse Brigade would be able to make a frontal attack from the trenches they occupied on Walker's Ridge.

The plan had some precautions built in: if the New Zealanders were delayed in capturing Chunuk Bair a minor assault would be considered instead of the full offensive. However, it would definitely occur 'unless orders are given to the contrary'.

Skeen also told Hughes and Antill reassuringly that while the attack on The Nek was underway other Light Horse units to the south would be attacking the Turks at Quinn's Post and Pope's Hill to keep the enemy diverted. These attacks, set for 7 August, would be preceded on the evening of 6 August by a major attack by the infantry on Lone Pine. This feint would make the Turks believe that the main Anzac breakout was being carried out from the south, which would be reinforced by another infantry attack on the position called German Officers' Trench at midnight. All this, it was hoped, would lead to enemy confusion before the 3rd Light Horse Brigade was called upon to attack The Nek, at four-thirty in the morning on 7 August. The action was also to be preceded by a heavy naval barrage against the enemy trenches.

There was much more to the overall grand plan for the August Offensive. Twenty-thousand men were to be smuggled ashore over three nights to the already overcrowded Anzac position before being shifted north to join in a massive assault on the Suvla plain. Altogether, 63,000 Australian, New Zealand, British and Indian troops would be fighting the enemy. The British generals were confident that the peninsula could be taken at last and the way opened for the Royal Navy to sail through the strait of the Dardanelles, across the Sea of Marmara, to Constantinople.

On 2 August the war diary of the 3rd Light Horse Brigade has another succinct entry: 'Conference with Gen Godley NZ & A re attack. Orders were seen and approved'.

Major General Sir Alexander Godley was in charge of the New Zealand and Australian Division. In May, the original commander of the Australians, Major General Sir William Throsby Bridges, had died from the effects of gangrene aboard a hospital ship after being shot in the thigh by a sniper in Shrapnel Valley. Godley, a thoroughly unpopular officer, was now also responsible for the capture of the Sari Bair heights and three subsidiary attacks. He was a bluff, haughty, horse-loving British general who remembered the significance of his birth year, in 1867, as 'the year Hermit won the Derby in a snowstorm'. He had been sent to New Zealand after the Boer War to run the New Zealand Army and to introduce a system of compulsory military training. He was 6 feet 2 inches tall, cold and aloof, now with thinning hair and a thick blond moustache. The New Zealanders detested him. 'Unsmiling with never a word of praise, his figure became the focus for all the grumbles and discontent', said Christopher Pugsley in his book *Gallipoli: The New Zealand Story*.

The Kiwis called him 'Make 'em Run Alex' because his wife, Lady Louisa Marion Godley, equally haughty and imperious, was supposed to have given him this instruction while reviewing a parade in Egypt. She was also said to have complained when wounded men from Gallipoli failed to lie to attention when she paid them a visit in hospital.

Antill, unsurprisingly, liked Godley, calling him 'a forbidding sort of man, but a good soldier'. In Egypt, Godley had told another officer during exercises: 'I particularly want you to understand that when I order your brigade to come into action . . . you have to do it, even if you think it is impossible'. With Godley it was a cardinal rule that orders were orders and had to be obeyed without question. Antill, who believed in the same principle, was the man to carry out the orders.

Godley wrote an autobiography late in his life that he called *Life of an Irish Soldier*. The book is 363 pages long and The Nek is mentioned only twice in passing, once almost as an afterthought. In the book, Godley pays tribute to Lady Louisa for sending him luxuries in Gallipoli that included 'eggs, ginger and Carlsbad plums'. These were a delicacy dating from the 19th century and took their name from a popular spa resort in Czechoslovakia.

General Godley's Carlsbad plums no doubt came in handy when entertaining visitors in the complex of dugouts he had established as his headquarters close to the sea and well away from the battlefields on the heights. 'I established my headquarters near the mouth of the Chailak Dere at No. 2 Outpost,' he wrote. You can still find some outlines of the headquarters today, shallow remains of deep holes scraped into the yellow soil of the first hill.

The general was very proud of his trench system hereabouts, writing that 'the criterion was that it should be deep enough for Godley to walk upright in and wide enough for McGlinn to walk in without touching the sides'. (Paddy McGlinn was a portly Australian officer).

And there at No. 2 Outpost Godley would stay through the battle that lay ahead. He had absolutely no idea of the conditions on the heights or the ground over which he was committing his troops to advance and conquer. In his book he says that at one stage during the battle he actually set out up the creek bed to find out what was going on, but 'an urgent telephone message turned me back and by the time I disposed of difficulties it was too late to start again'. Later he would go out to sea aboard a destroyer and view the action from afar through his field glasses. 'It is easy to be wise after the event', he wrote later, 'to begin with, our objective was too ambitious'.

Also writing long after the event, Jack Antill told Bean, as the latter was preparing the final draft of his *Official History*: 'From the official intimation of the proposed operations and right through the subsequent discussions and conferences, in the definite and reiterated judgement of the brigadier, his brigade-major and of regimental commanders, the projected attack on The Nek was foredoomed to failure. On the contrary, and in opposition to this view, both Anzac and divisional headquarters were confident of success'.

As the war diary records, on 2 August, Antill and Hughes met with Godley at his headquarters to get approval for draft orders for the 3rd Light Horse Brigade to attack The Nek five days later. Certainly, as Godley sat down with them in his foothill dugout, he was preparing to send the Light Horsemen into an extraordinary, impossible infantry action. He insisted that they would conduct the charge using fixed bayonets only, with no bullets in their rifle magazines – not even one round loaded up the spout. It was the kind of massed bayonet attack that might have been effective during the time of the Napoleonic wars but which had already been shown to be useless against modern weapons such as the Gatling gun during the American Civil War.

The plan must have seemed simple to those making it far away from the actual battlefield. Four lines, limited to 150 Light Horsemen each because of the narrowness of the land bridge, would charge across The Nek from Russell's Top and attack the Turkish trenches ahead in quick succession. The first two lines would be the Victorians of the 8th Light Horse, the last two the Western Australians from the 10th. The 9th – mainly South Australians – would stand by in reserve. The attack would also be supported by a battalion of the British Cheshire Regiment, which would help to consolidate afterwards, while two companies of the 8th Royal Welch Fusiliers would carry out a huge climb up the cliff from Monash Valley to the south in support.

The first line was to attack the Turkish trenches directly in front using homemade bombs and sharpened bayonets. The second line was to run past the first and take the nearest rows of trenches and saps dug into Baby 700, which loomed immediately behind. The third line would go on and capture the further trenches, while the fourth, equipped with picks and shovels, would either fight or dig in to consolidate the gains made. That final part of the plan was a little vague.

The scheme had been transformed into elaborate brigade orders for Godley's approval. Brazier said after the war: 'If you want to know how NOT to write an operational order you will find it in that order for the attack; as the Brigadier [Hughes] called it, a "comprehensive order". It took my adjutant an hour or two to copy it and almost detailed individual men to take specific machine guns!'

The order warned that the Turks' garrison at The Nek was 'not lightly' held and identified five positions where there were believed to be machine-guns commanding the ground. But there was the optimistic reassurance to the attackers that they would have 'the full assistance of naval guns and high explosive fire from the full strength of our howitzers and other guns'.

Hughes and Antill left Godley at the headquarters, Antill striding off up the long communication trench to prepare the set of orders for his squadron commanders. In the only reality check, the officer writing the 10th's war diary made his entry for that day: 'Sickness very prevalent. All ranks badly want a rest and change of diet'.

Fresh hope for the 10th was at hand. On 3 August, Hugo Throssell and his eighty reinforcements arrived at Anzac Cove. Hugo told an interviewer later: 'Those of us who had just arrived were fit enough to jump out of our skins, just spoiling for a fight'. They had arrived just in time for what he afterwards called 'that *fool* charge (the authorities wouldn't appreciate the adjective – they'd prefer another "f" and call it "famous")'.

The reinforcements were hero figures to the sick and suffering members of their regiment who they found on Walker's Ridge, camped in small dugout caves and sheltering in trenches carved out of the side of the hill that led to Russell's Top. The new arrivals were tall, tanned and, above all, healthy – Australians who had come to the aid of their mates.

Hugo had brought his fold-up Kodak camera with him and took some photographs of the ragged band of heroes that he found on the terraces of Walker's Ridge. Among them, of course, was his brother Ric.

There was no time for lengthy reunions, however. In the forward trenches on Russell's Top recently vacated by the New Zealanders to make way for the Australians of the 3rd Light Horse Brigade, Tom Kidd had been positioned as the brigade's intelligence officer since 1 August, peering across The Nek through a periscope, trying to assess the Turks' resources. 'Sleep is almost denied and the work is arduous 24 hours duty in the front line trenches and secret saps without sleep each alternate day and the bulk of my intelligence duties have to be prepared between the tours of trench duty', he wrote in his journal. Afterwards, he remembered that

> looking over the parapet before the charge impressed one with the immensity of our job. To my mind it looked an utter impossibility that

we could succeed unless providing a vigorous attack elsewhere drew off a considerable number of their garrison.

We knew the enemy possessed numerous machine guns covering every piece of ground which we would have to traverse and that the trenches were fully manned. Owing to the conformity of the ground we had one firing line only whereas the enemy had parallel and successive trenches, each trench overlooking the one in front, without interrupting fire.

Theirs was an ideal position and practically the Key defence to Battleship and the height of Chanuk Bahr [Bair] overlooking the Dardanelles. On the face of it, it was ridiculous to suppose the enemy would vacate his garrison at the Nek and Baby 700.

The Turks had the Nek and a line of trenches on our side of it. The sides were almost cliff like and practically unassailable. To assault these positions it was necessary for attacking parties to converge leaving a dense mass of men trying to squeeze through a neck of land about 50 yards wide whilst about a dozen machine guns played on them from the front and right . . .

In addition to this, trench upon trench was packed with riflemen with inter-relating fire.

The Australians' forward trench line was shaped roughly like a boomerang about 180 yards long, with sheer drops from cliff faces at either end. Eight main saps had been extended out in front, like fingers, towards the first line of Turkish trenches. On the left of the Australian front line was the 'secret sap', a shallow ditch without a parapet in front or a parados behind that provided some cover from the enemy. The uneven forward line sloped upwards, and the nearest Turkish trench was only about 20 yards from the most forward part of the Australian line; the distance extended to about 65 yards at the wings. The two sides faced each other to the right of the land bridge with little or no cover.

Kidd described the enemy's movements:

The Turks appeared to be feverishly consolidating their defensive positions and the movements of large parties could be detected and heard working in various sectors. It seemed obvious the Turkish command was anticipating an early offensive . . . Their position seemed formidable indeed.

In the rear of their front line of about 75 yards of uninterrupted fire lay trenches of successive alignments, almost parallel, each succeeding trench placed advantageously on higher ground, capable of cover fire and dominating the passage. Numerous saps at short intervals connected the trenches, thus facilitating the movement of their troops.

Assessing the 10th's morale, he wrote:

The eternal vigils, unceasing sapping, continuous sniping, exposure to unexpected and frequent bomb attacks, restricted water supply, nerve racking trench duty in the secret saps night and day, within bomb range of a vigilant and enterprising foe, the ever-present nauseous smell of the enemy dead lying exposed on the top, the contaminating fly and the prevalence of diarrhoea, had adversely affected the health of our troops.

Nevertheless, all ranks were in high spirits on the eve of the attack.

Antill had by this time drafted his own eight-page operational order, complete with capitals and underlines, although his words simply echoed Godley's commands:

In order to consummate the objective in view it is imperative that each individual clearly understands what is required and the general scheme of attaining it.

One thing must be clearly understood WE ARE OUT TO STAY – THERE IS NO COMING BACK.

The surest means are DASH and DETERMINATION.

No time to waste on prisoners – no notice of tricks of the enemy such as 'CEASE FIRE' <u>and there is no RETIRE.</u> ONCE OUT OF OUT TRENCHES OUT FOR GOOD and the assault once for all goes home.

The attack to succeed must be a surprise, carried out with a rush and WITHOUT FIRE.

> Should there be any doubt as to friend or foe, either of three passwords MELBOURNE, ADELAIDE or PERTH will be used and all so pre-warned.

As the 10th's reinforcements had arrived, four days before the scheduled attack, another curious order had been handed down to the Light Horsemen – an order that was actually cancelled in the case of the other troops. Signal Corporal John Brown noted in his diary: 'Packs, blankets, coats and tunics handed in. Going to charge Turkish trench soon. Issued with white cloth to sew on our backs and arms so that the artillery may distinguish us from the enemy'. The Light Horsemen were hence left with practically no clothes, except for their shirts, ragged shorts, frayed puttees and worn, scuffed boots, in which to fight. Nobody seems to have thought that the white patches might also provide Turkish snipers with bullseye targets.

Although seeringly hot by day at that time of the year, Gallipoli's temperature can drop sharply at night and plunge further near to dawn. For the three nights before the attack, the officers and men in the trenches were left without protection from the cold. They managed little sleep.

They were ordered to stow what they could of their belongings into kitbags. Bean wrote: 'Most of the men crammed into some corner among their clothes certain specially-treasured mementoes – a fragment of Turkish shell, some coins bought of a prisoner, a home letter, a photograph or two. There was no chance of taking such treasures with them; they expected to bivouac on the open hills'. He said the men were extraordinarily optimistic.

> The 3rd Light Horse Brigade had never yet seen any important offensive, and its troops accepted as almost certain the success of the big scheme, in which their attack was only a small part. They had so far experienced only the Anzac trench-warfare – eleven weeks of trench-digging and water-carrying; and when the orders for the attack arrived, all ranks became eager with the anticipation that within a few days they would have burst through the hitherto impassable trenches and would be

> moving through the green and open country. The prospect filled them with a longing akin to home-sickness.

Bean said the men were so excited about breaking out at last that a number who were really too ill for fighting managed to hide their sickness from the doctors. It must have been a relatively easy matter: the regimental diary records that on the day before the attack 'all ranks fully 45 per cent below their normal standard'. Sergeant John Gollan, a wheat farmer from Beverley, was too sick for his condition to escape detection, but he managed to persuade a doctor that he should stay on for the attack. Captain Vernon Piesse, one of the Guildford Grammar School old boys, had been sent away sick on 3 August but managed to get back from the hospital on the eve of the fight to rejoin his comrades, saying: 'I'd never have been able to stand up again if I hadn't'.

On 6 August the Light Horsemen stood on Russell's Top making final preparations for the charge scheduled to begin early the following morning. Fire steps were cleared, steps cut into the forward walls of the trenches to give a firmer footing and pegs driven into the parapets as handgrips to ensure a quick and simultaneous 'hop over' by each line of attackers. The 8th Light Horse was already filling the forward trenches, and the 10th was moving up the ridge behind.

Kidd was nursing a private grief. Already apprehensive about the outcome of the charge because of his observations as the intelligence officer, he had just received news that his youngest child, two-year-old Jacky, had died back at home in Geraldton. He wrote in his diary: 'Yesterday a letter from May informing me of poor little Jacky and the thought [that] oppressed me considerably was – could my dear wife stand a second shock . . . ?'

During the day there was heavy shelling from both sides. Marcus Coonan, one of three Coonan brothers in the regiment, was wounded. Within the month his mother had been forced to send an anguished telegram to the authorities: 'Please advice [*sic*] Christian name of Private M.J. Coonan wounded. Two sons same initial'.

By the time she received the reply stating that it was Marcus John – not Michael Joseph – who had died, there was another telegram from Melbourne: William Michael had also been killed.

In the afternoon the increasing roar of heavy gunfire, rattle of rifles and stutter of machine-guns away to the south told the Light Horsemen that the attack on Lone Pine was about to begin. When the trench whistles blew there, the men of the 10th could see Australian infantry advancing with fixed bayonets. The great August Offensive had begun.

During the following year Hugo told an Australian audience about watching the battle:

> It was my first experience of bombardment. Shrapnel shells came bursting over our trenches. I counted 20 or 30 shells bursting at once and as I watched them I thought how could any human being live through them.
>
> Presently someone gave the order to charge and the first line of khaki rose out of the trench and made for the enemy across the intervening shell swept country.
>
> It was most glorious to see these men jump over and charge with the bayonet.
>
> We could see them distinctly with the glass, line after line sweeping on and I never saw a man turn back.
>
> My hair was standing on end and I was just simply thrilled.
>
> We were on a gun station and were quite safe but in looking on I pushed forward and hurled against a man.
>
> This fellow turned round, saw me and said: 'Hullo Jim! How much crop have you got in at Cowcowing?'
>
> It brought me with a bump back to earth.
>
> I looked at him for a moment and said 'We have 250 acres and it's looking well.'

He added that the incongruity of the conversation was one of the things that had struck him most about Gallipoli.

That night, before the charge at The Nek, Hugo 'borrowed' a bottle of Scotch whisky from Major Tom Todd's dugout and arranged to meet Ric and the Chipper brothers on the cliff overlooking Anzac Cove. The *Northam Advertiser* reported what happened next, following a speech made by Hugo to the boys of his old school the following year: 'It was . . . the first occasion during his lifetime on which he had taken strong drink. They knew that in the morning they had to make a bayonet charge and he thought that something was needed to steady their nerves . . .'

The Throssell and the Chipper brothers moved to a spot on the cliff at Walker's Ridge and opened the whisky. They yarned together about their school days together until midnight, as they passed the bottle around. Hugo said 'the only unenjoyable part of it was the drinking of the whisky, which he candidly did not like. At midnight they shook hands all round and wished one another luck.'

The feelings of apprehension and foreboding before the charge of the Light Horse at The Nek were palpable. We have the last recorded words of two of the 10th who were about to die. 'Goodbye Cobber, I don't think I'll be coming back from this one', said Trooper Humfray Hassell to George Smith, who was standing in a trench behind him. Hassell was just twenty-four and came from near Albany, where he had been a stockman. A French dictionary was found in his kitbag afterwards; perhaps he had packed it for the time when the Light Horse would be riding through Europe on its way to Berlin. His words were almost echoed by Trooper Harold Rush, who was twenty-three and spoke with a soft Suffolk burr. He had been employed as an apprentice clothier before sailing to a new life in Australia as a farmer. Before going over the top he turned to a mate and said, 'Goodbye Cobber, God bless you'. His last known words were chosen by his father to be his epitaph, inscribed today on the headstone of his grave in the small, packed cemetery on the slope of Walker's Ridge.

8

'Push On!'

> Mate having said good-bye to mate, the third line took up its position on the fire step.
>
> CEW Bean, *The Story of Anzac*, 1921

THE PLAN STARTED TO UNRAVEL DURING the night, well ahead of the 3rd Light Horse Brigade's dawn offensive. The New Zealanders' attack on Chunuk Bair had disintegrated in the darkness and was running late. There was muddle and confusion surrounding other feints that were supposed to take place along the heights; some failed, while others had their orders changed throughout the night. The architects of the grand plan, Birdwood and Skeen, at Anzac Cove, had been in constant contact with Godley at his divisional headquarters. But in the dark and at such a distance it was almost guesswork as to what was actually going on. The commanders believed that the New Zealanders had achieved some success in their struggle to climb up to Chunuk Bair and attack Baby 700 from the rear, and that they now needed all the assistance they could get to hold them. The charge at The Nek would have to be just the frontal assault – not a converging attack. 'It's not the light horse I am anxious about', said Skeen. 'I think they will be all right. What I hope is that they will help the New Zealanders.'

'That night we filed into the trenches and turned in to get what sleep we could', wrote Corporal Henry Foss of the 10th.

'About 3 o'clock in the morning they roused us. I had slept fairly, considering, but did not feel fresh. After about half an hour's wait we commenced filing into position'. As the 10th jostled for space in the crowded trenches behind the men of the 8th, the next failure occurred. The regimental historian wrote:

> At 4 o'clock on the morning of August 7th the Regiment was quietly standing to arms awaiting the promised battering in of the Turkish defences by our artillery in conjunction with the naval guns. A destroyer, steaming close in shore, opened fire with a single gun in the direction of the Nek, and maintained, with as great a degree of accuracy as could be reasonably expected under such precarious conditions, a brisk fire till the half hour had expired.

Apart from the noise, as Foss wrote, the barrage was 'not very thorough and could have done little damage'. He continued:

> While there [in fire trench] D Troop of A Squadron filed past us. They halted for a while in front of us and I spoke to Gres. Harper and Wilfred, Bob Lukin, Hassell and Geoff. Lukin and some of the others I knew, little thinking that of all those chaps I knew well within half an hour Geoff would be the only one alive.
>
> They were cheery and confident, and soon passed on.

As the men moved forwards, there was an urgent conference of officers at Hughes's brigade headquarters. The officers were discussing a sudden, intense and continuing fusillade of rifle and machine-gun fire that had been directed by the Turks at the parapets of the trenches now filled with Light Horsemen. Antill recalled afterwards that:

> there must have been a score or more [machine-guns] in action at close quarters indicating a sure knowledge of our plans.
>
> Between the commencement of the fusillade, which never slackened a second, and zero [hour], two urgent telephone messages were sent to

> divisional headquarters describing the situation, which was stated to be a most serious development and urging the abandonment or postponement of the attack.
>
> The laconic reply was that the attack must proceed according to plan.

Whoever made that final order has not been identified. Antill later told Bean that it had been a 'callous and unforgivable blunder'.

Could the laconic voice have belonged to Godley? In his memoir, written nearly a quarter of a century later, he said that if he had to attack the heights of Sari Bair again he would do so very differently, concentrating on the capture of Chunuk Bair and boosting forces there to help the New Zealand Mounted Rifles to climb up by committing to that action the Australian Light Horse 'whose attack on The Nek met with such disaster'.

As the senior Light Horse officers met in the brigade's crumbly, makeshift headquarters, Alexander White made a gallant but fatal decision. The popular, sandy-haired commanding officer of the 8th Light Horse, ignoring pleas to the contrary, announced that he would lead his 300 men from the front. He had only recently recovered from a head wound and was perhaps still partly concussed. He had no coat on, and so in his stained, worn shirt and shorts he was indistinguishable from his troopers. Around his neck was a small locket containing a photograph of his wife, Myrtle, and their new baby, also Alexander, whom they called 'little button mouth'.

It was about ten minutes to zero hour as White held out his hand to the brigade major. 'Goodbye, Antill', he said as he hurried away to the forward trench, easing past his troopers, who stood ready for the charge on the fire steps, their bayonets fixed, assuring them as he passed that he knew they would all do well, do their best.

As the seconds ticked away, the last disastrous prelude to the disaster itself occurred. At 4.23 am – seven minutes early – the Allied bombardment, such as it was, of the Turkish positions ceased, 'cut short as if by a knife', according to one account.

The Turks at first couldn't believe it then scrambled to take advantage of the lull. They filled their trenches two deep, one line seated on the parapet, the other standing behind it, nestling their rifles on their shoulders, taking aim. Machine-gunners rattled off a few rounds as they fed the long ammunition belts into their Maxims, each capable of firing 600 rounds a minute. Some said there were thirty machine-guns aimed at the Australian trenches, but one Boer War veteran reckoned that there were 100 ready to scythe The Nek. Either way, the air itself was about to become 'hazy with lead'.

'Three minutes to go', said White, looking at his watch. And then, 'Go!' He leapt over the parapet with the first line of troopers as the trench whistles shrilled, and ran just ten paces before he fell, body riddled with bullets.

'The instant the light horse appeared, there burst upon them a fusillade that rose within a few seconds from a fierce crackle into a continuous roar, in which it was impossible to distinguish the report of rifle or machine-gun', wrote Bean. 'Watchers on Pope's Hill saw the Australian line start forward across the sky-line and then on a sudden grow limp and sink to the earth "as though", said one eye-witness, "the men's limbs had become string".'

At the time, Bean, the official war correspondent, was limping to his dugout. He had been wounded by a bullet to the leg and had just been treated at a dressing station beneath Walker's Ridge. 'The dawn was just growing and the shell shaped cliff around the Sphinx fairly bellowed with sound', he wrote in his diary. Everyone remembered the noise. Brazier thought that: 'a thousand sticks rattled against a thousand sheets of corrugated iron at the rate of a thousand revolutions a minute would hardly give a conception of what the sound of the guns were like'.

But it was what the machine-guns were doing that was the true ghastliness at The Nek. The horror and carnage at the top were awful. Every officer in the front line who went out with White was killed. Many of the Victorians fell back wounded into the trench before even clearing the parapet. Others managed to crawl back and tumble over but were still hit a second or third time and were killed. Practically all of the rest lay dead within 5 or 6 yards of the parapet. A tiny battlefield the size of three tennis courts had been swept again and again by the machine-guns, and the first line had been annihilated in thirty seconds.

Now came the thud of exploding bombs among the wounded, as they writhed in agony and screamed for help in the saps. Black cricket ball bombs and homemade jam tin bombs, full of nails and scrap, were thrown back where possible by the Australians still waiting their turn in the attack. Petrol bombs fell with dull crumps in no-man's-land, setting fire to the dead and wounded. Trooper Syd Livesey was with the 10th, waiting his turn to move forwards.

> I was one of the bomb throwers and I had two haversacks with five bombs in each, beside my rifle and 225 rounds of ammunition and food and water for 24 hours . . . The Turks were throwing bombs from a trench mortar in among us. It was terrible. We were so closely packed in the trenches that men could not get away from a bomb after it fell.

The 10th was stuck like a row of tin soldiers, tense and horrified, as the second line of Victorians moved forwards to take their place on the front line, clambering over their wounded mates, heaving themselves up towards the parapet. The noise was so great that they couldn't hear any shouted orders. The deadly cacophony had worsened, as two Turkish 75-millimetre field guns had found their range and were exploding shrapnel shells over no-man's-land as quickly as they could be loaded.

Exactly two minutes after the first line had charged to its death, the men of the second line, taking their lead from officers scrambling over the top of the parapet, climbed up and over and also charged to their deaths. Once again the rifles and machine-guns cracked and stuttered, cutting and shattering human flesh and bone. The dust of The Nek was becoming settled and muddy with blood.

The only grim mark of progress was that the dead and wounded lay a little further out, perhaps 10 yards or so from the front Turkish trench. The few survivors hugged the ground, took cover in small dips and hollows or sheltered behind the bodies of the freshly dead and the decaying corpses from the failed Turkish attack that had been made across the same ground only weeks before. In this new slaughter, when the eventual count was made, it was found that, in less than five minutes, of the 300 men of the 8th Light Horse who had charged only sixty-six had escaped being killed or wounded.

Through the dense cloud of dust that had been raised by the bullets of the Turkish machine-guns, Allied observers spotted a glimmer of success: a small red and yellow Allied signal flag was raised and waved from the Turkish lines. It was said later to have been carried there by Sergeant Roger Palmer, a former schoolboy athlete and 'man of splendid physique who stood out among the others'. The flag fluttered for about ten minutes before being torn down. It gave hope to some of those at the top: perhaps some men had secured a trench and were awaiting help?

It was the turn of the 10th. Bean wrote:

> The saps were crowded with dead and wounded Victorians who had been shot back straight from the parapet and were being carried or helped to the rear. Among the Western Australians, who occasionally halted to let them pass, every man assumed that death was certain, and each in the secret places of his mind debated how he should go to it. Many seem to have silently determined that they would run forward as swiftly as possible, since that course was the simplest and most honourable, besides offering a far-off chance that, if everyone did the same, some might at least reach and create some effect upon the enemy.

Brazier had already had the pipe knocked from his mouth by a stray bullet as he tried to gauge what was going on. The thick lyddite fumes from the high explosive bursting over the battlefield shrouded the scene in an acrid fog as the men of the 10th tried to take their positions in a forward trench clogged with dead and wounded. Brazier took advantage of the delay and a slight lessening of the enemy fire to raise a periscope and survey the killing field. He saw the troopers of the 8th in front of him, most either killed or wounded, those alive and able to move lying prone, waiting for a time when it might be safe to crawl back. Brazier saw no sign of a red and yellow flag in the front Turkish trench.

A young staff officer from brigade headquarters arrived and asked Brazier why he had not yet sent his men over the top. Brazier told him brusquely that he 'did not intend to send my men over until I had reported what I had seen and had my orders either cancelled or confirmed'. The lieutenant colonel hurried back down the finger-like sap to the brigade headquarters.

Hughes had gone off to a trench mortar position to peer through another periscope as he tried to come to terms with the carnage in front of him, which left only Antill in command at the headquarters. Brazier said afterwards that he found the Bullant 'with his back to the wall'. There followed a furious row between the two officers. There were no independent witnesses to the scene, but according to Brazier he told Antill that the 8th had not advanced more than 10 yards beyond their trenches and had possibly all been killed, and that the Turkish machine-guns had already cut the scrub level with the tops of the trenches. So would the acting brigadier confirm the order for the 10th to advance?

Antill said that he had received a report that the 8th had reached the Turkish trenches and had placed a flag there, so the Western Australians were to 'push on'.

Brazier insisted that not only was there no such flag but it was 'murder to "push on"' to which the Bullant 'simply roared – Push On'.

Brazier replied: 'Thanks, but don't forget I told you'.

The lieutenant colonel struggled back to his regimental headquarters. The look on his face must have told his officers what was coming. 'Very few men expected to get back and most of them had said goodbye to their pals', Brazier wrote later. 'For bravery each line was braver than that which went before. Death stared them in the face and not a man wavered.'

It was 4.45 am. 'I'm sorry lads but the order is to go', said Brazier to the troopers.

'With a smile it was received and with a smile the gallant band went over, leaping the parapet as one man', wrote Olden. The rifle and machine-gun fire rose again in the awful cacophony of death. Bean recorded that

> the 10th went forward to meet death instantly, as the 8th had done, the men running as swiftly and as straight as they could at the Turkish rifles. With that regiment went the flower of the youth of Western Australia, sons of the old pioneering families, youngsters – in some cases two and three from the same home – who had flocked to Perth at the outbreak of war with their own horses and saddlery in order to secure enlistment in a mounted regiment of the A.I.F. Men known and popular, the best loved leaders in sport and work in the West, then rushed straight to their death. Gresley Harper and Wilfred, his younger brother, the latter of whom was last seen running forward like a schoolboy in a foot-race, with all the speed he could compass . . .

'I saw the 10 L.H. come cheering and even laughing as men fell in dozens', remembered an 8th Light Horseman who was lying wounded in no-man's-land. Many of the first line of the 10th fell back, dead or wounded, into the trench they had just vacated. Others dropped riddled with bullets before they had crossed half the distance.

A few nearly made it. We gain further glimpses of the dead and dying, like freeze-frames in a film, from family records and from the accounts of those who survived. After that first line of the 10th charged, Phipps Turnbull, the Rhodes scholar, sent letters home no more; Leo Roskams did not return to the farm that, with his two friends, he had called Utopia; Harry Corker, the Liverpudlian, left his family the sole memento of a photograph he had given them of himself dressed as a cowboy at a fancy dress party; James Wilkerson's mother received the nineteen-year-old's identity disc and one halfpenny piece recovered from his body, but not until seven years later.

Geoff Howell, badly wounded, begged his friend Maitland Hoops to shoot him, but then a Turkish bullet finished him instead. Nearby, Robert McMasters was shot twice through the head, falling near Hoops, who had got two bullets through his own haversack and a piece of nickel opening a wound above his right eye. Like so many others, McMaster's body was never recovered.

On the left of the line, Sergeant Colin MacBean and Captain Vernon Piesse went out together. Piesse was the officer who was sick but had begged to be allowed to return from a hospital ship in time for the charge. They found themselves lying together in a small hollow as machine-gun bullets just cleared their heads. MacBean had a periscope with him and was looking, comparatively safely, towards the Turkish trenches when Piesse, who always thought of his men, said: 'I wonder how the rest of them have got on'. Unthinkingly, he put his head up and was killed instantly.

Sergeant John Gollan, the wheat farmer who had persuaded a doctor to allow him to return to the front from sick leave, was shot through the hand as he left the trench. Then in no-man's-land his leg was shattered by a bomb or exploding shell. He managed to crawl back to the front line but died in agony from his wounds three weeks later.

Staff Sergeant Major John Springall was a 43-year-old who had received four medals in the Boer War. He was kneeling on the parapet, facing the Turks, with his rifle in his hand when he was shot just beneath his row of South Africa ribbons.

Tom Kidd added to his reputation as the Bomb-Proof Kidd.

> I went over with my troop; it was necessary to move to the right front in order to gain the Nek.
>
> Moving some distance the pace was slow owing to the heaped up dead, rubble, bush and wire. A slight depression in the ground afforded

> us a little protection advantage of which had been seized by men of the 8th Regt who had escaped the holocaust.
>
> The row from bullets and bombs was hideous and in addition enemy 75's were pouring in a deadly fire.
>
> Just as we were forcing our way over the slight protecting rise the order to 'halt and dig in' was passed down the line . . .
>
> We lay as we were for about an hour with the deadly fire just brushing over our heads.
>
> Men lying in front, on right, left and rear of me were killed. These all seemed to be men of the 8th Regt – my own lads escaping with one man (only) wounded.

Trooper Charles Williams was one of those survivors. He had been a postboy at Mount Barker when he joined up. He remembered that

> I was in between the Sergeant and the Sergeant major and being the youngest fellow in the Regiment he said to me: 'Now listen to me, lad. There is no hope for us. So, as soon as you get over the top, lay down' – and I was pushed down. I wasn't allowed to lay down. I was pushed down and we fortunately got into a groove in the land and we laid there all night and all day. We couldn't move. There was that much fire and we eventually crawled back the following night.

The third line of Australians had been cut to ribbons; the survivors huddled in no-man's-land, sheltering in tiny dips and hollows or behind piled corpses. Among those who had found some shelter on the left, Major Tom Todd, in charge of the third line, managed to scribble a message on a piece of pink paper, which was passed back somehow to Brazier in his regimental headquarters. Todd asked for further orders, as he could not go on.

Brazier again desperately tried to stop the carnage. He hurried back through the trenches to the brigade headquarters only about 30 metres away, where he confronted Antill once more. Brazier was livid. As he wrote later: 'Nearly all my personal pals and fellow land holders and club men who, unfortunately for them were near my position' had just been killed in front of him.

Still Antill refused to budge, refused to listen, ordering him once again to 'Push on!'

Brazier asked the brigade major to write those words as a message for Todd, before repeating his earlier warning: 'Don't forget I told you'.

Antill scribbled something onto Todd's note, but Todd never received it.

Brazier went back to his regimental post, where he found another message, this time from Major Joe Scott, in charge of the fourth line on the right flank, saying that as he could not see how the task could be achieved, could he have further orders?

This time, Brazier decided to circumvent Antill, seeing no point in returning to the Bullant's dugout, which he described as his enemy's 'resort'. Instead, he forced his way back through the crowded trenches until he found a thoroughly shaken and confused Hughes at his observation post in a hole beside a trench mortar.

Brazier said later that he fronted Hughes and over the appalling noise of the battlefield 'informed him of the true facts of the case, of the confirmation of squadron leaders and the instruction of the Brigade Major to "Push On". To send any more men over, said the colonel of the 10th Regiment, is "nothing but b—y murder"'.

Hughes gave a puzzling half order, half suggestion that Brazier should take what men he could and 'go round by Bully Beef Sap and Monash Valley'. The brigadier general was suggesting that they call off the charge at The Nek and attack from an entirely different direction.

But while Brazier debated with Hughes, the fourth line of Light Horsemen was on the fire steps, bayonets fixed, ready to go over. Shouted commands could not be heard above the din of the rifles and machine-guns, so the signal to advance was to be a wave of the hand from Scott to his troop leaders, who would pass the wave on.

At about five-fifteen an officer turned up on the right side of the line. He had apparently heard Antill's order to push on and asked the troopers why they had not gone forwards. Total confusion reigned. The men took this to mean that the line had been ordered over the top, and they went forwards without waiting for the signal.

'By God, I believe the right has gone!' shouted Scott, somewhere near the centre, as The Nek erupted in another tempest of lead, noise again splitting the air like a rolling clap of thunder. The nearest officers looked towards Captain Andrew Rowan, a Boer War veteran, who signalled for them to go, at the same time raising himself and waving his hand, only to fall back dead from the parapet.

Hugo Throssell was commanding the extreme right of that fourth line. Afterwards, Sergeant John Macmillan, the giant with the heart 'as big as a cabbage', wrote:

> Before we charged Lieutenant Throssell said a few words to the troop and we listened intently, because every man had a fair idea of what we were going into.
>
> 'I am to lead you in a charge,' he said, 'and it is the first time I have ever done such a thing. If any man doubts me, let him step forward now, and he may go with someone more experienced.'
>
> Not a man stirred.

Hugo said later that a trooper called Dinsdale told him to keep his fingers crossed and 'he'd be all right'.

As Hugo leapt out and men around him began to fall, he realised the situation was impossible and ordered his men to throw themselves to the ground. 'We took the scanty cover of a little hollow, and lay there as flat as we could', said Macmillan.

> Presently he said, as loud as all could hear, 'A bob in, and the winner shouts.'
>
> And there, with the shells bursting all around us and the dead lying thick behind us, we proceed to 'sell a pony'.

> The boys all took their numbers, and I was just beginning to count when a shell came a bit too near.
>
> So we got the word to retire, and never knew on whom those drinks were. That's the sort of man he is.

Hugo recalled: 'We got out about ten yards and then lay there for an hour and a half until Major Todd sent word back that it was hopeless attempting anything and only throwing life away to remain there. Then we got orders to return to our trenches'. Yet Hugo kept his sense of humour. He said later that as he lay there one of his comrades had felt 'something trickling down his legs and had paled under the sensation'. Hugo asked the trooper what had happened and he replied: 'I can feel the blood simply gushing out of me'. But when Hugo looked he found that a shell fragment had blown off the cap of the trooper's enamelled water bottle and that the 'blood' was the contents of the bottle.

Other officers were also ordering their men to lie down. Livesey left this account:

> I was in the fourth line and I thought it would be the last line I would ever be in. I knew only a miracle could save a man here. We just got into the firing line and we got the word to go. And our officer, Jim Lyle, was the first man out.
>
> We scrambled out of the trench and rushed towards the enemy but half of the men were mown down before we got a dozen yards.
>
> And our officer cried out: 'It's no use: get down lads.' And we dropped on our faces.
>
> We got the order to get back the best way we could. It was like a dust storm. You could not tell who a man was 10ft away.
>
> I turned my head around to see the best way back and I could see the bullets hitting the ground all around me so I stayed where I was for about ten minutes until the fire died down a bit.
>
> I was expecting a bullet to hit one of my bombs any moment and blow me to glory or somewhere else. I wished those bombs anywhere but around my neck.

> When the fire eased off a bit I crawled slowly towards our trench. When I got within 6ft, I made a rush on all fours and tumbled head first into the trench.
>
> The trench was in a terrible state; dead and wounded men lying everywhere. Some were lying dead half in and half out the trench, some got a yard away, some got more, some were killed trying to get out.
>
> About 10 yards away from our trench they were lying in rows and heaps.
>
> It was awful. We could not get many of the poor chaps in and they had to stay there and rot.
>
> Most of them were never buried, unless the Turks buried them after the evacuation.

Sergeant William Sanderson, a former Scotch College boy who had become a surveyor, remembered how the machine-guns had cut the rhododendron bushes on top of Walker's Ridge to jagged spikes that grabbed at his puttees as he ran. He saw the Turks two deep in the trench in front of him. There was a machine-gun barking from his left and any number more sweeping the field to the right. 'The thing that struck a man most was if he wasn't knocked in the first three yards', he said later.

Trooper Fred Weston, an orchardist, fell dead beside Sanderson. He saw both Trooper Henry Hill, a farmer, and Sergeant Arthur Biggs, a goldminer, mortally wounded.

Sanderson tripped over a bush and landed on the Turkish parapet, noticing arms throwing cricket ball bombs over his head. One bomb blew back and hit him slightly in the leg. He saw two bodies on the parapet. They looked like the Harper brothers, Wilfred and Gresley, united in death at the end of their sprint.

After half an hour out there he saw Captain Phil Fry, alive. Sanderson waved to him and Fry saw him. Then Todd, who had survived the third line, crawled alongside Fry and shouted something like 'Retire the fourth line first'.

Sanderson came upon an 8th Light Horseman lying on his back calmly having a smoke, who invited him to share a cigarette, because 'it's too — hot'. Lieutenant Ted Henty, from the same regiment, was lying with his hip blown away by exploded bombs that he had been carrying in a bag. 'I can't bloody well stand it', he said, before Sanderson and the cigarette smoker managed to drag him into a sap, where he died. Turnbull was lying in the trench, dying, among other dead. 'About fifty yards of the line had not a man in it except the dead and wounded – no one was manning it.'

Trooper Jim Fitzmaurice, a stockman in his twenties, was also in the fourth line. He recalled that he had gone 20 or 30 yards before diving flat – 'if you lifted your head at all you would have got it. [You] went to ground and kept your nose to the ground and never moved. I didn't'. He lay waiting for orders, listening. There were about eighty men around him. After around forty minutes 'we got the order to retire. That came passed along the line several times and we retired with our noses still to the ground and fell back in our trenches. Turned round on our bellies and crawled back. I kept my nose that close to the ground, you know you couldn't get any closer'.

Love, Brazier's second-in-command, had wrenched his knee as he followed the fourth line out. He met up with Todd, and together they had crawled and limped back to the brigade headquarters, where Todd told a totally confused Hughes that he was going to withdraw the survivors. Hughes kept up his plaintive plea to 'try Bully Beef Sap', but there was no one left to carry out this mad plan, and it was abandoned.

Todd heroically crawled out again into no-man's-land to tell the survivors to return. Lance Corporal Billy Hampshire became a legend by going out five times to rescue the wounded.

All this time, Brazier had been waiting in a sap – 'a lonely sentinel watching with a periscope' over the scores of bodies that lay before him. The trenches around him were entirely empty.

At 5.35 am an officer and eight men from the 10th and a few survivors from the 8th tumbled into the sap beside him. They reported that no one had reached the Turkish trenches. It was now fully light. The massacre had taken just over an hour.

Ross and Lindsay Chipper, the brothers who had gone to Prince Alfred's with Hugo and Ric, and had shared a drink with them just hours before, were both dead. Ric himself was badly wounded in the chest. A trooper told Hugo later that when Ric had been shot he had called out: 'I'm done – but keep on! Keep on! Keep the ball rolling!'

In the trenches, Doctor Bentley was working frantically to save lives. Afterwards, his name was put forward, to be mentioned in dispatches for his efforts in the carnage and chaos that surrounded him that day, as the dirt trickled down on the wounded and the dying. He slapped a field dressing onto the wound in Ric's chest.

Those who had a chance of living were carried out first on the long haul down Walker's Ridge to the beach and were evacuated to the hospital ships offshore. As with the original landing at Anzac Cove, preparations for receiving the wounded after the battles of the August Offensive were woefully inadequate and under-resourced. The day after the charge at The Nek the medical control officer sent an urgent message to Anzac headquarters: 'Please arrange naval transport to evacuate from beach here 100 per hour for next 24 hours. Very urgent as wounded are dying for want of proper rest and treatment in hospital ships. Send all available stretchers and improvise as many more as possible. The condition of the wounded on the beaches in the Anzac areas is desperate'.

The casualty clearing stations were packed, and rows of wounded lined the shore waiting to be loaded into overcrowded barges and towed to already-full transports that had been converted to makeshift hospital ships. Then, as the onshore hospitals in Egypt and Malta filled up and temporary tented field hospitals became packed to capacity, there was no alternative but to press passenger liners into service and carry the wounded on to Britain. The journey from Russell's Top down to the beach was a fearful, jolting trip in itself, along the narrow track carved into the steep hillside with shrapnel shells exploding overhead.

It was on the beach that Hugo eventually found his brother, after hunting along the foreshore giving their signal, the piercing whistle that they had used to communicate with each other in the paddocks back home on the farm at Cowcowing.

Ric was in the last line of stretchers, 'grey, heavily bandaged, blood soaking through the field dressing on his chest. He couldn't speak. His lips were pressed together tightly, flecked with a froth of scarlet blood'. Hugo squatted beside him, gripping his arm, reassured by the recognition in Ric's eyes, and stayed with him until he could oversee the stretcher bearers carry him to a crowded tender.

For Hugo this was a defining moment. Now, as well as simply doing his duty in fighting the Turks, he had his brother to avenge.

Ric nearly didn't survive. He probably suffered from septic shock; with no antibiotics he was lucky to live. His medical report from a hospital in Egypt just over a month after he had been wounded read:

> Patient received a bullet wound in right side of chest. The bullet passed beneath the great pectoral muscle, and became septic. A large abscess formed, and had to be operated on. An abscess being opened and drained in three places. Patient is now doing well but is pulled down in health and needs a change.
>
> Disabled by bullet wound and abscess of right pectoral region. He can only raise his arm to shoulder level. Has lost over a stone in weight, and will not be fit for active service for at least six weeks.

The entry for 7 August in Hugo's war diary is laconic:

> Great charge of the 3rd LH Brigade on the Nek. 10th lost 7 officers killed & 96 men – 8th & 10th between them suffered about 450 casualties. Ric shot thro lungs & sent to Cairo – Capt McMasters took my position in mistake, he & 26 of his Troop were killed. No casualties in my troop – Night before Ric, 2 Chippers & self spent night on cliff

watching warships bombard (our 1st taste of Whisky – I stole a bottle from Mjr Todd), both Chippers killed.

The final count, according to the official war historian, was that the 8th Light Horse Regiment suffered 234 casualties – including 154 dead – out of 300 men. The 10th Light Horse Regiment suffered 138 casualties – including eighty dead – out of 300 men. Bean added: 'During the long hours of that day the summit of The Nek could be seen crowded with their bodies. At first here and there a man raised his arm to the sky, or tried to drink from his waterbottle. But as the sun of that burning day climbed higher, such movement ceased. Over the whole summit the figures lay still in the quivering heat'. They lay not only on The Nek – the August offensive had failed everywhere.

✠

It is April, just before Anzac Day, nearly 100 years later. A piercingly cold wind from the north sweeps across the slate-grey sea bringing freezing drizzle to the Ari Burnu cemetery on Anzac Cove. Behind the cemetery is the Sphinx and the long yellow line of Walker's Ridge, which leads up to Russell's Top and The Nek. They carried some of the bodies from the charge at The Nek to Ari Burnu for burial, down the track that had been carved into that yellow ridge.

There is no noise today except for the ceaseless rhythmic roar of the sea. Waves crash onto the pebbly beach only a few yards from the stone retaining wall of the cemetery and its sloping green lawn. Bright yellow and orange flowers are just appearing between the graves for another spring.

Three rows in, you can find some of the men of the 10th Light Horse lying together. The drizzle condenses, trickles and weeps down their headstones. Here are Hugo's friends. Trooper RRV Chipper, aged thirty-one, ('Greater love hath no man') lies next to Second Lieutenant Alexander Phipps Turnbull, aged twenty-seven ('In loving memory of our dear son'), who in turn is next to Captain AP Rowan, aged thirty-nine ('*Cresco per crucem*'). Then comes Second Lieutenant LJC Roskam, no age or epitaph given, shoulder to shoulder with Corporal LLS Chipper, aged twenty-eight ('Greater love hath no man'). And then, almost by himself, is Sergeant DFC Bain, aged twenty-nine, lying exactly where his brother Enie buried him, all those years ago. Enie, who survived to be an old man and to lead the Anzac Day parade through the streets of Perth, mounted on a grey charger, when he was 82.

Up on The Nek on this freezing April morning there is nothing much left to hint at what happened across this tiny sloping piece of turf on 7 August 1915. The rain, turning almost to sleet in the icy wind, drives across the cemetery here with its ten lonely grave markers, five of them in front of the limestone memorial stone engraved with the words 'Their name liveth for evermore'.

Three of the names are of 10th Light Horsemen. Two have the same surname but were apparently unrelated. Trooper Geoffrey Cantwell Howell, aged twenty-five, a British-born stockman, is believed to be buried here together with Trooper Raymond Howell, aged twenty-one, a farrier's floorman from Perth. They lie next to Trooper Ernest William Penny, aged twenty-two, also British born, a labourer from the tiny town of Wonnerup in the south of Western Australia.

More than 300 other Australians are buried beneath the springy turf here high up on The Nek. Nobody knows exactly who lies where. Their names are listed among the missing on the memorial at Lone Pine, names etched on stone that has now weathered into a red colour. Each one left a trail of human heartbreak.

Trooper Amos Leonard 'Ned' Doust, for example, was the mail contractor at Bridgetown in Western Australia. After the charge, his widowed mother, aged seventy, received a letter from the authorities saying that he had been wounded, but she couldn't find out anything more. Fred Stout, the editor of the local paper, took up the cause and spent months writing letters, trying to find out what had happened. Some survivors said that Ned had died, some that they had read in the papers that he had been taken to Britain, some that he had died on the voyage and had been buried at sea.

In December 1915 the official news that everyone had been dreading arrived: Ned had died of wounds on the day of the charge, in August. Ned's fiancée married eventually – but when she died, an old woman, Ned's engagement ring was still on a gold chain around her neck.

Louisa Evans, a widow, lost her two sons, Alexander George and Albert Lacey Evans, in the charge. They also lie somewhere under the sward at The Nek. Louisa took solace in a poem that someone from her community put as a tribute in the local newspaper:

> You answered the call of your country, boys,
> But the voice of the cables tell
> That two dauntless boys in khaki clad
> Were killed in the Dardanelles.
> We mourn your loss. Your action, boys,
> Sweet balm to your kinfolk bring
> For you are heroes, the boys who died
> For your country, and your King.

The wind rustles and sighs in the pine trees beyond the limestone memorial. There are no individual names here, no epitaphs, just that all-embracing 'Their name liveth for evermore'.

One task remains. A small bunch of wildflowers, gathered from so very far away, to be placed here at the foot of this memorial in Turkey. The flowers are tied with ribbons of blue and gold, the brave colours of the 8th Light Horse Regiment.

They were picked in the Australian bush by the grandchildren and great grandchildren of Lieutenant Colonel Alexander White, the leader of the charge at The Nek, and they have asked me to place them here.

The rain collects, drips off the memorial. There is no sound. Just the wind up here on the heights, far above the sea, the raindrops falling on the flowers.

9

Water into Blood

> Major-General Godley visited the gully and addressed as many of the men as could be collected. His speech was not a long one, but he told them what he expected them to do. One regiment had already failed to capture the wells; now the Rangers were to do it with the cold steel.
>
> Major Bryan Cooper, *The Tenth (Irish) Division in Gallipoli*, 1918

TWO DAYS AFTER THE CHARGE AT The Nek, as the stunned and shattered survivors tried to come to terms with what had happened, a formal board of enquiry was assembled in the back trenches of Russell's Top 'for the purpose of enquiring into and reporting on the Officers, NCO's and men of the 10th Light Horse Regiment (list attached) reported missing since the assault on the Turkish trenches on the Nek Anzac on the morning of the 7th August 1915'. It was a long list, and Brazier was keen to get his position on the record. He gave written evidence to a three-man board presided over by Love.

Brazier told how he had referred the matter to brigade headquarters before ordering his men to attack, 'although at this time there was a murderous hail of shrapnel, machine gun and rifle fire from the enemy and he felt quite convinced few if any would return'. Now he had 'personally seen with a periscope a great number of our dead outside the trenches'. He had caused the recovery of some of the bodies but considered it unwise to risk further loss of life in the operation. 'He is of the opinion all the missing are dead.'

There was no relief for Hugo and the survivors. They had lost half of their strength in the charge but were ordered to continue to man the trenches at the top. There were no fresh troops available to relieve them. Every man still alive was fearful of a sudden Turkish counterattack. Out in front of them, the bodies of scores of their mates lay rotting in the sun in no-man's-land, out of reach and unable to be dragged in. They were covered in a cloud of black, bloated flies, whose maggots feasted on the corpses. Seeing this added to the men's trauma and the horror of the ghastly carnage.

'The smell is dreadful', wrote Sergeant William Cameron of the 9th Light Horse, whose job during the attack had been to provide covering fire as a sharpshooter. 'Nothing can compare with decomposed human flesh for horror. The intervening space is lit by flares and bombs and several bodies have been burnt thus. It seems cruel, but from a health point of view it is better, whoever does the burning.' Another trooper remembered afterwards: 'Looking out on the dead was horrible. We were in a sort of coma – dopey. We never discussed it later. We couldn't'.

The remains of White and others who had led the charge were only about 10 yards out from the front trench, but despite 'gigantic efforts on the part of sappers to get to them' they could not be brought in. The relieving 20th Battalion finally recovered them in October. The brave colonel was eventually identified only by his pocket watch, slightly burnt and with a bullet hole through its cover: his membership tag of the Commercial Travellers Association was on the chain. His exact burial place remains unknown.

Love, president of the immediate enquiry, was himself lucky to be alive. Before going over the top, a trooper had tried to bayonet him. Trooper Charles Williams claimed that the night of the charge was the first time Love had been seen in a forward trench, and 'a man tried to put a bayonet through him as he said "I am going out and I am not coming back – and you are coming with me"'. Three or four other troopers grabbed the man before he could carry out his threat, and then 'he went over the top and we never saw him again'.

Who was to blame for the disaster? In 1929, Brazier, still a haunted man, wrote an article and a long poem for the Perth *Sunday Times* about the charge, saying that,

> had the official time not been bungled, the Eighth Regiment would have hopped over as the last shell burst from our own guns.
>
> The Turks' heads were then down below the trenches and as the distance across was in places less than 20 yards, they would have had more than a sporting chance of success. As it was, the Turks, knowing a charge was imminent, and seeing no one coming over, doubled the number of rifles that mounted their parapets.
>
> It is too late now to cast blame on anyone but it is generally recognised that brigade headquarters were at fault in not taking notice of the difference in time, and then compelling line after line to go to their doom. The official history confirms that view.

Brazier's epic poem contained the following verse:

> Into these shambles, now a bloody trench,
> With reeking lyddite fumes to choke their breath
> The Tenth filed in – grim, tense, determined –
> To show the world how men can still meet death.
>
> Beyond the power of men, their Colonel knew:
> Reporting thus, was ordered to 'Push On.'
> 'I'm sorry boys, the order is to go' –
> All knew they had to cross the Rubicon.
>
> Undaunted still they flung themselves aloft.
> To be hurled back like those who went before.
> ''Tis murder to push on,' their Colonel cried:
> And while he sued the battle ceased its roar . . .

> No tiny space in any scene of war
> Has yet contained so many heroes slain;
> Line after line, each braver than before –
> God's heroes all; so hallowed be their name!

Christopher Pugsley, a leading military historian, put the blame squarely on headquarters in his book *Gallipoli: The New Zealand Story*: 'The attack was suicidal and should never have been ordered. Birdwood and the Australian staff of the 3rd Australian Light Horse Brigade must bear the brunt of the blame. But it was Godley whom the Australians identified as the villain, and The Nek was renamed by the men "Godley's abattoir" '.

The abattoir was in full view, and for the survivors shock set in. Lieutenant Wilfred Robinson of the 8th described how men of his regiment seemed stunned and dazed: 'one was sobbing like a lost child three years of age, another laughed hysterically whenever we spoke to him'. Some men were incoherent and had to be sent offshore to rest in hospital.

The toll from physical sickness also continued to rise. Todd was evacuated with dysentery two days after the charge and was sent on to London to recover from exhaustion. He led a procession of officers leaving Gallipoli, with Love soon following him: he sailed from hospital in Egypt to Australia for six months' leave, to recover. Love, apart from being exhausted, had jumped into a trench at The Nek, hitting the inner side of his knee against a stone and apparently dislocating the joint. Then he went down with influenza.

One unnamed officer, quoted by Olden, wrote in his diary on 11 August:

> We now realise we have failed, at any rate for the present time, in our effort to reach the Dardanelles. This undertaking every man had personally set his heart on. What a terrible blow it is to know that it is a 'wash-out'!
>
> Before the attack the [10th] Regiment was buoyant, excited and hopeful. Now its aspirations are shattered like an electric globe. Our

> hopes are frozen tears. The men carry on and do their duty, but each man seems to be brooding over the possibility of 'what might have been'. He does not speak for fear of starting the same train of thought in his mate. He has not appreciated the fact that his mate is thinking exactly the same unuttered thoughts.

Hugo Throssell, like the bombproof Tom Kidd, came through the charge physically unscathed. 'We held our positions for nearly three weeks', Hugo wrote later about his time on Russell's Top. 'We had only half a gallon of water per day – a wash was out of the question. Fighting was continuous. We had no rest for the whole three weeks excepting a couple of hours' sleep snatched in turn in the trench. The men were tired to death, prostrated with sickness, vermin-infested.' Livesay recalled:

> We were in the trenches day and night working two on duty and two hours off. And the smell from our dead mates was awful. They were lying that close to our trenches that we could almost touch them with our rifles. We got a lot of the closest in the night, but as soon as the Turks heard a noise or saw any movement outside our trenches they would let their machine guns loose on us.

Water was uppermost in everybody's mind. On Anzac water was strictly rationed, and it was mostly of dubious quality. Fatigue parties were always on the move, toiling up to the heights with water tanks so that the soldiers could replenish their bottles. As the temperature soared, the need for more water, just to keep the men alive, grew desperate. Major Bryan Cooper, an Irish officer, wrote, 'there was, indeed, no object for which any man in the rank and file would more willingly fight in Gallipoli in August than a well'.

Cooper was with the Connaught Rangers, fighting on the Suvla plain to the north, and they were about to be thrown into battle there in an attempt to capture two spots marked on the map as 'Kabak Kuyu' and 'Susak Kuyu'. 'Drinking water was as precious as the elixir of life, and almost as unobtainable, but officer and man had the same ration to eke out through the thirsty day', wrote the English novelist AP Herbert, who served on Gallipoli. In the minds of the generals – and those of their men, collapsing from heat stroke – these spots were two beautiful wells, which, if captured, would be lifesavers. They imagined that the wells would provide a life-nourishing source nothing short of the biblical wells of Beersheba. The reality was somewhat different: at best they were places to water sheep and goats.

But there was another reason for the action just beyond the wells: they were at the foot of that small swelling in the Suvla plain known as Hill 60, half a mile inland from the seaside junction where the Anzac forces linked up with the Allies who had landed at Suvla Bay, 4 miles to the north. There was a thin line of outposts close to the sea that connected the two groups, and every day a messenger on horseback – and even on one occasion a battery of artillery – had to gallop along the foreshore from Anzac to Suvla, dodging and weaving to escape the enemy's machine-guns and the snipers in the hills above the beach track. The Turks held Hill 60. If the Allies could capture Hill 60 they could link up Anzac and Suvla properly, as well as giving the generals command of the strategically important Anafarta gap from the hill's summit.

On 7 August, when the great Allied offensive began, Hill 60 was so undefended that British and Australian troops wandering across it could easily have secured it for the Allies. But the situation changed rapidly later in the month. The British landed a major force at Suvla with the principal aim of establishing a winter base and the secondary aim of taking over the surrounding semicircle of hills and ridges, which overlooked the proposed base areas. Elderly generals dithered after the troops landed, and there were fatal delays. The Turks called up two divisions and counter-attacked, routing the advancing British force, which fled back across the plain, suffering huge casualties.

The Turks then took over the hills and ridges overlooking the plain and swiftly consolidated. At Hill 60 they began digging a maze of trenches around the summit and a major trench in front of the wells, to guard them. This was connected with their main position by a deep communication trench improvised from a water course. A little higher up in the foothills, at Hill 100, they dug more trenches for their infantry and built machine-gun nests that overlooked and could sweep the ground below.

Ironically, the persistent illusion among the Allies of the wells' importance was incorrect: there was apparently plenty of underground water available on the Suvla plain all along. Major General Beauvoir de Lisle, who reached Suvla on 15 August, later gave evidence before the Dardanelles Commission in which he said: 'You had not got to go down more than 15 feet before you got as much water as you wanted. On the shore, within 100 yards of high water mark you only had to dig the sand 4 feet down to get water . . . The difficulties about water were very much exaggerated'. Nobody, it seems, bothered to act on this information at the time.

On 12 August, a British regiment, the 9th Worcesters, tried to seize the Kabak Kuyu well but was swiftly beaten back by heavy Turkish fire. The Turks had already taken charge of the hill by that time. The news of the failure was noted in the diaries of men from the 3rd Light Horse Brigade up on Russell's Top, who were existing on half a gallon or less of water a day. The Bullant wrote in the official war diary on 17 August: 'Our own Brigade is getting very weak. There is little rest and no relief and hit badly after 13 weeks incessant and most arduous work requiring rest and change. Numbers are down and a good deal of sickness results from weakness and weariness'.

Antill totted up the figures for the brigade on 26 August. Of a total 2145 men who landed on Gallipoli, 313 had been killed, 333 had been wounded, and 617 were away sick. The number of 'effective bayonets' from the three regiments was just 540. Death continued to stalk them on the heights. An entry in the 10th's war diary for this time talks of the daily shelling from a Turkish .75 artillery piece: 'She is an absolute spitting cat and (today) killed two men and wounded one'.

Private Victor Portman of the 20th Battalion, which eventually relieved the 3rd Brigade on Russell's Top, recorded what they found in the trenches there:

> There was a frightful reek of death and huge black swarms of flies seethed over the place, living on the dead and poisoning the living. The trench walls in places were reinforced with dead men and everywhere on the surface of the ground were limbs and bodies, adrift in the debris of smashed rifles, bloody equipment and the flotsam and jetsam of the mad battles fought in the scrub and tangle of those harsh, forbidding slopes.

Perhaps because of these appalling conditions, new friendships were being forged in the trenches between Hugo and his men. They were the toughest of the tough, men who had either survived or who were joining or rejoining the 10th after The Nek. Tom Kidd and the Victorians Sid Ferrier and big John Macmillan remained, along with Syd and Hubert Gillam and Horace Robertson, the young Duntroon graduate, who suddenly found himself promoted to captain after 7 August.

Trooper Thomas Brooke Stanley, always known as Brooke to his family, was also there. He had been born near Sheffield in Britain in 1892, migrating to Western Australia in 1913. He had been sent off the peninsula suffering from bad diarrhoea after his first arrival at Anzac Cove in mid July and had arrived back from hospital on 8 August – the day after the charge at The Nek.

When he had first tried to join up in country Western Australia, Stanley's boss had told the local doctor to turn him down and had told Stanley himself that he'd be better off growing wheat.

> He was right but it wouldn't do for me, so I went to Katanning taking all my kit and guns with me and parked them at the station.
>
> I caught the next train to Perth, 200 miles away and there I was told to get four teeth out and I would be accepted. They gave me gas and when I came round three nurses and the dentist had me on the floor and assured me I would make a good soldier.

Harry Macnee had just been promoted to corporal. He was a stocky man and born leader in his thirties who had been the skipper of a pearling lugger out of Broome. He found himself alongside Sergeant William Henderson, a Boer War veteran and a careful man who had served with the Victorian Mounted Rifles before moving to Perth to practise as a legal manager and accountant.

Trooper Tommy Renton was a tough little miner originally from Liverpool in Britain. He had been working as a gold miner in the mid west of Western Australia when he joined up.

Trooper Frank McMahon was twenty-one but looked younger. He had gone off Gallipoli with a bad case of influenza on 31 July, which had saved him from the slaughter at the Nek. Back up on Russell's Top on 17 August, he told everyone that his one ambition now was to kill a German officer.

George Arthur Leake was the son of Western Australian premier George Leake. Along with Guy Sholl and Leo Roskams he owned the property Utopia near Kellerberrin. Leake's world had gone mad on Gallipoli: Roskams had been killed at The Nek, and Leake had been promoted on the battlefield to temporary second lieutenant to take his friend's place.

Together, the survivors of the 10th waited, day after day, to be relieved, existing in almost indescribable conditions. Although exhausted, they were still put to work trench building and tunnelling. 'Had a shrapnel bullet through the back of my trousers', reported Hubert Gillam matter-of-factly in his diary one August day. He had managed to get time off to go down to the beach and catch a few fish in the evening. The next day he wrote: 'Winds very strong and dust about something awful. Still crook with diarrhoea'.

While those left of the 10th waited, dreaming of some rest, in the top ranks of the 3rd Light Horse Brigade the bitter in-fighting continued between Brazier and his superior officers Hughes and Antill. Brazier blamed them for the disaster that had befallen his regiment. He believed that Antill was now trying to get rid of both

Hughes and himself, and to take command of the brigade. Antill, as we know, despised Brazier, while Hughes regarded the prickly lieutenant colonel as a disrespectful nuisance with a manner that was 'objurgate, litigious and sullen'. On 23 August, Hughes relieved Brazier of his command, because he was 'not satisfied with Colonel Brazier's action or explanation or general work and told him so'.

Brazier accused brigade headquarters of 'hitting him up' and said that he would 'sooner be out of it and transferred'.

Hughes told Godley of his decision at six o'clock that evening and on his return to headquarters sent for Brazier. The lieutenant colonel sent an orderly back with an impertinent note saying that any further communications between them should be in writing. It seemed like an impossible stalemate until, after more discussions, Godley's headquarters intervened, with the result that Brazier was reinstated to a shaky command of his regiment on 26 August.

As events transpired, he was very soon out of the way. And while Hughes remained in command of the brigade, it was command in name only. He was useless. Antill was the real boss. And he was an officer who had demonstrated at The Nek that he believed that orders were orders, and that orders were to be obeyed without question – especially orders from Birdwood and Godley.

Someone else might have argued that the men of the 3rd Light Horse Brigade, particularly those of the 10th Light Horse Regiment, were no longer fit or able to take part in action. But attention was now focused in another direction, well to the north of Russell's Top and The Nek, on the Suvla plain. Nobody with any common sense was in charge up there, either – only dim, pig-headed generals.

On 21 August, Hubert Gillam noted in his diary: 'Attack took place for possession of wells at 2.30 pm. Heard they succeeded'. The tragic and futile campaign for Hill 60 had begun. The water in the wells below the hill soon became bloody, then poisoned by the decaying bodies of those killed on the nondescript mound above and in the thorny scrub around it.

✠

The attack on Hill 60 was part of another grand plan designed by the generals. Beauvoir de Lisle had persuaded Hamilton that he could succeed – with one last attack at Suvla and by seizing the foothills of Scimitar Hill and W Hills – to secure an unbroken Allied front line across the plain. He intended to use two British divisions, both already nearly broken from incessant fighting, at this final attempt for a victory.

The British official history says that by this time, late in August, the Allied force at Anzac and Suvla was 'holding a frontage of roughly 20,000 yards with only 50,000 rifles [men]'. There was no hope of any reinforcements within a month to relieve the wretched, almost wrecked force, which was steadily dwindling through disease and casualties. The Turks, on the other hand, were believed to have 75,000 soldiers in the northern zone, and their numbers were steadily increasing as they poured fresh troops in. Despite these odds it was decided that the attacks would go ahead. Australian and New Zealand troops were to attack Hill 60, although all of the Anzac units were so weak after the heavy fighting earlier in the month that even to collect a force with the strength of a normal infantry brigade meant drawing detachments of men from more than four different brigades.

So, on the oppressively hot afternoon of 21 August, a composite force of around 3000 men was in place for the attacks, including Britons, Gurkhas, Irishmen from the Connaught Rangers, Kiwis from the New Zealand Mounted Rifle Brigade and Australians from the 4th Infantry Brigade. Although there was a preceding artillery barrage to soften the Turkish defences, it was ineffective; the guns were short on shells and did little except alert the enemy that an attack was imminent. The action had been planned for the afternoon, with the thought that the setting sun would shine in the Turks' eyes and blind them to the Allies' advance from the south-west. It was a vain hope, however, as the sky clouded over, shutting out the sun. Soon afterwards a strange and somewhat eerie mist rose from the plain, which then became woven into thick, acrid smoke as fierce fighting erupted and bushfires broke out, trapping the wounded and burning them alive, their own ammunition exploding on their bodies and tearing them apart. The attacks on Scimitar Hill and W Hills eventually broke down in panic, total confusion and ultimate failure.

As part of the attack on Hill 60, the Connaught Rangers were to take the two wells. Before the attack began they were addressed by Godley, who exhorted them to go into battle with 'the cold steel'. Godley was said to have 'an intimate knowledge of the Irishman to deliver such an address'. Two chaplains, Protestant and Catholic, also celebrated Holy Communion and gave the Irish soldiers absolution while 'the bullets of snipers were whistling overhead and ploughed furrows through the ground as the men knelt in prayer'. Captain Bryan Cooper described the final hours before the charge for the wells:

> Here and there a man muttered a prayer or put up a hand to grasp his rosary, but for the most part they waited silent and motionless till the order to advance was given. At last, at 3.40, the bombardment ceased, the word came and the leading platoon dashed forward with a yell like hounds breaking covert. They were met with a roar of rifle fire, coming not only from the trench attacked, but also from Hill 60, and from snipers concealed in the scattered bushes. Not a man stopped to return it; all dashed on with levelled bayonets across the four hundred yards of open country, each man striving to be the first into the enemy's trench.
>
> That honour fell to the platoon commander, Second Lieutenant T.W.G. Johnson, who had gained Amateur International Colours for Ireland at association football, and was a bad man to beat cross-country.
>
> Rifle and bayonet in hand, he made such good use of his lead that before his platoon caught him up he had bayoneted six Turks and shot two more. For these and other gallant deeds he was awarded the Military Cross.

The Kabak Kuyu well was seized, but soon there was a deadly and determined counterattack by the Turks, with heavy rifle and machine-gun fire backed by artillery shells. The Allied forces became mixed up and driven backwards down Hill 60, yet they managed to capture and hold a small toehold of trench at the foot of the hill and to secure both of the wells. 'Men went on as long as they were able to stand and fell, still facing the foe', wrote Cooper. 'From the wells below, their bodies could be seen, lying in ordered ranks on the hillside, with their bayonets pointing to the front.'

On the southern side 500 Australians made the dash across the creek bed valley known as the Kaiajik Dere in three lines, each man laden with 50 pounds of ammunition and equipment and also carrying a shovel or pick to dig in to the hill on the other side. They were mown down by the machine-gunners on Hill 100, who could see them from their slightly higher position in the valley. Major Charles Dare of the 14th Battalion led the second line. He reached Hill 60 with about forty survivors from the 150 men who had begun the sprint with him.

A fire was then started on the hill by a shell that burst among men from the Hampshire Regiment who had charged in to try to help Dare. The Turks had covered their bivouacs on Hill 60 with branches of cut scrub, and this tinder-dry fuel was spread beneath many of the dead and wounded. Soon the flames were exploding bombs and ammunition on the bodies, and bits of burning uniform and wood were falling onto more scrub, starting more fires. 'I know of no cases of wounded being burned', Dare wrote later, 'but witnessed many attempts of wounded trying to crawl from the fire being shot down by the Turks. Every man who moved was sniped at and if seen to be getting away was shot down by machine guns'.

Under the cover of the smoke rising from the fires, Chaplain Andrew Gillison, a Scottish-born Presbyterian minister, accompanied by Corporal Robert Pittendrigh, who had been a Methodist minister in civilian life, and the 14th's regimental doctor, Captain Henry Loughran, went out onto the slopes with stretcher bearers, braving the bullets to drag wounded away from the flames. The next day Gillison, who was waiting with his prayer book to bury some of the dead, heard groaning from a ridge in front of him. Ignoring a warning against moving out in daylight, he discovered that the cries were coming from a wounded British soldier being eaten alive by ants. Gillison called to Pittendrigh and Private Arthur Wild for help, and the three crawled forwards, reached the wounded man and had dragged him about a yard before a Turkish sniper opened fire, severely wounding the two ministers. Gillison died the same day, Pittendrigh a week later.

When night fell on 21 August, the local commanders realised that the tiny gains that had been established on Hill 60 could not be held or extended by the survivors of the first battle. They desperately needed more men. The Connaught Rangers alone had lost 157 officers and men killed, wounded or missing. Godley reluctantly agreed to send in a fresh battalion of Australians. These were inexperienced, ill equipped, unsuspecting and completely unprepared. 'We had no idea where we were going – everyone in the ranks thought it was the trenches', wrote Private Myles O'Reilly. He was a farmhand from Parramatta who had arrived on Gallipoli barely thirty-six hours before with his mates from the 18th Battalion. However, 'these troops came to the tired and somewhat haggard garrison of Anzac like a fresh breeze from the Australian bush', reported Bean. 'Great big cheery fellows, whom it did your heart good to see', wrote another Australian. 'Quite the biggest lot I have ever seen.' Bean continued, 'These fine troops had made a deep impression upon all who saw them, and brigadiers, anxious to relieve or support their tired troops, looked eagerly towards the "new Australians".'

Despite Godley's initial reluctance to commit these green troops to battle, at midnight on 21 August he received word at his dugout from his generals on the spot, Herbert Vaughan Cox and Andrew Hamilton Russell, that the Turkish communication trench on

Hill 60 should be carried at dawn, and that a fresh battalion should be used for the task.

The officers making these decisions had common bonds – they had both in their youth joined the British Army and trained as officers at the Royal Military College, Sandhurst. Then they had gone their separate ways.

Brigadier General Cox, son of an Anglican rector, was described in one history as an officer 'of controversial abilities'. Here he was, aged fifty-five, with a clipped moustache, battered cap at an angle, a red-faced veteran of the Indian Army who had taken part in campaigns including the Afghan Wars and the Boxer Rebellion in China. When the First World War broke out, he was given command of the Gurkhas and had arrived in Gallipoli in charge of the 29th Indian Brigade.

Brigadier General Russell, in charge of the northern Anzac sector, was a New Zealander and, although eight years younger than Cox, was the senior general. After winning the Sword of Honour at Sandhurst and serving briefly in India, Russell had returned to his home country and taken up farming. Russell had impressed General Godley when he arrived in New Zealand to form an army and so Godley appointed him to command the New Zealand Mounted Rifles when war came.

The battalion requested had already turned in for the night just north of Anzac Cove. The men were tired after working hard to establish themselves on their arrival on Gallipoli. Now they were woken 'in a leisurely way' and told they were in for a night march. Nobody told them where they were going.

For about four hours more than 700 men stumbled through the dark under the fire of stray bullets, heading north from Anzac and losing their way at one stage. Eventually, around dawn, they reached the scrubby spur called Damakjelik Bair, which looked across the creek bed valley of Kaiajik Dere, with its well, and on to Hill 60. The men were ordered to lie down, and they rested in trenches that had been inhabited the day before by the Connaught Rangers.

Lieutenant Colonel Alfred Chapman, who was a police magistrate in civilian life, and his officers went to the local headquarters to find out what to do next. They were given an impatient reception and told that they were overly late for the planned action. However, 'arrangements were hurried forward'. By candlelight, Brigade Major Guy Powles told them that the battalion was to make an attack and to do so with bombs and bayonets only.

Chapman interjected that they had no bombs.

Powles replied that they must 'do the best that was possible' without them. He handed each company commander a rough diagram of Hill 60 and then personally led the officers, followed by a long crocodile line of the men of the 18th, down over the spur, along the creek bed and onto flat land behind a gap in a ragged hedge. It was 4.45 am and almost fully daylight. Powles pointed to a low, dark smudge 400 yards ahead: the summit of Hill 60.

The order was given to the men to fix bayonets, charge their rifle magazines with bullets and form themselves into two lines. It was the first clue that the soldiers had received that they were about to carry out a full-scale attack against the enemy. A few minutes later, the attack began. It was the start of a fresh massacre. At least three Turkish machine-guns opened up from the top of Hill 60, scything through the confused men advancing from the wheat field below. Mauser rifles cracked from the trenches above, and cricket ball bombs began exploding among the Australians.

'Out we went tripping and stumbling among the undergrowth', wrote Private Joe Maxwell afterwards.

> What a tragic morning it was! We had never seen a hand grenade, nor had our officers. Ridges sprang to life. They began to crackle. Turkish machine-gun bullets pelted us. Rockets of dust burst and flew. That rapid ripping machine-gun rattle that we came to know so well raced up and down a ridge that loomed in the grey light ahead. Men fell into gullies and pockets. There were groans and thuds to right and left. You just held your breath and stumbled or crawled on.

O'Reilly had a surreal moment as, terrified, he panted his way upwards:

> I saw a German officer. He was holding a drawn sword in his hand – I fixed my sights at 200 yards and had a shot. It seemed to make him take cover though I waited for him to show up again.
>
> This went on until about 10 am when my rifle jammed. I was reaching for another when a bomb landed fair on my back. Fortunately it was to the left of the spine but even so I suffered agony.
>
> I found myself among six wounded and as the hours dragged on we suffered from thirst . . . About four, feeling weak, I tried to crawl away but could not manage and on looking around I could see three of the group had died and the other three had crawled away and I was alone.

At about six o'clock he was rescued by a lone New Zealander who dressed his wound and then helped him to where the stretcher bearers were. They had to double across one or two places when the Turks fired on them.

It was another ghastly disaster. The Turks bombed the men of the 18th out of any small lengths of trench they managed to capture and then forced them back down the hill. There, the Australians managed to cling on to about 50 yards of captured trench line to the left of the shallow toehold that had been won earlier by the New Zealanders. But Hill 60 was still held firmly by the Turks, and the 18th Battalion had been slaughtered. Of the 750 who had made the charge eleven officers and 372 men were casualties; over half of these had been killed. 'My platoon had diminished from sixty to seventeen men. Many a familiar and cheery face was missing. I was too sick to eat', wrote Maxwell afterwards.

Of the 3985 Allied troops that had been sent to attack Hill 60 on 20 and 21 August, 1302 were now dead, wounded or missing. A Gurkha officer, Major CJL Allanson, wrote in his diary on 22 August, after burying three of his officers: 'I want no more of the glories of war . . . I hope that we may not be yet in for another advance'. The next day he added: 'The whole place is strewn with bodies – Gurkhas, Australians, Connaught Rangers. The smell, another of the minor horrors of war, is appalling, the sights revolting and disgusting. Our work is so heavy that we cannot add to it by burying the bodies'.

But the generals had not given up on Hill 60. They were determined to capture it, no matter what. They were also looking for others to blame for the lack of progress in achieving this goal. Godley dismissed the 18th's failure with one imperious sentence in his memoirs: 'The result proved that it was too much to ask of inexperienced troops, with no opportunity for previous reconnaissance, and their attack failed'. He also wrote irritably of his annoyance at being out of 'proper touch' with what was going on at Suvla, with 'individuals passing from one corps to another' and 'the unusual spectacle of a mounted man galloping along the beach with messages to my headquarters'. He added: 'It was imperative that Hill 60 should be taken in order that the junction be made secure, and that the Suvla and Anzac fronts should be continuous'.

On 23 August, Hamilton cabled the secretary of state for war in London without his usual cheery optimism:

> The troops attacked with great dash and stormed the lower slopes of the hill in spite of strong entrenchments, but I regret to say they were not able to attain their objective not even to consolidate the position gained and yesterday found the whole line back to their original trenches except the left of the Australians where one battalion of Ghurkhas and new Australian Battalion continue to hold Susak Kuyu. Casualties not yet to hand, but I fear they amounted to some 6,000 in all.
>
> This renewed failure combined with the heavy total casualties since 6th August, and the fact that sickness has been greatly on the increase during the last fortnight has profoundly modified my position, and as you cannot now give me further reinforcements it is only possible for me to remain on the defensive.
>
> Naturally, I shall keep on trying to harry the Turks by local attacks and thus keep alive the offensive spirit but it must be stated plainly that

> no decisive success is to be looked for until such reinforcements can be sent.

'Harry the Turks' and 'keep alive the offensive spirit' . . . that was the thing now.

Capturing Hill 60 had become an obsession. Birdwood received permission to mount yet another attack on the summit. The problem was finding enough men to do it. As the Turks continued to spend all their nights digging new trenches and building up their defences around the summit, another Allied attack scheduled for 25 August was delayed until 27 August as the commanders tried to scratch together a force of 1000 physically fit men. To accomplish this they had to take troops from no fewer than nine different battalions. Dysentery was now so bad that they had to pick individuals instead of units. From the New Zealanders, for example, the Auckland Mounted Rifles could muster only sixty fit men for the attack, with Canterbury supplying ninety, Otago fifty and Wellington 100 – a total of 300 out of the original 2000 men.

Three groups were to carry out the attack. On the left were 250 Irishmen of the remaining Connaught Rangers, in the centre were the New Zealanders together with 100 survivors of the Australian 18th Battalion, and on the right were 350 Australians of the 4th Brigade. There was to be an artillery bombardment, which would begin an hour before the attack, timed for four o'clock in the afternoon on 27 August. But the gunners were ordered to be 'sparing of 5-inch shell, which is very scarce', and the barrage, when it began, was ineffective, merely warning the Turks that the Allies were coming again.

The guns fell silent at five o'clock. Then the whistles shrilled, and the infantry charged at Hill 60 once more. It was another massacre, dissolving into savage hand-to-hand fighting inside the maze of Turkish trenches, which now extended down the slopes.

On the right, even as the Australians of the 4th Brigade waited to charge from their trench across the narrow Kaiajik Dere, the

Turkish rifle and machine-gun fire was tearing the parapet to pieces above their heads. When the whistles blew, the first line was immediately swept away, and the second line soon met the same fate. The Turks were standing breast-high in their trenches, firing at the Australians like targets in a shooting gallery. The Turkish artillery also opened up, sending lethal showers of shrapnel balls across the battlefield. 'Shrapnel was falling everywhere, including in the trench and smashing up the bodies in a frightful way', wrote one officer. Two-thirds of the men and all except one of the officers were killed. The wounded survivors crawled back across the creek bed after dusk.

The Irishmen were also being decimated. War correspondent Henry Nevinson reported:

> The Connaught Rangers on the left, although much enfeebled by dysentery, charged upon the northern trenches with their customary enthusiasm. Torn by accurate shrapnel as they ran forward, they still fought their way into the first narrow trench and occupied it by 6 p.m. But all that evening and night, by the light of the crescent moon, the Turks stormed down upon them in successive waves, shouting their battle-cry of 'Allah! Allah!'
>
> At 10.30 p.m. they bombed and shot the Rangers out of the northern extremity, and drove them along the trench upon the centre. It was in vain that their own reserve (forty-four sick men!) came up to reinforce.

The Connaughts faltered after losing 152 out of 250 men.

In the centre, the New Zealand Mounteds were engaged in grim hand-to-hand fighting to gain ground trench by trench. The first line, of Canterbury and Auckland troops, took the front trench and threw out the Turkish dead and wounded to make way for the second line, of Wellingtons and Otagos. Then the New Zealanders charged on to try for the next trench. Small parties of the Kiwis threw bombs around the sharp angles in the trenches and then shot and bayoneted, bashed and rifle-butted their way upwards towards the crest.

Men from the 18th held in reserve were sent in, but the last 100 were used up in carrying picks, shovels and sandbags to help the New Zealanders to consolidate the ground they had won. Barely 100 men of the original 750 'great big cheery fellows' of the 18th who had marched around from Anzac on 21 August were left uninjured by the end of this battle.

However, the original toehold won on Hill 60 was looking more like a foothold here, though it was hard to discern who held what and how strongly.

Then, despite shell fire on the approaches to the hill, large numbers of Turkish reinforcements were seen arriving through communication trenches on the far side. They began flooding into the trench maze to bomb their way back again.

Reinforcements were desperately needed before the Allies' attack failed. The New Zealanders were told to stand fast. Their last hope lay with the Australian Light Horse: the men of the 9th and 10th regiments of the 3rd Light Horse Brigade were to be rushed to the rescue. They were the last men available to win Hill 60.

✠

The 9th Light Horse Regiment, having been held in reserve during the charge at The Nek, was relatively unscathed, except for losses due to attrition from enemy fire and sickness, and for the loss of its commanding officer, Lieutenant Colonel Albert Miell. The Boer War veteran had made the fatal mistake of lifting his head over the parapet to try to see what was going on during the charge, only to be shot and instantly killed. His place had been taken by the freshly promoted Lieutenant Colonel Carew Reynell, a 31-year-old vigneron.

Reynell led his regiment in a dash from Anzac to answer the call for reinforcements at Hill 60. They arrived at Cox's headquarters at nine-twenty at night on 26 August but were told to bivouac in the scrub and rest up for the next day. They soon learnt to be wary after Turkish snipers picked off a few of the men when they showed themselves in daylight the following morning.

On the evening of 27 August word came at seven o'clock to prepare to send men to support Russell, who was in charge of part of the attack on Hill 60. Bean said that they were led at night into 'an uncertain and excessively complicated position'. Second Lieutenant William Cameron was told to report to brigade headquarters as orderly officer and later recorded what happened next:

> I went round and reported to General Russell. Had not been there long when I got orders for our Regt. to supply 1 officer and 50 men for reinforcements on an important position, which they had taken during the evening after a prolonged artillery bombardment. These were supplied and sent off. An hour later they called for 100 more and 2 officers and later for 25. These were duly sent along and I reported back to Bde. HQ.
>
> I just got back when Colonel Reynell arrived behind me and asked the General to allow him to accompany his own Regt. This he was permitted to do, and after giving me some instructions for the 2nd in Command started off for the position; just as he left he turned to me and said 'Goodnight Cameron'.
>
> I do not know how it was but I felt a premonition that we would not meet again, and so it proved . . . During the night an attempt was made to take some more trenches.
>
> It was a gallant charge led by the Colonel and two Captains. On the command 'The Ninth Regiment will charge,' they leaped over the parapet and raced for those lines of Turkish trenches on Hill 60.

But again something went terribly wrong. The regiment's own war diary records that 'they appeared to lose direction in the scrub which abounds . . . came under a withering fire from rifles, a machine gun and bombs . . . and the party literally faded away'.

The colonel and his two captains were killed. Most of the troopers were killed or wounded. One officer, Lieutenant John McDonald, together with a sergeant major and three men, got back to safety, and about twenty other wounded crawled in during the night. McDonald, showing extraordinary bravery, returned four times to the scene of the disaster and managed to bring back another wounded man each time. A small party of 9th Light Horsemen attacking from a different direction after desperate fighting had managed to enter, if not entirely capture, 80 yards of trench, which was swept by machine-gun fire.

Bodies were left where they were. Survivors were told not to attempt even to go out to grab identity discs, as it was far too dangerous. Another long list of missing was created for another hastily convened board of enquiry on the battlefield.

As the sun rose on 28 August the survivors of the New Zealand Mounted Rifles and the 18th Battalion held some trenches on the western approaches to Hill 60, while the small party from the 9th Light Horse was holding on to the end of a trench that had been taken, then lost, by the 18th Battalion on 22 August and by the Connaught Rangers on 27 August. Both sides spent the day digging and reinforcing their trenches, and trying to snatch some rest before another night of attack and counterattack. There were occasional outbreaks of rifle fire, stutters of a machine-gun and explosions from a bombing duel.

It was another hot day. Clouds of flies swarmed over the fresh kill and rotting corpses in trenches and on slopes. The stench, said one New Zealand officer, could be scraped out of mouth, throat and stomach in chunks. The smell drifted from Hill 60 across the valley of Kaiajik Dere to the men who had recently arrived and were camped in the dugouts opposite, beneath the thorny scrub on Damakjelik Bair. The men of the 10th Light Horse, tired and thin, battered and ill, were to be thrown at Hill 60 in one last vainglorious, crazy attempt to capture the summit of this 'swelling in the plain'.

10

'Take and Hold the Trench'

> Fighting of the most desperate character, in which the men of the 10th Light Horse particularly distinguished themselves.
>
> CF Aspinall-Oglander, *Military Operations: Gallipoli*, 1932

On 26 August the men of the 10th Light Horse Regiment were ordered to leave their trenches high up on Russell's Top near The Nek and the nightmare scenes that surrounded them. At long last they were going to be relieved and, they thought, to break away and get some rest from their awful vigil on the heights.

There had been no relaxation. Tobacco for their pipes or hand-rolled cigarettes was in short supply and issued only once a week. The rum ration, which came out of stoneware jars lugged up the hillside, was stingy; one trooper wrote that 'it is only issued as medicine . . . An issue is about a tablespoon per man and after 24 hours in the trenches without a wink of sleep it is a Godsend, especially if the night is cold'. Conditions were desperate. The men were tired, hungry, sick and traumatised. 'We'd been holding the trenches, about 30 yards from the Turks, for three weeks and when reinforcements – a splendid crew of men from the 20th Battalion who had just landed on the peninsula arrived – we handed over the trenches with an easy conscience', Hugo Throssell said afterwards.

The troopers believed that they were about to march down Walker's Ridge to regroup and then set up a rest camp near Table Top, a flat-topped hill some way inland considered a comparatively safe place. The 3rd Light Horse Brigade had established its headquarters there. At about seven o'clock, on the 27th, dusk, a sad procession of around 180 ragged, thin men, the worn and shaken remnants of the 10th, began straggling down the steep slope of Walker's Ridge to the beach. 'There was difficulty in getting mules and we had to carry our own belongings – clothes, rifles, ammunition, sandbags, water-bags, picks and shovels', said Hugo. The men stumbled along in the growing darkness, weighed down by their burdens. The regiment's diary noted: 'Men tired and weak, carrying food, firewood, water cans in addition to rifles and equipment and 300 bombs'.

The surviving officers encouraged them along. They were still being led by Brazier: at last, after the agonies of The Nek, the founder of the regiment could be with what were left of his boys. Yet he may have been feeling apprehensive about living in close proximity to Hughes and the Bullant at their new headquarters at Table Top. But the 10th were at least out of the trenches, and we can imagine Brazier's pride and relief as he set out with his officers and men, probably carrying his favourite riding crop, with the curved cane handle, and with his revolver on his polished belt, going forwards again. Perhaps soon there would be a chance, once his men had been rested, to avenge so many of his boys, so many of their mates, who had been killed in the disaster of 7 August.

Once they had climbed down the track carved into Walker's Ridge and had reached sea level, the 10th moved into the deep and wide communication sap that had been dug almost parallel to the beach. From there the men headed north, to Godley's command headquarters. A track inland led from there to Table Top. But when the Light Horsemen reached the headquarters they found that there was a change of plan. As Hugo recounted:

When we got near Table Top the promised rest disappeared. Bullets were whistling round us and at 9 o'clock in the evening we were ordered to sling off our packs and just take our fighting gear and ammunition.

We expected to be right into a charge, but the order was countermanded and we had a long walk to Hill 60 towards Suvla Bay. Wounded men were passing us all the time on their way back from the firing line.

So the confused troopers of the 10th were ordered to pick up their gear again and begin another long march, their equipment clattering and banging like an old-fashioned tinker's cart doing the rounds of an outback station. The machine-gun section, weighed down by its load of weaponry, heavy mount, cooling cans and belts of ammunition, would do its best to catch up with the troopers later on. It was cold, wet and still dark as the 10th staggered northwards with their loads. 'I never felt so tired before', wrote Livesey. 'We were loaded like jack donkeys.'

'The country was sapped the whole way until the last half mile, when we had to get out into the open, and the bullets began whistling around us again', Hugo recalled. 'One of the mules was shot, but all our men – between 100 and 200 – got through. It had just been blind firing on the part of the Turks as they could not see us from over the hill.' Tom Kidd seems to have quite enjoyed the march. He wrote in his journal the next day: 'Olive trees grow wild and are now covered with unripe fruit. The thick tangled undergrowth consists mainly of dwarf oak covered with small acorns. It is quite a treat here in open country and fertile and that what a change from the close foetid air of the trenches. Plenty of shrapnel flying about but one can breathe the pure open air here, hence the preference'.

They halted on an open hillside – 'there was a sort of small prickly shrub growing on it, I remember', said Hugo – and decided to camp for the night. They were too tired to dig in and just lay down where they were and slept. They ignored warnings of the danger from bursting shrapnel shells coming from over the hillside. The warnings had come both from the Connaught

Rangers, in a secure position further on, and from the 9th Light Horse, who had fallen in with them in their march among the olive trees and had told them which direction to head for.

'It was a bitterly cold night and there was a lot of fighting going on', Hugo remembered. Later, the 9th went out to charge the hill: 'two or three lots of fifty men, with one lot wiped out to a man, their bodies being found heaped up some days later'. As for the 10th: 'We were not called out that night and did what we could to make our positions secure'.

They were not secure enough. There were no dugouts; they had scraped shallow holes – if they had had enough energy even to do that – in the open ground before a thorny ridge. At seven o'clock the next morning Turkish artillery spotted them and began shelling. One shell dropped directly among the men but luckily failed to explode. Others burst overhead, however, spewing their lethal showers. Soon there were severe casualties. Hugo had a lucky escape: 'I got a scratch on the leg but nothing to speak of'.

Then Brazier was hit. A lead ball struck him in the left eye, tearing away the iris and blinding him. They patched him up at Doctor Bentley's hastily assembled dressing station before leading him with the trail of wounded to Anzac Cove to be evacuated. Suddenly, with one small piece of shot, Brazier's military career was over.

Command of the regiment passed to Major Joe Scott, the only senior field officer left. By this time numbers in the 10th had become so depleted that A and B squadrons had been amalgamated as A Squadron, commanded by the popular – and prayerful – Phil Fry, and C Squadron was under Duntroon graduate Horace Robertson.

At ten past eight, as the wounded were being treated and the men of the 10th were scrambling to find fresh cover, word came that Russell wanted fifty men to 'hold ready and move at ten minutes notice'. Shortly afterwards the troopers were ordered to stand down again. Kidd observed that 'through being weeks in the trenches with very little sleep and as we had just completed a long march with heavy kit up it can be easily understood that we were not in very good fettle although the men were game enough for anything & had no time for grumblers'.

A new bivouac was selected, and all ranks dug in with renewed energy. The digging went on all day. At the same time others were rising to the occasion. Bean noted that one man cooked for the entire regiment and managed to produce a three-course meal at two o'clock, while another carted fresh water for 1½ miles. That evening, after drawing rations, the men stretched out with only their overcoats over them, waiting for more orders, as a heavy dew fell.

Meanwhile, at three o'clock that afternoon word had come that Godley wanted to see the officers of the 10th. They met together an hour later. Godley said that he wanted the 10th to take a trench on the summit of Hill 60. Hugo described the major general as 'a fine, tall handsome man' who told them that the trench had been taken twice before, but the difficulty would be to hold it. 'He made so light of it that I said: "Is it only one trench you want us to take?" and he said, very quietly, "Only one". Phil Fry winked at me behind the General's back and when we left him one of the fellows said it seemed as simple as going down to the Claremont Show.'

Major Powles showed them the ground ahead, as he had the 18th Battalion before its ill-fated assault on the hill. The objective was also spelt out in an operational order with a map grid reference: 'Take uncaptured trenches in centre and left of Kaiajik Aghala on N-W slope of Hill 60 92JH SW 100 yards'. Translated onto another trench map covered with capital initials and numerals and wavy lines marked in blue for British trenches and red for Turkish trenches, it meant capturing a one-hundred-yard section of a main trench, now coloured in red, labelled D-C.

'It looked like a maze', said Hugo, describing what he had seen.

> The trenches were so close together that it was impossible to tell which were ours and which were the Turks. The particular trench we had to

> take was partly held by the Turks and partly held by our fellows. These trenches are constructed in a straight line for about five yards, and then they bend back for a couple of feet, and then go on straight for another five yards. This is to prevent the enemy, on capturing a trench, from sweeping it from end to end with a machine gun. Well, in this trench our fellows had been steadily driving the Turks from portion to portion, erecting barricades of sandbags as they went. For five minutes at every hour they put up two pink flags to show the artillery just where the dividing lines were, and the Turks – seeking to mislead us – used to hoist flags as well.

The 10th's officers asked Powles to give them a closer view of the trench. Powles told Bean later that he had done so 'under the most difficult circumstances'. He had to take them down the hill opposite and then through a communication trench dug in the Kaiajik Dere valley. The creek bed and communication trench dug into it had wounded men and dead bodies lying in and around them after bad shelling by a Turkish gun on Abdul Rahman Bair. That trench, easily covered by snipers, machine-guns and artillery observing from positions on the ridges higher up the valley, led to the New Zealanders' toehold trenches and on to Hill 60. 'It was the worst walk I ever had', said Hugo.

> The trench we had to traverse was shallow and wide. A lot of wounded men were coming out and 75's were falling all around us. We came to one strip of twenty yards we had to cross that was commanded by a couple of snipers and we lost eleven men. It was then decided that only the squadron leaders should go out to investigate and the rest of us awaited their return.
>
> They got back at about seven o'clock and it was just after that with Capt. Fry I crossed that terrible twenty yards. We just doubled up and ran for our lives, treading on dead and wounded men. It was awful but we had to find out just what was before us.
>
> At 9.30 we got back to our men. We had a little refreshment and a 'tot' of rum, and told them we were to charge at 11 o'clock.

A general – possibly Godley or perhaps Russell (although he was sick) – then came along and addressed the troopers. There were barely 160 men left of the 180 who had marched down the hillside two days before – all that was left of the entire 10th Light Horse Regiment and the first reinforcements. Livesey put the number who went into action at even fewer: he said there were just 148 men capable of carrying a rifle. According to an account by John Macmillan, the general said that, 'a most difficult and important piece of work had to be done, and that we were selected for it. We were to take and hold a trench the possession of which was absolutely essential to the big operation. "When you get it," he said, "you must hold on to it like grim death. Men, I have every confidence in you" '.

But the officers were not confident about the attack. The situation was so difficult to comprehend that some were in favour of a further postponement. They went at ten o'clock that evening to see Russell, 'who was down with a touch of dysentery in a dug out'. Russell said that a postponement would give the enemy time to strengthen its position and that it was better to attack without delay. Russell's insistence that the operation 'must be carried out that night gave them the necessary confidence'.

The rest of the 10th waited. Water bottles had been filled, ammunition pouches checked: 200 rounds to a man. Magazines were full, bayonets sharpened. Every second NCO and trooper carried a sandbag containing ten cast-iron spherical bombs with fuses. All ranks carried at least two or three additional sandbags each.

At eleven-thirty, when the senior officers had not returned, everyone thought the operation had been called off for the night. But then Fry appeared to say that 'the General was very optimistic regarding our success, and thought that, as the Turks were digging themselves in, the longer we left them the harder it would be to shift them. I can tell you I did not fancy our chance of getting it [the trench] after the others getting such a doing', wrote Livesey.

One o'clock in the morning of 29 August was appointed the new time for the charge. The officers used watches borrowed from their men, and Fry borrowed a prized gunmetal signalling watch from Stanley. He told him to set it for exactly one minute to one o'clock.

Henry Foss wrote philosophically that he and a mate called Mac sat down and ate a couple of raw onions and a biscuit while they waited.

> A few minutes later the rest came up and we marched up the trench, the regiment mustering 160 bayonets. It was moonlight, so we could see pretty well. Without much loss of time we arrived close to where our take off was. The men in the fire trenches wished us luck as we passed. Orders came to keep our bayonets low for fear the enemy should see them glinting in the moonlight.

Stanley continued:

> I got a pick, fixed my bayonet and followed some other bloke who was simply following another bloke single file into a trench guarded by NZ's. The trench had once belonged to Turks. They had made a platform on which a machine gun could have rested. It was a handy step for us, one by one, to climb up and over and not a darn thing except quiet – still quiet.

'It was a glorious still, moonlight night as we formed up', wrote Robertson. 'Most of us were suffering from dysentery, but in the excitement of the next few hours, I at least forgot about it. My watch had given trouble, so I borrowed another from one of my troopers, and after synchronizing with A Squadron, stood ready to give the signal.'

Each of the two squadrons was to attack in two lines, with two troops in each line. The men of the first line were to assault using their rifles and bayonets, carrying three bombs each. The second line carried picks and shovels. It would be essential to dig frantically and erect sandbag barricades in the trench as soon as it was captured. Meanwhile, the remnants of the 9th Light Horse, holding on grimly to the small piece of trench that they had captured the night before, were currently sheltering there behind some sandbag blocks. They were to break out and bomb their way down the trench, meet up with the 10th and re-erect their barricade further on.

The first line of A Squadron, commanded by Fry, had George Leake and Colin MacBean in charge. Tom Kidd, with Hugo Throssell and Irwin Burgess as troop leaders, commanded the second line. Robertson was in charge of C Squadron but was short of officers. After selecting two other young lieutenants, Sweetapple and Howard, to accompany him in the first line and debating whether to lead the second line himself, he decided that a Boer War veteran, Sergeant Major Samuel McWhirter, should lead it.

One potentially troublesome Turkish machine-gun position had been identified before the attack. At ten minutes to one Lieutenant William Sanderson and four men laden with bombs crawled out of a forward trench at the foot of Hill 60 and took up a position in the scrub close to where they thought the gun might be.

'We lined up in the firing line about five minutes before one and fixed our bayonets', wrote Livesey. 'An officer was standing with a watch in his hand. We got orders not to fire a shot before we got out of the trench, and not to make a noise. At last he said "time's up, over you go lads", and we scrambled out of the trenches.' Kidd took up the story:

> Leaping over the parapet of our trenches (where we had assembled) precisely at 1am a momentary pause was made on top & the men formed a straight line in close order.
>
> In ordinary times this might have proved dangerous but as it happened it gave a sort of élan to the Charge.
>
> The Turkish trenches could clearly be seen in the moonlight.
>
> As arranged they were rushed quietly in order to make a complete surprise which really [*sic*] eventuates in our secta [*sic*].
>
> C Squadron was not so lucky and had many casualties between the trenches. Here Sgt Major McWherter [*sic*] was killed and Lieut Irwin

> Burgess lost two fingers from his hand. In the secta [*sic*], which A&B Squadron charged, the Turks remained in main fire line and these were either shot or bayoneted.
>
> I myself made rather an undignified entrance to the enemy's trench. As I made a leap over the parapet my foot caught and I landed on the trench bottom and on my head after wrenching my knee & back a bit.

Livesey continued:

> As soon as I got to my feet I could see a lovely row of lights along the Turks' trench. Their Mausers were spitting at us as soon as we started. Neil Conway was just in front of me going like a young kangaroo. As soon as we got close to the Turks we let out a blood curdling yell and I think it frightened 'Jacko' a bit.
>
> Anyhow they did not wait and meet us with bayonets. They were getting out as we were getting in, and there was no one more pleased than I was when I saw them getting out.

Hugo was waiting with the second line.

> I was in the middle of my troop of 24 men, only two of whom got through that night. I was telling them to look to their magazines and see that their bayonets were properly set when big McMillan [*sic*] – a chap standing 6 feet 6 inches – shouted that the line in front of us had charged. There was a fusillade of rifles. We could only get out of the trench one at a time, but we scrambled up and ran for our lives across the sixty yards that separated us from the Turks' trench.
>
> It was a strange sensation to leave the high walls and the confinement of the trench for the open air. We had timed our charge to the minute and it was a wonderful thing to see the fellows running across that strip of ground with bombs bursting all around them.

The second line cheered as it went over. A machine-gun immediately flashed like a torch signalling Morse code in the dark, and other Turks opened fire with their Mausers. Sanderson and his four men launched themselves and smothered the earlier identified machine-gun with their bombs, also killing the crew. Sanderson himself was shot in the back, a bullet lodging in his left shoulderblade; Bentley dug it out afterwards at the clearing station.

Hugo continued: 'Half way across I got my foot in a bush and fell, and, struggling up, struck something else and rolled over and over. But I was not hit, and running for all I was worth, hopped down straight into the Turks' trench. Our first line had got several of the Turks, but by the time we arrived all that were alive had fled'.

The 10th's casualties, mostly from the second line, were not more than about twenty by the time they had taken possession of their section of the trench. Two unrelated troopers called Hallett were among the first to fall, shot during the rush up the hill. Both were aged just twenty-two. John Hallett was a stockman born in Broken Hill, while Bert Hallett was an orphan from Britain, who had been sent to the Parkerville Home near Perth when he was nine years old along with his sisters, Fanny and Jane.

Harry Macnee, the pearler, recalled that 'the trench, so called, was only a shallow ditch, rather wide and full of dead men and equipment. Our first job was to try and deepen the trench, but this was extremely difficult, as it was a kind of hard pipe-clay, and the dead men took up a lot of space'. The trench was in fact almost choked with Turkish dead mixed up with the bodies of the 9th Light Horsemen killed the night before. 'These perforce had to be surreptitiously thrown out to enable our men to dig in', said Olden bluntly. 'The trench was little more than a ditch, the average being well under four feet, and contained no traverses.' Livesey also described the scene:

> Before I went to the front I had read lots of articles about the dead lying for days before they were buried but I could never believe it. I did not think men could put up with it. But after that day at Russell's Top and Hill 60 I can believe anything.

> We were walking over the dead and fighting over them all night. Outside the trenches they were lying everywhere, in front of us, behind us and on all sides. I never thought I would see such an awful sight.
>
> There were dead Australians, New Zealanders, Turks and Englishmen all mixed up. Some had been killed days before.
>
> For about 30 yards up one of the saps the dead were packed into it three deep. One of the parapets of the Turkish trench we took was built mostly of dead men instead of sandbags. As our men got killed we would just take hold of them, one by the arms and the other by the legs and throw them outside the trench. Poor chaps, they were no use to us after they were killed, but it had to be done.

The bodies of Lieutenant Colonel Carew Reynell and Captain Alfred Jaffray of the 9th were found, however, and put aside. They were recovered later and buried, and lie today in the Hill 60 cemetery, two of the few Light Horsemen to have marked graves. The troopers also found the body of Reverend W Grant, chaplain of the New Zealand Mounted Rifles, the who had been shot in the earlier battle while going out to tend to wounded men in the open.

Kidd and the young MacBean, in their section of the trench, were working their way over putrid bodies to link up with C Squadron when MacBean was killed. He ran into four Turks and killed two before a third shot him in the stomach. Sergeant Noel Kidson and Trooper Bill Hunter, following closely behind, promptly killed the remaining two Turks. 'We now commenced to consolidate with all tools available', wrote Kidd. 'Steps were taken to deepen trench, erect overhead traverses.'

The Turks began to fight back, at first with rifle and machine-gun fire. Fry ran along the parapet shouting instructions to his men, while they yelled back at him to take cover, until eventually some of them had to almost force him to get down to shelter. It was a desperate race against time for the men of the 10th to dig in, fill their sandbags and hold the trench against the counterattack. 'They tore into the white pipe clay of the trench floor – hard as cement – with their picks, filled and tied their sandbags and rushed them along to the barricade builders working under the very muzzles of the Turkish rifles and machine guns', wrote Olden.

There was one moment of light relief. Stanley recalled:

> Now we found something different. The texture of the ground was different. It was clay no more. Dry as a bone on that hill, our picks raised a fine grey dust. A whisper started and grew to a wail – Gas! Gas!
>
> It was nonsense of course but a bushfire never travelled faster. The amusing bit was that we'd all been issued with a piece of square flannel as an improvised gas mask. Instructions noted that some ammonia was needed – and there was only one source for that!
>
> Now I ask you, how can you expect any man to have any of THAT left when he has just charged across No Man's Land? No one was gassed, but we feared the worst.

As the men dug like rabbits, the casualty numbers began to rise. 'They got their wounded out of the trench as best they could', said Olden, 'the stretcher bearers behaving with splendid heroism. And now came the greatest test of all'.

11

'Who Said Retire?'

You will be glad to know the men died well.

Keith Murdoch, Gallipoli letter to Prime Minister Andrew Fisher, 1915

THROUGHOUT THE GALLIPOLI CAMPAIGN, THE TURKS had seemed to have an endless supply of easily thrown cricket ball bombs. The Turkish troops called them '*humberas*'. They were small and round, smooth on the outside but segmented on the inside like a chocolate block. When they exploded, each metal square was a potentially lethal jagged bullet capable of inflicting hideous wounds. These bombs were ignited by a fuse that normally took five seconds to burn. The fuse was usually lit by rubbing it on a brassard – a patch of material like the side of a matchbox attached to a soldier's uniform.

Sometimes, however, the bombs failed to ignite in this way, and the fuse had to be lit by hand.

In April 1915, following the initial landings on the peninsula, the Allied troops had been, at first, out-bombed by the Turks. The invaders had no proper workshops, no tools, lathes or casts, so they had needed to improvise and make primitive hand grenades. Jam tin bomb factories sprang up on the beaches at Anzac Cove and Cape Helles. Tins were filled by teams of soldiers with any explosive available and packed with pieces of iron, barbed wire, cartridge cases and anything else that came to hand. These bombs were ordinarily exploded by a short length of safety fuse lit by a match. Wax Vesta matches, sometimes stored by the soldiers in decorative metal holders like miniature cigarette cases, were waterproof and could easily be ignited against a solid surface, but troops also sometimes used lengths of smouldering rope hanging from their belts to light the fuses quickly in bomb battles.

The Australians had come prepared to Hill 60. Bean noted that 'for the first time in the campaign an entirely adequate store of grenades had been supplied, some 2,500 having been brought up to Damakjelik beforehand and two given to each man as he went'. These were not only jam tin bombs but also the newly introduced No. 15, or British Cricket Ball Grenade, a rough cast-iron ball 3 inches in diameter, filled with explosive. It had a screwed brass plug and iron carrying ring; there was a hole in the plug through which a fuse was inserted and then lit. These were crude bombs and not segmented on the inside, giving them a reputation for exploding into a few large, jagged pieces. Often they could be smothered by a blanket or half-filled sandbag, but, alarmingly, they could explode prematurely. However, they could be thrown further and with greater accuracy than a jam tin bomb, and that mattered a great deal on Hill 60.

✠

After sprinting forwards with the initial charge, tripping over, then scrambling to his feet and running again for all he was worth, Hugo Throssell had tumbled down into the trench only to see his friend Phil Fry running up and down on the rough parapet above him, helping and encouraging his men, regardless of his own danger.

> I yelled at him to jump down into the trench and he did. I posted myself at the corner of the trench. By looking round I could see the next five yards of trench. We were piling up sandbags and endeavouring to make ourselves safe. The Turks did not know how much of the trench we had taken, and it was not long before they came back into the five-yard section adjoining ours.

> One big Turk strolled in and stopped, giving me the finest target anyone could wish for. He fell, and others came in, and I got five of them before they discovered where we were.
>
> It was a bright moonlight night, though dark in the trenches.

Hugo was being modest. Bentley testified afterwards that two or three wounded men from Hugo's troop had told him that Hugo had personally killed not five but seven Turks.

The men struggled in a desperate frenzy to erect their first sandbag barricade and a few yards of overhead cover. The Turks, having pinpointed their location, began to open up with their Mausers and throw cricket ball bombs in earnest.

Hugo began to act like a superman, fighting mad, showing the devil-may-care spirit that soon made him a national hero and Anzac legend. He was now 'Fighting Jim', as some dubbed him afterwards – inspiring his men to superhuman efforts while on his way to earning the award for supreme valour, the VC.

Robertson later paid tribute:

> Hugo was to prove himself with a vengeance. Kidd's cool brain directed the fight, but Hugo's reckless active bravery met force with force and gave more than it received. There is little room in this machine fighting of today for the personal abandon and courage which were peculiarly Hugo's – he should have lived in feudal days.
>
> He was no idle leader while the trench blocks were made. He wielded pick and shovel, carried sandbags and inspired by example rather than words. When bombs ran out he it was who first started catching Turkish bombs and throwing them back before they exploded . . .
>
> In spite of his recklessness, he seemed to bear a charmed life. Bombs exploded all round him, and many fragments struck him, but he ignored these minor wounds and stuck to his post. And he succeeded.

Macmillan recalled:

> He stood there in the hottest part of the fight, a leader of men.

> His head was thrown back in the sort of exaltation that you always imagine in the fights of olden days, when it was honest man to man.
>
> His voice rang out cheerfully, 'Stick it out, boys. Get 'em good.'
>
> And not a man of us would have yielded a yard for the sure salvation of his immortal soul.

The casualties steadily mounted as Hugo's men rushed to answer his call. The Gillam brothers, Syd and Hubert, both died from their wounds after bombs flashed and exploded in black smoke within feet of them. Michael Coonan, one of three brothers in the 10th, was also dead – shot or bombed – lost forever. John Thornett, a stocky farm hand originally from Victoria, lay mortally wounded somewhere close by. Hill 60 was reaching out, with its iron shards and nickel-plated bullets, to affect the lives of people far away and for generations to come. Percy Seaman, for example, was bombed or shot down. He was a 37-year-old labourer who had reduced his age by five years when he joined the regiment. He was a widower, left with a little girl called Elizabeth Claire to bring up after his wife died, in 1907. He had felt compelled to ride away to war in 1914, leaving his ten-year-old daughter behind to be raised by friends as her adoptive parents. Six years later, Percy's mother wrote to the authorities to tell them that Elizabeth had run away after hearing of her father's death and had become a ward of the state of Western Australia until she turned eighteen. The writer had lost all contact with her granddaughter. The grieving woman added that she had sent two sons and four grandsons to the war, and exactly half those numbers had returned. Like most of the others from the 10th who died that night, Seaman has no known grave and is today forgotten. What happened to his daughter is also unknown.

Hugo was fighting in a scooped-out section of the trench with room for only about seven men. The section was 5 yards long, 4 feet wide and 4 feet 6 inches deep, with another foot of earth at the sides. They couldn't see the Turks, though they were only a few yards away, separated from them by the barricade. Hugo remembered:

> We had fixed up our sandbags as well as we could, but a lot of the bags had no string to them and as we placed them in position half the sand would run out. Although we could not see the Turks, we could see the tops of their bayonets, and we could see them striking matches to light their bombs. Soon the bombs began to fall in our trench and we had to pick them up before they exploded and throw them back again.
>
> That was a feature of the fighting that continued all night long.
>
> Our endeavour was to pick the bombs up quickly and hurl them back into the Turks' trench to explode there.
>
> Often there was not time for this and we just picked up the bombs and heaved them out of the trench. At times it was impossible to do even this and we had to lay down flat whilst the bomb exploded – and trust to luck.

The Turks launched their first big counterattack by throwing at the barricade a large bomb that appeared to be a biscuit tin filled with high explosive. It burst with a huge bang, blowing down the sandbags. At the same time a line of Turks, now clearly visible in the moonlight and crying 'Allah! Allah!', clambered out and made a rush for the Australian section of the trench. Macnee said that at one stage a German officer was seen on the parapet, urging his men on, 'but he was soon put out of action'.

The blast had destroyed the barrier, but after being driven back a few feet the desperate Australians managed to throw up another one, while the Turks melted away under a shower of bombs and heavy rifle fire. As Hugo wrote wryly afterwards, 'with the Turks within 5 yards of you, with only a couple of feet of sandbag barrier between, and with hundreds of them coming at you with fixed bayonets in the front, the chances of coming through that ordeal alive are very remote'.

The fighting was now close, bloody and awful. At one stage the former miner Tommy Renton chopped away with his bayonet any Turkish fingers that appeared on top of the barrier. Just as the first counterattack was beaten off, George Leake was shot through the head from behind. 'It was a shock to us but we were too busy to spend time worrying about it', one of the survivors said later. As Leake dropped dead, the men realised that there must be Turks in the trenches below their position as well as to the left and right. The small band of Light Horsemen was being attacked on three sides.

A quarter of an hour after the first counterattack, at about one-fifteen, a second shower of Turkish bombs rained down on the Australian section of the trench, and a longer line of the enemy, shouting 'Allah! Allah!', sprang from the night with the moonlight glinting on their bayonets, charging from the right. Again the attack was beaten back with a hail of Australian bombs and well-directed rifle fire. Although a few Turks almost reached the parapet, their bodies adding to the heap there, the attempt melted away. But this time Macmillan was wounded in the thigh. He lay on his back as one of his mates raised his shoulders, then propelled himself backwards down the trench with his good leg, talking calmly all the while, until they managed to drag him to safety and load him onto a stretcher. Afterwards, he suffered from what was described as 'foot drop' and walked with a stick for the rest of his life. And poor Fry, one of the most popular officers in the regiment, was killed, with no chance for a final prayer. Hugo explained:

> It was fairly easy to send the bombs back so long as we kept the bottom of the trench clear. All the fellows had been instructed that if they got wounded and had to clear out they must drop their equipment – rifles, ammunition, tucker, water bottles etc. – and leave them for us to use.
>
> Our practice was to put these things on top of the parapet out of the way but when three or four fellows got hit at once we could not do this and the floor of the trench became cumbered with stuff, amongst which the bombs fell.
>
> It was a bomb falling in this way that got Macmillan and killed Capt. Fry straight out.

> At another time I grabbed a bomb that had fallen amongst some equipment and just as I raised my arm to throw it out, my thumb caught on the equipment, and the bomb went right amongst our fellows.
>
> I called to them to lie down and none of them was hurt.

Chaplain Donald MacLean later quoted a survivor as saying:

> Whenever a bomb fell and we saw we couldn't get it out in time, we used to yell 'Down lads' and everybody would fall flat or squeeze into a corner.
>
> But this time neither Fry nor Macmillan could get far enough away and it got them both.
>
> After the explosion, Throssell shouted, 'All right, Phil?'
>
> Phil didn't answer and when Throssell bent over and raised his head he found it all soft.
>
> Death was instantaneous.
>
> Fry was only a handful but what there was of him was all man.
>
> He used to say his prayers every night and he lived every day as he prayed at night.
>
> There was a funny thing, too. When he came along the top of the trench he shouted: 'Give it to the beggars' and Throssell kidded he thought he was swearing and said, 'What, you swearing Phil!'
>
> Fry replied, 'I only said "Give it to the beggars".'
>
> He was a true Christian gentleman and a hero to boot.

With the death of Fry, Hugo was now in charge of this section of the trench, while overall command fell to Robertson. The young man, who eventually became a general, was already wounded – a bullet had shattered a nearby bayonet and the shards had sliced like razor blades down his face, which was weeping blood. He later wrote:

> Fortunately Lieut Throssell looked as if the Turks could never shift him while a seasoned South African veteran in Lieut Kidd was pitting his cool, shrewd brain against the Turks, and was forestalling every move they made.

> I could safely leave direction of the local situation to Kidd as long as I kept him supplied with men and material, and use C Squadron to narrow the frontage of Turkish attacks.

The 'Bomb-Proof Kidd' was cementing his nickname; this was his third heavy fight, after the sortie from Quinn's Post on 30 May and The Nek. Now this coolest and bravest of officers was holding his section of the trench, consolidating the position by digging deeper and then building bomb-throwing platforms out of the soft earth on the sides. He showed his initiative again in helping to beat off another counterattack by creeping out of the trench with a dozen men and surprising a group of Turks lying in the open and flinging bombs over the Australians' barricade.

According to Olden, Kidd had once again spared the life of a Turkish soldier, when his men first captured the trench.

> With that peculiar psychological trait in the Turkish character, coupled probably with worshipful admiration of a brave man, the prisoner indicated that he would like to render Kidd some service in return.
>
> In response to questioning, the Turk pointed out to Kidd the probable direction from which enemy counter attacks might be expected.
>
> Kidd made his dispositions accordingly . . . Throughout the night he remained in the vicinity of the barricade, seizing the enemy intention with lightning perception, and handling his men with amazing courage and ability.

The furious bombing from both sides went on all night. Explosions were accompanied by fervent cries to Allah, exultant coo-ees from the Australians, screams of the wounded and groans of the dying. 'Men were blown to pieces by bombs that night', wrote Livesey. 'Seventy got their arms and legs blown off.' The 10th Light Horse war diary says that on 28 and 29 August, Australians and Turks threw a total of between 3000 and 4000 bombs at each other. As usual, the Turks had a seemingly inexhaustible supply. But from his first aid station, Bentley had to call for more bomb supplies and then encouraged stretcher bearers to carry unused bombs back to the fight after they had brought in the wounded. Everyone had to be in this battle for any of the men in the trench to survive. Hugo recalled:

> At frequent intervals word was sent up to us to be sparing with our bombs as the supply was not unlimited and it was expected we would have to meet a counter-attack at daybreak.
>
> To prevent the Turks throwing our bombs back into our trench we timed them carefully. After lighting the fuse we counted slowly: 'One, two, three' then threw the bomb and the Turks never had time to handle it before it exploded.
>
> During the whole long night we never got one of our bombs back whilst we threw theirs back by the score to explode in their trenches. This went on for hours – heaving back their bombs and timing and throwing our own.
>
> Whenever one of our men fell we sang out for another.

Hugo seemed to be here, there and everywhere. 'He was in most things that night and kept us all going', one of his soldiers said afterwards, 'calling to us as if we were playing football. It was hearing him yelling "Come on you bonny boy! Come on boys!" that brought Frank McMahon along. He had no right to be on the extreme right, but when he heard Mr Throssell calling, he wanted to be in on the joke'.

McMahon, the boy with dark-brown hair and blue eyes, born in the little dairying town of Tongala in Victoria, started to throw bombs as easily as if he were pitching hay back on the farm. He continued to hurl bombs for most of the night.

Hugo described McMahon's end as 'tragic but glorious'. They had seen a German officer – 'his helmet was shining in the moonlight' – picking up clods of earth and throwing them at the Turks to urge them on. Sid Ferrier, the keen cricketer, and McMahon put their rifles up and got a sight of the German against the skyline. They fired simultaneously, and one or both killed him, each claiming the victim. McMahon said: 'It has been my ambition ever since I enlisted to get a German officer, now I am satisfied'. Then he stood up to get another shot, only to be shot clean through the head. 'As he fell back', said Hugo, 'a Turkish bomb crushed into the trench, and, exploding over him, blew him to pieces'.

Six weeks later what was left of McMahon's body was discovered by a Sergeant J Varley of the Welsh Horse. Varley searched the tattered uniform and found a pay book, a few photographs and a copy of a will addressed to McMahon's brother. So Varley wrote reassuringly to the brother, saying he had 'found the body by a small donga . . . He was found quite decent. By appearance he was shot though the head and the body was not molested. You can rest assured he is where a good fight was once put up'.

The good fight went on. The tiny band continued battling, slipping in blood and body parts in the trench. Whole corpses and bigger bits of bodies had to be heaved up and over the parapet to get them out of the way. Foss told of the congestion:

> Bombs were used freely . . . a continuous stream of these was passing up the trench – 'bombs and more sandbags' would be the cry – and up they would come.
>
> Those not on the look out were hard at work with pick and shovel, deepening and strengthening the trenches, while wounded men passed continuously down the trench, mostly wounded with bombs.
>
> The majority had to be carried, and this was a terrible job owing to the narrowness of parts of the trench and the men at work.
>
> I helped carry one man out and was about staggering before I left him.

Men came and went or slumped and fell. Covered in their own and others' blood, the troopers of the 10th Light Horse Regiment fought on and on. Trooper Hobart Douglas Firns, aged twenty, who had been a school monitor at Perth Modern, was shot dead after fighting nonstop for five hours. 'Finished at last after many narrow shaves and was like a wild man', wrote Stanley, who had been alongside him in the trench. A sergeant, hit by a bullet in the forehead, dropped dead at Stanley's feet before being dragged away.

In one small pocket of the trench with Hugo was Harry Macnee, who had returned to fight after having a head wound dressed. Macnee was ordered to leave again later, this time after being shot through the hand. Tommy Renton had to leave too, after being bombed in the knee. He later had his leg amputated at the thigh. 'Dozens of men came along to lend a hand, but were invariably knocked out', wrote Hugo. He thought the small band of men with him seemed to have charmed lives: 'although in the absolute thickest of the fight [they] managed to scrape through right up to the time we had the fight finally won'.

Hugo continued to stir and rally his men through all the nightmare scenes around him. One of his troopers said afterwards that the Turks were 'a bit afraid of Australians', and that Hugo thought the enemy might be under the impression that the men facing them now were not Australians but 'the same crowd that had given up the trench before'.

> So he yelled: 'Shout and yell boys and coo-ee like the devil,' and so we did.
>
> We coo-eed until you'd have thought we were a mob of drunken bushmen riding home from town on a Saturday night.
>
> It seemed to act, too, for although they outnumbered us eight to one and would have blotted us out by sheer weight if they had come on, they pulled up about 10 yards away, and then bolted back among the bushes.

The Australians' hold on the trench was precarious at best. Hugo was worried about the Turkish artillery, which was sure to begin work at dawn, firing shrapnel shells above the trench.

> We were making preparation to protect ourselves against shrapnel in the morning and sent down orders for timber and iron to make a shrapnel-proof cover. We took it in turns throwing bombs and working with the pick and shovel.
>
> They sent us only one piece of timber and some latticework iron, so we rigged the iron on top of the timber, stretched our overcoats on it and piled sand on top of them, making the best protection we could.
>
> Frequently we all took a spell for five or ten minutes – it almost seemed as though it were done by mutual agreement between the Turks and us.
>
> They would throw just an odd bomb or two and then we would pitch them back again without bothering them with any of our own; then they would liven up again and we would be at it for all we were worth.

Ferrier had put his shoulder out, perhaps playing beach cricket down at Anzac Cove sometime before the fight for Hill 60. But that night he transferred his cricket skills to the battlefield, fielding the Turkish cricket ball bombs, fuses still fizzing, and then fast-bowling them back into the enemy trenches. After he had thrown an estimated 500 bombs during the night, his shoulder gave way again, and he had to reluctantly abandon his aggressive bowling. Hugo remembered that:

> We were very cheerful all the time – lots of laughing and joking, and each of us had wonderful escapes.
>
> One bomb hit Ferrier on the elbow and failed to explode; a spent piece of bomb struck me on the knee and blackened it, but without drawing blood. Several times I was hit like that, one smack on the foot causing a lot of pain, but by some strange chance I escaped any serious injury.

Just before dawn the Turks launched their third and most serious counterattack, this time from lower down the slope of Hill 60 and to the right. As they left their trenches and crept forwards through the scrub, their bayonets were seen, glinting in the moonlight. Hugo called what followed 'our worst trial'.

> We were hopelessly outnumbered. We had started out with only 160 men, and many had fallen, whilst the Turks seemed to be in unlimited numbers.
>
> We who held the section of the trench on the extreme right next to the Turks had to get our men in the next section to take down half of their sandbag barricade so that we could hop over and give up the section when things got too hot.
>
> Twice we had to do this, giving up five yards of trench each time and replacing the sandbag barricade.
>
> Early in the counter attack I got a bullet through the back of the neck and a piece of bomb through the left shoulder. Not until long after did I know that a bullet had gone through my neck; it felt just like a blow.
>
> We could see the bayonets above the Turks' trenches just as thick as they could stick.
>
> Then they crawled out of their trenches and came straight at us.
>
> In the dim light we could see them against the skyline. I passed the word to our fellows and when the first of the Turks got to within ten yards we cheered and shouted, and standing up in the trenches, started firing as fast as we could.
>
> There was no thought of cover. We just blazed away until the rifles grew red-hot and the chocks jammed and then we picked up the rifles that wounded or killed men had left.
>
> Twenty yards was about our longest range and I have no idea how many rounds were fired; I think I must have fired a couple of hundred and when we were wondering how long we could stand against such numbers, the Turks turned and fled.

Stanley went to get more ammunition from a supply point, but Hugo told him to simply fill up his ammunition pouches from the bodies lying in the trench beneath their feet. This came, Stanley said, just as Hugo 'saw a great fine Turk hop out leading a file not towards us but straight across to our right. I got four, one after

Prince Alfred College Archive

Left: Hugo Throssell was the schoolboy hero at Prince Alfred College, Adelaide. He spent seven years there as a boarder, captained the football team and was an outstanding athlete and gymnast.

Bill Day

Right: The grand Throssell family mansion, Fermoy, at Northam in Western Australia. Here in the late nineteenth century, Hugo's parents George and Annie raised their huge family and hosted lavish receptions. Today, Fermoy forms the core of St Joseph's School.

Bill Day

Left: Hugo Throssell the athlete with his trainer in 1905. Between 1903 and 1912 he kept records of his running performances in Perth and in country towns. He also captained his local district football team, was an amateur boxer and took part in wrestling matches.

Guildford Grammar School

The Harper brothers Gresley (*far left*) and Wilfred (*far right*) flank cousins Dudley (Bob) and Geoff Lukin (*centre right*) soon after they all joined up. Within a year Geoff would be the only one left alive.

10th Light Horse Regiment Collection

The young soldiers of the 10th Light Horse Regiment's A Squadron B Troop are in a jovial mood as they eat a hearty meal prepared and served by volunteers at the Claremont showgrounds before the troopers embark for overseas service, November 1914. Many of the men in this photograph would be killed on Gallipoli.

State Library of Western Australia

The troopers and horses of the 10th Light Horse Regiment waiting to board transport ships that would carry them away from Fremantle to the Middle East.

Bill Day

Ric Throssell, Hugo's older brother. The two were described as being like the biblical characters David and Jonathan in their devotion to each other. Ric also had a mysterious side to him.

Hugo Throssell, the dashing young Light Horse officer, poses for this studio photograph. After later being awarded the Victoria Cross, he was an ideal model for the recruiting campaign.

10th Light Horse Regiment collection

Marg Mansfield, Jenny Quartermaine

Left: Major Tom Kidd mounted on his horse Bluey in Egypt. Soon he would be known as the 'Bomb-Proof Kidd' on Gallipoli for his lucky escapes as well as his coolness and bravery in battle.

Shirley Mercer

On arrival in Egypt the Light Horse trained hard, but took time off to see the famous sights. *From left*: unknown soldier, Bill Baxter, Hubert 'Hughie' Gillam and Ernest W McAulley.

10th Light Horse Regiment collection

Right: Lieutenant Colonel Tom Todd, the handsome Boer War veteran and former New Zealand All Black, who went on to command the regiment in Palestine after surviving Gallipoli.

The Bullant – Brigade Major Jack Antill, the martinet who was second in command of the 3rd Light Horse Brigade, photographed on Gallipoli Peninsula in September 1915. He gave the fatal order to 'push on', sending the 10th Light Horsemen to their deaths at The Nek.

Australian War Memorial G01330

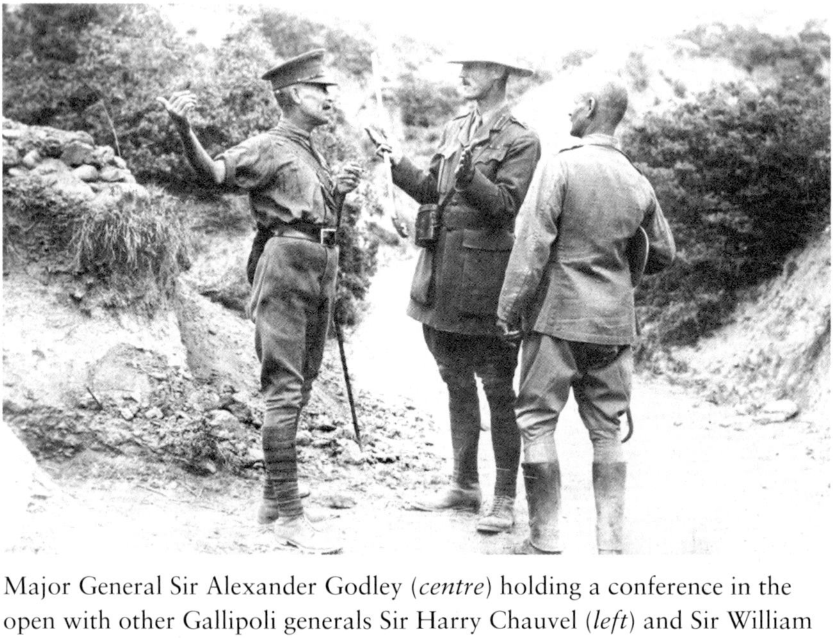

Australian War Memorial H15753

Major General Sir Alexander Godley (*centre*) holding a conference in the open with other Gallipoli generals Sir Harry Chauvel (*left*) and Sir William Birdwood on the Gallipoli Peninsula.

The 'Father of the Regiment', Lieutenant Colonel Noel Brazier, commanding officer of the 10th Light Horse Regiment.

Australian War Memorial P00783.001

Australian War Memorial A05402

Imperial War Museum MUN 3271

Above: A lethal 'cricket ball' hand grenade. Thousands were thrown, and many caught and hurled back at the enemy.

Left: Big John Macmillan, the giant from Gippsland, in 1915.

Right: Captain Phil Fry, the pious officer descended from Quaker stock, described as being Hugo Throssell's 'greatest chum' as he fought alongside him. Photographed here in the trenches on Gallipoli in 1915.

Australian War Memorial A05401

Jim Throssell

From Hugo Throssell's own photo album marked 'Russell Top Just Above Mule Gulley', showing exhausted troopers in the aftermath of The Nek.

Jim Throssell

From Hugo Throssell's own photo album. Tenth Light Horse troopers before the attack on Hill 60. The unsung hero, Sid Ferrier, is identified as the soldier on the far right.

Australian War Memorial G02078

The Hill 60 battlefield four years later. This is the scene of unburied human remains that greeted Charles Bean and his Gallipoli Mission when they returned in 1919.

Right: Katharine Susannah Prichard, who was a beautiful young Australian journalist and prize-winning novelist in London with an increasing interest in politics and socialism. She was about to interview Gallipoli hero, Hugo Throssell.

Karen Throssell

Australian War Memorial P00516004I

Hugo (*right*) and brother Ric in October 1915, recovering from wounds received on Gallipoli.

Jim Throssell

A toast in tea. Hugo and Katharine raise cups to each other in the London hospital grounds as Hugo recovers from his Gallipoli wounds, a botched operation and the bacterial meningitis which nearly killed him.

Jim Throssell

Left: Hugo's first outing from Wandsworth hospital, head swathed in a scarf as he is farewelled by an anxious nurse he called Dorothy.

Below: The scene outside Buckingham Palace on 4 December 1915, before Hugo had the Victoria Cross bestowed on him by King George V. Hugo (*second from left*) wears his scarf and plumed slouch hat, with his brother Ric to the right. Artist Tom Roberts is believed to be the man in uniform between them.

10th Light Horse Regiment collection

Right: 'Intimate strangers'. Hugo's schoolboy crush on actress Henrietta Watson led to their meeting in London after he had become the first Australian Light Horseman to be awarded a Victoria Cross.

National Portrait Gallery, London

Below: 'Lieut Throssell and "Tiny"'. Being awarded the Victoria Cross meant that Hugo was now not only a national hero but also a hero of the empire. He joined other colourful Great War Heroes in different sets of cigarettes cards.

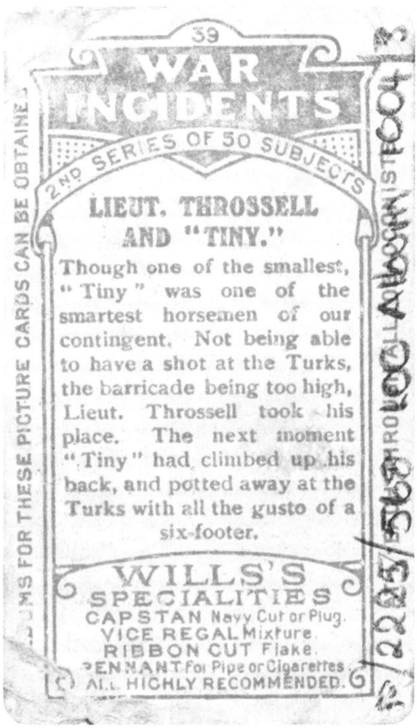

National Library of Australia

10th Light Horse Regiment collection

Left: A photograph taken after the capture of Jerusalem in January 1918. The Light Horsemen camped in a former school, and local children gathered to sell them food. Hugo is front centre of the photograph.

John Hamilton

Rose Charman's Cottage – Katharine's writing retreat at Emerald in the Dandenongs that became their love nest when Hugo returned finally from the war.

Right: A new life in Western Australia for the newlyweds. Hugo showed Katharine his home state as they set out on a whirlwind tour by motorcycle and sidecar in 1919 for their honeymoon.

National Library of Australia

Below: Hugo in slips while playing beach cricket on holidays at Rockingham. With their son, Ric, and his cousins Thea and Alan, this was a favourite place for the carefree Throssells.

Karen Throssell

The happy Throssell family at Greenmount, Hugo mounted on his charger Wyburn while Katharine steadies young Ric on a pony.

Karen Throssell, Patten Headlam

Always good with animals, Hugo teaches a pony to lie down on command while his son Ric looks on.

John Hamilton

On 19 November 1933, Hugo Throssell, VC, settled in a deckchair on this veranda, put his feet up on the latticework, and shot himself with his service revolver.

Courtesy of The West Australian

Hugo's military funeral was held the day after his death on 20 November 1933, his coffin carried on a gun carriage. Seventy people attended, including two fellow VCs.

another, falling like a row of dominoes, with the rifle. Henderson and Throssell got the rest'.

Hugo continued:

> In few minutes they came at us again, and the same thing was repeated. We had no machine guns and had to fire away with our rifles as quickly as we could.
>
> After the second repulse they changed their tactics and came at us from front, rear, and flank as well as getting behind us – between our trench and that occupied by the New Zealanders.
>
> Someone must have said something about retiring, though I did not hear it, and all round there were angry cries of 'Who said retire?'
>
> The hubbub was awful. Each man was determined to stick to the trench and along with the firing they were yelling and shouting like demons.
>
> The noise must have deceived the Turks as to our numbers, for they were all round us within ten yards, and if they had come on we would have been overwhelmed.

Just at this critical time, as dawn turned into daylight, five or six New Zealanders and some soldiers from the 18th Battalion on the lower side of Hill 60 could see properly what was going on and in particular the Turks attacking from the rear. They ran out into the open with a machine-gun, while at the same time Kidd charged from his section of the trench with a dozen troopers. The machine-gun, according to an eyewitness, 'made a cluttering and sputtering noise like a duck makes when it gets its bill into water and filters it for food. Throssell listened for a moment to make sure and then shouted: "Righto boys, there's no need to bother any more"'. The Turks indeed would not charge a machine-gun, and although there was a half-hearted fourth counterattack on the trench at about six o'clock the crisis was nearly over.

Just after daybreak the 10th's own heavy machine-gun arrived at last. A small section of men had carried it all the way from Russell's Top, along the beach and to Damakjelik Bair. Now it too opened fire, with 500 rounds a minute. The stream of lead could saw a man's leg off in a few seconds. 'There never was a sweeter sound to hear that pattering song of a machine gun when it's on your side – or an uglier one when it's on the enemy's', said Hugo.

Ferrier was still beside Hugo when the sun rose. He had apparently decided his shoulder was good enough to go back to work catching and returning Turkish cricket ball bombs. Hugo, meanwhile, was anxious again about the possibility of shrapnel showers from bursting shells. With a 'look after things, Sid, while I'm away', he went out of the trench by about 20 yards to gather more planks and galvanised iron for the overhead shelter. There was an evil *crump* noise of an exploding bomb. The Turks, getting wise to the Australians' tactic of returning their bombs, had begun to shorten their fuses. Ferrier had caught one with a short fuse, and it had gone off in his hand. It 'blew his arm to rags . . . an awful sight. Just tatters of flesh and bone and when Throssell got back and saw him it broke him up'.

Afterwards, Hugo wrote that, just as he was returning to the trench, 'young Ferrier came out with his right arm blow to smithereens. He said "Get the boys out of that, it is too hot altogether." He walked five or six yards and then sat down. There were no stretcher bearers, but someone gave him a "tot" of rum and he walked down to the dressing-room 300 yards away'.

Ferrier was then loaded onto a stretcher and carried along the awful lurching journey to a field hospital on the beach, where the arm was amputated, before he was taken aboard the hospital ship *Devanha*. After the amputation, Ferrier was consoled by a doctor about the loss of his arm. He was said to have replied: 'It's not the arm I'm concerned about; it's the sleeve. I spent two hours patching the bloody thing last night!'

As Ferrier left the battlefield, Kidd found Hugo dazed and bleeding. Stanley said later that a ricocheting bullet had struck Hugo and that he had 'bled like a pig'. Another trooper later told Captain Chaplain Donald MacLean that

> a bomb had burst in front of him and stuck splinters all over his forehead, and the blood had poured down his face and dried into cakes with the dirt and grime.
>
> Another one had splintered his hands, and you'd have thought by the look of them he had been killing pigs.
>
> Then, too, he had got a bullet through the neck on the right side, and his coat collar and shoulder was all blood from that, and his left shoulder had been torn by a bomb, and that was all blood too.
>
> In fact, he was just sweat and blood and dirt from head to foot, and, as though that were not enough, he was as lame as a cat from two other hits, one on the leg and the other on the foot.

Hugo recalled that Kidd told him that 'with so many dead men lying about I would be getting septic poisoning if I did not get my wounds dressed; so I went down and got fixed up'. He didn't leave the trench willingly, though. Robertson, the officer in charge, had to order him to go.

Bentley didn't like what he saw. On Hugo's left shoulder the muscle was cut almost to the bone, a bullet had gone through the right side of his neck from front to back, and splinters of bombs had peppered him all over. Bentley ordered Hugo out of the firing line.

Hugo ignored him. He said afterwards that he 'got some timber and iron for the shelters, and some periscopes, and returned, but I suppose I looked worse than I was with my hands all splintered from bombs and my face running with blood. Everything seemed nice and quiet so I told the boys I would go off and have a sleep'.

Robertson told a different story. 'He returned after his wounds were dressed, and I realised that the concussion of bursting bombs had made him light-headed, so I rather roughly ordered him out again, and said he was not to return.' This time Hugo obeyed. 'Dr Bentley had another look at me and packed me straight off to the hospital ship. I cannot describe the luxury of a bath, clean pyjamas, clean sheets and a comfortable bunk! I slept for hours and woke up with the beautiful face of one of those grand little Red Cross nurses bending over me.'

After Hugo left there were soon only two men in the disputed section of trench: William Henderson and Brooke Stanley. They would end up fighting for thirty-seven hours. Henderson had been catching bomb after bomb during the fight and because he was tall had thrown them back easily. Stanley had caught a bomb, but his hand had been knocked back and 'I heaved it over just as it went off and I got the blast – no wound – in my right ear'. He was badly concussed, however, and shaken. He wrote a letter afterwards to his father:

> The Lieutenant got a ping in the arm and went to have it dressed. Two of us now and bombs coming in steadily. One dropped beyond the bomb-proof among our poor fellows. It was impossible to get it out in time, so we two kept on firing, the bomb apparently blowing everything to a quick end.
>
> Inquiries for more men were not satisfied, so after daylight was firmly established we went back to the other fellows.
>
> Then this child showed his weakness and went cranky.

Stanley had collapsed from shock. He was evacuated unconscious and came to in the great Heliopolis hospital, in Egypt where he received ghastly treatment after complaining of headaches:

> Over my right ear to front forehead, since the concussion on Hill 60, I had violent headaches and odd bursts of black blood escaped through my nose but the relief was only temporary.
>
> Doc withdrew a length of flex wire and plug and needles. He plugged it into the nearest electric point on the verandah, backed me up to the wall and burnt the nostrils out with the immediate release of a flood of congealed blood.

The Stanley family still has the lid of a cheroot box on which, for lack of paper, Brooke wrote this reassuring message home:

> Dear Aunt Jennet and all
> Suffering from shock and debility result of last charge. Not hurt and not real bad.

> Guess I'm nearly as thin as you are but I've 'mafished' [finished] 4 poor Turks but never used the steel. Winning slow but sure. Weather getting cooler.
> Best love
> Brooke.

Almost unbelievably, Stanley returned to Gallipoli before the evacuation to fight yet again, eventually landing and being stretchered off three times. The Anzac was a different brand of hero.

On Hill 60, after Henderson and Stanley had been ordered out, Kidd took over the situation and consolidated a position 20 yards to the rear, with his men digging a wide bomb-throwing trench with protective ramparts to protect the throwers. 'All other officers withdrew to rest in bivouac' Kidd wrote in his journal. 'Being the healthiest animal I remained on duty and take command.' He remained on duty for day and night, during which 'we have a bomb fight practically from dusk to dawn but more than hold our own'.

There were more horrors. A new batch of bombs that the Australians were throwing, perhaps hastily manufactured in Egypt, turned out to have faulty fuses. Trooper Robert Spencer, a farmer and 'grandson of the first government resident of Albany', was the first to die after a bomb exploded in his hand. 'His two hands & one leg were blown off, both eyes blown out & stomach pierced. He was conscious for an hour & calmly gave instructions re personal effects', wrote Kidd. Trooper Archie Crowe, a survivor of The Nek, was next. His hand was also blown off and he, too, died of his wounds.

'Men were very tired & some in a state of stupor', wrote Kidd. 'Tonight I go down to bivouac to have short rest. Weary but damned pleased with myself. We had letter of thanks & praise from General Godley.' Kidd's only personal setback came when he discovered that someone had stolen his Boer War medals and a pair of gold cufflinks from a uniform jacket pocket he had left behind while he was away fighting.

The shattered remnants of the 10th Light Horse were required to hold their newly won position on Hill 60 for another ten days and nights against sporadic bombing and sniping before they were relieved by the British Northampton Battalion. They then staggered through another night march, ending up at the foot of Rhododendron Spur and digging themselves in once again. Their days as a fighting force on Gallipoli were over.

Exact figures vary as to the 10th Light Horse casualties on Hill 60. The regiment's war diary entry for 28 and 29 August says that 200 yards of trench was taken for the loss of fourteen confirmed killed, twelve missing and fifty-nine wounded: total casualties of eighty-five. But more men were cut down soon afterwards, as evidenced by the deaths of Spencer and Crowe. And Olden's regimental history says that the 10th went into action '180 bayonets strong' but could afterwards 'barely muster 70 efficients, and these, weak and exhausted, had almost reached the limit of human endurance'. Bean's official history of the war lists sixty-three of the 10th among 1148 Allied casualties from the battle. Finally, Neville Browning and Ian Gill in *Gallipoli to Tripoli* put the total casualties, killed and wounded, from the battle at seven officers and ninety other ranks. Of these, the authors say, three officers and thirty-nine other ranks died.

On the other side, one source puts the number of Turkish killed at 576. But on Hill 60 today farmers will tell you that local legend says the Turkish wounded were in such numbers that they were gathered together for treatment in huge casualty pits dug further up the ridge towards their strong point on Hill 100. How many of these casualties died?

When Bean returned to Hill 60 with his official Australian Historical Mission to Gallipoli in 1919 to answer some of the many remaining questions about the campaign the remains from both sides were still thick on the ground where they had fallen, or in piles of blackened, charred bones gathered by the Turks in funeral pyres. Even now in the scrub off the beaten track or on the edge of freshly ploughed fields in springtime the stark white bones of the men who died on Hill 60 come easily to the surface.

The VC is the highest award for acts of bravery in wartime, given to a person regardless of rank. It is awarded only for 'the most conspicuous bravery or some daring or pre-eminent act of valour or self-sacrifice or extreme devotion to duty in the presence of the enemy'. The medal was instituted in 1856 by Queen Victoria and made retrospective to 1854 to cover the period of the Crimean War. Designed in the form of a Maltese Cross, it is made from metal taken from guns captured from Russia at Sebastopol. The cross, with its simple words 'For Valour' inscribed below, hangs from a plain crimson ribbon.

Nine Australians out of a total of thirty-nine Allied soldiers and sailors – including a Royal Naval Air Service pilot – were awarded the VC for their bravery during the 1915 campaign in the Dardanelles. Seven of the Australians were awarded the medal after the ferocious fighting at Lone Pine at the beginning of August. Hugo Throssell was the last Australian to receive a VC, for his actions away from the Anzac stronghold on the Gallipoli peninsula at the end of that month. He was the first VC of the First World War from Western Australia, he was the first and only Australian Light Horseman VC, and he would be numbered among the first Australians to receive the medal from the hands of the king himself at Buckingham Palace.

Hugo's bravery on Hill 60 was almost immediately brought to the attention of Hughes through the flurry of letters describing the individual bravery of men of the 10th. Horace Robertson wrote:

> I wish to bring to your notice the splendid work of the undermentioned officer who took part in the assault made by the 10 LH Regt on the Turk trenches Kaiajik Aghala on Hill 60 on the 29th inst whose work I consider calls for special mention in despatches.

2nd Lieut Hugo Vivian Hope Throssell

This officer fought magnificently and I cannot speak too highly of the splendid work he did encouraging the men and by personal example keeping their spirits up although badly wounded himself at the time.

He had a bullet wound through the shoulder coming out at the back of the neck. He also had another wound on the right shoulder which laid open to the bone. In addition he had several wounds in the back from bombs and with all these wounds which must have caused him a lot of pain, he still carried on for a couple of hours refusing assistance and denying he was wounded until after all danger was passed when he went and had his wounds dressed and then insisted he was alright and returned again to the trenches and did another couple of hours work before he was ordered away by the medical officer.

James Bentley also wrote to Hughes:

I beg to draw your attention to the work that was done by Lieut Throssell at Kaiajik Aghala on the 29th instant.

As the wounded came out of the firing line to the dressing station each of them spoke in the most glowing terms of the work done by Lieut Throssell both by encouraging his men and by his example.

Two or three of his troop informed me that he had personally killed 7 (seven) Turks.

He was wounded (1) in the left shoulder which cut the muscle almost down to the bone (2) on the right side of the neck from front to back and (3) by splinters of bombs on various parts of the hands and face.

These wounds were received early in the morning and it was necessary for me to order him out of the firing line.

When he had been dressed he once more endeavoured to return to the firing line and it was necessary for him once more to go to the Field Ambulance.

From what I have learned from his wounded men his conduct deserves the highest tribute it is possible to give.

The 10th's commanding officer, Joe Scott, Tom Kidd and James Bentley were summoned to give sworn evidence as the required three witnesses at brigade headquarters in support of a recommendation that Hugo be awarded the VC. (After this, in one final tragedy for the 10th before they left Gallipoli, Scott was blown to bits, in early October, by a random shell.)

General Sir William Birdwood endorsed the recommendation, signing a letter on 7 September at Anzac headquarters at the cove for forwarding to London.

Hugo's VC citation read:

> For most conspicuous bravery and devotion to duty during operations on the Kaiakij Aghala (Hill 60) on the Gallipoli Peninsula on 29th and 30th August 1915. Although severely wounded in several places during a counter-attack, he refused to leave his post or to obtain medical assistance till all danger was passed, when he had his wounds dressed and returned to the firing-line until ordered out of action by the Medical Officer.
>
> By his personal courage and example he kept up the spirits of his party, and was largely instrumental in saving the situation at a critical period.

Many others from the 10th were recommended for awards. William Henderson, Harry Macnee, Tommy Renton and Brooke Stanley each, in time, received a DCM for conspicuous gallantry – a decoration established during the Crimean War and regarded in the First World War as second only to the VC. Their citations read:

> During the operations Sergeant Henderson rendered most valuable assistance to his Commanding Officer, and when the latter was wounded and ordered away he remained with one man only, and successfully held an important section. Finally, when relief arrived, he volunteered to remain, and was in the trench for thirty-seven hours, during which period there was almost incessant hand-to-hand fighting. He proved untiring, and displayed courage and devotion to duty beyond praise.

> He [Harry Macnee] displayed the greatest coolness and bravery in hand-to-hand fighting which took place during the operations, until wounded. He retired from the front line for time only sufficient to have his wound dressed, and then at once returned and remained until wounded a second time. He gave a fine exhibition of the highest courage and devotion to duty.

> No man of the 3rd ALH did finer work and his name [Tommy Renton] has been specially brought to notice by Lieut Throssell, VC who was decorated for his conspicuous service on this occasion. Trooper Renton displayed the greatest coolness, gallantry and resource under most trying conditions and subsequently lost his leg as a result of wounds sustained in action.

> He [Brooke Stanley] was one of a party which held an important part of the trench for thirty-seven hours consecutively, during which period there was almost incessant hand-to-hand fighting. He displayed great coolness and bravery, and when finally a withdrawal was necessary he was the last to leave the trench.

Eight men of Hill 60, including Hugo Throssell, Tom Kidd, Phil Fry and young Francis McMahon, were mentioned in dispatches for their gallantry and devotion to duty. James Bentley, later awarded a Military Cross, was cited for his work among the wounded both at The Nek and at Hill 60: 'He has never been absent from his duties for an hour and no medical officer could have carried out his duties more satisfactorily or with more credit'.

The hospital ship *Devanha* usually took three days to ferry the wounded from Gallipoli to hospitals in Egypt, but at the time Hugo was evacuated they were full after the August offensive. So the ship sailed on to Malta, but the twenty-seven hospitals and hospital camps that had sprung up on the island were also stretched to capacity. The *Devanha*, with some wounded camped on deck and the more serious cases packed into beds below, was forced to sail to Britain to unload the more badly wounded casualties, like Hugo, and Brazier with his injured eye, for specialist attention.

But Hugo lost no time in trying to ensure that the bravery of his men would be recognised. When the converted P&O passenger and cargo ship called at the island of Lemnos, he sent a letter back to headquarters singling out Ferrier, McMahon, Renton and Macnee 'for some special distinction' and saying that 'no honour could be too high'. He went on:

> As you know they held the extreme right of the captured trench from when we took it at about 1 am until about 7 and 7.30, despite the fact that this particular portion of the trench was bombed incessantly all night long.
>
> Whenever a Turkish bomb lodged in the trench these men immediately took it up and threw it out again, frequently succeeding in lobbing it back amongst the Turks. I saw this act performed not once, but dozens of times. They also played havoc with the enemy by throwing our own bombs.
>
> Many other men fought bravely but were unfortunate in being wounded early and so forced to retire. Others came along in the early morning and did yeoman service.
>
> Amongst others were Sergt Henderson, Burroughs, Eakins, Jones, Harris, Ainsworth, Sergt Macmillan, Ladyman, Steele and Horsfall, but the four I have just mentioned stand alone. They bore the brunt of the fighting over six hours and it was not until after the Turks had made their third and unsuccessful counter attack that they were all wounded about the same time between 7 and 7.30.
>
> The fact that we held the trench is, in my opinion, largely due to the splendid courage and accurate bombing of these glorious men.

In the end, of all the Hill 60 heroes only Sid Ferrier really missed out, probably because he died so soon afterwards. On 9 September, Chaplain Basil Bond wrote to Sid's father, John, in Carapook, western Victoria, from HM Hospital Ship *Devanha*, at sea:

I expect you will by now have heard the sad news of your son's death from wounds – Corp S.H. Ferrier, 176, 10th A.L.H. on board this Hospital Ship *Devanha*.

He came to us about Sunday Aug 29th from A.N.Z.A.C. having lost his right arm as a result of a bomb.

He did splendidly, and was so bright and cheerful – until a few days ago – and then tetanus set in and he died yesterday evening. He was so cheerful and were all so fond of him that we deeply regret his death. We were on the way to England with him, and he had been so bright, talking about his visit to the Old Country.

I can assure you he had the best of attention and care from Doctors' and Sisters' alike and all was done for him that human power could do.

I buried him this morning at sea, 10 miles S.S.W. of Cape Carveiro – Coast of Portugal – and about 30 miles N.E. of Lisbon as the crow flies.

His Colonel is on board – wounded and another officer sick, and several of his regiment – most of them well enough to be present at the funeral this morning.

His officer tells me he did splendidly the night he was wounded. He and two others held a trench against a whole horde of Turks – who were bombing them – they held it till long after the rest were wounded or killed, and he went on throwing bombs back, long after he was wounded, and until reinforcements came up.

I believe he has been mentioned for conspicuous bravery: I only wish he could have been spared to receive his award.

His possessions included

Disc
Pay Book
Note Book and Letters
Pipe

Please accept my sincerest sympathy in this your sorrow and sacrifice. He died a hero and a Briton. May God comfort you in your sorrow.

Hugo was heartbroken. He said afterwards that nothing had affected him more than Ferrier's death. He and Brazier watched as the body, sewn up in a blanket, was placed on a stretcher and covered with a Union Jack. The service was read, the stretcher tilted over the stern of the *Devanha*, and the body slid from under the flag into the waters of the Atlantic. Hugo then went to the side of the ship and 'cried like a kid. I couldn't help myself'. Later, from London, he wrote to Sid's mother telling her how he had located Sid aboard the hospital ship and that initially he had being doing splendidly.

> I told the doctor in charge of him about his great pluck and he took a special interest in him.
>
> We called at Malta, and I was with Sid when Lord Methuen, Governor of the Island, made his inspection, and the old General had quite a long chat with your boy.
>
> It was about that time that the awful tetanus got a hold on him, and although the doctors did all they possibly could to save him and his pluck never deserted him, he died quietly on the night of the 8th September.
>
> We buried him next morning . . . It was a nice little service; half a dozen of his wounded 10th Light Horse comrades being present together with the Colonel of our Regiment and myself.
>
> I used to spend a couple of hours with him every day, and I saw him just half-an-hour before he died. He was unconscious and the doctor told me that he did not think he suffered. He did not know me, but as I bent over the old chap the last word I heard him say was 'Mother'.
>
> I cannot tell you how I feel about it, dear Mrs. Ferrier. I have seen many brave men the last few months, and although there may be plenty of men just as brave, there never lived a *braver* man than your son.
>
> This is a wonderful war, and though your son has not been awarded, so far, any honour, it will be comforting to you to know that in the eyes of his comrades he earned the Victoria Cross dozens of times over.

Despite Hugo's prompting and recommendations, Ferrier received nothing. And what had he and so many other brave men died for? The bloody, heroic and desperate fighting for Hill 60 eventually achieved very little. Birdwood believed that the knoll had been captured and reported this to the commander-in-chief, Hamilton, who, himself desperate for a victory, exalted on 29 August: 'Knoll 60, now ours throughout commands the Biyuk Anafarta valley with view and fire – a big tactical scoop'. The next day Hamilton wrote:

> Still good news from Anzac. Seeing that the stunt was on a small scale, we seem to have got into the Turks with a vengeance.
>
> In falling back as well as counter attacking after we had taken Hill 60, the enemy was exposed to the fire from our trenches along the Kaiajik Dere. Birdie declares they have lost 5,000. We have taken several machine guns and trench mortars as well as fifty prisoners. Have sent grateful message to all on the spot.

It was an illusion. Even Godley, in his memoirs, conceded brusquely that 'enough of the hill was taken to secure our junction, though the actual summit remained in the hands of the Turks'. The truth was that half of the hill, including the summit itself – so hard to determine as a summit even today – and possibly even more was still held by the Turks. The summit shut out all Allied view of the slopes to the north. The seaward slopes had been captured and held by the Allies, which did give them a tenuous link to Anzac and a slight but vaguely useful view over the plain. It was the last big fight on the peninsula, and it ended in yet another stalemate. The official British war historian, Aspinall-Oglander, wrote:

> Many of the officers who took part in these operations expressed the opinion later that one more thrust would have completed the capture of the hill. But the truth seems to have been that the whole corps was now completely spent.
>
> The bitter fighting on Hill 60, still regarded by the Australians and New Zealanders as perhaps their sternest trial on Gallipoli had added the last straw.
>
> None of the units engaged had ever been so depleted as at the moment when the action began, and the men had only been able to carry on by sheer force of will.

> Their spirit, indeed, was so splendid that the higher commanders, judging from appearances, believed them capable of greater efforts than were humanly possible.
>
> Courage, morale, and the excitement of the moment enabled them to fight in flashes; but the prolonged strain at Anzac – the fighting, the heat, the constant debilitating sickness – had made too prodigal a call upon their store of nervous energy, and at the end of August the Anzac corps was temporarily incapable of further offensive effort.

Aboard the *Devanha*, Hugo nursed his wounds and mourned for Ferrier. The ship pitched and rolled as it skirted the rough waves of the Bay of Biscay and entered the stormy English Channel. It could have been a metaphor for the catalyst that lay ahead of Hugo: a woman. She was a person who rushed forcefully into people's lives, always inquisitive, instantly engaging, a whirlwind of ideas and opinions. She was tiny, only about 5 feet tall, a slim, pale creature with deep-brown sparkling eyes and fine, half-smiling lips. She wore her long, dark-brown hair piled into a wispy crown on her head. On 14 September 1915 – just over two weeks since he had descended from the bloody shambles of Hill 60 and still in shock – Hugo found himself in London, where he made a short entry in his war diary: 'Met Miss K.S.P.'

Part 2

Tragedy

12

Katharine and Hugo

I'll send you lavender,
To lay among your thoughts of me,
That I, forever in your dreams,
May dwell with fragrance – Breaths, undying,
Subtle, mysterious, and sweet –
Of these herb flowers I love so well.
Lo, I am a witch,
And weave the spell!

Katharine Susannah Prichard, 'The Earth Lover', 1932

KATHARINE SUSANNAH PRICHARD – 'MISS K.S.P.' – was born on 4 December 1883 in Levuka, Fiji. She arrived within the whirling winds of a hurricane. She lived a long, tumultuous and controversial life in which she became lauded as one of Australia's greatest and most extraordinary literary figures.

Katharine's father, Tom Henry Prichard, was a writer, a journalist – the correspondent for the Melbourne *Argus* and *Sydney Morning Herald* – and the editor of the *Fiji Times*. Her mother, Edith Isabel Fraser before her marriage, was a gifted amateur painter and delighted in reproducing the tropical flowers that surrounded her and Tom in their Fijian house, situated on a hill overlooking the brilliant blues and greens of the tropical sea.

Both sets of grandparents had originally arrived in Australia together, in the sailing ship *Eldorado* in 1852, the Prichards from the Welsh borderlands, the Frasers from Scotland. During the ninety-five-day voyage the two families became firm friends, and there was joy when there was intermarriage and the birth of grandchildren.

Katharine was the eldest child, followed a year later by her brother Alan, to whom she was especially devoted. Nigel came next, when Katharine was aged three, and immediately afterwards their father decided to give up his Fiji post for his young family's sake and return to work in Melbourne, where a fourth child, Beatrice, was born.

Tom became editor of the *Weekly Sun*, a popular social and political paper, for which he wrote a satirical column in rhyme. He also published a historical novel called *A Tale of Early Melbourne: Retaliation*, in 1891. When the paper changed hands, Tom disliked the policies of the new owners, as they moved the paper down-market and cut expenses. They in turn sacked him. 'He was broken in health as a result of over work and depressed by the failure of the paper into which he had put so much enthusiasm and vitality', wrote Katharine. At the end of the scrapbook of his cuttings from the *Sun*, Tom wrote:

Sunscreeds and Madcap Thymes
Written by me
T.H.P.
Who, with a sigh, adds
More fool I.

Depression set in. But when a job came up in Launceston he jumped at the chance of editing the struggling *Daily Telegraph* and moved his family across the sea once again.

For Katharine, free to roam in the hills and gullies of the Tasmanian bush, it was a glorious period, and her keen observations and developing imagination formed the basis of a semi-autobiographical children's book she published later called *The Wild Oats of Han*.

The idyllic existence did not last long. The *Daily Telegraph* folded abruptly. Katharine wrote later:

> I was about nine years old when coming home from a day in the bush with my brothers saw the family furniture piled on carts driving along the road and a red auctioneer's flag over the gate.
>
> Bursting with indignation, I wanted to know why other people had taken possession of our furniture.
>
> Mother was in tears. She told me we were going away. Father was ill and had no work.
>
> The furniture had to be sold because father and she had very little money.
>
> They were terribly worried. I must be a good girl and try to help.

The family returned to Melbourne and a borrowed house. Tom was so depressed that he could not work. Edith supported the family for a while by smocking children's dresses for wealthy clients or painting elaborate illuminated addresses for distinguished and important citizens. This first taste of acute poverty, indignity and social inequality made a deep impression on young Katharine. She remembered particularly her mother's distress when the baker called with a bill she couldn't pay. Katharine was sent to the door to tell the baker they would pay the next week and then wondered why he was so rude in return.

Tom recovered sufficiently to become editor of the *Australian Mining Standard*, but depression continued to reappear until eventually, in 1907, Tom committed suicide by hanging himself. The trauma of the event was so great that even sixty years afterwards Katharine could not bring herself to say how her father had died. 'In the end it seemed the struggle and frustration of many years had caught up with him. He could not sleep, and sat for hours with an empty sheet of copy-paper before him.'

When Tom had refused to eat, his family had gathered around him each morning to pray aloud for his recovery. That their prayers were unanswered was another defining moment for Katharine. She abandoned her religion afterwards, saying it was 'a farce, a tragic farce to imagine there was a God who could hear their prayers and would avert the sorrow which threatened us'.

After Tom's death Edith also became ill, but the children carried on at school. Katharine was very bright, and when she was fourteen she won a half-scholarship at South Melbourne College, founded by the poet JB O'Hara. She had already taken Latin as an extra at state school and was also learning French. Encouraged by O'Hara in her English studies, she began winning prizes for her writing and became editor of the school magazine.

Katharine became determined to be a writer, but her chances of winning a university bursary for further study were dashed when her mother went down with sciatica and was bedridden for six months. Katharine had to stay at home to care for her and do the housework. The Melbourne Public Library became the substitute for university, and she devoured the classics, reading in French and German as well. She attended night lectures at Melbourne University under Walter Murdoch, who sometimes wore a red tie, and met Rudolph Broda, a visiting Austrian socialist studying Australia's pioneering social legislation, ranging from adult suffrage to factory acts and free, secular and compulsory education.

Katharine's hopes soared when *New Idea* magazine ran a competition for a love story. 'I wrote "Bush Fires", knowing nothing about either love or bushfires', she recalled in her autobiography. But it won the prize, being published on 5 December 1903, and initiated her career as a journalist. 'Joy at the time reinforced my desire to be a writer. I decided, though, that I must know more about bushfires, love, and the country beyond the ranges.'

At nineteen and armed with a matriculation certificate she took off from home to become governess to a doctor's two children in

South Gippsland. Soon she was filling notebooks with descriptions of bush and town, collecting convict history, making observations of people, collating information and word pictures that were eventually gathered together in her novel *The Pioneers*. She was also finding out about love; she was pursued by an elderly European doctor who offered to give her German lessons. He kept calling on her, begging her to go to Europe with him. When she rejected his advances he rushed from the house, saying: 'You will never see me again'. He then took poison. He recovered, but the fear of causing such pain again remained with her.

A more agreeable experience occurred when Katharine took her next governess job, on an outback sheep station in the far west of New South Wales, 300 miles beyond Broken Hill and not far from the White Cliffs opal fields. She met the red-bearded son of the station owner, her ideal of an Australian stockman: 'tall, slender, reserved and sensible; walking with the graceful slouch of a man more accustomed to riding than walking'. She had promised herself that she would not fall in love or marry, but 'for a while Red Beard and I looked at each other as if we were a little dazzled by something inexplicable between us'.

Nothing appears to have resulted from this dazzle, although Red Beard did become the hero of Katharine's first piece of professional freelance journalism, a six-part romanticised version of her experiences, which was published in *New Idea* from May to October 1906 and called 'Letters from Back o' Beyond – A City Girl in Central Australia'. Red Beard starred in a scene in which he put his fists up to defend her when another stockman boasted that he had 'seen Miss Prichard's drawers' as she whirled in an impromptu tarantella at the station's fancy-dress ball. Perhaps it was a creation of her powerful imagination. The station owner later wrote to *New Idea* protesting about Katharine's descriptions of drunken revellers in outback pubs.

A male acquaintance from Melbourne with whom she had practised speaking French, and who had a daughter of her own age, became an admirer when they met in Sydney. Katharine called him her 'Preux Chevalier', or 'valiant knight', as he squired her around the city and raised his glass at dinner in the Paris Café to 'the time when you will be a famous writer in the real Paris'. Although she claimed that he did not kiss her or even press her hand suggestively, she was stirred by the way he treated her: not 'as an immature and insignificant damsel but, to my surprise, as an attractive and intelligent young woman'.

Katharine returned to Melbourne, where she took a job teaching small boys at Christ Church Grammar School. She would often walk through the Domain with an old friend of the family's – Alfred Deakin, a journalist who had witnessed the hanging of Ned Kelly and who was now the second prime minister of Australia. In those easygoing early years of Federation, when Melbourne was the country's capital, the prime minister often walked to work at Parliament House, sometimes riding his bicycle, sometimes catching a cable car.

In 1908, Deakin wrote a personal reference introducing 'Miss Prichard, a young Australian lady journalist of great promise', and Katharine sailed for Britain for the first time, supported by commissions to write articles on the Franco–British Exhibition in London for the Melbourne *Herald* and to interview celebrities for *New Idea*. London both beckoned and appalled her. On the one hand, she wrote, it was 'like an illuminated volume of poetry – a living history book', but on the other it was 'just the biggest, dirtiest, wickedest place I ever had room in my imagination for'. London was the location of her first political awakening:

> My experiences ranged from visiting the homes of the aristocracy and wealthy relations to excursions into the worst slums of the great city.
>
> I saw the extremes of wealth and poverty in brilliant receptions and children picking up food from rubbish bins.
>
> One article I wrote, *Toys of the Children of the Slums*, attracted a lot of attention. I had seen children playing with bits of wood and bone, or an old bottle wrapped in dirty rags and suggested, at Christmas time, an 'Empty Stocking Fund'. The '*Star*' and '*Daily Chronicle*' took up the idea.

The Queen gave her approval and for two years before the outbreak of the First World War, fleets of red cars left the newspaper offices stacked with toys.

It was said no child in the slums went without a toy for those Christmases.

But all the time I was wondering how the 'sorry state of things', which deprived men, women, and children of decent living conditions, could be changed.

I talked to writers and politicians, millionaires and hunger marchers, attended lectures, went to meetings, almost despairing there could even be any change in a social system designed to preserve the power and privilege of the rich and keep the working class in subjection.

There was a growing tide of unrest in those prewar years. Unemployed people rioted in Glasgow; hunger marchers filled Trafalgar Square. Marching women surged around parliament demanding votes for women. The Women's Social and Political Union was formed, calling for equality for women not only at the ballot box but also in the workplace and in pensions. The organisation even demanded paid wages for housework. It had been founded by the formidable Emmeline Pankhurst and her three daughters. One of them, Adela, travelled to Australia as a pacificist when the family split over allegiances at the outbreak of war in 1914. There, she became a founding member of the Australian Communist Party.

Katharine had grown up in a nation whose women (except Aboriginal women) had been enfranchised for the new Commonwealth parliament, in 1901, and had voted in the second federal election, in 1903. During her time in Britain she was asked to speak about the Australian experience. Her passionate speech notes for an address to the conservative ladies of the Primrose League of St Ives are preserved among her papers. After pointing out practical reforms achieved by women at home, including the treatment of women prisoners and the establishment of children's courts, Katharine told the ladies that, 'every day, the women of

Australia are making history, proving to the world that women's power in public affairs is for good; that when women vote a great power for the purification and betterment of public life is brought into play'.

Katharine lined up some notable celebrities for interviews, including Dame Nellie Melba's teacher Madame Marchesi, the writer George Meredith, and the Countess of Dudley, whose husband had just been appointed governor-general of Australia. She also travelled to Paris, to interview the famous actress Sarah Bernhardt – the 'Divine Sarah'. While there she stayed with Rudolph Broda, the socialist she had met in Melbourne, and his family. She met some Russian political exiles and became entranced by their idealism and dreams of a new social system that would sweep away the tsar, aristocracy and feudalism. She also met up with her old admirer the Preux Chevalier, and this time it became a fully fledged autumn affair, with rides to the opulent Palace of Versailles, gazing in wonder at the blue glow from the stained-glass windows of La Sainte-Chapelle, nights of laughter at the Comédie-Française and the Moulin Rouge, and candlelit suppers at Maxim's. She claimed later that her Preux Chevalier threatened to shoot himself when she told him the romance was over.

Katharine's London commissions came to an end, and after unsuccessfully freelancing for a while she went back to Australia and accepted a staff job on the Melbourne *Herald*, at first reporting the courts, then producing an article on a home for unmarried mothers, which caused a stir. She followed this by attending meetings of the Anti-Sweating League; she was moved by conversations with female 'white workers' – women who laboured under pressure running machines in shirt factories or took sewing home to earn a few shillings. She said later that this triggered the real awakening of her political consciousness and a determination to do something practical 'to prevent poverty, superstition and injustice wrecking so many lives. The rates of pay were scandalous and women told me that they were sometimes expected to submit to sexual intercourse with unscrupulous employers in small businesses, in order to obtain any work at all'.

Katharine did well at the *Herald* and was given her own page, attending events like the Melbourne Cup as the social editor. But in 1912 she resigned suddenly from the paper, because it was 'sapping my energy for creative writing . . . I became restless and dissatisfied'. She set out once more for London, travelling first through Canada and the United States, taking notes all the while for possible later use. She was convinced that no importance would be attached to an Australian writer at home until he or she had proved their ability to succeed abroad. This time she would succeed.

From a flat in Chelsea, Katharine worked hard to get back into print, at first with no success. Then one day she called at the offices of the *Globe* in Fleet Street with an article she had written about osier harvesting, the gathering of willow branches for use by basket weavers – an esoteric subject at the best of times. She told the editor that the article had been returned from nearly every newspaper in London and asked him what was wrong with it. He read the story through, said he liked it, and asked her for more articles, presumably of a more general interest. Soon she had won commissions to write for another five newspapers and periodicals and was also contributing to French publications in Paris. At the same time she was immersing herself in politics, joining the Women's Social and Political Union and carrying a banner in a march by 13,000 suffragettes through London. She also attended meetings of the Fabian Society, the Freewoman Discussion Circle and the Guild Socialists, and interviewed trade union leaders.

After about two years' freelancing, towards the end of 1914 she had saved enough money to take six months off and immerse herself in writing a novel. She hunted out the notes she had made when she had been a governess in Gippsland and, sticking a notice on her front door saying she had 'Gone to the Country', began writing 'all day and far into the night, often falling into bed, too tired to get there without holding on to the wall between the sitting-room and my bedroom'. The result was *The Pioneers*, described by a fellow writer, Henrietta Drake-Brockman, as 'a tale of first settlement, of escaped convicts, of courage, of corruption, of villainous shanty-keepers, of cattle-duffing, of murder, of the indomitable spirit that slowly brought to terms the hostile bush'.

Publishers Hodder & Stoughton had announced an All Empire £1000 Novel Competition, with prizes for the best Canadian, South African, Indian and Australian novels. To Katharine 'it seemed an opportunity which should not be missed, though I had no hope of winning with a first novel'. After waiting weeks – during which she spent time in Paris with the socialist Broda family again and attended a conference on 'The Regulation of Prostitution' – Katharine returned to London and a crushing disappointment. The afternoon post brought a circular letter from the publishers saying that her manuscript was not among the prize-winners and was not considered worthy of publication. It asked her to collect it at her earliest convenience.

But the next morning's post brought unexpected joy. 'The whole face of the world changed. A letter came from the manager of Hodder & Stoughton to say the printed circular had been sent to me by mistake. Far from my novel having failed to impress the judges, they were delighted with it. Would I please call at the offices of the firm that morning, as there was some interesting news for me.' She had won the prize for the best Australian novel: £250. It seemed a fortune. Katharine immediately started making plans to return to Australia.

> I wanted to go home. I thought I had done what I set out to do and that I could now live and work in Australia for the rest of my days. That was all I ever cared about. I did not want money, more than just enough to live and work on, and I did not want reputation as an English writer – I wanted to be part of the life and work of the Australian people.

First she had to cope with her instant fame. The British press trumpeted the fact that the Australian author of *The Pioneers* was a young and attractive woman living in London. Soon she was much feted and in great demand in fashionable circles. She was already well connected and also well known in Fleet Street. The war had begun, and, with the constantly grim news from the Dardanelles since the landings of April 1915, Australians and the new word 'Anzac' were on everyone's lips.

With the outbreak of war the year before, Katharine had already offered her services as a war correspondent to Serbia and had even tried to enlist in one of the women's auxiliary service corps that were in need of women able to cope with horses. When these led nowhere, she returned to some journalism. At the end of December 1914 she obtained permission to visit the Australian Voluntary Hospital at Wimereux, north of Boulogne, where Banjo Paterson was a volunteer ambulance driver and the noise of the guns could be heard thundering from the front. Her report appeared in March 1915, the same month in which 40,000 British and Indian troops attacked the Germans near Neuve Chapelle. The offensive was called off only on the third day, after an advance of a mile or so had rendered 12,847 men dead or wounded. 'What I saw in the hospital at Wimmereux [*sic*], only one of many in the war-devastated areas of northern France, I could never forget, or get over', she wrote later. 'If it is criminal for one man to kill another, I asked myself, how much more criminal are those responsible for the killing and maiming of thousands? In England I visited other hospitals for the wounded, and when Australians from Gallipoli began to reach them, heard infuriating accounts of the loss of life and bungling in that disastrous campaign.' But Katharine was still loyal, despite her misgivings. 'Neither I, nor anybody I knew had much sympathy for pacifists and conscientious objectors in that period of patriotic illusions about the war, the justification for it, and the need to win.' The sharp eyes of the young novelist turned to a novel sight on the city's streets.

> In uniform, the first Australian soldiers in London looked as if they belonged to a different race than the only men left in the streets. Of superb physique, sun-browned and arrogant, the Light Horsemen

> swaggered along, hats decked with emu feathers tilted at a rakish angle. Although they had been released from hospital after the treatment of wounds . . . it was difficult to believe they were a remnant of troops which had suffered heavy casualties on Gallipoli.

On 12 September, Hugo Throssell arrived at Southampton. He had apparently recovered amazingly quickly from his wounds but, after catching the train to London, was admitted to Number 3 General Hospital at Wandsworth, together with other wounded men from the 10th, including Noel Brazier and Harry Macnee, who needed specialist treatment. Hugo was suffering deafness in his ears 'from bombs', and an appointment was made for him to see a Captain Hastings a few days after his arrival. His medical notes reported that his wounds were either healed or nearly healed, but he was prescribed some medicine for diarrhoea, the persistent complaint among soldiers returning from Gallipoli. Then he was allowed to leave the hospital and see the sights.

Hugo met up with Tom Todd and four other convalescing officers for a tour of London. Todd had been evacuated with acute dysentery and was also at Wandsworth. That night he took Hugo to the Empire Theatre in Leicester Square. Another friend from the 10th limped along too for the evening's outing: Lieutenant Reg Cadden was a 43-year-old Boer War veteran who hailed originally from Sydney and had joined the 10th's reinforcements. A shrapnel ball had hit him in the knee on Gallipoli in June, which meant that he had escaped the horrors of The Nek and Hill 60. The Empire seated 2000 and was famous for its variety shows and spectacular ballets. For Hugo, the transformation from the horrors of Hill 60 to the gaiety and bright lights of the London stage must have seemed surreal. Perhaps it was during this evening that Todd had the idea that determined the course of Hugo's life from then on.

Todd was proud of his young lieutenant and wanted people at home to know about him and what had happened to the

Light Horse. He might already have had an inkling that Hugo had been recommended for a VC. Who better to tell Hugo's tale than Katharine Susannah Prichard, the young Australian journalist who had just made a name for herself by winning a top prize for her first novel? She would know how to write a piece and get it into the Australian newspapers. Todd invited Katharine to take tea with him and Hugo at the Royal Automobile Club on 14 September. The club is located on Pall Mall, a street noted for its gentlemen's clubs, and was built in the 'English Palladian style at its most sumptuously architectural'.

In those days lady visitors were first ushered into their own grey-painted drawing room where they could be met safely and then escorted into the dining areas.

Katharine was taken past the porter in his green livery and frock coat in the club's front hall, past cabinets full of gleaming silver motoring trophies and a gently ticking grandfather clock, through a dining room with marble pillars, gilded frames and five grand Italianate landscape paintings, and out onto the terrace overlooking the private walled garden that today still overlooks The Mall. Military bands play in the distance on their way to the changing of the guard at Buckingham Palace to the right from the club and there is often the clattering of hooves outside the garden as the Household Cavalry with their silver breastplates go to and from Horse Guards Parade. Katharine recalled that first meeting:

> It was a glorious sunshiny afternoon with lilac and laburnums in bloom below the terrace. Colonel Todd [as he became] introduced me to a young Australian soldier he was proud of, although I did not know why at the moment . . .
>
> Hugo said afterwards he had fallen in love with me as I walked along the terrace towards him. And I, certainly, was lifted out of my usual aloofness by the gay, irresistible manner of this young soldier.
>
> 'Let's go riding in Rotten Row,' he proposed blithely, after we had been talking a little while. 'You can ride, of course, I'll get the horses.'
>
> 'I haven't a riding-habit,' I protested.

'Never mind,' he insisted. 'You can fix a skirt on one leg, and another on the other for divided skirts.'

'But women don't ride astride in the Row,' I told him. 'It's just a parade of horses and riders in the most correct and decorous fashion.'

'We'll show them,' Hugo declared happily, 'how Australians can ride.'

I was not enthusiastic about creating a sensation on Rotten Row, but unable to diminish Hugo's delight at the prospect. It didn't happen, thank goodness, because he was going [back] into hospital the next day, and I was leaving for Australia within a few weeks.

There was an indefinable attraction to each other, though, at our first meeting. Hugo drove me back to my flat and I promised to go and see him in hospital. Colonel Todd, who came with us, was perturbed by what he thought were symptoms of love at first sight. Bluff and forthright, he declared: 'You can get engaged to him, if you want to, but you can't marry him till the end of the war.'

At the time nothing was further from Katharine's thoughts than getting engaged. She didn't believe that Hugo's thoughts had travelled so far, either. In any case, she was soon diverted. Her youngest brother, Nigel, a doctor, arrived aboard a hospital ship from the Dardanelles. He had volunteered for service with the Royal Army Medical Corps, attached to the British 29th Division, which had suffered enormous casualties on Gallipoli. He spent a few happy days with Katharine in London, camped in her flat.

Meanwhile, Hugo was in Wandsworth Hospital preparing for an operation. On 16 September he had seen the specialist, Hastings, who had decided that a nasal condition, not bomb concussion, was the cause of his deafness. This required an operation to straighten his nose and remove his adenoids. It sounded straightforward, but something went wrong. The procedure took place under a general anaesthetic on 22 September, and almost immediately Hugo was fighting for his life against bacterial meningitis. His medical records tell part of the story:

> Temp. rose to 100 night of operation. Some drowsiness with intervals of restlessness – with intense headache and stiffness at back of neck – and increasing pain in temples. Condition persisted and increased from 23rd to 29th. Vomiting began on 28th (night) green bilious fluid brought up without effort – sick seven times in course of 30 hours. Delirious at times on 27th, 28th and 29th . . . at his worst on evening of 29th.

He was calling out for someone in his dreams . . . 'Katharine! Katharine!'

On 2 October the doctors could report that Hugo's temperature had fallen rapidly, along with his pulse rate. His sleep was very broken, although he had slept well the previous night for the first time. The back of his neck was still stiff and sore. He was 'easily excited'. On 13 October his records say: 'Steady progress. Stiffness of neck practically gone. Still very easily excited. Twenty minutes walk yesterday. The mental condition is not normal. Old friends say he is "500 per cent more excitable than usual"'.

What does modern medicine make of these records? Professor Tony Costello is a pioneer of robotic surgery in Australia, a fellow of the Royal Melbourne Hospital and affiliated with the Department of Surgery at the University of Melbourne. His brother, Brian Costello, is an ear, nose and throat specialist in Melbourne. They examined Hugo's records, and Tony Costello reported that:

> This man was a very robust, athletic sportsman who went to Gallipoli. He was wounded in Gallipoli and repatriated to England. Whilst he was in London he en passant had an operation which was to straighten his nose. I don't think this had anything to do with his war wounds. The technique of nose straightening at that time was that a sharp blade was passed up the nose and rotated high in that area. One of the hazards of that particular procedure was that the blade could perforate the meningeal lining of the brain and enter the brain in the frontal cortex. Clearly in the case of Hugo he had severe bacterial meningitis following this procedure, which suggests he had a perforation of his brain cavity

> at this procedure. His behaviour was described following this as erratic and characterised by periods of great excitability.
>
> In summary I think he had a severe brain injury as a result of this particular procedure performed on him in London following his gunshot wound to the neck.

Hugo wrote in his war diary: 'Nearly Mafeesh'. It was soldiers' slang from the Arabic they'd heard in Egypt meaning 'finished'.

Katharine, too was misled as to the cause of the meningitis. Todd told Katharine that Hugo had developed meningitis 'as a result of that neglected shoulder wound' and that he had been calling for her in his delirium. But she could not go to Wandsworth until he was permitted visitors.

On 17 October he was allowed a special visitor who had news for him. 'Old Ric arrived, had a close shave but convalescent'. Ric sat by Hugo's bedside and told him that he had been awarded the VC. His name had been posted in the *London Gazette* two days earlier.

Hugo left no record of how he felt about receiving the VC or how he reacted when Ric gave him the news. The laconic entry in his war diary says only: 'Given V.C.' He rarely wore the medal after the war. His son later recalled 'going with him on one Anzac Day march when the VCs marched at the head of old diggers in St Georges Terrace and sometimes the sons tottered along beside them and I did that. And then he just had the little purple tab on his coat. I didn't ever see him wearing it himself and it just used to sit in a drawer at home'.

Hugo expressed formal gratitude for the honour in speeches that he made afterwards, but over and over again in official reports, in letters he wrote privately and in interviews he gave publicly he insisted that the real heroes were the men who had fought alongside him.

This is not to say that in Britain, and in Australia later on, he was entirely the humble hero. He certainly enjoyed a hero's rewards and the attention he received, especially from the ladies.

He posed for studio photographs with the simple deep crimson medal ribbon sewn onto his new, well-tailored uniform jacket, and with an officer's cap worn at a rakish angle or a slouch hat with the tuft of emu feathers perched jauntily on his head.

Ric was now thinner and greyer looking. He had been in hospital in Egypt and had been 'nearly Mafeesh' too, when his chest wound had become infected. After pulling through, he had been sent on to Britain and admitted to the Reading War Hospital, about 40 miles west of London, on 5 October. He had received there the bad news that Hugo was gravely ill. He had struggled to acquire permission to leave his own hospital and travel to his brother's bedside.

Katharine saw the news about the VC in the newspapers and sent Hugo a telegram of congratulations. Then a sister at the hospital rang her to say that Hugo was disappointed she had not been to see him and that it would be good for him if she could come to the hospital. A friend once wrote how soothing Katharine could be: 'She is gentle and her voice is soft and sweet . . . her face is sensitive and strong'. Katharine wrote: 'Of course I went and was conscience-stricken to see Hugo still in bed, looking wan and with his head wrapped in a warm scarf. More discomfited when he grasped my hand and said: "Why didn't you come before? And you didn't even write"'.

After she had told him about her brother's visit and Todd's warning that visitors were not permitted, 'soon we were chattering as if the undercurrent of that inexplicable attraction flowing between us needed no explanation'.

Hugo had been reading *The Pioneers*, and Katharine sat back expecting to be complimented. Instead, Hugo the bushman pulled her up short when he told her she had made a mistake in the first line of the book. She had called a covered-in dray a 'wagon', though a dray had only two wheels and a wagon four. Katharine was just explaining that her publisher had asked her to use 'wagon' because British readers wouldn't know what a 'covered-in dray' was when Ric walked in to join them. She was now smitten by two brothers.

> The brothers were David and Jonathan in their devotion to each other. Ric, a splendid looking man, broader and taller than Hugo, had the same Australian-ness I admired in them both, a virility and the air of horsemen accustomed to deal with men and beasts, fearlessly, straightforwardly: a natural grace and bearing and manner I had not found among all the men I met in London.
>
> 'Ah, the sort of man we ought to breed from,' said a withered old general of Ric one day.

But Ric went back to his hospital, and Katharine kept calling at Wandsworth. 'Hugo told me about the fighting in which he was wounded and about the charge on Russell Top where Ric had been wounded. From Colonel Todd, too, I heard about these actions. He was full of enthusiasm for what Hugo had done at Hill Sixty.' Katharine set out nineteen questions about his experiences on Gallipoli for Hugo to answer – 'such a callous thing to do under the circumstances', because he was obviously in shock and his mind was wandering. His medical notes say that he was still showing signs of 'mental excitability'. He continued to wear a woollen scarf around his head and ears – it remained there for weeks after the operation – and complained about her cold hands when she went to see him. He said he could not sleep. Katharine told him to think of a river flowing peacefully, quietly, in the moonlight. In answer to her questions he almost babbled as he told her that he

> preferred to think about that river with the moonlight in it and a girl sitting on the bank with 'cold hands' and the other thing that follows naturally. I awoke to find it was a mosquito singing and 'Babette' was taking my pulse, and asking why it had jumped from 82 the previous night to 112? But you've forgotten what you wrote me about rivers and mosquitos so what's the use anyway and besides this is no. 1 and I can see no. 19 looming up to me on the last page.

The answers rambled between the 'fool charge' on 7 August and the events on Hill 60: 'I bank on bombs and would like to see every man practise throwing a five pound weight for half an hour or so a day'. In reply to one question he answered:

> About 170 of the 10th charged – if course I'm only going on hearsay about the muster when we came out, but am told only 25 were fit for work. Many husky fellows when once they got away from the scrap, although they were not hit at all, just dropped dead to the world for the time being. It surprised me how few were *killed* that night.
>
> Don't forget to put in a word for old Johnny the Turk – we bear him no grudge – they can fight and are good sports. They enjoy a joke, such as putting up a notice for our benefit re 'Fall of Warsaw' – waving a miss when we fire at their periscopes etc. Most of the tales you hear of atrocities are moonshine.

Katharine typed up her notes of his responses to her questions but found it was 'impossible after all to repeat the story as I heard it. Glances and gestures, a voice vibrating with emotion recreated those hours of suffering, the barren hills and the moonlight of Gallipoli'. Instead, she went to see John Macmillan, also recovering in London, who told her how Hugo had won the VC. But he had already given an interview, to the London *Daily Mail*, describing the action on Hill 60; when this was printed on 27 October and reprinted around the empire, Katharine decided not to go on with her own writing project.

Congratulatory messages and telegrams poured in to Wandsworth Hospital and were conveyed to the new hero's bedside. The Western Australian Legislative Assembly passed a special resolution placing on record 'its great appreciation of Lieutenant Throssell's merit and gallantry'. The member for Irwin, James Gardiner, remembered Premier George Throssell and remarked that 'he used to be called the "Lion of Northam" and if the spirit of the father was hovering over this House tonight he would be glad to hear us say that the Lion of Northam had cubs, and that one of his cubs had brought honour to this State and to the race from which he sprang, as well as to the father and mother who bore him'.

One of Hugo's troopers wrote from Harefield Hospital, which had been established in a British manor house to treat wounded Anzacs:

> 'Tis late to offer congratulations but you know you have the goodwill of the boys who fought by your side that night and phrases written on impulse sound empty but we 'The Boys' know the mark of distinction is 'fair dinkum' and one which you must wear on the most prominent part of your chest for the symbol and wearer belong to the 10th A.L.H. and so do we, and we are very proud of the fact.

Hughes cabled from Cairo: 'Brigade desires convey their highest appreciation your magnificent performance bringing lustre and credit to Light Horsemen STOP Hearty congratulations your well earned award best wishes speedy recover STOP Hughes General'.

Hugo made a slow but determined recovery. A photograph survives showing him as a frail-looking invalid, head swathed in the scarf, body wrapped in a thick quilt. He is in the hospital grounds, taking afternoon tea with Katharine and another woman, with a nurse alert and watchful close by. Katharine and Hugo are raising their cups to each other and looking into each other's eyes.

There was no time for anything to develop romantically between them, however. Katharine was now determined to get back to Australia and exploit her new-found fame as a prize-winning author.

> Only a few days remained before I was due to sail. He insisted on coming to see me at the flat. The sister said he practised walking a little every day in order to come. I was afraid six flights of stairs might be too much for him, and begged her not to let him risk them if he was not well enough.

Hugo arrived, and we said goodbye in the midst of my luggage, packed cases of books and belongings. I couldn't believe there was more in his feeling for me than a sort of bushfire flare that would pass. So we parted, shaking hands, sadly, without any acknowledgment of an emotional stir between us.

13

Hail, the Conquering Hero Comes

Fighting Jim
It's a proud day for you, and prouder for us
So do you forgive us this bit of a fuss?
That we're making of you, Northam's own H.V.T.
And added to that is a well earned V.C.

You always loved scrappin' you cannot deny
And a twenty foot ring looked good to your eye
That you fought like a good 'un and beat your man too
Is what we expected 'Jim' Throssell to do

So when Father Bull got fighting, of course
You made one of the famous and gallant Light Horse
And when Johnny Turk from his trench was pushed back
You made the world ring with a new name 'Anzac'.

Poem printed on postcard, 1916

On 4 December 1915, King George V made a very short entry in his diary: 'Gave 7 Victoria Crosses, 4 Australian ones'. On the same day Second Lieutenant Hugo Throssell made a similarly short entry in his diary: 'Was decorated at Buckingham Palace by George Rex'.

The small-scale investiture was due to the king's being in recovery from a serious injury. On 15 October he had been across the Channel paying a visit to his soldiers on the Western Front when his horse had reared suddenly and then fallen on top of him, breaking his pelvis. Later in the war, when he had recovered, he held big investitures – 400 medals at a time – in the grand Ballroom, but on this damp London day he received the heroes in a smaller reception room.

Hugo arrived warmly wrapped in a double-breasted three-quarter-length greatcoat, head still swathed in the scarf, with his regulation riding breeches, leather leggings and boots complete with spurs. It was a 'cheerless, drizzling morning'.

Alongside Hugo were three Australians awarded the VC for their gallantry during the battle of Lone Pine: Lieutenants William John Symons and Frederick Harold Tubb, and Private John Hamilton. A newspaper reported that

> the heroes passed into the Palace yard without receiving any welcome from the public, but the cordiality of the King's welcome atoned for it. The King is still weak, but he warmly shook each soldier by the hand, and congratulated him on winning the proud distinction.
>
> Lieutenant Tubb describes the ceremony as follows: – 'We were ushered into the King's presence singly. "I am proud to meet you," said the King, shaking me warmly by the hand. An official read out the account of what I had done or was supposed to have done, and the King again shook hands with me, and said, "I have over 2,000,000 men fighting in my Navy and Army, but only 138 Victoria Crosses have been awarded. I tell you that for you to appreciate how rare is the distinction amongst my brave men." The King inquired kindly about my recovery.'
>
> Private Hamilton said: –'The King makes you feel his interest in you. He is something like a father who is proud of his son. He asked me a lot of questions – where I came from, how old I am, and what business I was in before I enlisted. I told him, and he said he was very proud of me, and I felt that he meant it.'

Hugo's impressions were recorded later. He was underwhelmed by the occasion. 'I was shown in alone and we just had a sensible little chat. The King is just like any ordinary English gentleman.'

A photograph taken outside the palace shows Hugo wearing his slouch hat perched on top of the scarf around his head. He is with Ric, also in a worn slouch and an old single-breasted overcoat. And there is another smiling, moustachioed face in the photograph: that of Hugo's unofficial driver and batman, his new and most unlikely friend, the famous Australian artist Tom Roberts.

Roberts, a member of the Heidelberg School, painted alongside artists like Frederick McCubbin, Arthur Streeton and Charles Conder. He was commissioned in 1901 to paint the scene of the opening of the first Commonwealth parliament in Melbourne's Royal Exhibition Building. The British-born artist decided to finish the giant work in London, and returned to live there with his family in 1903.

One evening in 1915 an officer walked into the Chelsea Arts Club to recruit volunteers for the military hospitals. Twenty-five signed up, including Roberts. He had actually turned fifty-nine in March 1915, but he lowered his age dramatically, shaved off his beard of thirty years and, keeping – perhaps colouring – his moustache, was accepted as an orderly, living in at the giant Wandsworth Hospital.

The hours were long and arduous. One Monday he was on duty from six in the morning to ten past ten at night without a break. On Sundays he was supposed to work without lunch. His wife, Lillie, said that he spent one night at home in every fortnight. His main duty was to act as a messenger, delivering telegrams and doing shopping for wounded officers. Later he was promoted from private to corporal and was put to work in the dental department, acting as a nurse and doing everything from 'cleaning instruments, keeping records, arranging appointments and collecting the vomit' as patients recovered from the gas anaesthetic. He said that the saddest cases were the shell-shocked men, who were 'a bit like children. Trembling and shaking'.

On the verge of collapse after his first stint at the hospital, Roberts was given a fortnight off. On his return to light duties he found himself assigned as unofficial batman to the new VC winner. He said that London was 'as in a dream' to the traumatised Hugo. They became firm friends as Roberts took him around the city and made introductions. Hugo affectionately called him 'Colonel'.

✠

Hugo's visit to Buckingham Palace was not his only outing. Suddenly he was famous, and everyone wanted to know him. He was almost overwhelmed. Wills's Cigarettes cards quickly added him to their set of twenty-five Great War Victoria Cross Heroes. He was described as 'seven feet of gallant manhood' and pictured holding a rifle and fixed bayonet defiantly, with the bodies of dead Turks piled around his feet. On 10 November the agent-general for Western Australia, Sir Newton Moore – described as a 'burly, bustling politician' – had swooped on the bewildered hero on the first day he was allowed out of hospital. Roberts delivered Hugo to London's docklands as a guest of honour at a grand luncheon celebrating the arrival in London of the Western Australian government's newest acquisition – the motor ship *Kangaroo*, which had been launched from Harland and Wolff's shipyards in Glasgow. The ship was special because she could carry enough oil to travel to Australia and back to Britain without refuelling.

Sir Newton had assembled 'a numerous company' on board the ship. The various speeches concluded with a toast to Hugo. Sir Newton said that he knew 'Lieutenant Throssell did not desire to make a speech as he had only that day been discharged from hospital but he wanted to congratulate him upon the honour conferred and to add that all Western Australians were proud of him (Applause)'.

Poor Hugo had to respond, and he did so by saying that if any honour was due to him it was equally due to

> his four comrades who stood so loyally by him on that fateful day in August – he referred to Ferrier, who died on the hospital ship to England, McMahon of Kelleberrin, Macnee and Renton. The last mentioned had had one of his legs amputated on the previous day (Lord Mayor's Day) in the Wandsworth Hospital while Macnee paraded the streets on the same day in the Lord Mayor's procession. He thought they all deserved to be rewarded, for they stuck so loyally to him throughout the fight (Applause).

Within days Hugo was at another huge reception, this time at the Anzac Buffet, which provided free meals and entertainment to convalescing soldiers.

On 20 November Mrs Minnie Rattigan and her volunteer ladies gave a reception for the four Australians just awarded the Victoria Cross by the king, together with some members of the crew of HMAS *Sydney*, which had destroyed the *Emden*. This time the guest speaker was a man noted for his oratory – the High Commissioner for Australia Sir George Reid, a veteran politician, former premier of NSW and the man who had served as the fourth prime minister of Australia.

Sir George did not let his audience down. 'Men of the Victoria Cross, in the name and on behalf of Australia, I salute you!' he began. 'You have lived to receive that rarest and highest form of decoration which is associated with the name of one of the noblest monarchs the world has ever seen, Queen Victoria.

'Perhaps the moments of your deadliest peril were your happiest.

'The King of Terrors made a thousand deaths for each of you but in spite of all the thunderbolts he launched you stand before us not only alive, but looking splendidly vigorous.'

Once again Hugo was asked to respond to the main speaker, and what he said was like a stream of confused consciousness. Only six days before, an army medical board had found that he was still showing signs of 'mental excitability'. A journalist reported what Hugo said verbatim:

> Young Frank McMahon – he was only about 18 or 19 – came into our part of the trench and I said to him, 'What are you doing here?' He said 'I heard you were calling for bags and I want to be in this show.'
>
> 'Can you throw a bomb, Mac?' I said. Now, throwing bombs is not as easy as it looks. A cricket ball weighs six ounces, and you know the effect of throwing that for long if you are not in form. These bombs weigh four and a half to five pounds. Mac went on throwing bombs all night.

Hugo went on to recount the Hill 60 action and how young McMahon had died before imploring his audience: 'Tommy Renton has just had a leg taken off at Wandsworth General Hospital, and if anyone would like to do a good turn they can't do better than ask to see him. No braver man ever lived'.

Hugo sat down. The audience cheered again. The reception ended with a concert in which 'several soldiers of the Australasian contingent showed notable musical and histrionic ability'.

There were happier diversions for the hero. A photograph album that survives from the time shows him surrounded by pretty nurses as he convalesced. Two photographs of him being helped into a car by a nurse are hand titled 'My first drive from Wandsworth' and, enigmatically, 'Dorothy May Or May Not'.

While he was in Wandsworth, he also wrote again to the actress Henrietta Watson, his boyhood crush, 'just saying I had not found the gold mine nor the bird's nest, but as soon as I was well enough she could expect a bearded bushman to be knocking at her door and announcing himself as "Northam Jim"'. No details survive of their first meeting or the depth of their relationship afterwards. Presumably, Roberts ferried them around London on outings.

Later, Hugo told Katharine that as a result he and Henrietta had met often during his convalescence and visited theatres together. He had even gone to her home, where she had shown him the dilapidated envelope addressed in pencil: 'Miss Henrietta

Watson, Actress, London'. 'Of course,' he told Katharine, 'in a proper story we should have got married and lived happily ever after, but this is a true story so we remained the best of friends, or, as she aptly put it – "intimate strangers"'. *Intimate Strangers* became the title of one of Katharine's best-known novels.

Hugo noted in his war diary meeting Henrietta in the hospital soon after his 'close shave'. There are also notes about meeting 'Rena' and 'Sara' and receiving a birthday present from 'Molly'. The diary shows that as Hugo began to feel better he embarked on a furiously paced tour of Britain, taking in Scotland, then going across the sea to visit Ireland and the ancestral Throssell seat at Fermoy and taking part in 'Irish hunting (bank jumping). Land delightful'.

At one stage he travelled with his Light Horse friends Reg Cadden and Tom Todd to Sussex, where they stayed at the home of a Mr Stevenson, a retired Ceylon tea planter. 'Throssell is the lion of the neighbourhood,' wrote Cadden, 'everyone vying with each other to do him honour . . . Mr Stevenson and his friends have motored us all over the country, and when we arrive at a house and the owner understands the Australian V.C. is in the car, the fact is quite sufficient and we are at once treated as was the prodigal son'.

At the end of January 1916, Hugo returned to London to see Ric sail for Egypt. Ric was going back to the war, having recovered sufficiently from his chest wound to be passed once more for active service. Sergeant Ric Throssell was soon afterwards promoted to second lieutenant and sent on an officer's infantry course.

Towards the end of February, Hugo was staying at the fashionable Ivanhoe Hotel in Bloomsbury. A photograph in the Australian War Memorial collection taken at the time shows some eighty members of the Australian Army Nursing Service posing for a group shot outside the same hotel. Hugo once said that there had been all sorts of rumours about him and that 'it was true that in England he had nearly fallen victim to Cupid's darts'.

On 24 February he wrote to Roberts after returning from a trip to Scotland:

> Dear Colonel:
> Yr last copperplate connected with me in the land where Wallace Bled & it looks as tho' I've missed seeing your boy & I'm sorry – I expect to be doing the big trip shortly & would like to meet Mrs Roberts before I sail so how would next Sunday 27th suit?
>
> I'd like to bring 'the Niece' too if you don't mind – if OK ring or write me yr adds to the Ivanhoe & we would have lunch in town & then paddle out to yr place and 'put me feet on the "ob" for a couple of hours or so'.

We do not know who 'the Niece' was, but Hugo also talked about fitting in a couple of days' sightseeing with Roberts, if he is still available, signing off 'Hip Hip Hugo Throssell'.

Less than a week later, Hugo had an appointment with the medical board at Wandsworth Hospital. The three-man board found that 'he is still somewhat nervous and suffers from continuous headaches. In view of his meningitis the Board is of the opinion that he should have extended leave'.

✠

On 17 March, Hugo sailed for Australia via South Africa aboard the Cunard liner *Ascania*. He had six pages of names and addresses in his private journal of the families and friends of those who were staying behind. He would write to them or go and see them if he could while he was in Australia. Among the names in his book was Miss Katharine Susannah Prichard of Emerald or 900 Malvern Road, Armadale, Victoria.

The Australian Army's recruiting office intended to make the most of Hugo's return. The AIF was facing a shortage of men. At the beginning of 1916, in the wake of the Gallipoli debacle and as the war escalated on the Western Front, the Australian casualty rate was increasing, while, despite a direct appeal to all eligible men to join up, the number of volunteers was declining.

Thus Hugo was going to be used in a mounting political campaign over the need for conscription. He would be 'a stirring figure in riding boots, breeches, the emu feather-tufted slouch hat, the modest purple tab of the Victoria Cross on the left breast of his tunic. He had only to appear for enlistments to improve', said Major General Michael Jeffery, the Western Australian governor and governor-general. 'There was an easy gaiety about him that complemented the popular image of the Light Horseman. He had a roguish grin that seemed to suggest a shared secret.'

Hugo slipped into Fremantle almost unnoticed on the eve of the first Anzac Day, 1916. 'Arrive home and glad to get there', he wrote in his diary on 24 April. The first thing he did was buy a Tatt's ticket.

The next day there was an Anzac Day luncheon at the Perth Town Hall with an overflow crowd in the nearby St George's Hall. It was in the Town Hall that Hugo was noticed for the first time. At the conclusion of the reading of the king's message by the governor, Sir Harry Barran, who proposed the toast to 'Anzac Heroes', 'Lieut Throssell V.C. entered the hall and was greeted with thunderous applause'. But when Hugo went on to St George's Hall a reporter noted that he was 'unknown to most in the room'. He listened politely as a member of parliament told the gathering that 'the anniversary of 25 April, 1915, should be a red-letter day in the life of Australia forever (Cheers)'.

A journalist from the *West Australian* caught up with Hugo at his hotel. Hugo was quite clearly ill and reluctant to give an interview. The reporter was disappointed. 'Physically, although the effects of his wounds and subsequent illness have left their mark, he is a splendid specimen of the Australian race. Yet this young stalwart, who, with his comrades for hours faced a rain of Turkish bombs, shrinks from recounting the story of his heroism in cold type.' It was with the 'greatest difficulty' that the reporter 'extracted a few facts' and a curious expression. 'Really I can't tell you much', said Hugo. 'I don't want to speak about myself. I'm a "boom". It's the other fellows who deserve it.' Throughout the interview he kept reiterating that he was a 'boom'. Gradually, though, the journalist

> snatched a glimpse of that trench on Hill 60 where only two of Throssell's troop of 24 returned unharmed.
>
> 'I could tell you . . . about the way our boys held that trench that night. Fight! God, they are fighters.' And here the young hero, who had been reclining on a lounge, sat up straight and his eyes shone as he spoke of the men of Australia. 'The Australians are absolute living marvels,' he said. 'I have seen them fight and get cut to pieces; I have seen them fight and win; I have seen them on hospital ships, suffering agonies – and that's the place to learn of suffering – but they have come up smiling every time. They are always cheerful and always bright. There may be as good fighters in the world, but I'll swear there are none better.'
>
> The interviewer strove to get the lieutenant to tell of his own exploits. 'You were pretty badly wounded,' he ventured. 'No,' came the reply. 'I was wounded in seven places that night, but not badly. I was covered in blood, and looked horrible, which made the fellows think I was seriously wounded. One bullet went clean through the back of my neck, just missing the spinal cord and the other wounds were caused by bombs. The luck I had! Men standing near me and next to me were blown to pieces or lost limbs, were killed outright, whilst I only got flesh wounds. It was horrible – ghastly. I have seen some terrible things.' Here he broke off again to tell of what his comrades did. 'Seven hours we held that trench. The Turks threw scores and scores of bombs that lobbed amongst our fellows, but they caught them up and hurled them back again. I know that the Victoria Cross has been given for throwing back a single bomb, but I saw four of our boys throw them out for seven hours solid. I recommended them for recognition, but they got nothing. The Turks counter-attacked three times that morning. We were helplessly outnumbered, but we stuck, and we won and the Turks ran and ran.'

Hugo recited his litany of names – Ferrier and McMahon, Renton and Macnee, Steele and Fry and Eakins. He repeated those names – and others, too – but especially the first four, at every opportunity from then on. He would not speak about himself.

Later, in 1916, he told his story at length, as he recuperated and gathered himself together. He dictated it in the study of his brother Lionel's grand mansion, Uralia. Looking out onto a rose garden and an avenue of palm trees he gave a full account of the battle for Hill 60. He did it for charity: the account was published in a beautiful little book entitled *Westralia Gift Book to Aid YMCA Military Work and Returned Nurses Fund by the Writers and Artists of Western Australia.*

When Hugo first arrived home, however, he was still sick. Although he looked fine physically, he was permanently mentally damaged and traumatised. Until the end of his life he desperately feared a return of the meningitis. He was haunted at night by the scenes he had witnessed on Gallipoli. Post-traumatic stress disorder had yet to be recognised; counselling was unknown. The medical board in Fremantle found only that he had spells of dizziness and was suffering from 'nervousness, sleeplessness and headaches'. He was ordered to take three months' leave and undergo further treatment.

Hugo stayed in Perth for a few days, and a reception planned in his hometown of Northam was postponed. Diplomatically, the illness of one of his sisters was given as the main reason for the change, but the *Goomalling-Dowerin Mail*, which circulated in the area around his old farm at Cowcowing, also referred to the 'hero's indisposition'.

On 2 May he felt well enough to return home. As the train steamed into Northam, hundreds of admiring friends packed the platform, led by a crowd of Throssell relatives and civic leaders ranging from the resident magistrate to the heads of the town's churches. As the crowd cheered, the mayor, AW Byfeld, drove the hero to the Town Hall and a hastily organised civic reception. 'Although no invitations had been issued or public announcement made, the function was very largely attended.'

And so began a months-long marathon of receptions and speeches. Hugo was a Northam hero, a Western Australian hero, a South Australian hero, an Australian hero and a hero of the British Empire. Everyone wanted to laud him, to be close to him.

At this first – of two – civic receptions in his honour in Northam, the main speech was given by the local member of parliament HP Colebatch, who proposed Hugo's health and suggested that local experiences had stood him in good stead.

> You will perhaps pardon me recalling to your mind the restive, almost rebellious spirit in which you received the order that delayed your departure from Australia, and the still more bitter disappointment under which you frowned during those dark weeks in Egypt after your regiment had gone to the front.
>
> Perhaps these things like your sound training on the college ground in Kent Town, your endeavours on the football field, the plucky fights that won for you the amateur boxing championships of these districts, and your still more valiant struggle against relentless nature on the then inhospitable shores of Lake Cowcowing were merely a part of the necessary preparation for the deed that was to win for you the highest honour a soldier can gain on the field of battle, and give to your town reflected glory that must not be allowed to fade.

There were ringing cheers before Hugo modestly replied. He paid tribute to an 'ex-Northamite' and athlete, a Mr Hughes of the postal service, who, before Hugo had left Perth originally, had given him a letter of introduction to a friend in Cairo. Hugo said he hadn't read the letter until one day in Egypt when he had been feeling particularly 'rotten' about having been left behind with the horses. In his letter, Hughes had called Hugo a fine athlete who would make a name for himself, if he had the luck to pull through. Hugo told the crowd that the letter had cheered him up and shown him how a man might be helped by 'kindly words of praise and encouragement'.

But his speech was abrupt. He said he wasn't going to make a speech telling of his experience on this occasion. He only wished to thank the local people for the warmth and kindness of their reception.

Two days later Hugo and Lionel motored the 70 miles or so to the town of Dowerin and to the flat wheat lands with their endless far horizons. There was another cheering crowd when they reached the dusty town at midday and then a lunchtime reception in the dining room of the local pub. It was a long way from the king's study in Buckingham Palace only five months earlier. The *Goomalling-Dowerin Mail* reported details of the visit, which seems to have had a calming effect on Hugo. He took the Victoria Cross with him, which was handed around with reverence wherever they stopped in the bush.

> The same afternoon the two brothers proceeded to Cowcowing making several calls at farms on the way to renew old acquaintances. This afforded the returned soldier a very pleasant afternoon and it was seen that he was delighted again to meet the many good folk with whom he had previously come into contact.
>
> Afternoon tea was partaken of at Mrs McCashney's homestead, after which Mr Leslie Hall's place was reached where the evening was spent.
>
> Friday morning was devoted to a ramble round the Throssell Bros farm and a general inspection of the settlement where so many happy and strenuous days were spent by Hugo and his brother prior to the outbreak of war.
>
> At noon lunch was enjoyed at Mr and Mrs Bennett's home and in the evening (accompanied by Mr and Mrs Leslie Hall) they motored to Korrelocking.
>
> At the Agricultural Hall over 150 people had assembled and as the guest entered the room the gathering joined hands and sang Auld Lang Syne in a very hearty and inspiring manner.
>
> Mr Shakeshaft occupied the chair and in a very glowing speech welcomed the hero to Korrelocking and also a local returned soldier . . .

> The remainder of the evening after refreshments had been handed round was devoted to singing, music and dancing.
>
> As Lieut Throssell left the room, three cheers were given.

The next day the two brothers bumped their way back along the rough, unmade road to Northam; the *Northam Advertiser* told what lay ahead: 'Very complete arrangements are being made for the public welcome to be tendered to Lieut Hugo Throssell V.C. at the Palace Theatre next Wednesday evening. The Premier and members of the State Ministry and Parliament are expected to be present and the function will be the most brilliant ever held in Northam'.

On the Wednesday morning Hugo was taken on a tour of Northam's schools. He was still troubled. Curiously, at one school he told the children about the night before the charge at The Nek, how he had shared a bottle of whisky with his friends. It was 'the first occasion in his lifetime on which he had taken strong drink, something was needed to steady their nerves before a bayonet charge the next morning . . . The next morning at about 4.30 the advance was made and a quarter of an hour later both the Chipper boys were dead and his brother was shot through the lung'. At this point Reg Cadden, who was with Hugo at the time, quickly stepped in to talk about the glorious 10th Light Horse.

That night the Palace Theatre was packed to overflowing: about 1200 attended. A huge 'Welcome' sign was hung over the entrance, and the street outside was festooned with flags. Two banners reading 'Welcome Home To Our V.C.' and 'Northam Schools Hail You' had been unfurled along the theatre's walls. The *Goomalling-Dowerin Mail* described the scene, paying tribute to the ladies of the town, who had

> excelled themselves in converting the theatre into a veritable floral bower. The walls of the great building had been relieved of their bareness by the deft and dainty touches of artistic decorators and

> from ventilators and every niche hung beautiful sprays of greenery and flowers.
>
> Rich carpets were placed with exquisite taste upon the granolithic floors, while luxuriant roses, dahlias and other rich and rare blooms were reposed with delicate idea upon pedestals within the room.
>
> The most handsomely furnished homes had sacrificed their furniture, their easy chairs, their lounges and settees, to assist in converting the theatre into a state of homey restfulness to suitably receive one who is the idol of his people.

The idol arrived soon after eight o'clock accompanied by Lionel and Cadden, once again there to lend him support. The wild cheering went on for minutes, interspersed with shouts from his old football team mates: 'Good Old Federals!' One journalist wrote that 'this frantic cheering took hold of the gathering with such feverishness as to deeply impress the guest, who smiled good humouredly throughout'.

The speeches soared. There was a fresh burst of cheering when Private John McMahon, an aged veteran of the Crimean War of 1853, with medals glistening under the new fangled electric lights installed in the theatre, rose and told how proud he was to be present alongside Hugo.

'Lieutenant Throssell is a man of whom Northam should be proud. It is not every man who had had the honour of earning a V.C. on his breast, and it is not every town that has the privilege of laying claim to such a hero', said the old man.

Reg Cadden soon had the hundreds hushed as he recounted Hugo's exploits on Hill 60. The Light Horse officer asked: could they imagine what it must have been like with their trenches and those of the enemy almost touching? 'The boys' had told him that it was Hugo's 'cheering on' that enabled them to hold the trench that they captured and held. They also told him that Lieutenant Throssell lay on the top of the parapet with a rifle and 'potted brother Turk as he came along . . .'

When the speeches ended, the *Kalgoorlie Western Argus* reported,

> upon rising Lieut Throssell, V.C. was unable to proceed for several minutes, there being volley upon volley of cheering. He appeared to be exceedingly shy and nervous. A nearby pot plant suffered severely during his opening remarks, for he unconsciously plucked many leaves from its stalks.
>
> He found voice to say he really did not know what to do to thank them for their generous reception and their flattering remarks.
>
> He had felt similarly nonplussed in London on one occasion when about to speak to an audience.
>
> He sort of broke the ice by telling them he was a farmer, whereupon a facetious member of the gathering sang out: 'You ought to be able to talk till the cows come home.'
>
> He had been obliged to reply that this farming had been done at Buckley's Tank, via Cowcowing, and that at Buckley's Tank there were no cows to come home. (Loud laughter.)

It was a disjointed speech in which Hugo said he couldn't tell his audience much about the fighting in the trenches, because they knew all about it. But he did want to knock down a rumour. Raising his voice, he shouted: 'Can you ladies at the rear of the hall hear me? I say I am not married!'

The celebrations for Northam's most famous son continued into the night. There was a musical program, then everyone sang 'God Save the King', and 'dainty refreshments were then dispersed, after which the floor was cleared and dancing indulged in until about midnight'. The grand heroic tour had begun.

What was the reason for that sudden shouted assertion that he was still single? At the other end of Australia in Melbourne was a new literary heroine – that gentle girl with the soft, sweet voice who had soothed him in London and helped to make him feel well again. Perhaps Hugo was telling Katharine that he was coming to her.

✠

Katharine needed some breathing space before she saw Hugo again. On her way home to Australia she had become smitten with a charismatic Marxist scholar who was later dubbed the 'playboy communist'.

Guido Carlo Luigi Baracchi was born in Melbourne, the son of Pietro Baracchi, an astronomer from Italy, who was in charge of the Melbourne Observatory, and his Victorian-born wife, Kate. He had a conservative upbringing – Melbourne Grammar, classics at Melbourne University – then travelled before the war to Europe where he became a convinced socialist.

He returned to Australia to take a leading part in the anti-war movement, helped to found the Victorian Labor College, joined the International Industrial Workers and was jailed in 1918 for 'making statements likely to prejudice recruiting' and 'attempting to cause disaffection among the civil population'. He was a foundation member of the Communist Party of Australia.

A charming, handsome man with fair hair and blue eyes, Baracchi was the original lothario. His biographer, Jeff Sparrow, in *Communism: A Love Story* says that after Baracchi died, in 1975, aged eighty-eight, a lawyer scrutinising his will said that 'the deceased had led a colourful life, having had at least two de facto relationships with women as well as being legally married four times. It appears he had four children, one of which was legitimate and three of which were illegitimate'.

But communism, said Sparrow, always remained Baracchi's great love. He saw in it a vision of a different world that 'burned itself into his soul' and stayed with him all his life. His meeting with Katharine helped her to go forwards on the same journey, to embrace communism with the same spiritual conviction and fierce passion of a religious convert.

Did Hugo know about the apparent love affair that developed, along with deckside political conversations, aboard an ocean liner? According to Sparrow, he was suspicious enough after the war to always refer to Baracchi as Katharine's 'greasy, hand-kissing dago'.

The liaison began because Katharine decided to stop off on the way back to Australia and visit her younger sister, Beatrice, known as 'Bee' or 'Twinks' to the family. Beatrice had married a former Bendigo bank clerk called Patten 'Pack' Headlam, and they had moved to Ceylon (Sri Lanka) to try their luck in business. The move was a success, and they lived in grand colonial style on a property with house servants and estate workers, managing large company rubber and tea plantations.

At about the same time Baracchi had accompanied his university friend Tristrim Buesst from Melbourne to Fremantle. Buesst was on his way to enlist in Britain. The farewell party aboard ship in Fremantle was so lively that Baracchi passed out and came to only when the ship was miles out to sea. He disembarked at Colombo, where a tea planter took him in until the next P&O liner called that could ferry him back to Melbourne. When he boarded the ship Baracchi was wearing borrowed tropical whites and a pith helmet. Only when the voyage was underway did Katharine discover that the handsome young man was not a planter or some kind of conservative reactionary but a kindred spirit with advanced political views – 'the knight-errant of Australian radicalism', as Stuart Macintyre described him.

A fluttery on–off love affair seems to have possibly developed between Baracchi and Katharine in the first few months of 1916, when they were back in Australia. But Baracchi had more than a wandering eye: 'his marital and romantic arrangements were in a constant muddle', according to Macintyre. At one stage Katharine took a cottage by the beach for a month to get away from it all. She wrote that it was good to 'stretch my arms over the sea and swear that I belong to the world – and to no man'.

On her arrival in Australia, Katharine had been toasted as a literary heroine. The first Australian author to have won a major prize for literature abroad was received as if she was an Australian cricket captain bringing home the Ashes. 'Miss Katharine Prichard is the woman of the moment in Melbourne this week', the magazine *Punch* trumpeted, 'and we are just tumbling over one another to say "we are proud of you, and welcome home"'. Katharine later wrote: 'There were many welcome home parties and receptions by literary organizations. Greetings and warm-hearted congratulations poured in from hundreds of unknown readers. I could never have imagined people would be so responsive to the success overseas of a young writer belonging to them'.

The premier of Victoria, Sir Alexander Peacock, gave a Cabinet luncheon in her honour and presented her with a free rail pass for six months. The New South Wales government quickly followed suit. She visited an aerodrome to inspect new war planes and was taken up for a spin. There was a poem written in her honour that concluded:

> But there's no place like the old place
> To home returning eyes,
> *Isn't it good* to be home again
> Under the old blue skies?

Now Hugo and Katharine were both home in Australia, if at other ends of the continent. Soon they would be together.

14
Love and War

As a vase of earthen ware
I am filled to the brim
With the golden wine
Of my joy in him.

Katharine Susannah Prichard, 'The Beloved', 1932

AS THE *ADVERTISER* OBSERVED, HUGO THROSSELL might have been a Western Australian Gallipoli hero but he was 'almost equally well known in South Australia where he was educated at Prince Alfred College'. On 7 June he arrived in Port Adelaide, and now South Australians could claim him as their own.

At the port itself there was a cheering reception for him at the local town hall and the overwhelming adulation continued after the train from Port Adelaide steamed into Adelaide's grand Railway Station on North Terrace just over an hour later.

The crowd here was led by the young state Labor premier Crawford Vaughan, who had strolled across the road from the state parliament buildings opposite together with his brother Howard, his attorney-general.

The Vaughans were both old Prince Alfred boys, and by their side waiting with them in a place of honour to greet the hero was Hugo's old headmaster, the trim bearded Frederick Chapple, wearing a formal suit with a stiff collar and a homburg hat.

And now it was a Prince Alfred College show all the way into the city. The crowd rushed Hugo as he emerged from the station, desperate to shake his hand. There were cries of 'Lift him up! Lift him up!' and two burly soldiers carried him shoulder high to the front car of a motorcade of more than twenty cars, which drove slowly through the city streets with cheering spectators lining the route to his old school in Kent Town.

Here the new headmaster, WR Bayly, the staff and 350 boys cheered him onto the grounds and into the assembly hall, where his VC was reverently taken from him and taped to the lectern on stage for everyone to see.

The boys listened spellbound as their headmaster told them of what had happened on Hill 60 and there was even more cheering when the headmaster announced there was to be a half-holiday in Hugo's honour. He then invited the hero to spend the night at the school, just like in the old days, when he was a boarder.

Hugo spent the night in the old boarders' dormitory, had breakfast with the boys and attended morning assembly. Then he headed eastwards again.

Hugo had written to Katharine to say that he was planning to visit her in Melbourne. The news must have sent her into complete confusion. She was just getting over her passing romance with Guido Baracchi and had told her mother that she didn't want to marry anyone, that she was married to her work. And then there was the emotional blackmail that her middle-aged former lover the Preux Chevalier had forced upon her after their fling in Paris, making her promise that she would never marry and threatening dire consequences if she married anyone but him.

Hugo swept all of this emotional baggage aside, bounding into Melbourne like a knight on a white charger galloping to her rescue. Katharine wrote: 'They were days of whirlwind love-making from the moment Hugo arrived'.

He had caught the overnight express from Adelaide and arrived in Melbourne on 20 June 1916, where he booked into the opulent

Menzies Hotel, regarded at the time as one of the world's finest hotels.

The spark that had flashed between Hugo and Katharine during their meetings in London now flared into a roaring Australian bushfire.

Katharine relived the moment later, in her novels. In *Black Opal* she described two lovers coming together: 'There was no hesitancy, no moment of consideration. As two waves meeting in mid-ocean fall to each other, they met, and were lost in the oblivion of a close embrace'. And in *Working Bullocks* the heroine tells of the 'urge and surge of her being to his, and of his to her'. She scrawled in one of her notebooks: 'Few women have the strength of mind to be frankly sensual'. Theirs was an explosive love match: a strapping and virile Light Horseman, a wartime hero, and a wispily beautiful literary heroine; a born conservative from the landed gentry thrown into war, and a radical woman of the suburban middle class already rebelling against the established order. It was, indeed, a match.

They needed to get away from Melbourne, away from the public eye, to be alone together. But Hugo had more official duties to attend to, and Katharine accompanied him to receptions, as well as to the theatre to see shows like *The Country Girl* and *Iolanthe*, while at the same time introducing him to some of her literary friends.

Everyone wanted to meet Hugo. No sooner had he arrived in Melbourne than a reporter from the *Argus* called on him at the Menzies Hotel and tried to get him to talk about Hill 60. Hugo was evasive. 'It was an all night "stunt" and it would take all night to tell', he parried. He didn't want to talk about himself. He said he was lucky and once again deflected the reporter's questions from himself, singling out Ferrier, McMahon, Renton and Macnee for mention. Deflecting attention and changing the subject became habitual responses to questions about the war as he travelled from reception to reception, although at one event a journalist observed that 'at times his recollections made it difficult for him to speak, and he was visibly affected as he mentioned the names of those who had the misfortune to be killed'.

Katharine took over. She needed to get him away from all this, give him some rest. She took him first to the prim two-storey Victorian family home in Armadale to meet her mother and her brother Alan.

Mrs Prichard had been working away on her pieces of Honiton lace, decorations that were called 'berthas' for wedding dresses. She had told her daughter that some day she would wear the lace, when 'Mr Right will come along and you'll have to marry him'. As Hugo was introduced, Katharine wrote, 'Mother fell in love with him' while Alan had remarked that it looked as though the lace would now be hers to wear as a bride.

Alan was only three months away from joining up with the 59th Battalion, bound for France. He told his sister before he left that Hugo was a fine man and she should marry him. But Katharine was in turmoil. She wrote: 'Still, I could not bring myself to break a promise to the Preux Chevalier that I would never marry. He had threatened to shoot himself on the day I married anyone else. I told Hugo about this commitment, but he would not accept it as reason for separating us. "I'll kidnap you if I've got to!" was his comment'.

So they went by train to a love nest about 30 miles south-east of Melbourne, close to Emerald, in the beautiful Dandenong Ranges. 'It was a place where she could work and dream,' her son wrote in his biography of his mother, *Wild Weeds and Wind Flowers*, 'a place where she could listen to the yearning of her own heart and confide her fears and joy in the words of poems. Emerald was home to Katharine'.

It was also home to other well-known writers and artists attracted by the quiet beauty of the Dandenongs. A writers' colony was established there during and after the First World War, the focal point of which was Rose Charman's Cottage, about a mile from the Emerald township, nestled away in seclusion at the end of a long avenue of oaks, elms and maples. Two big lime trees marked the entrance to a cottage garden surrounding the small, white-painted wooden house. In the surrounding rich brown soil everything grew: apples, pears and persimmons, huge cream magnolias and rich-red roses. On the property was a gully with tall gum trees wearing garments of peeling bark; the surrounding bushland was alive with the sound of whipbirds and the flash of mauve, blue and red parrots. This became Katharine's home.

It had been originally built in 1908 for Rose Charman, the unmarried daughter of pioneers. It had a sitting room, kitchen, two bedrooms and a makeshift laundry on the back veranda. A primitive wood stove cooked the food and boiled the water for the claw-foot bath. Rose lived in the cottage until she was wooed and won by the manager of a nearby nursery.

The cottage's first literary occupants were Louis and Hilda Esson. Hilda, who practised in the hills as a doctor, was a childhood friend of Katharine, and when the Essons vacated the cottage and moved to another on a nearby hillside, Katharine had begun using it to get away for an occasional quiet week of writing. She loved the place.

Perhaps her spirit sometimes still calls there. In 2010 the owners of the cottage, which still exists and had just been lovingly restored, complete with wood panelling and the claw-foot bath, told me that the home always felt full of warmth and love. Sometimes, they said, they almost believed they had seen a small, slim figure flitting through the garden under the enclosed veranda, where she wrote.

Katharine wrote passionately of the 'psalmist of dawn' at Rose Charman's Cottage, the yellow robin leading the chorus until 'the native thrushes awoke. A cuckoo's quavers flew with their wild sadness; whipbirds, golden-breasted whistlers, all the warblers, wrens and tree-creepers, tossed their ripples and runs into the air, while magpies and butcher-birds fluted and yodelled, kookaburras laughed and hooted away in the back hills'.

In time, Katharine bought the cottage, and it was there that she began work on one of her best-known novels, *Black Opal.*

She also rented the cottage to two other well-known writers and intellectual friends, Vance and Nettie Palmer. It was from the cottage that Nettie wrote a prize-winning book called *Modern Australian Literature*. She also wrote, perceptively, that 'Jimmy Throssell was broken by the war; he was broken already when he returned here on leave in 1916. Then he went back to the desert campaign'.

Hugo had decided it was his duty to return to the war. He needed to persuade the 10th's regimental doctors at Claremont that he was fit enough to go back to the front line.

Before he left Melbourne for Western Australia he told Katharine that he could not marry until the war was over. 'Too many of the men he had known had left widows or, worse, gone home a wreck, no good for anything ever more. He was determined that no woman of his would be tied to some pathetic cripple if there was anything he could do about it.' Katharine responded: 'More stirred than I had ever been, I cursed myself for letting Hugo go back to the battlefields with no more than the memory of kisses and our last passionate embrace. Was it the end of this brief madness? Would Hugo survive the war? Would he ever return to overwhelm me again?'

The answers lay ahead as Hugo once again plunged into a period of bitter frustration, waiting and waiting while others sailed for the front. There seemed to be some disagreement among the doctors as to exactly how fit he was and whether he should go back at all.

On 15 September, Hugo faced a medical board in Fremantle that noted he had 'nervousness, sleeplessness and headaches later. General condition now good. Some tremor still present. Tongue slightly furred. Heart normal. Recommend: Fit for light duty . . . [in] about three months'. More frustration. How to fill the time? A striking portrait of Hugo made by the Scottish painter Duncan McGregor Whyte in Perth towards the end of 1916 shows him as the hero in uniform, VC ribbon on his chest, hands on hips, jaw thrust out, looking defiantly, almost glaring, at the world. The eyes, though, seem sad and troubled. The portrait is now held in the Northam Arts Centre.

From Egypt, Ric, back with the Light Horse, wrote to another Throssell brother – probably Cecil – whom he called 'Doc':

> I've had a couple of longish letters and a lot of photos from Jim the last month. I don't know what to wish about him at all. If he's not himself he should certainly not come here, but I know what a scratch camp is like and know exactly how he feels about Claremont. In his last he said he was about fed up already.
>
> There appears to be little chance in life of the L.H. ever leaving Egypt and of course there is really no work for them in France as mounted men.
>
> These desert stunts are not half bad, ever so much better than these damned fixed camps where you get a crowd together and just get interested in them and off they go only to make room for a fresh lot to begin all over again.

On 31 October, Hugo also wrote to Doc:

> A line Doc while I wait my train. I asked for a board this a.m. and was passed as 'fit' and am just off to H.Q. to see about getting away with the next lot of reinforcements inside a couple of weeks.
>
> This is no game for me and I just feel I'd like to be right into it or right out of it, so put up a few words that the Heads smile on my proposition this afternoon.
>
> Hip Hip. Will be home before I sail for certain.
>
> All the luck.
>
> Jim.

The board found that his 'general condition now good, no tremor. Sleeps well. Eats and feels well. Pulse slow and regular. Recommend return to duty. Fit for active service'. Even so, it was not until 22 January 1917 that he could note in his war diary that he had sailed from Fremantle as the officer commanding troops aboard Transport A45, the *Bulla*, a converted captured German prize ship. Also aboard were Sergeant Cook and thirty-two men: the 23rd Reinforcements of the 10th Light Horse Regiment.

The 10th had eventually limped off Gallipoli during the evacuation on the night of 13 December 1915 with 150 men. What remained of the 3rd Light Horse Brigade was shipped back to Egypt. There wasn't much left. Hughes, the ditherer, had been invalided home to Australia, and Antill, the martinet, had taken over. At the end of November the Bullant had crowed that he was the sole original officer left in the brigade. Only about 130 other ranks remained of the original 1900 that had landed at Anzac Cove in May.

In Egypt the 10th had to be rebuilt almost from scratch. The commanding officer was now Hugo's old friend Tom Todd, promoted to lieutenant colonel. He had to build a brand new regiment. Reinforcements kept arriving from Australia, fit and keen and ready for action. Wherever possible the new troops and squadrons were commanded by veterans, like Horace Robertson. But Hill 60 was still reaching out to claim victims: Tom Kidd – the 'Bomb-Proof Kidd' – had to be invalided home at the end of 1916 when diarrhoea and sickness turned to cholera and complete exhaustion.

The long Desert Campaign lay ahead. The infantry on the Western Front may have been bogged down in trench warfare and suffering horrendous casualties, but, as Robertson noted, 'if the Australian troops in Egypt and Sinai missed something of artillery barrages, they found equivalents in the long years of sand, heat and natives'. One trooper, trying to describe it, wrote: 'Long rides, fatigue, sleepless nights, in a grim wilderness, one of the harshest regions in the world. The country offered no sustenance and little water, while blistering heat and blinding sandstorms were a common occurrence'.

The climate was almost unbearable, and the incidence of disease very high. Evacuating casualties often meant using camels to ferry patients hundreds of miles to the rear. Sickness was endemic: as many Australians died in this desert of disease as of wounds. Sir Henry Gullett, a former war correspondent turned historian, described the general conditions during the long campaign:

> Water was scarce, the heat oppressive, and the dust perpetual and suffocating. Thirty thousand troops, most of them mounted, moved constantly over a limited area of light clay soil for many rainless months. The dreaded khamsin [a strong, hot southerly wind] added to their trials. The men rode and lived and slept in a fog of dust, which seldom lifted.
>
> The monotonous diet and the absence of vegetables brought about a severe epidemic of septic sores. Few men, from the commanders down, escaped this evil, and at times the majority of the men in a regiment would be swathed in bandages.

For Hugo, another real-life nightmare was beginning. Although recovered physically from his wounds but still suffering mentally, he was sent to an unrelenting campaign that took even more of a toll on him. Yet it started with such joy: on arriving in Egypt, on 16 February 1917, Hugo was reunited with his brother Ric. There was much to catch up on: news of home and family in Northam, the trip Hugo had made to their farm at Cowcowing, life as an officer for Ric. But Robertson, for one, had noticed a difference: 'He was a different Hugo. There seemed to be the same exterior, but his eyes showed pain, and we all realized the bombs had left their mark'.

Hugo rejoined the 10th alongside Ric on 3 March, after being kitted out for the desert conditions and selecting a horse at base camp. The new regiment was already battle hardened after some major engagements, including meeting its old enemy the Turks at Romani the previous August and at Magdhaba in December, when it was engaged in a classic mounted operation in which hundreds of Turkish prisoners were taken.

Hugo later paid tribute to the Australian horses that carried him and his men through the barren, blighted landscape:

> Their powers of endurance were remarkable. Water supply proved the greatest problem in the desert, the Turks destroying the wells as they retreated.
>
> During one period of 10 weeks during which the heat was well nigh unbearable, the animals did not average one drink per day. Frequently they ran into a second or third day without a drink sometimes being without water for 50 hours. No horse carried less than 20 stone with rider and equipment, and sometimes there would be no opportunity of removing their burdens for days.
>
> Sometimes the animals were in such poor condition they would chew the harness upon them and it was not an uncommon sight to see them chew one another's manes and tails.
>
> They were simply wonderful the way they stood up to it on their rations.

After the battles to drive the Turkish forces back from the Suez Canal, and with the Sinai desert under control, the British forces under the indecisive General Sir Archibald Murray were given authority to push beyond the Sinai and into southern Palestine by crossing the enemy line that had been established between the fortress of Gaza and the frontier town of Beersheba.

Gaza was strongly held by the Turks and was dominated by a steep hill called Ali Muntar. There were natural defensive barriers to be overcome by any attacker – the town was surrounded by closely cultivated fields enclosed by thick hedges of prickly pear cactus up to 5 yards high, which flanked narrow laneways and formed a maze that in places was 2 miles deep. The first attempt to capture the fortress, on 26 March – known as the First Battle of Gaza – was a debacle. It was followed by a second attempt, which commenced soon after mid April and was also a disaster. The British forces deployed totalled some 70,000 men, while the 10th Light Horse's 450 men played small but significant roles in each assault.

In the first battle, the 10th moved out before dawn in a thick fog and took a Turkish outpost with little opposition. The Light Horsemen then halted and waited for orders to continue while the infantry went forwards. But the foot soldiers, delayed by the fog, were cut down as they struggled to break through the cactus hedges that surrounded the city. Other Anzac dismounted troops managed to shoot and hack their way through the maze and into the town and headed for the Great Mosque in the centre. British and New Zealand troops were then beginning to win the forward slopes of Ali Muntar with a series of bayonet charges.

But to everyone's amazement – including that of the Turkish commander of the Gaza garrison, who had been blowing up his wireless station and stores in anticipation of defeat – the British generals commanding the operation gave the order for their troops to retire. In the muddle and confusion the generals had become worried about Turkish relief columns that had been sighted on their way to reinforce the garrison, and then they started to be concerned about how their horses could be watered beyond the town once their forces were in the desert again.

The order to withdraw was received with dismay and disgust by the Light Horsemen, who pulled out, with the 10th acting as rearguard. The disgruntled men had thought the battle won, although the British infantry had suffered some 3000 casualties, often through being caught up in the cacti like flies in a spider's web and then picked off by snipers.

Encouraged by London to continue the Palestine offensive 'with a view to the occupation of Jerusalem', the British commanders then prepared for the Second Battle of Gaza. Heavy siege guns arrived by train. When the British artillerymen boasted that they could 'blow Ali Muntar into the sea', a Light Horse officer is reported to have said: 'That hill reminds me very much of Achi Baba at Gallipoli. I remember Achi Baba was to be blown into the sea many times, but it always seemed to bob up again'. There was another portent of what was to come. On one battle map the slopes of a feature named Savage Hill were called The Nek.

The plan consisted of a massive frontal attack by the infantry with the Light Horsemen striking eastwards on a 6-mile front to prevent Turkish reinforcements being sent in. Two thousand gas shells were to be fired; it was the first use of gas in the campaign on this eastern front. Another new weapon, the Hotchkiss machine-gun, was issued at one per troop: twelve per regiment. Each was capable of firing strips of .303 ammunition at a rate of up to 500 rounds a minute. The greatest excitement of all was described cynically by one officer as 'the Crowning Joy of the Army, the Hope of the Side, the mysterious, much advertised, irresistible, war-winning TANK'. Six were shipped out from Britain. Hugo snapped a photograph of a tank commander posing beside one of the lumbering machines, which had been named HMS *Pincher*.

The Second Battle for Gaza was, in fact, doomed from the start. 'The army, which awaited the dawn of April 19, was one filled with forebodings', wrote Gullett. 'Men who have been for some time in the field are quick to perceive the true feelings of their immediate leaders and infantry and mounted troops alike had at this time little faith in the High Command or in their own capacity to overrun the Turkish position.'

Gullett wrote of the prelude to the second battle. An early bombardment failed to disperse the enemy. The gas shells also failed – they were useless in high temperatures, and a coastal wind dispersed and blew away the gas. The tanks failed as they became scattered along a wide front, clanking forwards at 4 miles an hour, easy marks. They were gutted by well-aimed high explosive shells. Infantry attacks failed as machine-guns mowed them down. The Turks then counterattacked, and their artillery fire was deadly.

Men in the 10th's forward observation post had watched in amazement for two days before the battle as dust-shrouded lines of Turkish infantrymen had crossed open desert to their next objective – Atawineh – without a shot being fired at them by the British guns. On 19 April the 10th was ordered to join the other two regiments of the 3rd Light Horse Brigade in the fight. Once again they were ordered to leave their horses behind and to fight as infantrymen. They were to move forwards through fields of barley towards the stronghold of Atawineh, knowing that the 3000 Turks who had so recently passed this way into a network of surrounding trenches would be waiting for them.

'We began to realise that we had walked into a trap', wrote Olden. 'The enemy knew the ranges of our positions to a nicety, and had waited until our line had reached them before he unloosed the full fury of his resistance. Shrapnel, high explosive, machine gun and rifle bullets swept the ridges and the re-entrant behind them along which any supporting troops had to pass.'

The battle raged all day. The orders were that the 'holding attack' must be sustained on Atawineh so that Turkish troops in their trenches there could not be released to reinforce the garrison at Gaza. There was fierce hand-to-hand fighting. At one stage, according to Ian Jones in his history *The Australian Light Horse*, B Squadron of the 10th was pinned down in front of a major redoubt. Hugo Throssell told a sergeant to order his troops to fix bayonets and charge over about 270 yards. The sergeant responded by telling him 'not to be so bloody foolish', and the troops stayed where they were. The regiment had already lost half its men from the firing line. Later in the day the brigade was reinforced for a large-scale bayonet charge, and the few survivors of the original charge at The Nek disbelievingly prepared themselves for another massacre. But it was called off. The 10th held on.

'The steady stream of wounded going back told its tale and the Turks – particularly their gunners – seemed to be fighting with renewed vigour', wrote Olden. 'Their salvoes of shrapnel and percussion shells were delivered with regularity and precision; their machine gun and rifle bullets tore up the ground increasingly, whilst their aeroplanes held sway in the air and swooped and bombed and shot down opposing aircraft as the fancy pleased them.'

The Second Battle for Gaza had been lost. At dusk came the order for the Australians to abandon their positions and retire. A final burst of shell fire swept the 10th Light Horse. There was a head count a mile back, when they reached safety and their tethered horses. 'A number of the horses had been killed during the day by shell-fire and aeroplane bombs, but, gloomily enough, here were now plenty of riderless ones to spare.' The firing line of the 10th Regiment now numbered 35,' said Olden. It was the costliest day for the 10th since Gallipoli. One officer and seven other ranks were killed, twelve officers and eighty other ranks wounded.

Among the wounded officers was the commander, Todd, who had been shot early in the day. A bullet had passed through his eyelid, slightly damaging the eye, then through the bridge of his nose before lodging near his cheekbone. The handsome and debonair figure was now a shattered soldier, temporarily blinded and speechless. The desert dust troubled his eye long after the doctors had patched him up and the army had awarded him a bar to the DSO he had already won in the Boer War.

And Hugo had also been wounded again. Cadden wrote home for him to reassure the family in Northam: 'Hugo was wounded early in the fight and first got hit in the flesh of the thigh and then soon after in the foot. His wounds are slight and he will soon be as well as ever. Hugo did very well in the fight and carried on after receiving his first wound'.

Ric, however, was reported as missing. Hugo had no chance to go looking for him, to give those long piercing whistles they'd used on the paddocks at Cowcowing, before it was confirmed that Ric, that one officer, was dead. Anglican chaplain T Daimpre wrote:

> Lieut Eric Throssell was killed in this battle during a terrible burst of shrapnel. He was about the most beloved and respected officer in the 10th and there is profound regret over his loss.
>
> His brother, the V.C. man, was wounded in leg and arm – not badly. He passed me as he came out of it, riding on a horse to the hospital. He was looking cheerful and gave me a shout of recognition. He did not know then about his brother.

The details were given later to the Australian Red Cross Society Wounded and Missing Enquiry Bureau. There are differing accounts of Ric's death in their files:

> No 720 Trooper Ditchburn said he saw Lt Throssell after he had been killed. He had been shot through the brain and was lying with his face against his left arm as though asleep. By his position death must have been instantaneous – it was about 4.30 in the afternoon of 19th April.
>
> No 2096 Trooper C.B. Claxton wrote saying he saw Lt Throssell killed by a shell on 19th April. He was hit in the stomach and informant was present when all papers and other articles were taken from his body and handed to a trooper of 10th Light Horse.

The troopers then had to retire from the area, because the Turks were occupying the ground, but another informant said that Trooper Woods, the lieutenant's groom, had told him that 'early the next morning a "burying party" went out, found the body and buried it where it was found'.

After the war, in 1919, Ric's body was exhumed when the then Imperial War Graves Commission collected Allied bodies from the desert, identified and reburied them. Ric Throssell lies at peace today in the Gaza War Cemetery. There are 2500 graves amid the clipped lawns and neat rows of rosemary, oleander and purple-flowering jacaranda.

Ric's death was obviously a personal disaster for Hugo. He had been sending a steady stream of letters to Katharine, and, as he was the censor of his soldiers' letters – the envelopes came marked 'passed by the censor, Lieut Hugo H.V. Throssell' – he could be both informative and frank. Katharine said the letters reflected his war-weariness and disillusionment. 'Hugo was broken up by his brother's death. I could write little to assuage his sorrow.'

It took three months for Hugo's wounds to heal, and he spent time brooding. At some point he remembered the letter that Ric had given to him before leaving Australia. It set out matters that needed attending to in the event of his death, including some small bequests to their sisters. It also contained a riddle.

Ric had always been something of an enigma and kept things close to himself. He was broader and taller than Hugo but much more reserved. His letter included the puzzling instruction to 'buy a plain gold brooch £5 & inscribe "Liebe" [my love] . . . forward to Agnes Caspers, Montague St, Goulbourn [*sic*] from me – Katie Scott will know her address if she has left. Also send Katie £10. Buy a wristlet watch about £5 and inscribe "from Ric" with date & send it to May Thomas poor little girl'.

Hugo had discovered from an unidentified nurse in Britain that she had been married to Ric briefly in Perth, seven years before, but that the marriage had lasted only a year. Hugo wrote about it to another brother: 'I was able to send her a couple of snaps the lad had kept of her and she wrote to me "so my Ric has gone. I'm doing night duty again and the girl who was on this job died suddenly last week – how I now envy her." Poor girl.'

All in all, Gaza had almost knocked the stuffing out of Hugo. 'I was in hospital during the Gaza battles when Hugo came in wounded from the battle in which his brother Eric was killed', wrote Robertson. 'Eric's death saddened him greatly, but he went back to duty as determined as ever.' He was still mourning when he returned to duty, but the army promoted him to captain. However, for the rest of his war Hugo acted more like an automaton than a hero. The strange joy of battle, the dash, the inspiring bravery that had carried him and his men through at The Nek and Hill 60 were gone. The entries in Hugo's war diary as the Light Horse battled its way into Palestine are mostly dry recitations of facts: positions taken, casualties suffered, enemies killed, ammunition expended. He recorded no more 'great charges' – only occasional observations about the tough men who rode and fought with him through the desert. 'One man on being carried away badly wounded on hearing some words of sympathy from a mate said "Yes, my luck is dead out, for a chap will never again get a chance of such bonza shooting"', he wrote after one operation, in which he noted that 151 Turkish corpses had been counted afterwards and 38,000 rounds of ammunition expended. 'Another fellow was shot through the tongue and as he walked into the dressing station simply remarked: "They've made a —ing parrot of me!"' The neat note alongside records six officers and seventeen other ranks wounded that day. Two had died of wounds.

For the year before he returned to Australia, Hugo was either riding or fighting, or he was back in hospital. His medical record is a litany of suffering and is often distressing to read. His insides were being eaten by tapeworms.

Loss of appetite, weakness, dizziness, stomach cramps, diarrhoea and headaches – these are the symptoms when someone is infected with the human tapeworm, either through drinking contaminated water or by eating an intermediate host such as undercooked pork. The worm has a head with four muscular suckers and a crown of small hooks that latch on to the gut. It can grow to an incredible 30 feet, and if untreated it can work its way into muscle tissue and internal organs, causing cysts and disease.

Hugo had noticed that he was passing segments of the worm in October, but it wasn't until January 1918 that the stomach cramps sent him to hospital. He was given a course of medicine, and four days later he passed a worm 6 feet long. In May he was back again, this time passing a worm 9 feet long. It was noted that it came out 'complete with head'. It may have been the fighting that prevented Hugo from seeking treatment earlier. One of his favourite sayings after the war was that you had to 'crack hardy like a Light Horseman', no matter how sick you felt.

After the famous mounted charge on Beersheba by the 4th Light Horse Brigade late in 1917, the 10th Light Horse Regiment received orders to join British units for the final advance and capture of Jerusalem, led by General Sir Edmund Allenby. After two weeks of fighting, in which the 10th took the steep and rocky hills overlooking Jerusalem, the city surrendered, on 9 December. It had rained for three days beforehand, and the men found themselves fighting through mud instead of the usual dust.

Hugo and his regiment rode down from the hills in formation, along an ancient Roman road and into the Holy City. They were most unimpressed by what they found when they got there. Gullett described it as being in

> an indescribable state of filth. Excessively crowded and undrained, and with most of its main thoroughfares covered and therefore unpurified by the sun, the old city had been for centuries one of the most nauseating and verminous areas in the world; and even the open and pretentious new town beyond the walls was scarcely less revolting to the senses. To the habitual uncleanliness of a lazy, unproductive, parasitical people – most of them living by a traffic in manufactured holy relics and shoddy souvenirs, and by the general prostitution of religion to tourists of three faiths and many races – had for three years been added the primitive habits of the Turkish soldiery.
>
> So offensive was Jerusalem that even the most ardent Christian in the army who visited it at that time remembered that visit with feelings of horror.

Allenby formally entered Jerusalem on 11 December. In 1898 the German Kaiser Wilhelm II had visited Jerusalem, entering on a white horse through a huge new gateway that had been built into the city's stone walls to accommodate him and his massive retinue, which rode alongside him with raised banners. By contrast, Allenby ordered that the surrender ceremony should be marked by 'severe plainness and simplicity'. He drove up to a side entrance to the old narrow Jaffa Gate in his Rolls Royce staff car, got out and walked through a small honour guard of troops, 'not dressed as for ceremonial parade, but in fighting trim, with the mud of the hills on their ragged clothes, the lines on their faces and the hollows about their eyes telling of the long-sustained strain of marching and battle'.

Near to the gate itself stood Captain Hugo Throssell VC and thirty troopers of the 10th Light Horse, in a special place of honour. 'It was a wonderfully impressive ceremony,' Hugo recalled, 'remarkable chiefly for its simplicity'.

Hugo stood alongside fifty British troops, thirty Italians, twenty French, twenty New Zealanders and around twenty Indians. Once the general was inside the Jaffa Gate he proceeded to the Tower of David, where a proclamation was read in English, French, Italian, Arabic, Hebrew and Russian placing Jerusalem under martial law but also assuring the inhabitants of the city of their safety and 'immunity from molestation' by the victors.

Hugo sent a postcard home from Jerusalem to a young nephew. It did not show the moment of triumph, but simply a photograph of his thin-looking uncle and some of his Light Horsemen relaxing on the steps of a school with some children offering them food. He wrote: 'The house was a fine big French school but the Turks used it for a hospital and when we came we were very glad to live in it while the heavy rain was on. There were hundreds of ragged little boys and girls everywhere selling their goods'.

The Light Horsemen were also sending specially printed Christmas cards home to Australia, with a verse entitled 'Coo-ee':

Here's a 'Coo-ee' Sister Billjim
From a Billjim overseas
Where there ain't no scented Wattle
And there ain't no Blue-Gum trees

We're among the wavin' date-palms
Makin' Jacko Turkey-trot,
And send sincerest Christmas Greetings
From this Gawd-forsaken spot.

Allenby's capture of Jerusalem was a triumph, and it lifted spirits everywhere in the British Empire. But it proved to be only the halfway mark in a long campaign. Hugo did not see the end of it. No sooner had he recovered from the tapeworm than he caught malaria in the mosquito-infested Jordan Valley. The disease made him helpless, with recurring bouts of fever. For over six months in 1918 he was in and out of army hospitals, malaria clinics and convalescent centres, spending up to seven weeks at a time in Port Said, Cairo, Jericho and Gaza.

The means to go home appeared at the end of July, when a cable arrived at the Australian Army headquarters in Cairo from the headquarters of the AIF Fifth Army in France that read: 'Defence desires present war Victoria Cross winners return Australia on furlough to enable them to spend few months there and help in recruiting'. On 4 September, Hugo sailed from Suez aboard the HMAT *Suffolk* as officer-in-charge of troops returning to Australia on leave. By 8 October news of the hero's imminent return was out, with the *Kalgoorlie Western Argus* speculating that another career lay ahead: 'An effort is being made to induce Captain Hugo Throssell, who is on his way back to the State, to contest the Swan Federal seat'. But after the *Suffolk* called at Albany on 10 October, an application that had been lodged on Hugo's behalf was quickly withdrawn, ten minutes before closing time.

Hugo was on his way to Melbourne, armed with war souvenirs and photographs from Gallipoli and Palestine to be made into slides for a proposed lecture tour to aid recruiting. He also had something far more important on his mind: Katharine.

This time it would be for keeps. He had cabled her from Egypt, telling her that he was coming home. As the *Suffolk* meandered its cautious way through the Red Sea and across the Indian Ocean, he sent a barrage of messages to 900 Malvern Road, Armadale. Katharine recalled:

> Cable followed cable from every port on his journey. The telegraph boy was kept busy running up and down our garden path. On the day Hugo's ship steamed into the bay, he sent me several wires. Mother and

Ethel were in a fever of agitation. I still felt afraid to commit myself where Hugo was concerned.

But when Ethel opened the door and he stood at the foot of the stairs, a tall, masterful figure in uniform – returned from the maelstrom of war – my irresolution vanished. He held out his arms, and I walked down the stairs into them.

15

Home from the Hill

You are the fragrance of the lemon trees,
The stars, the whistling of the starlings,
The autumn air, and the blue of the sky.
You are everything of joy and beauty:
Everything of joy and beauty is the thought of you.

Katharine Susannah Prichard, 'Your Name', 1932

HUGO AND KATHARINE WASTED NO TIME before heading for their love nest, Rose Charman's Cottage, in Emerald. Katharine called Hugo 'a deliriously exciting and romantic lover'. An extraordinary chemistry had brought together a conservatively raised upper-class hero from the Western Australian countryside and an intellectual writer and developing social activist from middle-class Melbourne. However, they did share common interests, from riding horses to attending the theatre and a love of music. They also loved the bush and would later enjoy a semi-rural lifestyle together.

Katharine, late in life, told her granddaughter Karen that she was attracted to Hugo by 'his passion, his energy, his love of life and the fact that despite his upbringing he was a down to earth Aussie bloke'. She also wrote: 'Virile and forthright, Jim was always a source of inspiration to me; a personification of Australia'.

Karen Throssell does not see their class difference as having been a potential obstacle to Hugo falling in love with Katharine. 'There are many examples of people from privileged backgrounds who come to the position, one way or another, that their privilege is unfair and end up working to change things for the underprivileged. And Katharine was such an eloquent advocate for her cause, how could he not be convinced?'

The relationship that developed between them, however, seemed to be based on a very strong physical connection, and well into their marriage Katharine still wrote powerful, passionate love poems like these verses from 'Lips Of My Love':

Adventurous lips
That o'er me rove,
So swelling soft
And smelling like the rose,
Lips of my love! My love!

Lips of the bee
That cling,
And fall from clinging,
Yearning,
Drunk with bliss!

Dear lips
That to me prove
My body
But a chalice, white,
For your delight,
My love, my love

Oh, I am faint
When your lips hang on mine,
And there is ecstasy
In their mute questing,
Easting, westing,

So
They are gentle
As the brooding dove,
Fierce as twin birds of prey,
Lips of my love! My love!

She owned their cottage now; it had been bought for her by her mother with some money that Alan had bequeathed after being killed in France. Whenever possible Katharine went to Emerald to 'absorb some of the vigour and beauty of the world as an anodyne to realization of the woes of the world', and to write a new novel, *Black Opal*, with material she had collected on an outback trip that had included the opal fields of Lightning Ridge.

The year 1917 had been important for Katharine. Her political activism had continued to grow, as she became a campaigner for social justice. She had been involved in the fiercely divisive anti-conscription campaign the year before. One evening, as she was crossing Princes Bridge in Melbourne, she had seen newspaper posters about the Bolshevik revolution, which was consuming Russia. It was her 'road to Damascus' moment, a blinding flash of revelation. She wrote later:

> Until then, despite all my wanderings and searching, I had not heard of Karl Marx or Communism.
>
> I lost no time in finding out all I could about them . . . I felt like some watcher of the skies when a new planet swims into his ken.
>
> Finding this exposition of Communism was like discovering a new world; a world with a social system created by the organised workers so they could use their hands and brains for the welfare of their country and people . . .
>
> Organizations for peace would triumph over the horrible mania for war which Capitalism uses as a profitable investment.

The war was consuming the world, consuming them all. Hugo had been wounded again and Ric was dead.

Katharine and her mother became focused on their worry and fears for Alan, fighting at the time on the Western Front. In December came the moment they had been dreading. Katharine read the yellow telegram that was delivered to their home by a small messenger boy. Alan had died of his wounds after being hit by a shell near Steenwerck, in Flanders. He lies today among the 1700 soldiers buried in Trois Arbres Cemetery. Katharine wrote: 'I hated the war bitterly and furiously and every circumstance which threw men into this madness of slaughtering each other'.

By the time Hugo returned from Egypt, Katharine was reading the works of Marx and Engels with the passion of a new convert well on the way to becoming an evangelist. She said her mother at the time was disturbed by her interest in the revolution in Russia and her socialist ideas and had told her that her father had never believed in socialism. 'He didn't read this book, I'm sure', Katharine had retorted. 'And he didn't go through this war. If he had understood that a system of production for profit is the basis of wars, in our time, he would have been as anxious to change it as I am.'

Katharine told Hugo of her political views and claimed that he simply 'accepted them with me'. She was caught up in his ardour and passion. While they were still in Melbourne, every morning flowers arrived at the family home in Armadale. Any day they did not meet, love notes were delivered by express messenger. Katharine basked and glowed in his company. 'Such a gallant, striking figure he made as he strode through the streets. If we dined in town, I could hear the whispers going round: "Throssell, V.C." and crowds collected to cheer us as we passed.'

Hugo spent time in Melbourne receiving further specialist treatment for his malaria. A month after his return to Australia he was still suffering from shivering fits and waking with heavy sweats. He also had new official duties to perform. He visited the Melbourne stock exchange and was given 'a most enthusiastic reception'. Only about eighteen months before he had been persuaded to 'relate his thrilling experiences at Gallipoli'.

Now the members sat entranced as Hugo told them of the adventures of the Light Horse in the desert and of being there for Allenby's triumphant entry into Jerusalem.

But Hugo had only Katharine on his mind. He was still apprehensive, still did not want to commit to marriage until the war was definitely over. In the meantime he asked her what kind of engagement ring she would like. Katharine replied that she had seen a case of brilliantly coloured Queensland butterflies mounted on a corkboard in a shop. 'I told him that I thought the passion of our love was like the colour and wings of the butterflies', she wrote. "But they're dead," he exulted, "and we're alive!" His tempestuous love-making made me feel that there was nothing more important than to be alive and in love.'

But her mother was quite crestfallen when Hugo told her that her daughter wanted butterflies instead of a ring, so Katharine eventually ended up with a Western Australian pearl set with small diamonds, and the tropical Queensland butterflies.

November came. Katharine wrote:

> We had been spending the day at Emerald, and were walking to the train at twilight, when flares lit up the distant hills.
>
> Hugo gazed at them, a strange expression on his face. So moved and silent, he was, as flare after flare cast a yellow light across the sky.
>
> I asked anxiously: 'What's the matter?' thinking the flares might be reminding him of bomb explosions and the havoc they cause.
>
> His arms folded round me. 'The war's over,' he said, 'those are armistice rockets. We can be married now. I won't have to go away again.'

'The war left what Churchill called a "crippled, broken world"', wrote Adam Hochschild in his book *To End All Wars*. 'The full death toll cannot be known, because several of the governments keeping track of the casualties had dissolved in chaos or revolution by the war's end. Even by the most conservative of the official tabulations – one made by the U.S. War Department six years later – more than 8.5 million soldiers were killed on all fronts. Most other counts are higher, usually by about a million.' Hochschild said that more than 21 million men had been wounded. From a population of fewer than 5 million, a total of 416,809 Australians had enlisted: 40 per cent of all Australian men aged between eighteen and forty-five years. Over 60,000 had been killed, and 156,000 wounded, gassed or taken prisoner.

In 1918 an entire government department – now the Department of Veterans' Affairs – came into being in Australia to try to look after those who were carried or had managed to walk or hobble home. The first artificial limb factory was opened at the Caulfield Hospital in Melbourne. Eventually, Australia had six of these factories.

Thousands of men ended their lives in sanatorium wards or boarding houses, still coughing from the gas. Other men were hidden away. Sergeant Martin O'Meara, a stretcher bearer, was awarded a VC for his bravery in the charnel-house that was Pozières in 1916. For four days during heavy fighting he brought in wounded officers and men from no-man's-land. He was both physically wounded and mentally shattered himself. By the war's end he was 'required to be kept in restraint' in the secluded Claremont Mental Hospital near Perth. Evidence was given to a 1919 parliamentary select committee that he was restrained in a straitjacket from four-thirty every afternoon and was not released until eleven the following morning, because there was only one attendant on his ward at night. O'Meara died alone, from 'chronic mania', in 1935. He had spent sixteen years in that straitjacket.

Nearly 4000 men passed through the 10th Light Horse Regiment of Western Australia. Nearly 300 were killed and just over 700 wounded. For many survivors, the 'returned men', the end of the war meant the beginning of a new struggle, for stability, and a total readjustment of their lives. What had they fought for? It was a question that many of them were asking.

As Hugo stepped off the Great Western Express to spend Christmas 1918 with his family he was met by a reporter from the

Western Mail anxious to discover how the state's first VC winner in the war was faring. It had been more than two and a half years since he had made his first return, wounded, from the front. 'Out of work, but never so pleased to lose a job in my life', was his response. Hugo was in good spirits and chatted to the journalist about everything from 'having a fly in a Bristol fighter travelling at no less a speed than 150 miles an hour' to the wonderful work being done by two Australian women volunteers in running tea rooms in Egypt and making lemonade for the troops serving in Jerusalem. He continued:

> I have had an opportunity of seeing troops from many parts of the world in this war and better fighters than the Australians I have never seen.
>
> They are second to none when they get up against real hardship.
>
> In travelling around since my return to Australia I have noticed a tendency to slow down the despatch of comforts.
>
> I just want to say, if my opinion is worth having, that this is the time when they will need support from home more than ever they did before.

In January 1919, Hugo was back in Melbourne, to be married. He was back in style again. This time the hero and celebrity was staying at the grand Australia Club with its pillars and mosaic-tiled entrance hall. Around the corner was Collins Street and a short walk east to the Registry Office. Katharine had insisted there should be no church and no clergyman for her wedding. What little lingering faith she may have had in God after her father's suicide had been shattered by Alan's death on the Western Front. Hugo appears to have felt much the same, so they decided that the wedding would be held in the registry office and be as plain as plain could be. The press was not told about it and only caught up with the news of the celebrities nearly a week later, reporting that 'the ceremony was exceedingly quiet'.

And so Hugo and Katharine were married on 28 January, with her mother and brother Nigel and a few close relatives and friends as witnesses. They somehow managed to reduce Katharine's age a little (she had just turned thirty-five) so that they were both shown to be thirty-four years of age on the official record. They had a reception at Katharine's home in Armadale, where her aunt Lil had decked the house with big branches of sweet-smelling white magnolias from her garden.

Katharine and Hugo then drove to the hills and Rose Charman's Cottage for their honeymoon, oblivious to the worldwide flu epidemic that had just arrived in Australia and the bushfires that raged through the Dandenongs that summer. Katharine had a picture of Achilles holding a shield and javelin in the cottage. 'You like that bloke?' Hugo asked her.

'He's my ideal of masculine beauty', she responded.

She found Hugo standing on the kitchen table the following morning, holding the lid of the rubbish bin for a shield and the broomstick for a javelin. '"Won't I do instead of that peanut?" Collapsing in laughter I assured him he was the only peanut in the world for me. So it went, in the gay camaraderie of our first years together, with fulfilment for both of us, in our love and confidence in each other.'

✠

Hugo and Katharine decided to move to Western Australia and start a new life together after he was officially discharged from the army early in 1919. Although it may have seemed more logical for Katharine to have stayed in Melbourne with her connections, friends and beloved cottage at Emerald, she seemed content to do what wives were wont to do then – follow her husband. As her granddaughter Karen observes today, 'Despite her later independence she was, in fact, far more conventional than you would think about gender politics'.

So they decided to move west. Hugo still owned property there and was a farmer at heart. Katharine perhaps saw it as not only a new adventure but the opportunity – soon fulfilled – to gather new material for what would become an outpouring of creative writing. They would decide to set up home in the hills near Perth.

Roughing it on the property at Cowcowing, pioneering in the dry country, was no longer attractive to Hugo, now that Ric had gone. And Cowcowing, without even a proper homestead, was no place for a growing literary figure to live. Physically, farming would have been too demanding for Hugo as well. A medical board in February found that he was still experiencing minor attacks of malaria, although his wounds were not causing any disability. 'Appears restless and nervy', said the doctors. 'General condition good. Further improvement to practically complete recovery may be expected in time.'

Postwar reality soon set in. Hugo's 50 per cent disability pension was reduced to 35 per cent. By the end of the year he was receiving £1 6d a week, his wife 10s 3d – a grand total of £1 10s 9d. But they were madly happy and deeply in love. 'My husband is truly, I believe, the best thing that ever happened to me', Katharine wrote to a friend.

No sooner had they arrived in Perth than Hugo set out to show Katharine his home state, from the small farms and giant karri trees in the south-west to the broad flat lands of the wheatbelt and the rich-red desert sands leading to the goldfields. Encouraged by one of his brothers-in-law, Perc Armstrong, a motor-racing champion, he bought an Indian motorcycle with a wickerwork sidecar. They roared off together – the dashing hero, Captain Throssell VC, and his winsome bride – charming everyone they met. They travelled as far as Cowcowing. 'The journey was gorgeous', Katharine wrote. 'Every stockman and drover on the road knew Jim – and of course it was a case of pull up and have a yarn with everyone! "Hullo Jim" from the men on the road and "come and see my missus" from Jimmy after the first few minutes.'

After their adventure they continued their honeymoon at Wandu, a sprawling, rented ten-room house on the upper slopes of Greenmount, about 12 miles east of Perth. 'We lived in only two or three rooms and on hot summer evenings disported ourselves like Adam and Eve in the garden.'

Katharine was anxious to continue to educate her husband politically.

She had already impressed him with her passion and earnestness about the cause of socialism, the promise that a new system of running society would take the profit out of war, lessen the chance of it happening again, and give more people equal opportunity. Now she gave him a book to read called *Socialism: Utopian and Scientific* by Friedrich Engels, the German philosopher and Marxist theorist. 'Often there would be a yell of: "Hell, girl, what the blazes does this mean?" I would go out to explain, his arms stretched out, and usually our political discussions ended in love-making. Jim had never heard the arguments for socialism before and said he "couldn't fault them".'

Hugo had never had to worry about money before, let alone politics. His conservative father had always made sure that the family was well provided for. Hugo had always been comfortable; now he felt positively rich. When he had been discharged the army owed him the tidy sum of £150 in deferred pay. Hugo noted vaguely on one official form that he had interests in his father's estate. He had also secured a job as the soldiers' representative on the Western Australian Land Settlement Board, at a salary of £300 a year. It was a good start. They expected that royalties would come in from Katharine's writing, too. Within two years her novel *Black Opal* was to be published in London with a royalty of 10 per cent on British and American sales and 'threepence per copy sold in the colonies'.

But there were also debts. During four years of drought at Cowcowing before the war nothing had come in against the brothers' bank loan. Hugo scrawled on a form that he owed £450 to the Agricultural Bank and another £600 to the National Bank. Some money went to buy their new hillside home at Greenmount, a small dwelling at 11 Old York Road, together with 140 acres of well-grassed paddocks across the road. The land sloped to a creek bed from a knoll called Sugar Loaf. Hugo intended to farm some of it, plant an orchard and subdivide the rest.

The house was similar to Rose Charman's Cottage: a modest square weatherboard with two bedrooms and a wood fire in the kitchen. In time the Throssells built verandas where they could sit or sleep out, especially in summer, with views of the lights of Perth twinkling in the distance. The verandas were eventually covered in sweet-smelling climbing roses, wisteria, jasmine and honeysuckle, together with grape vines. Hugo planted a rose garden and terraced flowerbeds amid which he built a writer's studio for Katharine. It contained a stone fireplace, and jarrah bookcases still marked today with Katharine's handwritten signs – 'Novels', 'Plays', 'Lectures', 'MS of Published Novels' – and a plain writing desk. Here she wrote well over a million words for publication, first drafting them in her small, pointed handwriting and then typing the manuscripts herself. 'The happiest years of my life were spent in our home at Greenmount in the West. My best literary work was done there . . . In those halcyon days we could not have believed that for us the future held so much misfortune.'

The misfortune began on Peace Day, 19 July 1919, the Allies' red-letter day celebrating the signing of the peace treaty with Germany in June. There was enthusiastic support for the celebrations throughout the empire, with a huge victory parade in London that marched past the new Cenotaph, in Whitehall. Australia followed suit, and in Western Australia, the town of Northam invited its own son, Captain Throssell VC, to lead a victory parade through the streets during the day and to speak at the official celebrations that evening.

The speech would be made against a national background of political unrest and division around the subject of socialism. Returning servicemen had found a changed Australia. Women in the workforce had taken jobs that had been previously occupied by men and employment was generally hard to find. There had also been a growth of organised unionism. Some soldiers who found jobs grew disillusioned over poor working conditions and pay and so joined workers and unions to campaign for an equal share of wealth and a classless society.

But many other returned diggers strongly opposed the socialist movement that seemed to be sweeping the world. They clashed especially over the union appropriation of the red flag, the symbol of the Bolshevik movement that had staged a revolution and installed a communist government in Russia. These diggers who had risked their lives in the First World War did not want to see anything approaching a communist revolution in Australia.

The idealists – like Katharine, and perhaps to a lesser extent, Hugo – believed that the only way to stop future war was to change the system. As their son Ric wrote, 'It made him sick to think there were people who had made money out of it. Katharine was right. There had to be an explanation . . . what for? Jim Throssell wanted to know the answers, like so many of the men who had been through the war'.

As he thought about what he might say at the Peace Day celebration, Katharine obviously went to work on him if not manipulating him then certainly strongly influencing his possibly weakened mind. If Hugo had not met Katharine and had simply returned to his pre-war country roots and attitudes, the speech that was to follow would probably never have been made.

'Katharine encouraged him to make a stand', wrote Ric. 'If he was going to strike a blow for socialism, that would be the time to do it. She helped him to write his speech and heard him try it out. It was a fine statement, she assured him. She was sure that it would make a great impression. He was a natural speaker, easy and relaxed before a crowd. He had the knack of winning people, treating them all as friends – and they would be in Northam, of course. There wouldn't be too many who'd agree with him, he knew that. But there wouldn't be a man-jack there who didn't know Jim Throssell.'

They seemed to have swept away any doubts about the wisdom of what they now planned. But this was not the time, nor Northam the place, for a political speech. Peace Day was a patriotic occasion, a time to give thanks, a time to remember the fallen, a time to rejoice that the war was really all over at last. It was not an occasion for any kind of political polemic, especially as they had chosen an audience well to the right of the political divide. There wouldn't be a socialist amongst them and any returned man present would be utterly against the idea. All of his conservative country family would be attending, together with his father's old conservative friends and colleagues, including the current premier, James Mitchell, himself a Northam man. It was a disaster waiting to happen.

The victory parade through flag-bedecked Northam got underway at one-thirty. Thousands of townspeople and farming families from far around lined the streets along the route to the oval at East Northam, where a football match was to follow the parade. Those marching were led by the Salvation Army brass band. Then, mounted on a big bay gelding, came Hugo in full Light Horse uniform, sword in his right hand, bronze VC glinting slightly on his left breast. Hugo was leading a squad of his troopers. Behind them came a relative, Sister Throssell, riding in a car with 'three maimed soldiers', and another thirty local returned men in uniform. Following behind were army cadets, Northam's motor ambulance and the fire brigade's motor reel vehicle. The Red Cross Society had also turned out, in a horse-drawn drag. Soon, according to the report in the *Northam Advertiser*, it seemed that the whole town was falling in behind Hugo and the others, from tradesmen with their displays on the backs of trucks and people riding in decorated motorcars to adults in fancy dress and comic costumes, who were vying for prizes. At the football ground the speeches were brief in order to start the game on time.

At eight o'clock, between 1200 and 1500 people gathered in Northam's narrow main street, in front of a large platform that had been erected outside Tattersall's Hotel. A massed choir from the town's churches sang, the Salvation Army band played, and, after everyone in the crowd had joined in with 'God Save the King' and 'Praise God, from Whom All Blessings Flow', the speeches began.

Father O'Donnell spoke about peace in Australia; Premier Mitchell talked of the need for everyone to work to return the country to normal. Then Hugo rose, and the crowd cheered and cheered. Their hero, their nation's hero, home for good. At first he said how wonderful it was to be back in Northam and to receive dozens of warm-hearted handshakes. He told a few stories about his exploits on the local football ground and in the boxing ring. Then, suddenly, the mood changed. The crowd's warmth towards the speaker gave way to a frozen, disbelieving silence. What Hugo was saying now was later described by Jan Goodacre as 'akin to Christ returning to the Mount and telling the multitudes he had lied'. The *Northam Advertiser* reported that Hugo had changed his demeanour and had become 'intensely earnest'.

> He said during the past five years he had seen much of the world. They had known him as a sort of irresponsible lad, but he claimed now to be a man. Nearly five years ago he had rode through the streets of Northam in charge of eighteen men, who were among the first to enlist. With him were the late Harry Eaton and the speaker's brother Eric. Of that eighteen, seven were lying either in Gallipoli, Palestine or France. His hearers would realise the feeling within him when greeted by happy faces on his welcome home.

Then he spoke the words that made the crowd gasp: 'War had made him a socialist'.

Katharine wrote afterwards to her friend Nettie Palmer: 'You could have heard a pin drop. Jim himself was ghastly, his face all torn with emotion. It was terrible – but magnificent'.

The *Westralian Worker* called it a 'veritable bombshell'. Its sister paper in Queensland headlined the front page story: 'Hugo Throssell, V.C. Declares Himself a Socialist: A "Bomb" at a Peace Gathering'. The story began: 'There was probably no more astounded gathering in any part of the Commonwealth than the mob of patriotic Tories who had gathered together in Northam (W.A.), on Peace Day, "to celebrate" when Captain Hugo Throssell, V.C. – a scion of one of West Australia's "very best" families – declared himself to be an out-and-out Socialist'. There followed the full text of the extraordinary speech, which not only dumbfounded the audience but had widespread ramifications far beyond Northam.

> 'The war has made me a man!' proclaimed the soldier-orator. 'I have come to speak to you as a citizen!' . . .
>
> 'The war has made me a Socialist. It has made me think and inquire what are the causes of wars. And my thinking and reading have led me to the conclusion that we shall never be free of wars under a system of production for profit, with its consequent over-production, periodic crimes, unemployment and the struggle for markets.
>
> 'I am convinced that only the reorganisation of society on the basis of production for use and for the well-being of the community as a whole can give any assurance of a permanent peace.
>
> 'I want to work for peace because I know and have seen the horror of war. If only the people who say they want peace would do the logical things to bring it about, there would be no wars.
>
> 'As it is, to-day the Peace Treaty leaves us at the mercy of the system that makes wars. After four years of war, after the loss of 8,000,000 lives, with a total of 18,000,000 wounded, of which 6,000,000 are permanent wrecks; when Great Britain has shouldered a debt of £8,000,000,000, of which Australia's share is something over £285,000,000 it is still possible for individuals to make colossal fortunes by the manufacture of armaments and war materials.
>
> 'While it is possible for unscrupulous men, profiteers, and manufacturers of war materials to profit by war, we will always have wars.
>
> 'If we do not want war, we must change the system of production for profit, and organise not for the benefit of a few people but of the community as a whole.
>
> 'The subject is too big a one to deal with in a few words to-night. But I wanted to say that the only real way to celebrate peace is to do the things which will make for peace. Think; talk to people who are opposing the system of production for profit, study books on the subject, and test what you read by the facts of everyday life.
>
> 'Don't bother about what the daily newspapers or the people interested

in maintaining the system of production for profit may say. You've heard what they've got to say all your lives. Go to the other side! Get their point of view. Then do what is necessary to make your convictions realities, and work for the conditions which will make it impossible for any to make fortunes out of war. Recently-published statistics have shown that, while the incomes of the wealthy and interest-drawing classes have doubled themselves during the war, the incomes of ordinary working class people are no more than they were before the war.

'You will not find this way of working for peace a popular one. You'll find it most unpopular, because all our institutions have grown up under the wing of this system of production for profit. But if we want peace, if we want to do the things which will make for a permanent peace, we must do away with the system of production for profit, and reorganise our life in common on the lines of production for use and for the well-being of the community as a whole.'

A bugler sounded the last post after Hugo had finished his speech, and the crowd melted away. The Throssell family sat stunned and embarrassed. The returned soldiers felt somehow betrayed. Hugo had turned his back on both his town and the countryside's conservatism. He had preached revolution.

The feeling ran so deep that it was not until 28 August 1999 – just over eighty years since Hugo had made his speech – that a modest cream-brick memorial to him the size of a backyard barbecue was unveiled in Northam by the governor of Western Australia, Michael Jeffery. He said that 'it is probable that rejecting the values of his peer group was the reason no memorial existed [before] for Throssell'.

✠

Hugo and Katharine returned to their cottage in Greenmount after the speech. The die had been cast: politically, they were outcasts, pariahs.

Not long afterwards the wharfies went on strike, scab labour was brought in by the government, and Katharine was down on the docks firing up the strikers. A year later she joined a handful of people in the Perth Trades Hall to form the Western Australian branch of the Communist Party of Australia.

There is no evidence that Hugo became an active member of the party himself; rather, he found it hard to keep up with his wife as she moved further and further to the extreme left. He settled into a supportive role at home, sometimes accompanying her and protecting her when she was heckled at public meetings. Nevertheless, he was under suspicion. The forerunner of the Australian Security Intelligence Organisation watched both Hugo and Katharine from 1919. The voluminous ASIO records held by the National Archives of Australia show that Katharine was under close surveillance from then until she died, fifty years later. Hugo's very own country began spying on him four months after he made the Northam speech. The opening two pages of the first ASIO file, of 127 pages, on Katharine are devoted to Hugo. On 24 November 1919 an agent wrote under Commonwealth of Australia letter-head from Perth to a Major HE Jones in Melbourne:

> In compliance with Circular No 1, the following report is submitted: – CAPTAIN HUGO THROSSELL, VC The latest recruit in the ranks of the Social Democrats is Captain Hugo THROSSELL, V.C. and he now speaks on the same platform as Monty Miller and Ben Jones in Perth and Fremantle.
>
> Many attribute his leaning towards Socialism to his wife's influence, but he states he saw the need of such principles whilst on service and on his return to Australia. However he was struck on the head at Gallipoli and further he was a victim to Cerebro-spinal Meningitis, his mind perhaps having been affected.
>
> On his return to Australia he married a Miss Kathleen Susannah Pritchard [*sic*], well known in Melbourne as a novelist. I am attaching a cutting from the 'West Australian' of the 20th. It is concerning a lecture on Socialism, which Mrs Throssell delivered in Perth on the 19th instant.
> Yours faithfully,
> R.H. Weddell.

On 2 March 1921, Weddell wrote again, this time to the director of the Investigation Branch of the Attorney-General's Department in Melbourne:

> Captain & Mrs Hugo Throssel
> In reply to your W 209 of the 22nd ultimo, I have to state that Captain Hugo THROSSEL, V.C. and Mrs K.S. THROSSEL, nee PRITCHARD, concerning whom I reported to you in my 19/1/113 of the 24th November 1919, are residents of Greenmount, situated in the hills around Perth.
>
> Captain THROSSEL is a member of the Discharged Soldiers Settlement Board under the Discharged Soldiers' Settlement Act, and has been representing the soldiers for two years. He possesses property in and about Northam and is a member of a well-known West Australian family. His father, the late George Throssel, was at one time Minister for Lands in this State and was also the Premier.
>
> THROSSEL is not regarded as a strong minded individual and he is thought to be influenced by his wife, who has achieved fame as an Australian Novelist. Mrs Throssel holds advanced views on Socialism, and gave a lecture on the subject in Perth in November 1919.
>
> Captain and Mrs THROSSEL are residing in a beautiful home in the hills and both of them are regarded as visionaries, the humorists having it 'that they sit on the lawns in the early morn and write blood and thunder'.
>
> I have met THROSSEL and it is my intention to 'draw him out' on the subject of Communism, and, if successful, I shall report same.
>
> A medical authority informed a friend of mine that he would not be surprised if THROSSEL went 'off his head' at any time, so it is evidently his wife who must be regarded as the more dangerous [spelling errors in original].

Were the agents somehow right in their conclusions that Hugo was now not 'a strong minded individual' and liable to go 'off his head' at any time? Was it a direct result of Hill 60? Or had the suspected brain injury from the botched operation at Wandsworth or the meningitis changed him so that he became more vulnerable and easily influenced – especially after he fell in love with Katharine and then professed publicly that he had become a socialist? Whatever the answers, Hugo was being watched by the country he had fought for.

After this the spies turned their full attention on Katharine. The first file on her bulges with copies of intercepted letters to and from Greenmount, intelligence reports on meetings of the Communist Party, details of her passport, press clippings and anonymous tips to the authorities.

Oblivious to this secret attention, Hugo and Katharine settled into a happy life together at Greenmount. In December 1919, Tom Roberts came home from London. His last wartime job in Wandsworth Hospital had been to make and colour artificial noses for soldiers with ghastly facial wounds. His ship entered through Fremantle, and he wrote the next day to his wife and son, still in London:

> The first touch of Australia – I must tell you of it, while the feeling of it all is fresh. Just one word – ideal. It had the sensation that as a child you thought it would be going to Heaven; I don't exaggerate. Throssell and Mrs, waited for us till near the evening – a car, the air fresh and smelling of the land and the burnt grass of the roadside. The old gums, you know them, like lace against the warm moonlight sky. The road winding through the bush, by cottages and bungalows . . . I watched the VC feed the ducks and fowls and milk the cow. A breathless stillness over all.

Katharine began writing books in earnest in the 1920s, finding continual new inspirations. A trip to a country race meeting and a visit to a sawmill in the south-west, for example, provided her with the inspiration for a novel called *Working Bullocks*. She was also writing pamphlets and speaking at meetings for the Communist Party. While Katharine wrote, Hugo pottered about his farm.

They both loved horses and rode along the bush tracks and gullies of the Darling Ranges.

Hugo's medical records, however, show a slow and steady decline in his health. In 1921 he was still suffering from attacks of malaria, and he told the doctor that 'strenuous work knocks him out and he gets very shaky'. The following year he complained of shortness of breath and heart palpitations: 'the slightest thing that irritates him produces an attack. Cannot do hard work . . . has good days and bad days'. His pension was increased to 40 per cent disability.

Professor Tony Costello, the present-day surgeon who examined Hugo's medical records, commented, 'It is reasonably easy to understand that this man had severe problems post war. Not that these would not the least have been caused by his episode of bacterial meningitis and the brain injury from the blade being inserted into his frontal lobe I would suggest. He also had malaria and cardiac failure . . .'

This was the time that Hugo began dreaming up money-making schemes. He had noted the streams of cars and buses that came up from Perth to the hills at the weekends crowded with families on a day out in the national park, which blazed with blue leschenaultia, red and green kangaroo paw and other wildflowers. Hugo believed that such people would buy blocks of land in Greenmount if they were properly promoted.

He increased mortgages on the property at Cowcowing – although he still owed the bank money – to raise the capital for the deposit to buy up most of the land along the York Road in Greenmount for subdivision. Hugo was confident that this would pay for itself in sales and set about having signs painted, which he plastered along the hills road offering quarter-acre blocks for sale on £100 deposit and easy terms. The first blocks were snapped up, and Hugo thought the speculation was on its way to a great success. A career in real estate beckoned.

Then came a new happiness in their lives. At dawn on 10 May 1922 their son, Ric Prichard Throssell, was born in their home at Greenmount while Hugo anxiously paced around the garden outside. There had been no hesitation in their deciding that the little boy should be called Ric, after Hugo's beloved brother.

Katharine celebrated the birth in an unusual way. She wrote to Ric much later telling him about it: 'My heart sang all the Magnificats you can imagine. Then I saw you so fat and red and lovely and they bathed you beside the fire and I said: "Put on his Bolshevik gown, please." That was the little gown I had embroidered with wheat ears and a hammer and sickle'. The emblem of communism so fervently embraced by his mother stigmatised Ric throughout his life.

Ric entered a home already alive with children's laughter – that of his two cousins. Katharine's sister, Beatrice, whom Katharine had visted at her home in Ceylon, had two children – Thea and Alan. In the true colonial custom of the time it had been decided to send the children home to Australia to be educated. They stayed at first full time at Greenmount with their aunt Katharine and their uncle Hugo, the tall, loving figure they knew as 'Unk'. Later, while attending school as boarders, they spent their holidays with the Throssells, sometimes by the sea at Rockingham, where beach cricket was a favourite game, and were reunited with their parents in Ceylon only once every two years.

In 2009, Thea recounted some of her recollections of Unk:

> Hugo taught us about animals. To have no fear and to respect animals. He taught us how to ride and he was a wonderful rider himself.
>
> He brought his own horse down from Northam, a beautiful big horse called Wyburn.
>
> He'd lead the horse with us three kids all sitting on his back. Then he bought a pony for Ric to ride when he was only about three or four.

Thea remembered Katharine's writing room – the writing table, the typewriter, some upright chairs. 'That's where she escaped most days to do her work and we kids were kept well away by Unk to make sure we didn't go round that side of the house shrieking and yelling. When she was working he made sure she had peace and quiet.'

Hugo showed Thea his VC, which he kept in a chest of drawers; 'it was remarkable in its plainless, it wasn't a glossy thing, it had a certain feel'. But he would not be drawn out about how he came to have it, or about the war. 'I think all of us kids would have liked to hear him talking more about his experiences, but he wouldn't or couldn't.' Thea said that there was a restlessness to him. He always seemed to be going away, sometimes to the east, to the great wheat lands, where he could seek out the company of returned men like himself as their representative on the Land Settlement Board and yarn with them about things that only those who had gone away to the war could understand.

A string of new works came out of the writing room. A short story called 'The Grey Horse' was be well reviewed, as was the novel *Working Bullocks*, published in 1926. But earnings often didn't match the words of praise. The first royalty cheque for *Working Bullocks* amounted to £23 and Katharine had already paid a typing bill for the finished manuscript for £25. She told a friend that she made just 7 or 9 pence on the American edition.

When Ric was four, Hugo arranged for him and Katharine to stay on a station in the north-west, near to where he had spent his jackarooing days. Katharine and Ric travelled to the end of the railway line at Meekatharra and then by truck another 400 miles to Truree Station, beyond the Ashburton River. The result of this stay in the heat and red dust was the prize-winning play *Brumby Innes*, two short stories and the foundation for one of her best known and most controversial novels, *Coonardoo*, whose theme was the tragic love affair between a white station owner and an Aboriginal girl.

Hugo and Katharine were both involved in the research for her novel *Haxby's Circus*. Katharine had always wanted to write a story based on a bareback rider in a small travelling circus who had once been brought in to her doctor brother Nigel's surgery with a broken back. When they saw the big tents of Wirth's

Circus going up by the railway station down from Greenmount, at Midland Junction, Hugo met with George Wirth and arranged for Katharine to travel with the circus on a tour of some of the state's country districts. In return, Hugo agreed to take part in a daredevil circus act.

A new sharp-shooting act had recently been introduced, with a group of 'Cossacks' circling the ring on horseback, picking off balloons with single rifle shots at full gallop. When Hugo took part, a roll of drums sounded, and the ringmaster announced that a volunteer was needed for a feat of marksmanship hitherto unequalled throughout the world. Hugo stepped forwards and was introduced, and the ringmaster explained that the gallant captain would hold his gold wedding band between two fingers as a target. Firing over his shoulder, 'Boris the Cossack' would sight the ring through a mirror and shatter a bottle placed beyond it. It was apparently a trick.

Although Gladys Wirth had given her assurances that there was nothing to worry about, the act looked very dangerous. When the sharp-shooter fired and missed, Gladys stepped into the act. She grabbed the rifle, fired again, and the bottle shattered. It took some time to find the wedding ring. An assistant concealed behind the target had knocked it violently from Hugo's fingers.

There was lightness and fun in the air. The small family at Greenmount was happy and seemingly secure. Nobody was worrying much about money, least of all the Throssells. Those blocks in the hills were going to sell. The royalties for Katharine's works would come in eventually. And Hugo had the land settlement job. In late 1927 they decided to celebrate by taking a trip to the eastern states. Hugo organised an official visit to New South Wales 'as a soldiers' representative of the West Australian Land Settlement to inquire into land settlement conditions', while Katharine put on a fabulous party in Melbourne to thank the Wirth family for allowing her to travel with them.

Hugo and Katharine were in their element, feted as celebrities. The Governor would later that month invite Hugo, along with a handful of other Victoria Cross medallists, to a Remembrance Day luncheon at Government House.

Louis Esson, a writer and dramatist, wrote to Vance Palmer, one of Katharine's literary friends:

> Kattie and Jimmie arrived this week and will leave for a week in Sydney after Cup Day. They are both in excellent form.
>
> Jimmie, who is enjoying every moment of life, insisted on us jazzing; so I had my first lesson on the night when Squizzy Taylor and Snowy Cutmore had their duel to the death at the other side of the Gardens.
>
> I had the honour of being Kattie's dancing partner. I had never seen her looking so well or in such gay spirits.
>
> She gave an extraordinary party last night at the Green Mill, a party, as Bill Dyson said, that nobody except Katharine could possibly have conceived.
>
> It was for the members of Wirths Circus, with whom she travelled in the West. They were interesting people of different nationalities, American, German, Danish, Norsemen, trapeze artists, bear-tamers, head balancers, mixed in with Dyson and Bancks, Tom Roberts and other highbrows.
>
> The ladies were delightful; and there was dancing, and an elegant supper, with sparkling hock and whisky under the tables in the boxes.
>
> Dyson announced himself a wombat-tamer and Jimmie never missed a dance.

Everybody was jumping to the latest dance craze, the 'Varsity Drag', and singing along to the top hit for 1927, 'I'm Looking Over a Four Leaf Clover'. But Katharine and Hugo's luck was about to run out.

16

Against the Odds

They used to tell me I was building a dream, and so I followed the mob.
When there was earth to plough or guns to bear, I was always there right on the job.
They used to tell me I was building a dream with peace and glory ahead.
Why should I be standing in line, just waiting for bread?

Say, don't you remember, they called me Al; it was Al all the time.
Say, don't you remember, I'm your pal?
Buddy, can you spare a dime?

Yip Harburg, 'Brother, Can You Spare a Dime?', 1931

ON TUESDAY 29 OCTOBER 1929 – FOREVER afterwards known as Black Tuesday – the stock exchange crashed on Wall Street in New York. The effect sent ripples of misery across the world that gathered into waves signalling the beginning of the Great Depression and a new battle for survival as far away as Australia.

'Every person I met in every station of life, from elevator boys to reputed millionaires has been hit, the majority of them ruined', Edgar Wallace reported to his paper, Britain's *Daily Express*, from New York.

After the crash, readers of the *Western Mail* in far away Perth could share in a letter written by a Dr Lincoln Graham in New

York to a friend in Sydney: 'Dr Graham said that he was tired of listening to stories of ruin. Suicides were much more numerous than were reported in the newspapers. Office boys, servant girls, barbers and labourers were involved'.

But even before the devastating stock market crash things had been getting tough in Australia. Unemployment had been at 10 per cent; by mid 1930 it was at 21 per cent and peaked in mid 1932, when almost 32 per cent of Australians were out of work. The impact on the country, both socially and politically, was profound. Many people lost their homes and were forced to live in camps on the fringes of cities and towns. Thousands of men had to leave their families and went on the track looking for work, any kind of work, in the country.

The political divide grew wider. On the left the communists, socialists and like-minded organisations banded together to fight forced house evictions, while on the right nationalistic and quasi-fascist groups like the New Guard, which boasted 50,000 card-carrying members, many of them returned soldiers, were formed to fight communism. The New Guard even had plans for a possible coup d'état against the Australian government.

In Western Australia, where unemployment hit 30 per cent, there were hopes of relief after a bumper wheat crop. But the wheat price collapsed, leading to militant union action of withholding deliveries and preventing the forced sale of bankrupted properties.

Hugo and Katharine found themselves plunging from carefree days into a worrying new sullen world. Ironically, *Coonardoo*, published in 1929, won equal top prize in the first *Bulletin* novel contest, which had propelled Katharine to new fame. *Haxby's Circus* came out the following year. They desperately needed money from royalties. Katharine wrote to friends about the minute cheques she was receiving from her publishers in Britain after being taxed both in London and Australia.

There was some welcome prize money from *Coonardoo*, but that soon disappeared when Hugo insisted that his wife take a holiday in Broome and Singapore. She was tired not only from her creative writing but also from what had become constant work for the Communist Party. The Commonwealth Crimes Act of 1914 had been added to in 1926 and was invoked in an effort to curtail certain communist activities, and Katharine told friends half-jokingly that she might any day find herself in jail.

Ric continued to play around the house and among the fruit trees in their orchard at Greenmount. Chickens pecked and ducks paddled around the pond. In a paddock there were some cattle and horses branded with the mark Hugo had registered in 1926 – ⌶1T– the lazy H for Hugo and the T for Throssell.

'I had no sense of my parents' anxieties as the slow decay of the Depression engulfed them', Ric wrote later, in his biography of Katharine, *Wild Weeds and Wind Flowers*.

> I did not see the moods of exhaustion that swept my father's spirit; I did not know how the idyll of their life together soured. The camp for the unemployed at Black Boy just below our home had no meaning for me. The men and women in black-dyed Army greatcoats who tramped up the York Road looking for an hour's work or a meal were strangers. My world seemed full of the good things of living: the shadows passed me by. Life was still a circus, and ours 'the lightest, brightest little show on Earth'.

Hugo's passion for land had, in Katharine's words, 'involved him in reckless expenditures and obligations to the banks'. In December 1925 he had received a letter from EA McLarty, the general manager of the Agricultural Bank in Perth, saying that Hugo's main source of income other than his war pension, as the soldiers' representative on the land settlement board, was drying up:

> Consequent on the discontinuance of Soldier Settlement, which will obviate your attending office more than one day per week, the Hon. The Minister has approved of the present salary arrangements being discontinued, and in lieu thereof you will be paid three pounds three shillings

> per sitting, being the allowance paid to other members of the board. The new arrangement will operate as from the beginning of the coming year.
>
> I take this opportunity of placing on record my appreciation of the valuable services you have rendered the Department and soldier settlers. Your duties have always been carried out with ability and tact, and the result has been that your association with the management and staff has been of a most harmonious nature. I am pleased that you will still be associated with the Board.

Through a friend, Hugo then managed to get a humble desk job at the bank, travelling down from the hills each day by bus or dashing through a paddock to the level crossing, there to swing aboard the last carriage of the train as it slowed on its way into the city. But the 'harmonious nature' of relations with the soldier settlers did not continue. Katharine later blamed her own political activities – and Hugo's support of them – for what transpired, as the political gulf between left and right continued to widen and attitudes grew hard and bitter during the Depression. The returned men had long memories and had neither forgiven nor forgotten Hugo's speech on Peace Day in 1919. Behind the scenes, the Northam sub-branch of the Returned Sailors and Soldiers Imperial League of Australia, founded in 1916, known familiarly as the RSL, before later name changes, had been moving against him. Some regarded his embrace of socialism as nothing short of treason. In 1930, Premier James Mitchell sent a handwritten memorandum to McLarty at the Agricultural Bank:

> A deputation from the R.S.L. headed by Colonel Collett requested the right to suggest an appointee as representative of the soldiers under the Soldiers Settlement Scheme.
>
> They complained about Captain Throssell's lack of interest in the Soldier Settlement and said they objected to his continuance as their representative.
>
> They went further and asked that Mr Throssell be requested to resign. I promised to submit their request to you for report. I think you

> should mention the matter to Mr Throssell so he can make any reply that he wishes.

Hugo resigned as requested – choosing the next Anzac Day to do so, to make a point. He noted: 'It is not true that I have lacked either interest or personal service in the interests of soldier settlers under the Scheme. During the last ten years, no soldier has applied to me for whom I have not done everything in my power. Many letters of gratitude I have received bear out this fact'. But it was no good. He had lost this job permanently, despite his protestations. The secretary of the Northam sub-branch sent him a letter that said: 'Don't let the thing worry you too much Jim, – as life is made up of disappointments & one has to just smile through them all'.

The decline in Hugo's health seemed to accelerate in tandem with his increasing worries. In January 1929, Doctor JS Yule had noted on his Repatriation Department record after examining the 44-year-old ex-soldier: 'Not much trouble from wounds. Just at present feeling very well, but last year very bad. Depressed, sleeping badly. Heart gives some trouble. Cannot sleep on left side . . . fluttering sensation after excitement. Manner somewhat nervy and looks somewhat older than stated age'. The following year he wrote: 'Thinks heart not too good, can do no strenuous work. Can't sleep on L side. R eye giving a lot of trouble lately, lot of pain at night'.

His war time wounds and the effects of meningitis were catching up with him. He would complain about tiredness in the back of his neck if he drove very far, which he attributed to his meningitis.

Hugo had been wearing glasses for reading for the past five years, because he had failing vision in his left eye. But with the appearance of the pain in the right eye, in 1931 a fresh examination was ordered from a specialist, Claude Morlet. He discovered a small fragment of metal – almost certainly a piece of bomb from Hill 60 – imbedded in the cornea. What's more, he also noticed other small metal fragments imbedded in the skin of Hugo's limbs.

A prescription for new glasses was given to Hugo, but he would have to pay for them himself. The metal fragment in his eye was not a 'recorded disability'. A Doctor CW Courtney was quite definite on the matter: 'I do not consider patient eligible to receive glasses at Departmental expense'. So when GF Yeates, a Perth optician, presented an account to the department for 12s 6d for spectacles supplied to Hugo on 2 April 1931 he received this amazing reply: 'Receipt is acknowledged of your account for twelve shillings and sixpence (12/6) for glasses supplied to the above named ex-soldier, and in reply thereto I have to advise payment of your account by this Department is declined as Mr Throssell's eye condition has not been accepted as being caused by war service. He has already been advised of this decision'.

Pressed for a second opinion, the specialist who had initially said the corneal injury was 'reasonably attributable to . . . bomb explosion on 29-8-15' then said 'corneal injury, though modifying the refractive power of the eye to some extent is not producing any gross refractive error' before going on to discuss the effects of advancing age on eyesight. Dr Courtney then reiterated his first ruling. Hugo wasn't going to get a pair of new glasses at departmental expense. This callous treatment can only have further sapped Hugo's spirit.

Hugo and Katharine may now have needed a break from each other. When they took Ric and the other two children for a holiday at Rockingham, Katharine seemed distracted. She had begun work on a new novel, a story about a family helplessly trapped in the Depression and the disintegrating marriage of sensitive and talented Elodie Blackwood and her devoted but inadequate husband, Greg. The book was called *Intimate Strangers*, the phrase that Henrietta Watson had used so long ago to describe her own relationship with Hugo. At the very beginning of the novel Katharine describes Greg having night sweats, haunted by the horror and nausea of his wartime experiences in the trenches.

> He had come home; not permanently incapacitated the repatriation doctors said: only suffering from nervous strain, hardships of the campaign and so on. Astounded to find himself alive, when he had seen so many men blown to pieces about him, Greg felt it was indecent, somehow, to survive them. It had taken him a long time to live among people who knew nothing of dug-outs and countrysides blackened by shell fire, men lying smashed and dying in unutterable confusion: to live among people who talked of 'honour and glory' in connection with the colossal atrocity beside which all other atrocities were a flea-bite: to hear fools talk of 'paying for the war'. As if it could ever be paid for. Such damnable suffering and loss of life. He loathed the whole civilian population which had driven men like sheep to this shambles: the farce of a civilization which maintained itself by war: was cheerful, pious, and made money out of the beastly business.
>
> He had brooded over it: brooded almost to madness. But to live, a man had to have work and wages. He had contrived to secure them . . . But he was caught in a rut: couldn't see beyond it, or any chance, now, of having the sort of life he had promised himself. Any more than Elodie.
>
> During the last few years, he and Elodie had settled down to a more or less matter-of-fact jog-trot of spirited trace-mates, broken-in to each other. They pulled, pretty well, on the whole, with occasional lightnings to clear any sultry atmosphere.

Was this a reflection on the relationship between Hugo and Katharine at that time?

In real life Katharine's letters from Greenmount to her friends in the eastern states screamed of her 'weariness and protest' during this time, according to her son Ric. 'I wish to goodness I could shake the dust of this humpy from off my feet', began one.

> I've been working, so hard, and badly, because Jimmy is dashed hard up and fretted to frazzles over it. Has little debts amounting to something like £4,000 and for the first time since I've known him has gone down to it, dropped his bundle and funked; really I can't stand that – weakness, and I don't expect it of Jimmy. I'll carry my own and his bundle, but a lot

> will be lost in the doing. It always is – Damn! Damn! Damn! And again Damn!
>
> And I milk the blasted cow and feed the chooks – make the jam and kill and pluck the blasted brutes – and it seems a very good idea to sit on the veranda and drink beer. Only there isn't any beer!

Hugo battled on, mood swinging up and down, as the Great Depression hit hard. There were 'brainstorms', periods of irrational excitement, and sudden wild bursts of optimism over get-rich schemes: anything to pull them out of the mess. The real estate business had collapsed, and as his son wrote, block after block of land in Greenmount and land he had apparently inherited in Northam was mortgaged to meet arrears of rates or debts. Hugo also lost money from speculating on wheat futures. The schemes became more desperate. There was a new kind of potato slicer that might take off; it didn't. Then he discovered a device to take the hard work out of lifting wheat bags; a similar device had already been patented. There was hope of an oil find in the northwest; Hugo bought shares in a prospecting company that dug up a greasy substance that turned out to be not oil but a worthless type of wax.

The Rural Bank had introduced a 'pay or go' drive against farmers in the wheatbelt. The mortgage on the Throssell brothers' property at Cowcowing was still unredeemed, and now the tenant farmer couldn't make the payments. Hugo took Katharine and Ric on the long drive to Cowcowing to see if he could lend a hand getting in the crop and salvage at least a few pounds from yet another wreck.

They camped in the one room iron-roofed shanty with hessian walls that was the homestead, with a bush shower rigged outside near the dam. Hugo shot rabbits for the stew pot, and Katharine cooked meals on an open-air fireplace. After a week they were all covered with a red, itching rash, perhaps from fleas, or possibly caused by the chaff dust that swirled around them. After a week they headed home to Greenmount, tired and despondent.

What would Hugo try next? The answer seemed simple enough – though a godsend – when the opportunity arose: gold!

✠

On 13 June 1930 the *Kalgoorlie Miner* reported a new gold find near Widgiemooltha, 300 miles from Perth. A well-known goldfield prospector, Mickey Larkin, and three other men were on the track of a new alluvial field where the gold was continuous, if unspectacular, with samples varying from 4 pennyweights to about 1 ounce per ton. Before the end of the month the find had been christened 'Larkinville' after Larkin picked up a nugget the size of a man's palm.

By October the rush was on, with five goldmining leases and thirty prospecting areas taken up.

Peter Bridge told the full story of Larkinville and its great gold rush in his history *The Eagle's Nest*. Larkin and his mates had by November recovered gold worth more than £300, and men were pouring in from all over Western Australia to have a go at it and, they hoped, dig their way out from under the Depression.

Hugo and Katharine were no exception. 'For a long time my husband and I had been promising ourselves to rush to the first rush which looked like the real thing, and so armed with miner's rights, picks, shovels and dishes, we started for the alluvial diggings beyond Widgiemooltha', Katharine wrote in an article that appeared in the Perth *Daily News* on 3 December that year. Hugo had taken leave from his desk job at the bank; Ric had been parked with some aunts. For Hugo this was the chance to get himself out of financial trouble; for Katharine, the chance to find background colour and characters for her later goldfields trilogy, *The Roaring Nineties*, *Golden Miles* and *Winged Seeds*. Katharine continued her description for the newspaper:

> Within the last month or so, two hundred men have swarmed to the rush, it is said. The pegs of mining leases and prospecting areas are scattered through thorn bush, snap-and-rattle, sandalwood and camel brush, for

> a mile or so on either side of the main camp. But there is still plenty of room for enterprising prospectors. Along the lead, where the dry blowers and shakers are panting and rattling all day, the claims stretch for half a mile or more. On them, most of the men can show little bottles of ounce and half ounce specimens, although some say they have been working for three weeks without 'seeing her.'
>
> About these claims, the digging is rarely more than half a foot or a foot from the surface, and gold is found in the loose wash of the old creek bed, or lying about on the ground to be 'specked' by the first sharp eyes, which recognise it from any other rusty pebble. When some old prospector, red with dust, unfolds a sock, or a dingy piece of flannel, to show the twisted effigies of pre-historic pancakes and wild pigs in bright gold, weighing five or eight ounces, you understand why his hand trembles and his eyes are bright.

She might have been describing her husband. Hugo had caught gold fever in the red dust. Just before Christmas 1930 he pegged some ground near Larkin's original find, learnt how to use the dry blower to extract specks of gold from the dust, and promised to be back. The *Kalgoorlie Miner* reported that on 27 November

> an enjoyable camp fire concert was held at Larkinville on the eve of the departure of Captain H. Throssell, V.C. and Mrs Throssell, of literary fame.
>
> The musical and elocutionary contributions were infinite and varied, and in keeping with the atmosphere of a camp fire concert. As an interlude a waltz and the old Fitzroy Quadrilles were essayed on the gravely ground, at the risk of sprained ankles, the dance music being supplied by an accordion, violin and guitar, with a petrol tin for drum effects. Mr and Mrs Throssell thoroughly enjoyed the novelty as did the amused spectators.

After the singing of 'Auld Lang Syne' and the national anthem, Hugo and Katharine were duly elected honorary members of the Larkinville Progress Association.

Back in Greenmount for Christmas, Hugo gave his son a little gold nugget he had found at Larkinville. It was shaped like the map of Australia and was no bigger than a thumbnail.

Then, on 14 January, came the discovery that had Hugo completely throwing in his desk job and hurrying back to Larkinville with his old Ford loaded to the roof with tools, supplies and camping equipment. Jim Larcombe, the seventeen-year-old son of a veteran prospector, had found the biggest gold nugget ever discovered in Western Australia on a day so hot that he reckoned the temperature was 'about 115 degrees in the waterbag'. They called the nugget the Golden Eagle. Jim's father told a newspaper reporter:

> When the lad gave me the slug, I walked out of the hole with it in my arms and called out 'Sluggo'.
>
> As prospectors came running from all directions a man in the next claim shouted, 'the man's mad he only thinks it a slug.'
>
> I lifted the slug above my head but it was too heavy and I let it drop. Men came from everywhere. They were like a flock of sheep with four or five dingoes behind them.

The nugget was 78 pounds of solid gold. One man could just bear its weight on a shoulder, though father and son were more comfortable carrying it together, one on either side, to the bank. The Golden Eagle was put on show in the Kalgoorlie Town Hall, and a shilling was charged to view it, the proceeds going to assist the unemployed; £47 was raised in just two hours. The nugget was eventually sold to the government for the astounding figure of £5438 4s 2d. Today it would be worth about $2 million.

Hugo threw himself into the task of trying to find another Golden Eagle. He held a quarter-share in a piece of ground once held by the original prospector and a third-share in another prospecting area at Widgiemooltha; he also applied for another 24 acres of ground 7 miles from Larkinville. But the magical glow spread by the wings of the Golden Eagle soon faded. There were no golden eggs. The rush was over. One of the main tracks through the straggly settlement of bush-timber, corrugated-iron and hessian shacks now had a sign up: 'Struggle Street'. On 14 April the *West Australian* reported:

> Only a few men are on gold . . .There have been no large finds recently, although Mr. Hugo Throssell secured about £50 worth of gold a few days ago . . . The rumour that many men were starving could not be conclusively proved, although a few are existing on scanty rations . . . Many men were leaving daily, but taking their dryblowers and shakers with them – an indication that they intend to continue their search in some other region.

But Hugo had paid £100 to Mickey Larkin for his quarter-share only a month before. He was at least £50 down now, probably much more. It was time to go home again: another disaster.

Ric remembered his father's homecoming vividly. There were no presents except for some sweet-smelling sandalwood logs for Katharine and a pocketful of quandong nuts for the little boy to play with.

> He wanted to clean up first, he said, soaking off the red earth of the gold-fields. His arms and shoulders were burnt brown. It was as if his body had been scrubbed white below the line of his singlet. His face and neck looked like a ruddy copper mask. I passed him the towel. His hair seemed more grizzled with grey than before. He covered his face as if he were hiding.

Hugo showed Ric his wedding ring, reduced to a sliver, and said that there was more gold there than he had seen in the past month. 'He was thin, his eyes hollowed by weariness, and his neck corded by the strain of swinging the pick day after day.' Ric recalled how his father had then sat at the head of the table, silent and withdrawn.

In August, Katharine wrote to a friend: 'I'm worn to frazzles myself, not sleeping and trying to work – au despair about everything. Jim with no job and colossal debts, having to be sheered-off and cheered off nervous breakdown all the time . . . Working myself to keep things going'.

They tried to improve their situation. There were debts of over £4000. At one stage Hugo was forced to ask his son to hand back the nugget he had first brought home from Larkinville: it would fetch £12, and Mum and Dad needed the money. Katharine continued to try to cheer Hugo up with pep talks. There was still the 40 per cent pension coming in and the occasional small royalty cheque. They would not starve at Greenmount: they had their own cows and chickens, fruit from the orchard, vegetables from the garden. She told him: 'You mustn't let this beat you. You've got Ric to think of. We've got to see that he gets a good start, a better world than we've ever had to live in'.

There is some evidence that the Repatriation Department had treated Hugo for depression on at least two occasions by 1932. A June examination recorded that he was 'worried about his health. Unable to sleep lately. Gets headaches resembling the pains he had with meningitis on service. Everything is a worry and he is a nuisance to himself and his friends. Brain will not seem to work properly. Has lost weight and feels flabby – disinclined for exertion . . . despondent and depressed-looking'. A recommendation was made that he enter an unnamed hospital for observation. The diagnosis was 'neurasthenia', an obsolete term now but defined at the time as 'a psychological disorder characterised by chronic fatigue and weakness, loss of memory and generalised aches and pains thought to result from exhaustion of the nervous system'.

It appears that perhaps through a combination of the treatment he received, Katharine's encouragement and a slight change in their fortunes Hugo's old optimism returned. Although his old job at the Agricultural Bank had since been made redundant as the state government slashed costs, a friend managed to find him a temporary place with the government as inspector of fertilisers. It would mean a lot of country travel, but, with one in three now unemployed, Hugo jumped at the chance.

Ric remembered his father's show of triumph when he was given the job. He marched onto the back veranda at Greenmount with his coat slung over his arm, flourishing the Gladstone bag that he carried on his business trips to Perth, and threw open his arms, exclaiming: 'Hullo, old chap! How do you like the new inspector of fertilisers?'

Katharine responded with a kind of puzzled sympathy: 'Oh Jim . . . isn't that wonderful, darling!'

The title sounded grand; the reality was travelling to tiny towns and taking samples of superphosphate, potash, and blood and bone for analysis. Ric went with his father on one of the trips only to discover Hugo's frustration, how his singing aloud on the long drive through the bush petered out into brooding silence. He sensed his father's despair at the futility of a job fit only to 'earn a crust . . . It offered no hope of relief from the debts that weighed upon him; not an earthly chance of freeing Katharine from the household cares that consumed her vitality'.

✠

In March 1932, Katharine's one-time lover and fervent communist Guido Baracchi sailed into Fremantle, on the way to the Soviet Union with his latest conquest. She was Betty Roland, a pretty young Melbourne journalist and playwright who had run away from her husband of ten years to go to this promised land. After their ship berthed, Baracchi and Roland travelled to Greenmount for the day, together with a fellow traveller and writer, Bertram Higgins, to visit Katharine and her family. In her 1979 autobiography, *Caviar for Breakfast*, Roland left a fascinating appraisal of the state of Hugo and Katharine's relationship at the time.

> She is a close friend of Guido's but I had never met her though admired her as one of Australia's most celebrated writers. She came out of the door to meet us, lifting an orange fringe that dangled from her hat and kept away the flies. She is gentle and her voice is soft and sweet

and I seemed to see a hint of sadness in her eyes. No one could call her beautiful but her face is sensitive and strong.

She led us through the house where she has her own special sanctuary, a small stone cottage in the orchard, with a fireplace, a large window that lets in plenty of light, many books, and a table where she works. It seemed an ideal place in which to do so. We sat there talking for a while and then her son, a handsome dark-eyed boy called Ric, came in from school.

'This is Ric, my son,' she said to Guido and her face lit up with pride. The boy was rather silent and obviously devoted to his mother.

We went inside for lunch and met her husband, Captain Hugo (Jimmy) Throssell, V.C. He is strikingly handsome, tall and powerfully built. He was the first holder of the Victoria Cross that I had ever met and appeared to live up to every ideal of a hero, yet, somehow, he roused my sympathy.

He seemed uneasy and uncertain of himself, as though he did not belong. Katharine sat at one end of the table with Guido on her right and Bertram on her left, at the other end Hugo with Ric on one side and myself on the other. The boy ate in silence, his eyes fixed on his plate, taking no interest in the guests, and the father was as silent as the son.

There was a lot of animated talk at the other end of the table, in which I took no part. Towards the end of the meal Hugo – Jimmy – roused himself and picked up a pot of jam.

'Try some of this,' he said to Guido. '*My wife* made it, I can recommend it.' It was an attempt to assert himself as a husband and I fancied I saw a shade of irritation pass across his wife's face, but she hid it under an indulgent smile while Guido thanked his host, helped himself to jam and pronounced it excellent. Lunch over, Ric went back to school and Hugo Throssell, V.C., returned to his ploughing in the orchard.

How did Katharine, dedicated Communist that she is, come to marry a man like Hugo Throssell? What have they got in common? She has no respect for soldiers and a Victoria Cross to her is not so much as an award for valour as an indication that the recipient is an expert at killing other men. It must have been his handsome, swarthy face, his virile masculinity, yet she refuses to use his name. She is never Mrs Hugo Throssell,

> always Katharine Susannah Prichard, poet, playwright, novelist, sometimes the Maxim Gorky of Australia, never a mere wife. It must be very difficult for him. Yet it is plain he adores her.

This judgement seems a little harsh. Katharine certainly revelled earlier in the marriage in being known as Mrs Hugo Throssell and seen on the arm of the Gallipoli hero. Even as her own fame grew, while she wrote professionally under her own name, it seems that she was known generally as Mrs Throssell, sometimes with the clarification of 'known in literary circles as Katharine Prichard'.

A collection of Katharine's short stories, *Kiss on the Lips*, was published in 1932, and when the government unexpectedly resumed some of Hugo's unsold blocks to build the Great Eastern Highway near their home, there was also a welcome cheque. Ric was sent off to be a weekly boarder at Wesley College until the money ran out again and he had to return to the nearby state school as a day boy.

Katharine's political activities grew in step with the rise in unemployment. When there was a mass protest rally of the jobless in Perth, some known communists in the crowd were arrested. Katharine sold a brooch given to her by her father to put up bail for a communist friend charged with inciting the crowd by waving her arms and crying out: 'Three cheers for the working class and down with the dirty police curs!' Ten days later, while Hugo was away in the country on one of his inspection trips, police arrived at the Throssell's home early in the morning as part of a series of raids on premises believed to be occupied by communists. They seized a quantity of literature from Katharine.

But Katharine was totally committed to the cause. The world had to be changed. She yearned to go to Russia, to see the results of the revolution, to experience the Soviet Union for herself. The opportunity to do so arose when her sister, Beatrice, in Ceylon, wrote to say that her husband was retiring from the plantations and that she planned to take her daughter, Thea, who had just finished school in Perth, on the European grand tour. She begged Katharine to meet them in London and go on to Paris with them as their guide. What was more, she was sending money towards the fare.

Hugo was all for the idea. His wife had been suffering under the constant strain of caring for him, writing her books, looking after Ric, and now being persecuted by the authorities for her political beliefs. She was suffering from migraine attacks, taking to her bed for days in the darkened front bedroom of their cottage. She desperately needed a break. She could meet both her British and her American publishers in London, and if she had the chance she could go on to the Soviet Union. Hugo told her: 'I'll never forgive you if you don't try and see what's happening there. We must know whether what we've been told is true'. So Katharine decided to go abroad for six months, 'on the understanding that Jim would do nothing while I was away to make me regret leaving him'.

The Investigation Branch of the Attorney-General's Department was keeping close tabs on Katharine. They asked the police to report if she had applied for a passport to visit Berlin on behalf of the Friends of the Soviet Union. The check was made: her passport was currently not valid for travel to European countries but it could be endorsed for travel somewhere else. On 15 May 1933, Mr Woods, a customs agent, reported to the Investigation Branch that Katharine was sailing for London on the P&O liner *Baradine* on 22 May. 'Says purpose holidays – duration 12 months'.

By mid July, Katharine was aboard a small steamer called the *Jan Rudzutak*, bound from London to Leningrad. Katharine's grand political passion had begun to be fulfilled. It was the beginning of 'the greatest event of my life', a 30,000-mile journey through Soviet Russia and Siberia that would last until November. As the ship left the mouth of the Thames someone began to sing:

> a girl cleaning brasses in the alley way. In the forepeak, a man's voice joined her. From all parts of the ship voices took up the song. Soon the

> whole crew was singing. Every day the chanty kept breaking out, gathering a score of voices and falling away into the silences of the dim sea. But it wasn't a chanty I was told. 'The Song of the Red Army,' popular all over Russia, and the seamen, and seawomen, sing it when they're homeward bound.

Comrade Katya was going home. This account comes from her book *The Real Russia*, a 300-page paean of unremitting praise and adulation for the new Russia, its people and its system of government. The book was published in 1934 and is a compilation of a series of articles written on Katharine's return to Australia for her old paper the *Melbourne Herald*. She also made radio broadcasts from Moscow to Australia during her visit.

Like other sympathetic writers and intellectuals from around the world who visited the Soviet Union at the time, she eagerly swallowed everything and anything that was fed to her by the authorities. Some of her article titles give the flavour of her reporting: 'Collective Farm Sketches – "The New Life" in Siberia', 'A Woman Engineer Tells Her Story', 'Comrade Baby and His Mother Have Precedence', 'Domestic Happiness the Rule Despite Easy Divorce'. It was pure propaganda and journalistically delusional. The true but unreported story was that millions of Russians were dying of starvation in a fearful famine. Some historians believe that at least in part the food shortage may have been engineered for political purposes, smashing the resistance of peasant farmers to the government's policy of collectivism. British historian Robert Conquest estimated that in 1932 and 1933 at least 7 million people died from hunger in the European part of the Soviet Union, and 5 million in the Ukraine. News of the famine was suppressed by the regime as anti-Soviet propaganda until the break-up of the Soviet Union, in 1990–91. The famine was followed by the brutal Stalinist political purges of the latter 1930s, in which millions more people were sent to forced labour camps or were deported, while hundreds of thousands were executed. Altogether, according to Conquest, the total number of deaths caused by the Soviet regime 'could hardly be lower than some fifteen million'.

Katharine apparently saw nothing of this. She was taken to the Theatre of the Revolution, where she watched a play called *Grain* and much admired the production.

In August, Katharine arrived on the doorstep of a one-bedroom flat in Moscow, home of Guido Baracchi and Betty Roland. 'Only those who have spent a considerable time in an alien land can fully understand what it means to see somebody from "home"', Roland wrote in her diary. 'She is Guido's friend, not mine, and I had only met her that one day at Greenmount but I threw myself into her arms with a loud cry of joy and came close to shedding tears. She was almost as emotional, and when Guido came hurrying out to join us we practically danced a *carmagnole* in the dingy corridor.'

Katharine was after a bed. She had been put up in the crowded and expensive Lux Hotel, a place reserved for party members by her Soviet hosts, but was finding the atmosphere depressing. There was only one bed in the flat, but two mattresses. They drew lots, the winner to have the bed and a pallet, the loser to have the floor and a thicker mattress. Katharine lost; Baracchi and Roland shared the bed. 'A strange *ménage à trois*!' wrote Roland. 'I hope she is not aware that the situation acts like an aphrodisiac on Guido. I beg him to restrain himself but this has no effect. He still works till midnight almost every night but K.S.P. and I retire at a more reasonable hour. We must present a strange sight, each with an open umbrella over our heads, while Guido pours over his books.' She just hoped that Katharine – 'a serene person with a soft voice and gentle smile' – was sound asleep by the time Baracchi closed his books and came to her bed.

Roland wrote that Katharine was 'tremulous with happiness' about joining a writers' delegation to Siberia. Here was the 'fulfilment of her dreams . . . Only occasionally does she suffer some misgivings, especially when she has been mixing with the Lux fraternity and has been disturbed by their cynical attitude, or has seen an example of bureaucracy. The undisguised struggle for personal advantage shocks her profoundly; she had not expected to find it here and talks about it in a hushed voice and with an air of disbelief'.

Katharine had not expected to stay away so long from Australia, and Roland found her to be considerably troubled. She had reservations about the trip to Siberia and felt that she should return home, as there were 'many problems' there. A loud alarm bell had just sounded: 'Jimmy had written to say he is turning their place at Greenmount into a "dude ranch" and she is aghast at the idea, fearing it is another of his impractical schemes that will end in failure'. But she decided to ignore the alarm and proceed with her trip. She couldn't have come so far as a true believer only to miss this chance of seeing an important part of her promised land. It was hardly likely that she would be back.

The great adventure in the huge, cold vastness of Russia lasted for two and a half months. Katharine returned to Moscow at the beginning of November, looking thin, tired and pinched with cold. Roland said that she was 'sadly disillusioned' after her travels and that none of her former optimism remained. But these sentiments were not reflected in Katharine's broadcasts or published reporting.

Katharine was longing to go home and spoke to Roland of the pretty house at Greenmount, of Ric and Hugo waiting there to welcome her. 'How good it is going to be to see them both again', she told Roland.

> 'My Jimmy's been so good to me, so understanding. Putting up with all my pranks.'
>
> Her voice was tender and glowed with a gentle happiness.
>
> 'He shot some possums and made a pair of fur-lined boots for me and, like a fool, I left them in London, never dreaming that I'd need them. When I've been blue with cold in Siberia I've thought of them. What wouldn't I have given to have them then! How he'll scold me when

he hears about it. And for getting thin. He'll fuss over me and make me eat all kinds of nourishing food to "fat me up" again when I get home.'

Roland wrote that this was a different Katharine, and she contrasted her with the Katharine she had met at Greenmount. There, she had been a little patronising to Hugo, had been inclined to brush him aside, while Hugo had been uneasy and nervous, excluded from all the things that she and Baracchi had discussed. 'Now she has learnt to recognise his worth and I do not think he will ever feel humiliated again.'

Baracchi and Roland said goodbye to Katharine – 'a thin, tired figure carrying a battered suitcase, hugging her coat around her in an effort to keep out the biting wind' – and watched her struggle up the gangway to her ship, the *Felix Dzerzhinsky*, on its last voyage to London before the Baltic froze over until the next spring.

Just before she left Moscow, Katharine posted a letter to Ric at Greenmount:

My Darling Little Son
I wonder did you hear me on the air last night? It would have been about 9 o'clock in the morning in Melbourne. You should have been listening. I know Daddy would have tried very hard to hear the broadcast.

I sent him 2 wires, really, one that was returned from Greenmount, Queensland.

Would you believe it – nobody knew Hugo Throssell, V.C.

I was so angry because I wanted Daddy to hear the message from me first thing on his birthday.

In about three days now, darling, I'll be leaving here and starting on my long journey home. It seems such a long way and such a long time.

But soon you'll be giving me hugs and kisses and I'll be telling you about everything.

17

Mafeesh

What is the market price of valour? In a medal and coin shop on Adelaide street the clerk said: 'No, we don't buy them. There isn't any demand.'

'Do many men come in to sell medals?' I asked.

'Oh, yes. They come in every day. But we don't buy medals from this war.'

'What do they bring in?'

'Victory medals mostly, 1914 stars, a good many M.M.'s, and once in a while a D.C.M., or an M.C. We tell them to go over to the pawnshops where they can get their medal back if they get any money for it.'

Ernest Hemingway, 'War Medals for Sale', *Toronto Star Weekly*, 8 December 1923

It is hard to discover when exactly Hugo had the biggest brainstorm of all: the idea to stage his very own rodeo to get himself out of debt and save the family home at Greenmount. It must have struck him forcibly not long after Katharine sailed to Russia, in May 1933. Perhaps he wanted to show her when she returned that he could still be a hero to her.

Hugo and Ric were desperately lonely together in the weeks after Katharine left. Ric had just celebrated his eleventh birthday when she waved goodbye. 'My Dad and I would have a bit of breakfast together; he didn't say much; turned over the pages of the *West* while he drank his coffee without his usual comments on the day's news', Ric wrote later. 'There were letters from London, Paris and Moscow. Photographs of curious shaven-headed youngsters at a Russian school; pictures of Katharine in ankle boots and a long cloth coat posing with a group of foreign writers with whom she travelled through Siberia . . . Katharine in earnest discussion with the director of the cinema train which took her through the Urals; Katharine in earnest discussion with the peasants on a collective farm; wearing proudly her Udanik medal for outstanding workers.' Ric said that the foreign letters and photographs somehow made being by themselves worse, serving simply to remind father and son that she wasn't there.

Once, they climbed out of bed early to hear Katharine broadcasting from Russia on a neighbour's short-wave wireless set. 'We managed to catch a few phrases among the crackles of static before her voice faded again into the senseless jungle whistle and chatter of the sound-waves. We walked down the hill, silent and disappointed. My father put his hand on my shoulder. "Never mind, old chap. She'll be home again soon," he said.'

Just before Katharine had departed, Hugo had been to the Repatriation Department for a check-up. The doctor had reported that he was 'very much improved but several nights since Anzac Day has noticed palpitations at night'. The nightmares of The Nek, Hill 60, Gaza and his brother's death had been triggered once again. Now, when those horrible nights returned, Katharine was not there to soothe and comfort him. He missed her sorely.

> He caught the train home from Perth in the evenings, gazing out the window trying to think as the narrow-gauge railway rattled through the succession of Perth suburbs. At least he didn't have to see those fool signs he had put up along the main road making a mug of a man. They were faded now, clattering loose in the wind:
>
> BLOCKS 4 SALE.
> EASY TERMS.
> HUGO THROSSELL AGENT . . .

All the same, if only things eased up a bit. He was sure that was the answer. It was the only way left now. It was good land, worth twice as much as he needed to pay off the bank. Some day it would be worth a packet. Anyone could see that. Not just for weekenders. People would be living in the hills and travelling down to Perth each day for work, instead of packing into the suburbs. Houses side by side. Red iron roofs. Picket fences. Backyards full of junk. It was rotten luck that money was so tight. If he could only persuade the bank that they just had to hang on for a bit.

Hugo knew he couldn't stave off the bank's threats of foreclosure by plodding away at his job as inspector of fertilisers. If only he could find a way to wipe out the debt before Katharine returned and surprise her with good news at last. In America, President Roosevelt had begun to introduce his New Deal, economic reforms to pull the nation out of depression. When he took the oath of office, on 4 March 1933, unemployment was at 25 per cent and the state governors had closed every bank in the country so that no one could cash a cheque or draw on their savings. The New Deal ignited a new feeling of optimism in the world. The top-grossing film was *Gold Diggers of 1933*, and soon everyone was humming the catchy new tune:

We're in the money,
We're in the money
We've got a lot of what it takes to get along!
We're in the money,
That sky is sunny
Old Man Depression you are through,
You done us wrong!

Hugo was seized by the mood. It took him over completely. He could be in the money again and shake off the depression. All he needed was a big attraction to get Perth people to travel up into the hills; then he'd be able to sell the blocks of land. His thoughts turned to a young visitor to Australia that he had met who had told him about the dude ranches in America, where ordinary people could pretend to be cowboys. The ranches had sprung up all over America since the end of the First World War, the interest spurred on by the popularity of Western movies and the huge growth in affordable automobiles that carried people away from the cities. Why not in Australia?

'The thought came back into his mind like a recurring dream', wrote Ric. 'Perhaps if he started a dude ranch, with trail rides through the hills, they'd come for the novelty of it. Cowboys in sombreros and leather chaps. Rides where there were good blocks going. You could use the brand name just as they did in America.'

The humble Greenmount cottage was to be transformed into the Lazy ⌶1T Ranch. Lazy H for Hugo; one for just one; T for Throssell. 'It had a real ring to it. And the more people you could get coming up from Perth the better the chance of selling the land. More and more excited by the proposition, he calculated that it would only take twenty or thirty sales to wipe out the four thousand pounds overdraft.'

Hugo threw himself into planning. 'As the scheme developed, the rodeo took more and more of his attention, until it became an end in itself. His original purpose was lost in everything that went into making a show.' Hugo had realised that simply a ranch name and riding horses wouldn't be enough. There would have to be a full-scale rodeo to attract the crowds: a Wild West show complete with buck jumping, cattle drafting, trick riding and lassoing, other animals on show, food, drink, music, a band. It had to be big! The ideas tumbled out of him and grew by the day both in scale and expense. He did not have much time. If the show was to attract the right crowds, everything would have to be ready when springtime was approaching, when the hills were green and the wildflowers were beginning to come out, the bush soon vibrant with red and green kangaroo paw and Katharine's favourite blue leschenaultia. It would be too late in summer, when the heat bounced upwards from the coastal plain, the hills were burnt brown and the bush was brittle, crackle dry and full of clinging bush flies. No one would come to Greenmount then, and no one would be in any mood to buy a bush block. They'd all be off to Perth's beaches to swim and surf. So timing was everything. He would work through the mild winter, get the acts and everything else together, and open his show early.

Hugo fixed the morning of Sunday 30 July 1933 as the official opening date. For two months he worked feverishly to put the extravagance together. He built stockyards on a wedge of land beside the creek that had a natural amphitheatre of steeply sloping land on three sides, which would house rough benches made from railway sleepers. Horse lines were put up in the triangle of land near the cottage. He bought horses for the ring events and steers for the buck jumping, ten ponies and riding hacks, a white donkey and a couple of mules, along with the saddlery. Hugo thought it a nice touch to name each animal after one of Katharine's novels or stories.

As he rushed along with his plans to organise the rodeo – which in his mind was approaching the greatest show on earth – his list of attractions, and his costs, grew. He had employed former soldiers to build the stockyards and other buildings, so now there were wages to be paid for half-a-dozen hands plus fees for the rodeo performers. He also had to buy stock feed, and refreshments for the crowds he expected would visit. And extra cash was needed for prizes, to attract the buck jumpers, stockmen and jackaroos, from farms and outback stations. Later, he added novelty events such as clay pigeon shooting, archery, hill climbing for motorcycles and sports cars, and stunt flying by an air force pilot to his list of attractions. A leaflet that Hugo had printed to advertise the event gives an idea of the size of the scheme; the erratic, rambling text indicates the strain he was under.

To All Horse Lovers,
The Lazy ⌶1T Ranch on the 13 m. peg, York Road, Greenmount, is now a going concern. The Journalistic branch of the R.S.L. is taking a hand,

and a proportion of profits. It has been arranged for the official opening to take place at 11 a.m. on Sunday, 30th July.

There will be Clay Pidgeon [*sic*] Shooting, the William Tell Act, and at 2.30, for those who fancy the smell of petrol, Motor Bike and Sporting Car Climbing Competitions, over the Freak Hill.

Some of the boys will try their hand with a Lassoo [*sic*] and Stock Whip. Black fellows will throw Kylies and make fires.

Barney, the *Butting Billy Goat*, may play his part, as may also *Bill the Bantam.*

The main attraction however, will be the Buck Jumping Exhibition.

Several horses with reputations are here. *Elsie the Kicking Mule* has arrived, so has *Clarice the Donkey*, with her half dozen mates. There are 4 steers that will find their way to Midland Junction if they can't buck off their brands.

The round yard has been erected in the Natural Amphitheatre beside the running creek.

Arthur Jones, who won the £25 Championship Cup at White City will ride, so will Curly Cooves, of 10th Light Horse fame, Snowy Watts and Nipper, the Kimberley Boy.

Send your Outlaws along; freight paid this end.

These lads guarantee to ride anything with hair on.

George Mellor and his R.S.L. Band will enliven proceedings.

Lunch and Afternoon tea available. Make certain of Turkey and Scalded Cream, by booking ahead.

Classy Trail Ponies are available at 2/6 per hour at all times. Considerable reductions for Parties and Week-days. Horses include old '*Abergwain*' second in Perth Cup and '*Lord Machree*' the noted Hurdler. '*Kiss on the Lips*', the skewbald stallion, leads the ponies, with '*Han*', the chestnut with silver tail and mane as favourite of his Harem, while '*Working Bullocks*', the mule, stands ready packed to take the turkey to the Luncheon Rendezvous, and a couple of Donks are available for the kiddies.

The honour of your presence pretty lady, pretty gentleman.

ONE CHARGE ONE BOB

HUGO THROSSELL

Hugo ignored both advice and pleading from his friends and his bank that he was getting out of his depth. Everyone shied away from the scheme, and nobody would invest in the venture, despite his efforts. He insisted that at the very least the investors would get their money back. No one believed him.

Soon, Hugo was so far committed to the rodeo that he could not pull out, even if he had wanted to. He thought that if he cancelled it now, it would be like throwing away what little money he had. He tried to convince the bank that his rodeo was worthy of another loan. The bank, however, demanded something practical as collateral. In desperation, Hugo offered the family's house and its surrounding block of about 1½ acres as additional security for the money, despite having promised Katharine before she went overseas that he wouldn't touch the house. But Hugo rationalised that he would be able to pay off this new loan from the first land sales before Katharine got home, so there was no risk.

He was still working for the Agriculture Department, hoping he would not be sent off on another country trip as inspector of fertilisers. There was no chance of being allowed to take paid leave in these tough times. In his office his colleagues were noticing that he seemed to be spending all of his time on his own rodeo business, making telephone calls, writing letters – not on the business of the department.

Hugo seems to have completely ignored or forgotten about officialdom, with its rules and regulations. A letter that he sent to the Greenmount road board asking it to level the public land near the front of his cottage, which he needed for his horse lines and visitors' parking, met with the frosty response that he should try the main roads board instead. But Hugo went ahead anyway and cleared the land, erecting a thatched 'kraal' and kiosk on it without waiting for official permission.

Then Hugo's foot was crushed by one of the horses he had corralled at his 'ranch'. The animal lent its full weight on it, breaking two of the small bones on the instep. He was forced to walk on crutches with his foot in plaster: he couldn't put any weight on it. The injury was so painful that he told Ric: 'By cripes it hurts old man. Worse than anything in the war'. At least it meant that he could take time off work from the department. He hobbled around their home writing letters, shouting down the telephone, trying to organise supplies, equipment, stock, and sorting out all of the other little details.

A few days before the opening, Hugo's negligence towards official permits began to catch up with him. Perhaps he should have known that the authorities would be onto him when he mentioned 'black fellows' in his flyer. On 28 July, AO Neville, the chief protector of Aborigines, wrote to Hugo:

> I understand that you are holding a Rodeo at Greenmount on Sunday next, and that included in the programme are several items in which the performers are natives.
>
> Allow me to point out that you do not appear to have obtained permission to employ natives in this capacity, and I would advise that it is a breach of the Aborigines Act to do so without first securing the necessary permit.

Then, on the eve of the rodeo's grand opening, he received a letter from the Greenmount road board ordering him to remove the 'kraal' and 'all buildings and temporary structures' from the land close to his cottage within seven days, as they were in contravention of building regulations.

One frantic letter from Hugo written on the eve of the opening survives. It was to his friend and neighbour Mrs Ross, who ran tea rooms just up from Greenmount.

> I have sent young Spurling down to Mrs Birch to say my spring-cart is on its way to collect cups and saucers as arranged, and we'd hire the trestles and copper as well, if available. He has just returned to say Mrs Birch told him to tell me that the Greenmount Progress Association held a meeting last night, and decided not to let anything out at all.

Didn't you tell me that you definitely fixed yesterday for the cups and saucers, and that the trestles were available and that the only thing in doubt was the copper?

Never mind now, but please act quickly as all shops will be closed in two hours. Ring Boans or anyone you can think of.

I'll hop down to town immediately with old Liz and ring you from Perth and pick up anything you can get hold of. Bolger didn't bring the copper, nor did Padbury's Store send the empty petrol tins as ordered; but leave this to me.

The three-poled tent is up and looks well. I've rung Millers for timber and Bloget can knock up a few tables in lieu of the trestles.

The truly devastating news, which also came about through Hugo's lax approach to officialdom, arrived early on the morning of the opening, Sunday 30 July. Police from Midland Junction dropped by to warn Hugo that as the rodeo was a Sunday performance no charge could be made for admission. He could take up a silver coin collection, but this must go to charity. They handed him a lawyer's letter that advised:

The holding of Sunday entertainments is regulated by the Police Act Amendment Act 1902, (2 Edward VII, No 31), and it is provided by Section 9 that if any person without the consent in writing of the Chief Secretary opens or uses any premises for public entertainment or amusement on a Sunday, and to which persons are admitted by payment of money, or by tickets sold for money, or if a charge is made for seats, or a collection of money is made, such person is liable on summary conviction to a penalty not exceeding £50.

As Hugo rode out to greet his visitors he must have known in his heart that he was ruined. But he sat erect, a proud Light Horseman again in the saddle, wearing a crisp white shirt with casually rolled sleeves, faded cord riding breeches and one of the gleaming tan riding boots that he had worn to Buckingham Palace seventeen years before. His other foot was in a white plaster cast.

Throughout the day he was everywhere – ringmaster, marshal, boss of the ranch – greeting important visitors from Perth, urging on his band of performers and pseudo-cowboys. It was a brave show of leadership.

About 2000 people flocked to the ranch that day. On the surface, the charade appeared a triumph. The local paper, the *Swan Express*, headlined it as: 'Greenmount's Greatest Day'. The report read:

> Beautiful weather last Sunday greeted the success of the greatest enterprise Greenmount has ever experienced when the Lazy Hit Ranch, upon which Mr. Hugo Throssell, V.C., has expended much money and labor, was opened to the public, for the purpose of assisting the funds of the R.S.L. and Greenmount charities.
>
> Though the event was an outstanding success, a loss was sustained owing to the heavy initial expenses; and a series of such functions is needed to fulfil the purposes of the promoter. We understand, however, that Captain Throssell is making personal donations towards the good objects referred to.
>
> There were about 2000 visitors, a greater number than has previously assembled on the Greenmount heights. Never before have so many motor cars been seen in Greenmount, and the parking along the side of the York road was quietly effected, although no traffic police were visible.
>
> Happy, laughing crowds wended their way from the station, having come by special train; buses were filled with visitors, and throughout the day cars brought their quota.
>
> During the morning and afternoon a 'plane droned overhead and executed graceful evolutions.
>
> Motor-cycles and racing cars roared and buzzed up the steep ascent to the top of Greenmount in the competition for two cups donated by Captain Throssell, these events being under different management.
>
> Prominent City men were loud in their praises of the attractions and sports provided by the enterprise of Captain Throssell, which they declared were the finest they had ever witnessed; and they are anxious for many more to be arranged.

> Only experts could have negotiated the bucking horses and the wild cows; a novice would have been quickly made a cot case, if nothing else befel him.
>
> A bounteous luncheon was dispensed in a large marquee, and pleasant afternoon teas were served.
>
> There was fun for all, old and young, who were offered their choice of hiring horses, archery, clay pigeon shooting, stock whip cracking, cattle branding, hill climbing events, bicycle racing, aboriginal kylie throwing, etc., and after an invigorating day on the hills they returned home pleasantly weary, leaving the heights and valleys to again drowse in the creeping shadows of eventide.

The daily press was equally enthusiastic. 'The Lazy H Ranch has come to stay, and on future fine Sundays it is assured of a large patronage', wrote one reporter for the *Daily News*. 'Captain Hugo Throssell, V.C. and his band of returned soldier helpers have struck upon a unique manner of entertaining Sunday pleasure seekers and as a result of yesterday's efforts, charity will benefit considerably.' Another reported: 'The novel programme presented certainly attracted large crowds and Mr Throssell is to be complimented on organising a novel and interesting attraction, the proceeds of which were donated to deserving purposes'.

But the most deserving cause of all, Hugo Throssell, did not receive a penny in profit for his labours. Not one block of land was sold. People, including whole families, had thrown only threepenny and six-penny coins into collection bins, many ignoring the 'one charge one bob' (shilling) proposed in the advertising dodger. Some had even scoffed the afternoon teas for free.

Ric wrote that during the day his father's face was drawn, there were hollows under his eyes, and his lips were tight. 'Mooning about in my cowboy outfit, I felt out of everything. I thought my Dad's foot must have been hurting him. He didn't say anything, just told me to see if I could give a hand somewhere, as if I were in the way.'

Not long afterwards, Hugo asked his son if he would like to go and stay with some friends, the Newmans, for a while. He explained that he wasn't going to be home much, that Mrs Newman would look after him and that he could go to school with her boys. Besides which, as Ric wrote, 'there wasn't much fun at home any more'.

Four days after the opening, Hugo wrote a delayed reply to the secretary of the Greenmount roads board about the order to remove the kraal, apologising and saying that he had been 'extremely busy on organization work and have been handicapped considerably with an accident to my foot. I am still under medical treatment from Colonel Juett, the bone specialist and Dr Buttsworth, the local doctor'. He went on:

> I very much regret to hear the Board's decision and if this ruling is maintained, it will necessitate quite a number of returned men who have been employed here for some time, loosing [*sic*] their jobs.
>
> Which please, is the building you wish me to remove? Do you refer to the bell-tents or to the picturesque booth which has attracted much attention?
>
> You will remember that you charged me 2/6 and granted me permission in writing last year to erect a 10x20 plain galvanised iron motor garage on this very same block, which was so unsightly that my wife gave me no rest until I had the thing removed.
>
> I do hope you will not force the issue and I certainly would have appreciated a hint from some of the members, who must have noticed some of the soldiers working for weeks on this job, that the Board had decided some time ago to have my structure removed, and saved me a great deal of expense in the matter in these very hard times.

As an almost pathetic postscript, Hugo added: 'I thank you, Sir, in staying your hand with regard to your threat to summons me for my non-payment of rates. As you are aware my annual rates to your Board are around the £70 mark, and that amount takes some finding'.

I hoped to have been able to have made some money by holding these healthy and happy Sunday afternoons on my property, and so pay off my indebtedness to you, but the Chief Secretary's Department notified me that permission was granted to charge last Sunday – only on condition that 100 per cent of profits were to be devoted to approved charities.

Two weeks after the rodeo's grand opening, Hugo received a letter from the director of the Department of Agriculture, EL Sutton:

With reference to your engagement in this Department's Inspector of Fertilisers etc. I regret having to advise that owing to the fact that the necessary money had not been provided in our estimates, it will not be possible to give you further employment.

Therefore, your engagement with this Department terminated on the 29th June, the date from which you were forced to absent yourself from the Office owing to an accident.

I certainly hope your foot is improving and that you will soon be able to use it again.

Hugo now was desperate. He had to keep the rodeos going in an attempt to sell his blocks of land. But he was attracting fresh enemies. Just as he received the sacking letter he wrote to his general practitioner, Doctor Buttsworth, asking for help.

The Chairman of the Greenmount Road Board has this morning called on me in an unofficial and friendly capacity to inform me a petition is being signed to compel me to close down my horse-lines owing to the frightful stench emanating there from.

Only yesterday a lieutenant in the Militia Forces congratulated me on the cleanliness of my lines and he has inspected them again this morning with equal satisfaction.

Three ladies examined the Ranch at my request today, one of whom served four years at the Base Hospital, Fremantle, with the Returned Soldiers, but could find no disagreeable odour, though my house is nearest to the source of complaint.

> The chairman, or any of us, could not discover one single fly, and although we sniffed hard, we could smell nothing but boronia and wattle-blossom, nor was one fly visible in the horse-lines, due probably to the fact that the fly-spray is used twice a day.
>
> I immediately, however, reported the matter to Health Inspector Toll of the Abattoirs and Inspector Grey at the Midland Town Hall, and invited them to visit the Lazy Hit at any hour.
>
> Excuse me for writing at length, please, but as Mrs Throssell is away in England, I am particularly anxious to avoid the possibility of any risk of our child contracting a foul disease.
>
> In the absence of disagreeable odours this morning I was informed that the major trouble occurred in the evenings, so could you find it convenient please, to inspect my lines at any hour tonight most suitable to you?
>
> The three rabbits that I'm holding on sale for a returned soldier, unemployed, with a sick wife and two children have, I understand been blamed for the nuisance. However they yielded no unpleasantness this morning, and I gave instructions for their immediate return to their unfortunate owner, if so desired by the petitioners.

Buttsworth duly called and afterwards gravely wrote a reassuring note: 'At your request I have inspected the horse lines in question. I have found them quite clean, and they do not constitute a danger to public health'.

Under pressure from all sides, Hugo mentioned nothing of it when he wrote a cheerful letter to Katharine just a week later, on 21 August, telling her to take her time in returning to Australia, even suggesting that she travel via New York. Perhaps he was trying to buy some time in the vain hope that he could somehow fight his way out of the mess.

> Katharine Prichard is fairly on the map and I'm proud to know her and call her my friend. One thing that I want to impress on you is not to hurry home and to take every advantage of getting the information you want.

> We are so well and happy that it would be a thousand pities for you to tear back and not see something of Hollywood and the doings which will be so helpful to you and your work, and don't forget that if your reports of the Bolshies is a favourable one that the wise guys will only be too ready to say that you scampered through the place in 5 minutes and could not possibly be in a position to form any opinion of the working conditions of such a vast country.

He told her that he had a 'million interruptions' but that 'this Lazy H is some hum-dinger'. He assured Katharine that 'things are going smoothly now', and the staff was by this time down to two stockmen and the Sunday helpers. He had put on another show, 'cutting out the band and the aeroplane and just concentrating as you would advise on buck-jumping, pure and simple', and had still attracted close to 2000 people. 'Everyone expressed themselves as delighted and now as there is very little expense attached to the concern we have decided to run the show every Sunday.' (He did not mention to Katharine quite how the show was being funded, or would be in the future.)

The letter to Katharine amounted to brave words. Officialdom was out to close down the show completely. Was this a political decision? Did Hugo have enemies at work within the government because of that speech he made back in 1919, or was it because his wife was well known as a communist? Or was it a combination of both? Whatever the reason, a letter dated 31 August from the Chief Secretary's Department arrived, informing Hugo that he could no longer even take up donations to keep his rodeo running. No money could be collected now in any shape or form. 'I would point out it is illegal either to make charge or solicit voluntary contributions in the absence of either being approved by the Hon. Chief Secretary . . . It is unlikely that permission to make a charge for admission to similar affairs in the future would be granted to you and the same applies to the taking up of a collection in any form.'

Hugo kept trying. On 9 September the Chief Secretary's Department wrote again:

> In reply to your application of the 8th instant, I hereby convey the permission of the Hon. Chief Secretary for a collection to be taken up at Sunday afternoon entertainments to be held at the Lazy H1T Ranch, Greenmount, subject to the condition that such entertainments must not commence before 2.30 p.m.
>
> This permission is given for the period ending 31st December this year, and is subject to withdrawal at any time at the discretion of the Minister.

Now they were restricting the hours of operation.

Hugo began to seize at straws. In mid September he turned to the Returned Sailors' and Soldiers' League of Australia proposing a joint venture at the ranch: a show that could extend into the evenings. He found it difficult to set down his expenses so far, but 'up to date I have tried it entirely on my own and have been handicapped by a crippled foot and lack of capital, with considerable opposition from the powers that be'. Nevertheless, he tried to sound optimistic: 'Apart from this, I have now sold my wheat farm for cash and so have every prospect of selling my Fermoy property at Northam'.

> My foot is mended and the show is a going concern. We have six donkeys, a number of decent buck-jumpers, two mules, a mob of cattle, shooting gear, gun cartridges, throwers and clay birds, a dozen decent hacks and ponies with necessary saddlery, bell-tents, an excellent buck-jumping yard with all necessary crushes and stock-yards combined, with seating accommodation, yards for a sheep-dog trial, ideal spot for a tennis court, creek cricket pitch etc, while the Freak Hill is declared by the W.A. Motor Bike Association and Sporting Car Club, to be ideal for their competitions.

On the opening day of the rodeo, he declared, over £70 had been taken at the gate and another £10 for afternoon tea. (Of course, it had all been donated.) There had also been sales from items like chocolates and oranges.

Hugo's imagination was now again in over-drive. Engineers had advised him that his creek could be dammed at no very great cost and that 'much could be done in the evenings throughout the summer'. Totally confused, totally desperate, his mind must have been in turmoil with yet another 'brainstorm'. Hugo's thoughts suddenly turned back to Gallipoli. That was it! People were always asking him what it was really like to be on the peninsula. Why, he could re-create a small slice of the Gallipoli landscape here in the hills of Perth. The soil on Greenmount wasn't the same – more red gravel than the yellow, crumbly clay of Russells Top or Hill 60 – but easy to dig. Trenches! Dugouts! Saps! The Lazy Hit Ranch could be turned into an Anzac war experience, of course without the bombs and without the horrors. But there could be shooting – yes, real shooting – down there by the creek.

Hugo wrote: 'It has also been suggested that the engineers might practice on digging trenches and a dug-out where war trophies could be exhibited and the public shoot from the trenches with a periscope rifle at disappearing targets across the creek – a la Gallipoli . . . A Gun Club could be formed . . . and I feel a good deal of money could be made for the Anzac House funds.'

There was no response from the league, which must have been dismayed. Who would want to be reminded of Gallipoli?

The rodeo eventually petered out. It was last advertised for 10 September but it seems it may have struggled on later, Ric writing that 'crowds dwindled as the heat of summer hit the hills'. The costs continued to mount. Hugo was forced to admit defeat and sell the gear and livestock for whatever he could get, so that he could pay off his two stockmen.

Hugo descended into despair. He retreated within himself. He left Ric with the Newmans, telling him that it wasn't too far to walk to school and that it was only until his mum came home, which wasn't long now. He promised to visit Ric whenever he could. At first, he couldn't face staying in the empty cottage at

Greenmount alone, amid the smoking ruins of his rodeo. He couldn't be bothered cooking for himself, either. So for two weeks he moved in with the homely Mrs Ross in the tea rooms up the hill. But then, concerned for both of their reputations, he moved back home. The electricity had been cut off, and there were final notices threatening to disconnect the telephone. Letters demanding payment tumbled out of the mailbox. On 4 October the National Bank of Australasia wrote:

> Further to our letter of 23 February last advising the Under Secretary of Lands had repeatedly written us regarding outstanding rates on this lease, we would advise he has again written us under date the 29th ulto that the amount of rates outstanding now are £26-15-8 and requesting a remittance of same. We understand that you had made arrangements regarding this overdue payment and we should be pleased with your advice so we can reply to their letter.

'I saw little of my father', recalled Ric.

> I would walk through the orchard after school . . . and find the house empty. I fossicked for Minties among what was left of the kiosk's supply of sweets in one of the big veranda cupboards; played with the remaining bows and arrows, or wandered aimlessly through the house just looking at the things I knew. There was strangely little comfort in a handful of free sweets. The house was a lonely place.

One day there was a letter for Ric in the mailbox from his mother, blissfully unaware of the catastrophe at home, dated 16 October and written from Moscow:

> My Darling Little Sunny Bunkin
> I arrived back here from Siberia the day before yesterday & yesterday got my letters 2 from you and 3 from Dad.
>
> I nearly ate them. A month since I heard from you. Dad will tell you all about the wonderful things I've been doing here – going down coal mines at midnight and for aeroplane rides.

Katharine prattled on about her visit to a children's theatre. She added: 'Kiss Dad, for me – and look after you both, won't you? – because I simply couldn't bear it if you weren't both quite well'.

On 9 November, Hugo presented himself at the Repatriation Department for a check-up. Doctor S Herriot made notes:

> Not sleeping well – heart feels too big, occasional palpitation on exertion – dull pain in left side of chest.
>
> Right eye occasional pain.
>
> Has ague at times, usually at sundown. Gets very tired back of neck, usually noticed after exertion.
>
> Is financially worried.
>
> History obtained with greatest of difficulty. Does not wish to discuss his complaints.
>
> Improvement since last review has been nil.
>
> Unemployed – has only worked Agricultural Bank 10 weeks and run a few rodeos during past year.
>
> Nervousness and inability to sleep.
>
> Introspective but has apparently good control of himself.

One Saturday early in November, Hugo made arrangements to meet Ric in Perth for a day's outing together. It was the first time his son had seen him in weeks. Hugo told him he would meet him off the bus, as he had some business to attend to in the city first.

That morning Hugo took a leather case from the jarrah chest of drawers in the front bedroom. The drawer was filled with Katharine's bits and pieces, her mother's silver brooch, her amber beads. In the case was his VC medal, dark bronze lying on yellowed cotton wool, crimson ribbon crumpled and twisted. Hugo put it in his pocket and caught the train down from the hills.

Later, Hugo went to the bus station and met his son. They walked together to the Ambassador Picture Theatre, a place with a red-carpeted stairway, heroic plaster statues, artificial stars in a night sky when the lights went down, and a mighty wurlitzer organ that rose from under the stage to play triumphantly happy tunes before the pictures began.

Strangely, Hugo paid for their two seats in the cinema. It was strange because all First World War VC recipients held a gold pass in the shape of the medal, which entitled them and their families to lifetime free admission to many theatres and variety venues. Perhaps Hugo had sold the pass to give him enough money to pay for a whole day's treat for his son.

> I sank into the lounge seat and waited impatiently for the film to begin. My father was sitting silently beside me. It was good to be with him. I looked round to him happily. He seemed miles away, staring. He didn't know I was there. Later, when the lights had gone down and the film had begun, he took my hand.
>
> 'Do you love your old Dad, son?' he asked me. Of course I did. He knew that. And anyway you shouldn't talk during the film should you?
>
> The pawnbroker had offered him ten shillings for the Victoria Cross. The knowledge of his failure overwhelmed him.

18

Last Post

The tumult and the shouting dies;
The Captains and the Kings depart;
Still stands Thine ancient sacrifice,
An humble and a contrite heart.
Lord God of Hosts, be with us yet,
Lest we forget – lest we forget!

Rudyard Kipling, 'Recessional', 1897

ON SATURDAY 18 NOVEMBER 1933, HUGO made a new will, naming George Withers, the city accountant, his estate's sole executor. He bequeathed everything to Katharine. On the back of the will he wrote: 'I have never recovered from my 1914–18 experiences and with this in view, I appeal to the State to see that my wife and child get the usual war pension. No man could have a truer mate'.

George, Hugo's brother-in-law, was concerned about Hugo's mental state. He decided to accompany Hugo home after he made his new will in the city and spent that night with him at Greenmount. Withers had experienced Hugo's fluctuating moods: 'He was very subject to brain storms, a very little excitement would upset him . . . He had one of these brain storms and threatened he would never come to my home again. He used to dread going to bed as he had the most horrible thoughts as soon as he would lie down'. Later, Withers described the evening of 18 November:

On arrival there were two other men at the house named Douglas Dickson and Harry Welsh who had come to assist to burn the grass around the house which was completed about 7.30 p.m. that evening.

The deceased drew my attention to his madness in starting his Rodeo Stand which he called Throssell's Folly. He said the expenses were very heavy and ran him further into debt. He said if he had any pluck he would blow his brains out.

He said his wife left everything in perfect order when she left and there was no need for him to start the Rodeo and 'I was mad to do it'.

He seemed very worried as to what she would think when she came back from England where she was at the time.

He said she would find everything in a muddle and he was far better out of it.

Later we went up to the 'Log Cabin' and had tea there about 8 p.m. and stayed to midnight.

After tea he seemed a little brighter and was telling fairy tales to Mrs Ross's child.

About 11 p.m. we had a cup of tea and left for home at midnight.

He asked me where I wished to sleep. I said on the veranda.

He gave me a couple of rugs and then he went away and had a shower and rub down and said how fresh it made him feel. He then told me how good it was for me to come up and stay with him, and said good night and stated that he was going to sleep in his wife's room.

These were the last words I heard him speak.

✠

Early on the morning of Sunday 19 November Hugo got out of bed in the front room of his home. He reached behind a hook in the hallway and felt beneath his old officer's overcoat for the holster. Carefully, he removed his army-issue .455-inch Mk IV Webley pistol, broke it open to check that all the chambers were loaded, then swung open the flywire door and stepped outside across the bare jarrah boards of the back veranda.

There were magpies carolling at the dawn from the gum trees around the cottage and kookaburras chuckling and laughing from the bush below. Hugo glanced at the garden, past the rose bushes to the writer's cottage he had built for his beloved Katharine. She could keep writing now undisturbed; there was no need to worry about him any more.

He settled in a deckchair, bare feet up on the veranda's handrail, and put the gun to his right temple.

One shot.

A momentary shocked silence.

Then a flurry of wings and the sound of crows cawing in alarm in the distance.

Withers found Hugo shortly after ten past eight. While Hugo had been sleeping in the back bedroom, opening to the back veranda, George had been sleeping at the front of the house, on the front or side veranda. He had expected Hugo to call him early, to help with some more burning-off around the cottage, but as there was a strong wind blowing he had assumed the task had been postponed. Strangely, he hadn't heard the noise of the gunshot.

> When I got up I went out to look for him. I found his bed had been occupied then I went about the yard searching for him. Not finding him I came back into the house, opened the passage door and found him lying in the deck chair in his pyjamas with his feet up upon the lattice work and a big wound on the side of his right temple.
>
> A revolver was in his right hand resting on his right shoulder. A large pool of blood was on the veranda and he was still bleeding and breathing heavily.
>
> I was stunned at first and called to him but got no reply. I then rang the telephone exchange and asked to be put on to a doctor. Dr. Rockett replied and I asked him to come along as quickly as possible and described how to find the place.

Rockett arrived at Greenmount. He later described what happened next: 'He was still alive on my arrival. There were three or four pints of blood on the veranda and deck chair. With Mr Withers' aid I removed him to a couch where he expired about ten minutes later. I then found the bullet lying on the veranda behind the chair. I then found the note in the book case'. Hugo had left a note on a shelf next to Katharine's books: 'I can't sleep. I feel my old war head. It's going phut, and that's no good for anyone concerned'.

Rockett had known Hugo for twenty or thirty years and was aware that he had suffered from meningitis, which frequently caused 'deranged mentality and patients frequently suffer from fits of depression and a little worry is frequently exaggerated'.

At Greenmount now there was nothing else George Withers or Dr Rockett could do until Constable William Brooke arrived and removed the body to the West Midland morgue in Mr Snell's mortuary van.

In 1933 funerals were usually conducted as soon as possible after a death.

The next morning the *West Australian* ran the headline: 'War Hero's Death: Late Capt H. Throssell V.C. Found with Bullet Wound in Head'. The news flashed across Australia by press telegram and around the world by cable.

Ric was staying with an aunt at the Newman family's big house. At first his gentle aunt, comforting him between her sobs, had told the eleven-year-old that 'Daddy's had an accident, Ric'. The son later remembered thinking that his father must be in hospital, perhaps after a smash. Perhaps he might have been blinded. His dad would now expect him to be a brave boy and look after him until 'Mum comes home'.

They seem to have hidden the truth from Ric who, the next day was left alone in the house with a cousin, while the rest of the family went out, probably to the funeral. It was only then Ric discovered the newspaper with its stark headlines folded on the arm of a chair. 'My father was dead. I ran out of the house and fell crying and crying on the grass.'

The death notice read: 'On November 19, 1933 at Greenmount, Hugo Vivian Hope Throssell, the dearly beloved husband of Katharine and devoted father of Ric. Youngest son of the late Hon. George Throssell. Aged 49 years'. The obituary said that since his return from active service Hugo had been 'in indifferent health and the circumstances of his death indicated he was suffering severely from old war injuries'. The military funeral and burial were to be held that very afternoon.

Frantic cables had been sent to Katharine in London, on her way home from Moscow, but they were somehow delayed in finding her. It isn't clear exactly how she discovered the news. One story says she was alone in a boarding house and learnt from a newspaper that he was dead; another has it that she read it on a news poster while on a bus. But for years afterwards she nursed a terrible doubt, which she eventually confided to Ric. She had left the unfinished manuscript of her novel *Intimate Strangers* in her workroom at Greenmount. Perhaps Hugo had seen it there and read it, and had understood himself to be the unwanted husband, Greg. In the original version Greg killed himself. In the version Katharine published, in 1937, she changed the ending. Elodie discovers Greg asleep with a half-finished suicide note and a revolver by his side. She wakes him up, and there is a happy ending.

In real life, at around the same time that Katharine was reading of Hugo's death, his funeral was commencing at the Karrakatta Cemetery in Perth. About seventy of his former comrades from the 10th Light Horse lined up alongside a host of military and civic dignitaries, and two other First World War heroes from Western Australia: Jimmy Woods of the 48th Battalion and Tom Axford of the 16th Battalion, both of whom had been awarded the VC for their gallantry during the fighting in France in 1918. The *West Australian* covered the story:

> At the cemetery gates a firing party drawn from the Royal Australian Artillery stood with reversed arms as the hearse passed between its ranks to the waiting gun-carriage, which was drawn by four horses and

manned by members of the permanent Army Service Corps. Reverently the flag-draped coffin was lifted on to the gun-carriage and the pathetic souvenirs of the late Captain Throssell's active service – his Victoria Cross and other war service medals, his weather-beaten plumed Light Horse hat and sword were placed on top of it . . .

Then at a slow march the sad procession moved to the graveside. At the head of the cortege marched the firing party, carrying their arms reversed. Then came two trumpeters, the chaplain, and the bearer-party, comprising warrant-officers of the Australian Instructional Corps. The gun-carriage with its burden followed, the pall-bearers marching and a sergeant of the Army Service Corps riding beside it. Behind came a party of police, led by Inspector McLernon and then the men of the 10th Light Horse who had fought with Captain Throssell at Gallipoli and in Palestine. They were led by Captain J. A. B. Phillip. Many of them showed the scars of war, and not a few came on crutches, showing that even the disability of a lost limb could not keep them from paying a last tribute to their old comrade. In the ranks of the great crowd that followed behind were members of Parliament, representatives of the legal profession, the sheep and wheat industries, business houses, returned soldiers' organisations, and other bodies. Save for the clanking of trace-chains and the half-muffled hoof-beats of the horses, the long procession moved in deep silence. Light rain fell as the cortege drew up at the graveside. Someone offered the chaplain the protection of an umbrella, but he brushed it aside, and the rain streamed down his surplice. Water dripped, too, from the shrubs on to the flag-covered coffin . . .

In the course of a simple and impressive address at the graveside, Mr. Collick [the chaplain] said that all present had come to lay at rest a beloved friend and a brave man. 'We all know the circumstances of his death,' he said. 'It was very sad, but you can all be sure that he did not know what he was doing. He suffered from meningitis after being wounded and he was never the same afterwards. He was a man of too high a courage and with too great an idea of devotion to duty to have done what he did while knowing what he was about. He died for his country just as surely as if he had perished in the trenches.' All sections of the community and representatives of other churches, the chaplain

> continued, had expressed to him their grief at the loss of a brave man and a Christian gentleman. 'His gallantry in action earned for him the distinction of being the first West Australian to be decorated with the Victoria Cross – the highest military honour the King has the power to bestow,' he concluded. 'It is with deep regret that we lay to rest such a fine type of West Australian. As you place your tributes on the grave say with me, "Father forgive him, for he knew not what he did".'
>
> At the conclusion of the address the last post was sounded, the firing party fired three volleys over the grave and the trumpeters then sounded the reveille. The firing party then presented arms and the service was at an end.

And so Hugo Throssell was laid to rest – as he rests today – in Grave 304 in the Anglican section of the Karrakatta cemetery in Perth. Today a patch of sand bordered by grey granite blocks with fading letters on a weathered granite headstone.

On 11 December, following an inquest into Hugo's death, the coroner found that he 'came to his death at his residence, York Road, Greenmount by a bullet wound on the head self-inflicted whilst his mind was mentally deranged due to war wounds on 19th November, 1933'. An examination of his financial affairs later showed that he had owed nearly £10,000 and had just £11 10s 7d in the bank.

Extraordinarily, Doctor CW Courtney of the Repatriation Department disputed the coroner's finding the following year in a review: 'Despite the Coroner's finding it is probable that constitutional and post-war factors were mainly responsible for death by suicide. If war service were a contributory factor, the degree of such contribution would not be greater than 25 per cent in my opinion'. He suggested seeking another opinion, but this action was apparently not pursued.

Katharine quickly leapt to her late husband's defence:

> The facts, I think, are well known. Nervously and physically, my husband's magnificent constitution was impaired as a result of war service.

The Medical Board has the record of his wounds and periods in hospital for meningitis and malaria; but I resent the idea that his mind was in any way deranged. He feared that it might become so.

When he was first employed, as soldiers' representative on the Land Settlement Board, and had a full time job, he never suffered from the depression which assailed him when it became a one day a week engagement. After the war, he was left with obligations on his own and his brother's farm to meet, and tried desperately and in many ways to fulfil them. The Returned Soldiers' League executive was directly responsible for the loss of even this one day's work a week – as the file in relation to its contemptible action on that occasion will show.

Since then, my husband suffered, at recurring intervals from sleeplessness and the pressure of financial anxieties. On two occasions we consulted Dr Alfred Webster and he was several times examined by officers of the Medical Section of your Department. In November 1932, after an incident which foreshadowed what has happened, a temporary appointment was found for him in the Agricultural Department, and immediately his health improved. When that appointment was withdrawn, he attempted to earn a living by organising a rodeo in the hills. In my absence, he was not able to withstand the torture of another crisis of sleeplessness and financial embarrassment.

I am convinced that he believed he would be insuring a pension to me and my son by his last act – although he had promised me that this would never happen.

I consider that his 'grateful country' made it impossible for my husband to live. He thought he had to die to provide for his wife and child. As far as I am concerned, I could not accept anything that cost him his life; but I feel I have no right to interfere with what he sought to do for his son.

My own health is uncertain and I may not be able to provide for our boy who is eleven years old.

But she would live a long and extraordinary life after the tragedy.

Katharine arrived home in Australia on Boxing Day 1933, just over a month after Hugo's funeral. Customs and police met her on board the SS *Baradine* at Fremantle. In a secret memorandum they reported to the Investigation Branch of the Attorney-General's Department in Perth that 'the examination of Mrs Throssell's luggage was conducted privately and without any undue unpleasantness'. The following month, in turn the director, HE Jones, wrote to a blacked-out address, presumably in Canberra: 'Mrs Katharine Susannah Throssell arrived in Fremantle on 26 December 1933. Her baggage was carefully searched and only three novels in Russian were found. She also had some copies of International Press Correspondence, which is on our prohibited list, and these were confiscated. It may interest you to know that her husband, Captain Throssell VC, committed suicide last November'.

Katharine nursed her grief in her own way. She had already earlier in her life endured the heartbreak of her father's suicide – and now her husband had taken his own life, too. The writer Henrietta Drake-Brockman, who knew her well, said, 'Katharine Susannah Prichard was called on to exercise the fortitude with which she had so often endowed her characters; there was her son to bring up, her husband's debts to pay. Outwardly she never faltered, although for some time she was unable to return to creative work'. Her son wrote, 'Like the bush creatures she loved, Katharine kept her wounds to herself, hidden away in some secret place until the hurt was healed. She felt too deeply for it to be seen by others. It was impossible for her grief to become a public display. Only to the closest friends would she sometimes speak of the tragedies in her life and, later, to me'.

The official watch kept on Katharine intensified as she threw herself into her work for the Communist Party. 'Only my belief in the need to work for the great ideas of Communism and world peace helped me to survive a grief so shattering', she later wrote.

She remained a complete and unwavering communist until the day she died, rejecting any criticism of Russia or the Soviet Union as 'capitalist propaganda'. Her granddaughter Karen, who visited Greenmount as a teenager, remembered sharing a bedroom with a bust of Stalin. Katharine also campaigned for causes ranging from Aboriginal rights to a nuclear-free southern hemisphere.

Katharine lived in the cottage at Greenmount for most of her life, except for a period during the Second World War when she moved to Sydney and became a member of the Central Committee, the Communist Party's main policy body. Afterwards, she returned to Perth, drawn by the hills. She managed to sell some of the surrounding blocks of land to prevent foreclosure on the Greenmount property, thus saving the cottage for her home base.

By the time Katharine published her autobiography, in 1963, she was recognised for at least thirteen novels, three collections of short stories, a book-length children's tale, a travel book, two plays and two collections of verse. She had been translated into at least thirteen languages, and the number of articles, essays and political polemics that she wrote were legion. In 1951 her admirers nominated her for the Nobel Prize for Literature.

In 1964, Katharine suffered a stroke. This paralysed her right hand, but undeterred she taught herself to write with her left hand, and later with her right again, but needed some help with the typing of her manuscripts.

Late in life she befriended the young pianist David Helfgott, who visited the cottage on Fridays and played for her on the family's upright piano.

Katharine had an idea of how history would remember her. She carried out a systematic combing and burning of her personal papers at Greenmount towards the end of in her life, a task that was completed by her son. She destroyed most of Hugo's letters to her and even her own father's love letters to her mother. But voluminous amounts of material remained, and they form one of the great collections of the National Library of Australia.

Katharine died on 2 October 1969, shortly before her eighty-sixth birthday. She had a communist funeral with the red flag with its hammer and sickle covering her coffin, and an armful of blue leschenaultia on top. Members of the Throssell family who attended were surprised to find themselves singing 'The Internationale' from what they had thought was a hymn sheet. Her body was cremated and her ashes scattered in the Greenmount hills, where she and Hugo had lived and loved and ridden their horses together. According to Ric, she had once written that it would be good to become part of the earth and 'perhaps nourish a wild flower'.

Ric sold the Greenmount property after Katharine died, and it passed through the hands of a couple of private owners before lobbying by Katharine's friends and the Fellowship of Australian Writers led to its purchase by the state and the establishment of the Katharine Susannah Prichard Foundation, in 1984. The cottage is now known as 'Katharine's Place' and, with additional studios outside, is run as a writers' retreat. There is no sign that it was once also the home of Hugo Throssell. His memorial at Greenmount is quite separate, a small shelter, perhaps where the 'kraal' once stood, built almost diagonally opposite the cottage and alone on public land.

Afterword

THE SAD LITTLE BOY WHO HAD learnt the details of his father's death from a newspaper never quite got over it and went on to have a tragic life of his own.

Hugo's old schoolmates from Prince Alfred College had set up a fund to pay for Ric's school fees, and later Ric would present Wesley College with his father's sword, the tip of the blade deliberately blunted, specifically for safe keeping and as a symbol of peace. He went on to teachers' college on another scholarship before enlisting in the Army in 1941 and then was accepted as a cadet diplomat in the Department of Foreign Affairs.

Canberra decided it would be a good idea to post Ric to the Australian delegation in Moscow; he had an entree as the son of an idealistic Bolshevik. Unlike his mother, Ric was not enamoured of Russia, and this posting haunted him for the rest of his working life of over forty years; his first wife, Bea Gallacher, became ill and died painfully in hospital from a little-known disease called polyneuritis.

Later in Canberra, he developed a love of the theatre, which he may have inherited from Hugo. Ric went on throughout his life to enjoy being an actor, producer, director and playwright with the Canberra Repertory Theatre. He wrote some twenty-three plays, including *For Valour* based on his father's tragedy, as well as three novels and editing three volumes of his mother's articles, speeches and stories. As well as writing the biography *Wild Weeds and Wind Flowers* about Katharine, Ric also wrote his own autobiography, *My Father's Son*, in which he tried to come to terms with his father's suicide, and detailed his own life and persecution by using Freedom of Information laws to explore ASIO records held in the National Archives.

Ric had remarried, and after a further overseas posting to Brazil he returned to Canberra with his small family to serve in External (later Foreign) Affairs for the next thirty-one years. But he was not sent overseas again for twenty-eight years – suspicious years of relentless surveillance by the authorities.

In 1954 came the Petrov Affair. The Menzies Government granted political asylum to a Soviet diplomat, Vladimir Petrov, who admitted to being a spy and named names, including those of the Throssells, mother and son. Ric was called before the subsequent Petrov royal commission and quizzed about his contacts with Russians in Australia. The commission cleared him of spying but he remained under suspicion throughout the rest of his career, fighting to clear his name.

When Ric was eventually posted overseas again as a diplomat in 1980, he decided to put his father's VC into safe custody and was astonished to find it was then valued at $25,000 for insurance purposes. Four years later Ric decided on a controversial action – donating Hugo's VC to the People for Nuclear Disarmament. He wanted it to become known as the Peace Cross. Ric declared Australia could become a 'sanctuary for sanity'. 'My father believed he fought in 1914–18 in a war to end all wars. At the victory parade in 1919 he declared his commitment to peace', he said. The People for Nuclear Disarmament would use the money raised by the sale of the medal to bring the case for neutrality to Australians' attention.

The decision caused an immediate public furore. The RSL immediately jumped in and offered $38,000 so that the VC could be placed in the Hall of Valour of the Australian War Memorial in Canberra alongside another 34 VCs then on display. But the national president, Sir William Keyes, was fearful that the figure might not be enough if the medal went up for auction. Others rallied to a national fundraising appeal.

Eventually the Throssell VC was sold for $42,000, with many small donations contributing to the purchase, including $4250 from the 10th Light Horse Regiment itself. Two members of the regiment were present when the medal was handed over to the Australian War Memorial on Remembrance Day, 1984. The People for Nuclear Disarmament spent the money on making an anti-nuclear film called *The Pursuit of Happiness*.

There is a bitter irony in the value of a VC today, remembering Hugo's vain attempt to pawn his medal in the depths of the depression and being offered only ten shillings for it. The last privately owned Gallipoli Victoria Cross, awarded to Captain Alfred Shout, was sold at auction on 24 July 2006 for $1.2 million. It was purchased by Kerry Stokes, who presented it to the Australian War Memorial. The nine Australian Gallipoli VC medals, including the Throssell VC, went on a national tour in 2010. They were insured for $15 million.

Fresh speculation around Ric and spying arose in 1996 with the release of the so-called Venona cables, the secret US intercepts of Soviet diplomatic cables, and Ric took legal action against a major newspaper over its allegations about him. His daughter Karen has also been forced to defend her father more recently.

Ric's wife Dodie was seriously ill with cancer when she died at home in Canberra on 21 April 1999. Ric chose to die with her on the same day. He was 76. A death notice read bitterly: 'Did any Australians suffer more from our resident McCarthys?'

Comrades in Arms

The four men who were awarded the Distinguished Conduct Medal fighting alongside Hugo Throssell at Hill 60 all survived the First World War.

Brooke Stanley became a successful dairy farmer in Western Australia after having first carved out his land from a raw bush block. In later life, he studied Braille and translated books for blind students, becoming a powerful advocate for returned servicemen and the Farmers Union. He wrote his lively memoirs, together with a fiftieth anniversary history of his small country church, before his eventual peaceful death in 1969 aged seventy-seven.

Harry Macnee finished the war as a commissioned officer with a Military Cross, and went back to Broome to own a fleet of pearlers, including *Kim*, *Claudius*, *Warrawong* and *Betty Margaret*. He also became a member of the WA Transport Board before dying in 1960 aged seventy-three.

William Henderson was also commissioned and after the war became general secretary of the RSL in Melbourne before dying of illness in 1921 at just forty-one, after only a short time in the job.

Tommy Renton's leg was amputated at the thigh and took thirteen months to heal. He also survived a heart attack in hospital. Yet he battled on back in Australia, working at odd jobs, including being a nightwatchman in a factory, until he died aged seventy-seven in 1944.

Tom Kidd – the 'Bomb Proof Kidd' – survived the First World War and went on to serve as an air raid warden in the Second World War. He was still fighting (in this case the Repatriation Department over pension matters) when he eventually died in 1957 as a much loved great-grandfather aged seventy-eight. His ashes were scattered in a rose garden, which is today only a short walk from his friend Hugo's grave.

Dr James Bentley was Mentioned in Dispatches for his work on Gallipoli. Later he served in France, and he was awarded the Military Cross for conspicuous service in the field. He was recalled in 1918 to become medical superintendent at the Claremont Hospital and was later appointed Inspector General for the Insane – he would be in charge of five mental institutions during a long and distinguished career as a psychiatrist. Dr Bentley died in Perth aged eighty-two.

Big John Macmillan returned to Victoria to settle at Metung. He suffered from 'foot drop' for the rest of his life, caused by nerve damage from his wound at Hill 60. He always required a stick to walk, but when Melbourne had a police strike, he became so incensed he offered his services as a special constable and was seen ably directing traffic in Swanston Street, supported by his stick. He died in 1950 aged eighty-one.

Lieutenant Colonel Tom Todd, CMG, DSO and Bar, the one-time New Zealand All Black who had introduced Katharine to Hugo, survived the war, sickness and being wounded at Gaza only to die of heart failure while on leave in Cairo in January 1919. He was forty-five. Among his effects shipped home to a brother were a guitar and a set of bagpipes.

Colonel Noel Brazier retired with his bung eye back to Capeldene, his farm in Western Australia's south-west, there to breed horses and to take up his pen. For years the peppery old colonel would fire off letters aimed at the men he felt were responsible for the 'bloody murder' at The Nek. In the early 1930s he became a passionate supporter of a move for Western Australia to secede from the Commonwealth. A gruff character well-known around Perth, he would eventually die in 1947 aged eighty.

Brazier's nemesis, the Brigade Major Jack Antill, 'The Bullant', was promoted to brigadier general after Gallipoli and went on to serve with the Light Horse in the Sinai. Showing what was called a 'lack of quick decisive action', he was set on to France to command infantry on the Western Front, but his health broke down and he returned to Australia. He retired as a major general, laden with suitable honours, and died in 1937 aged seventy-one, after co-authoring a play with his daughter called *The Emancipist*.

Brigadier General Frederick Hughes would also retire as a major general and, after evacuation from Gallipoli due to sickness, would busy himself around Melbourne with business and civic affairs. He died in 1944 aged eighty-six.

General Sir Alexander Godley, who presided over both The Nek and Hill 60, outlived both these subordinates, dying in Oxford in 1957 aged ninety. His career after Gallipoli included being responsible for yet another disastrous attack at Passchendaele.

Memorials

A visitor to Western Australia today has to search long and hard to find a memorial to Hugo Throssell, VC. There is his final resting place, of course, beyond the manicured green lawns and rose beds of Perth's Karrakatta Cemetery. He lay in a bare and unkempt sandy grave with a barely legible headstone, which has since been tended to. There are no bugle calls at this grave on Anzac Day, no red poppies laid here on Remembrance Day. Dry and withered flowers in a plastic container and a small faded Australian flag stuck in the sand at one corner of the grave are the only signs that this one is different from the rectangles of sand that surround it, the only evidence to show that a few people from today's world, amateur historians, have sought him out. At Greenmount on 24 February 1954 the strange isolated granite and tile shelter was opened by the general officer commanding the army in Western Australia, Major General Rudolph Bierwirth. The shelter has a plain cast plaque. It was a long time coming: in 1936, Katharine suggested to the local council that a memorial tablet and fountain be erected on the spot.

In 1998 a group of Northam citizens led by Lloyd Nelson decided it was time to give Hugo a memorial. Their vision was to have a life-size statue of the hero overlooking the main thoroughfare through the town. But they ran into opposition. As Nelson said: 'Memories are very long in country towns. They never forget. If you took a vote, half would be for him and half against'.

Eventually, on 28 August 1999, the governor of Western Australia, Michael Jeffery, officially unveiled the Hugo Throssell VC Memorial. It is a modest affair: a plain cream-brick structure, barely chest high, carrying the legend 'Courageous in War. Steadfast in Peace', near the spot where Hugo made his 1919 speech. In March 2012 the Shire of Northam, after more debate, decided to rename the Avon Mall the 'Hugo Throssell Walk'.

Northam also holds a splendid portrait of Hugo painted by a visiting Scot portrait painter Duncan McGregor Whyte, who came to Australia between 1916 and 1921 and accepted commissions.

The portrait has not been exhibited publicly for some time and is in storage in the local Arts Centre.

In 2010 a memorial plaque was unveiled at nearby Jennacubbine at the place where Hugo once rode with the Jennacubbine Mounted Rifles before the First World War. The re-enactors from the 10th Light Horse Bunbury Troop took part, including Kay Fry, the great-niece of Captain Phil Fry, killed at Hill 60. The Fry family are today firm friends with the family of Trooper Brooke Stanley, who won the D.C.M. at Hill 60. Descendents of both families have ridden together in Anzac Day parades.

When Colonel Noel Brazier returned from the war he built himself a sundial on Capeldene, his property near Kirup. The Brazier family has had the sundial rebuilt with new memorial plaques to the colonel and one of his sons, Arthur, who died as a prisoner of the Japanese in the Second World War. The memorial was unveiled in 2012 with members of the present-day 10th Light Horse taking part.

The Tenth Light Horse

The Tenth Light Horse still exists and proudly remembers its hero, Hugo Throssell.

A Squadron 10th Light Horse is today an Army Reserve armoured unit, part of 13th Brigade based at the large Irwin Barracks at Karrakatta, an inner Perth suburb. A portrait of Hugo, together with his citation, hangs in a place of honour in the 'Throssell V.C. Club', where soldiers from the 13th Brigade get together and welcome visitors – including, quite recently, Corporal Benjamin Roberts-Smith, awarded the Victoria Cross for his gallantry in Afghanistan. In August 2011, A Squadron hosted an inaugural dinner to honour The Nek, which now promises to be an annual event. Officers of the squadron served the soldiers in recognition of past sacrifices.

In Perth's King's Park there are three Honour Avenues of flowering gums, beneath each of which is a plaque honouring a Western Australian soldier who was killed and buried in a foreign field.

The original concept of the avenues was to provide bereaved spouses, parents and relatives from all over the state with a place to grieve their loss. Ric Throssell has his own tree, but Hugo died at home, so was not eligible. However, in 2003 it was decided that Hugo should have his own tree; he died for his country, after all.

And so, every year, on the Sunday before Anzac Day, the troopers of today's 10th Light Horse Regiment make their way down the Honour Avenues to the granite obelisk that is the memorial to the 10th. They call it the 'Old Boys Parade'. After a service, the youngest trooper steps forwards and lays a sheaf of wheat at the foot of the memorial, in recognition of the horses who never returned. Then the parade moves to a giant pine tree alone about 15 yards behind the obelisk. There, another soldier steps forwards and places a small bunch of flowers on a plaque that reads: 'In Honour of Lt Hugo V.H. Throssell, Victoria Cross, 10th Light Horse Regiment. Awarded for Gallantry Hill 60, Gallipoli, 1915. Dedicated by Members of 10 L.H.'

EPILOGUE

Çannakale

The benign sea sighs
Now, it's just blood red poppies
On those young boys' graves.

Crumbling cottages
How many young sons were ploughed
Into that black soil?

Cigarettes, chocolates
Trench-tossed instead of bombs
That is the real message.

– Karen Throssell

Karen Throssell, granddaughter of Hugo and Katharine, wrote this verse after she visited Gallipoli in 2008 as an Australian peace ambassador at the invitation of Emine Erdoğan, wife of the Turkish prime minister.

Acknowledgements

AN EXTRAORDINARY NUMBER OF KIND PEOPLE in many different places have helped to make this book. Let me begin by acknowledging and sincerely thanking Karen Throssell, granddaughter of Hugo and Katharine, without whose cooperation this book would not have been possible. Not only did Karen believe in the project after we met, but she then helped in every possible way, including – as the literary executor of both her grandmother's and her father's estates – giving me access to their papers and permission to quote from their works.

I also wish to especially thank other members of the extended Throssell family for their help and interest. I especially thank Karen's brother Jim Throssell, as well as John Throssell, Bill Day and Kim Edwards. On the Prichard side of the family I thank Patten Headlam, who met me in Brisbane in 2009 and introduced me to his remarkable mother, now the late Katherine Beatrice 'Thea' Headlam, niece of Hugo and the last person able to recall him alive and well in the happy days with Katharine at Greenmount. Mrs Headlam died in April 2011, a week before her ninety-fifth birthday.

In Western Australia my initial enquiries were helped by Tim Lethorn at the State Records Office, Niamh Corbett at the Parliamentary Library, Gary Billingham in the Perth office of the National Archives of Australia and the friendly staff at the J.S. Battye Library of West Australian History. In the National Archives' head office in Canberra I was given every assistance by a staff led by the director-general Ross Gibbs and the assistant director-general Anne Lyons. I thank all at the National Library of Australia, especially Beth Lonergran in the Manuscripts Section, together with all those who toil behind the scenes to put invaluable material such as the Trove collection online.

I have been helped once again by that remarkable institution the Australian War Memorial, led by its director Major General Steve Gower and my old friend, tutor and walking companion, Gallipoli expert and head of military history Ashley Ekins. I also especially thank my friends Peter Burness, First World War expert and definitive writer on The Nek and the history of the Victoria Cross, and Nick Fletcher, who has helped me again with his prodigious knowledge of armaments, particularly this time with bombs and fuses. I also thank others from the Australian War Memorial including Dianne Rutherford, Garth O'Connell, Janda Gooding and Diana Warner, not forgetting veteran Bill Fogarty, pointing the way on Gallipoli to new insights. And I give a special thank you, too, to the Department of Veterans' Affairs, particularly Ian Kelly, Cheryl Mengan and Mike O'Meara.

On the other side of the world I would like to thank two Gallipoli experts from the Imperial War Museum for their help: the oral historian Peter Hart, whose work *Gallipoli* contains the words of many who fought there, and the principal historian Nigel Steel, for his kind permission to use an extract about Hill 60 from his book *The Battlefields of Gallipoli Then and Now*, which has been republished as *Gallipoli*. Phil Dutton from the museum's Department of Photographs and Films also helped.

I thank Foster Summerson, editor of the *Gallipolian* magazine in Britain, for his help and interest, and Graham Wilson, research officer of *Sabretache* magazine, the journal of the Military Historical Society of Australia. I also thank Claudia Edwards of the New South Wales branch of the Returned and Services League for unearthing invaluable 1930s copies of *Reveille* magazine with first-hand accounts by the men of Hill 60.

Back in Victoria, theatre historian Frank Van Straten helped to track down Henrietta Watson, while Daryl Povey and Jan Lier of the Casterton Historical Society led me to Stuart Ferrier, great-nephew of Sid Ferrier, forgotten hero of the 10th. I thank Stuart for his great help. Similarly, John Bate and Bruce McMaster of the Morwell Historical Society led me to Sheila Moody, Shirley Tanner and Rob de Souza-Daw for the story behind John Macmillan. In Emerald I received help from Jenny Coates at the Emerald Museum; Chris Britton, a descendant of Rose Charman; and Peter and Marion Verbeeten, the recent owners of the cottage that was Hugo and Katharine's love nest. It was a memorable day when the Verbeetens arranged to show granddaughter Karen Throssell and me over the home where Hugo and Katharine were together when the First World War ended.

A fortuitous meeting on Gallipoli with Marg and James Hewson of Allans Flat revealed the diary of Colonel Charles Dare, and Jennie Hollander provided more details from her family records. I again thank Doctor Ross Bastiaan, AM, of Merricks North for his interest and help. My old friend Jon Dwyer, an art expert, gave help and advice on portraits of Hugo, as did a colleague, Arthur Spartacus, while another old friend, expert numismatist and medal collector Gerhard Reimann-Basch shared his knowledge of the Victoria Cross.

Rachael Elliott searched the records of the Australian Club for when Hugo stayed there, and Donna Bishop and Tony Henningham from the Herald and Weekly Times Pty Ltd library were always there to help. Charles and Hamish Cameron and Anne Macarthur shared the records of Sergeant Major Colin Cameron of the 8th, killed at The Nek, while Jeff Pickerd, the expert on the 8th Light Horse, whose grandfather was badly wounded in that battle, was an old friend always willing to share his knowledge and research. So too was Kristin Otto, author of the fascinating book *Capital*, about Melbourne at the time of Hugo and Katharine; Kristin spurred me on every time I called on The Avenue bookshop in Albert Park.

My great friend and supporter Major General David McLachlan, AO, state president of the Victorian Branch of the Returned and

Services League, gave enormous assistance, which ranged from contacting his friend, the former governor-general Major General Michael Jeffery, AC, and prevailing on him to unearth a copy of the speech he made when dedicating the Throssell memorial in Northam in 1999. David also helped access old Returned Sailors and Soldiers Imperial League of Australia records on Hugo and the purchase of his Victoria Cross after it had been donated to the Campaign for Nuclear Disarmament.

At the Melbourne Shrine of Remembrance, I have always received help and support from many, including particularly Chief Executive Denis Baguley and Curator Jean McAuslan.

I particularly want to thank some medical friends for their expert advice. Doctor Peter Stratmann cast his experienced eyes over the reports of Hugo's deteriorating medical condition, while pioneer robotics surgeon Professor Tony Costello and his brother Brian, an ear, nose and throat specialist, examined the records and reviewed historical surgical procedures to come up with the surprising conclusion that Hugo was the victim of a botched operation in a London hospital and the operation's aftermath.

I acknowledge the strong support I received from Prince Alfred College, its headmaster Kevin Tutt and archivist Tony Aldous, and I thank the school for permission to use material from its official history and for supplying a range of illustrations to choose from. I also thank Chris Read in the Research Services of the State Library of South Australia for tracking down contemporary newspaper reports.

I was helped by an immense range of people in Western Australia, starting with the headmasters of major schools who led me to archivists Barbara Van Bronswijk at Wesley College, Peta Madelena at Scotch College, Rosemary Waller at Guildford Grammar School and Bill Edgar at Hale School. I want to particularly thank Andrew Pitaway, archivist for the City of Fremantle and First World War buff, and the amazing Sandra Playle, who guided me to Hugo's grave when we first met up at Karrakatta Cemetery, along with Chris and Shirley Durrant, two other amateur historians. For several years now Sandra, as well as researching family records and military history, has made it her business to visit a number of almost forgotten soldiers' graves in Karrakatta Cemetery, when she can, to try to keep them tidy. She places flowers on Hugo's grave each time she calls by.

I also acknowledge the contribution to research made by Neville Browning and Ian Gill in republishing Arthur Olden's original history of the 10th Light Horse, *Westralian Cavalry in the War*, and in privately publishing their own history, *Gallipoli to Tripoli*, in 2011. I thank them both for their help and for sharing their knowledge and the illustrations they have collected over time.

I want to thank A Squadron, 10th Light Horse Regiment, Es Salt Lines, Irwin Barracks, at Karrakatta, for making me so welcome. In particular may I single out Captain Duane Nurse, second-in-command, and Kaye Attrill, curator of the 10th Light Horse Unit Historical Collection. Some of the collection has now moved to the Army Museum of Western Australia at Fremantle, and it was there, when I first called, that I was helped by Director Graham Horne and later by Captain Wayne Gardiner, the assistant manager.

At Greenmount, when I first visited I was helped by Karen Kuentsler, the coordinator of the Katharine Susannah Prichard Writers Centre, and later by Shey Marque, the secretary. Barry Healey, who coordinated an annual Hugo Throssell Anzac Day Peace Commemoration for the Hills No War Alliance, was also of assistance.

I was helped in Jennacubbine by Joe and Cathy Bowen and Michelle Patton. In Northam, among those who went out of their way to be of assistance were the staffs at the Visitors Centre and Shire Offices, together with Kay Lansmeer, secretary of the Northam Historical Society; John Bird, the former principal of St Joseph's School (once the Fermoy mansion); Sue Dawson at the Northam Arts Centre; and John Proud, editor of the *Avon Advocate*.

Richard Brazier, who farms near Northam and is the grandson of Colonel Noel Brazier, kindly gave the family's permission to access and quote from the colonel's records. I pay tribute to the late Peter Brazier and his wife, Kerri, who also helped me.

I acknowledge and thank Professor Don Garden, environmental historian and president of the Federation of Australian Historical Societies and of the University of Melbourne, for his kind permission to use material from his definitive work *Northam: An Avon Valley History*. I also thank Elizabeth Forbes for permission to use extracts from the history written with her mother, Eva Braid, about the Koorda district, *From Afar a People Drifted*, and to Peter Bridge, publisher of the Hesperian Press, for his kindness in allowing me to use material from his book about the Larkinville gold rush, *The Eagle's Nest*. I also thank the Wyalkatchem Shire Council, publisher of the history *Wyalkatchem* by John C Rice, for its help. My appreciation and thanks also go to Jeff Sparrow for allowing me to use material from *Communism: A Love Story*, his biography of Guido Baracchi.

I particularly want to thank Merle Henning, secretary of the Koorda Historical Society, and her husband, Malcolm, for their kindness, hospitality and help. They insisted this total stranger stay at their wheat farm and took him in hand for a grand tour of the district, which included calling at Cowcowing and visiting John Martin, who now farms the flat paddocks that were once cleared by Hugo and Ric Throssell, when John's ancestors were the next-door neighbours.

The hunt for descendants of the men who fought with Hugo on Gallipoli was made easier with the help of many people. Brett McCarthy, editor of the *West Australian*, and Jenny Kohlen, compiler of the paper's popular 'Can You Help?' column provided the key to the door when they agreed to place an item in the *West* on 8 March 2010. As a result of this appeal and other enquiries in Western Australia and elsewhere I received invaluable help from (listed chronologically) Keith Morris, Phil Sullivan, Tony Bozich, Marg Mansfield, Kelly Graham, Jenny Quartermaine, Jim Livesey,

Robert and John Harper, Pam Praetz, Norm Corker, Nick Di Campi, Robert Hardwick, Wally Bamford, Beverley Campbell, Judy O'Neil, Margaret Paterson, John Sweetman, Lawrence Macnee, Joyce Brian, Shirley Mercer, Cindy Wood, Margot Bentley, Alan MacBean and Wendy Fry. I particularly want to thank Marg Mansfield and Jenny Quartermaine for supplying and allowing me to use the records of their ancestor Tom (the Bomb-Proof) Kidd, Jim Livesey for Syd's accounts, Shirley Mercer for the Gillam brothers, Wendy Fry for the records of her great-uncle Phil Fry, and an especial thank you to Margaret Paterson, who remembers her grandfather Brooke Stanley with such affection. Margaret not only provided me with valuable material for this book but as a result was herself moved to make a pilgrimage to Hill 60 to see today's pine grove where Brooke once fought and was wounded, later to be awarded the DCM for his bravery. Judy O'Neil, an amateur genealogist, provided immense help in tracking down descendants and, in some cases, even had the great pleasure of introducing the third generation of Gallipoli families to each other.

John Waller and his daughters, Michelle, Christine and Laura, at Boronia Travel, the battlefield specialists based in Victoria, organised all of my six visits to Gallipoli and are simply the best in the business. On Gallipoli I enjoyed the hospitality of Kemal and Çenk Pazarbasi when I stayed at the Kum Hotel, while in Kocadere Köyü, Eric and Özlem Goosens have also shared their hospitality and local knowledge at their Gallipoli Houses. Walking Gallipoli with Kenan Çelik OAM is one of life's great experiences, and I have also been helped by other professional Turkish guides including Serap Saçik Akis, Özgur Erdoğan, Hasan Gūnduḡar and Gençay Ücok.

Professor Geoffrey Blainey has, as ever, given me his wise counsel, suggestions and gentle encouragement, and my friend Les Carlyon, who wrote the definitive book *Gallipoli*, has always been my inspiration as a writer and available for consultation, willing to share his knowledge and give invaluable help and guidance.

John Tidey – author of *Class Act: A Life of Creighton Burns* – a class act himself, has always there for me through my life, and other friends who have given me support in different ways (in many cases listening patiently) this time around include Father Michael Elligate, Commander Gary Jamieson, John and Janet Calvert-Jones, Julian Clarke, Peter Blunden, Phil Gardner, Simon Pristel, Alan Armsden, Damon Johnston, Ed Gannon, Jill Baker, Russell Robinson, Geoff Easdown, Geoff Wilkinson, Neil Wilson, Patrick Carlyon, David McMahon, Hayley Taylor, Trudy Mickelburough, Carmel Evans, Steve Edwards, Campbell Sorell, Wayne Dowd, Denise Setton, Doctor Vera Polgar, Belinda Downie, Warren Joel, Pat Stone, and Vice-Chancellor Professor Linda Kristjanson and Professor Ken Chern at the Swinburne University of Technology.

Others who have helped me on this book's journey include Bruce Pike, Greg Zakharoff, David Williams, Norm Manners, Rear Admiral Ken Doolan, Air Vice-Marshal Alan Reed, John 'Pedro' Dunlop, Tony Barber, Kim Phillips, Gary Snowdon, Mick Stone, Brigadier Chris Roberts, Lieutenant Colonel Russell Linwood, Commander Terry Makings, Chief Petty Officer Doug Higgins and members of Melbourne's Turkish community, especially Umit Ugur and former Consul-General Aydin Nurhan.

I would like to thank Tom Gilliatt, director of non-fiction publishing at Pan Macmillan, for believing in the Hugo Throssell project, for his great encouragement and for driving the book towards publication with the wonderful team of professionals at Pan Mac, especially Managing Editor Catherine Day, copy editor Penny Mansley and Libby Turner who turned an unwieldy manuscript into this book, as well as publicist Jace Armstrong.

Lastly, I thank my family for putting up with me when I became absorbed once again in the place they call 'Sepia Land' and either disappeared on my travels or became lost in time among the books and papers in my study. To my amazing wife, Charlotte Kay, the original Southern Belle, and the Ballard family, my sons, James and Matthew, Marnie and Jade, and grandchildren, Kimberley and Jack. My love, always.

Bibliography

Books

A Brief History of the Çanakkale Campaign in the First World War (June 1914 – January 1916), The Turkish General Staff Directorate of Military History and Strategic Studies, Ankara, 2004.

Adam-Smith, Patsy, *The Anzacs*, Thomas Nelson, Melbourne, 1978.

Arthur, Max, *Forgotten Voices of the Great War*, Ebury Press, Great Britain, 2002.

—— *Symbol of Courage: A History of the Victoria Cross*, Sidgwick & Jackson, London, 2004.

Ashmead-Bartlett, Ellis, *Ashmead-Bartlett's Despatches from the Dardanelles*, George Newnes Ltd, London, 1915.

—— *Some of My Experiences in the Great War*, George Newnes Ltd, London, 1918.

—— *The Uncensored Dardanelles*, Hutchinson & Co., London, 1926.

Aspinall-Oglinder, CF, *Military Operations Gallipoli*, vols 1 & 2, History of the Great War, The Imperial War Museum in association with the Battery Press, Nashville, republished 1992 (1932).

Austin, Ron, *Cobbers in Khaki: The History of the 8th Battalion 1914–1918*, Slouch Hat Publications, Melbourne, 1975.

—— *Wounds & Scars: From Gallipoli to France, the History of the 2nd Australian Field Ambulance, 1914–1919*, Slouch Hat Publications, Melbourne, 2012.

Austin, Sue & Ron, *The Body Snatchers: The History of the 3rd Field Ambulance 1914–1918*, Slouch Hat Publications, Melbourne, 1995.

Australia in the Great War: Individual and Social Responses, New Century Antiquarian Books, Kew, 2003.

Australian Dictionary of Biography, Australian National University, Canberra, 1979, 1983 and online.

Australian Imperial Force: Staff Regimental and Graduation List of Officers, Government Printer, Melbourne, 1914.

Bain, Evan (Enie), *The Ways of Life*, Elder Smith Goldsborough Mort Limited, Perth, 1976.

Bean, CEW, *Anzac to Amiens*, Australian War Memorial, Canberra 1948.

—— *Gallipoli Mission*, Australian War Memorial, Canberra, 1948.

—— *Official History of Australia in the War of 1914–18*, vol. 1, *The Story of Anzac*, Angus & Robertson, Sydney, 1921.

—— *Official History of Australia in the War of 1914–18*, vol. 2, *The Story of Anzac*, Angus & Robertson, Sydney, 1924.

—— (ed.), *The Anzac Book: Written and Illustrated in Gallipoli by the Men of Anzac*, 3rd edn, UNSW Press, Sydney, 2010.

—— and Gullett, HS, *Official History of Australia in the War of 1914–18*, vol. 12, *Photographic Record of the War*, Angus & Robertson, Sydney, 1923.

Benson, Sir Irving, *The Man with the Donkey*, Hodder & Stoughton, London, 1965.

Billiere, Sir Peter de la, *Supreme Courage: Heroic Stories from 150 Years of the Victoria Cross*, Abacus, London, 2005.

Birdwood, Field Marshal Lord, *Khaki and Gown: An Autobiography*, Ward, Lock & Co Ltd, London, 1941.

Blainey, Geoffrey, *The Causes of War*, Sun Books, Melbourne, 1977.

—— *A Short History of the World*, Viking, Melbourne, 2000.

—— *A Shorter History of Australia*, Vintage, Melbourne, 2000.

Bou, Jean, *Australia's Palestine Campaign*, Army History Unit, Canberra, 2010.

Bourne, GH, *The History of the 2nd Light Horse Regiment, Australian Imperial Force, August 1914 – April 1919*, Northern Daily Leader, Tamworth, NSW, 1926.

Bowes, Joseph, *The Aussie Crusaders: With Allenby in Palestine*, Humphrey Milford, London, 1920.

Braid, Eva & Elizabeth Forbes, *From Afar a People Drifted: The Story of Koorda, a Wheatbelt Settlement*, Elizabeth Forbes, Perth, 1997.

Brenchley, Fred & Elizabeth, *Mythmaker: Ellis Ashmead-Bartlett, the Englishman Who Sparked Australia's Gallipoli Legend*, John Wiley & Sons Australia Ltd, Brisbane, 2005.

Bridge, Peter J, *The Eagle's Nest: Larkinville, the Golden Eagle, and the Great Depression*, Hesperian Press, Western Australia, 1999.

Bridger, Geoff, *The Great War Handbook: A Guide for Family Historians & Students of the Conflict*, Pen & Sword Books Ltd, Great Britain, 2009.

Broadbent, Harvey, *The Boys Who Came Home: Recollections of Gallipoli*, ABC Books, Sydney, 1990.

—— *The Fatal Shore*, Viking, Melbourne, 2005.

Browning, Neville & Ian Gill, *Gallipoli to Tripoli: History of the 10th Light Horse Regiment AIF, 1914–1919*, Quality Press, Western Australia, 2011.

Buley, EC, *Glorious Deeds of Australasians in the Great War*, Andrew Melrose Ltd, London, 1915.

Bull, Stephen, *Trench Warfare*, PRC Publishing, London, 2003.

Burness, Peter, *The Nek: The Tragic Charge of the Light Horse at Gallipoli*, Kangaroo Press, Kenthurst, NSW, 1996.

Butler, AG, *Official History of Australian Army Medical Services*, Australian War Memorial, Melbourne, 1938.

Cameron, David W, *Gallipoli: The Final Battles and Evacuation of Anzac*, Big Sky Publishing Pty Ltd, Sydney, 2011.

—— *'Sorry, Lads, but the Order Is to Go': The August Offensive, Gallipoli, 1915*, UNSW Press, Sydney, 2009.

Çanakkale Battles, Publication of Chief of General Staff Military History and Stategic Study, Ankara, 1998.

Cannon, Michael, *The Long Last Summer: Australia's Upper Class before the Great War*, Nelson, Melbourne, 1985.

Carlyon, Les, *Gallipoli*, Macmillan, Sydney, 2001.
—— *The Great War*, Macmillan, Sydney, 2006.
Carlyon, Patrick, *The Gallipoli Story*, Penguin, Melbourne, 2003.
Carthew, Noel, *Voices from the Trenches*, New Holland, Frenchs Forest, NSW, 2002.
Carver, Field Marshal Lord, *The National Army Museum Book of the Turkish Front 1914–18*, Pan Books, London, 2004.
Çelik, Kenan & Ceyhan Kok (eds), *The Gallipoli Campaign: International Perspectives 85 Years On*, Çanakkale Onsekiz Mart University, Çanakkale, 2005.
Clapham, Marcus (ed.), *Wordsworth Book of First World War Poetry*, Wordsworth, Herts, UK, 1995.
Clark, Manning, *On Gallipoli*, Melbourne University Press, Melbourne, 2005.
Cochrane, Peter (ed.), *Remarkable Occurrences: The National Library of Australia's First 100 Years, 1901–2001*, National Library of Australia, Canberra, 2001.
Cooper, Major Bryan, *The Tenth (Irish) Division in Gallipoli*, Herbert Jenkins Ltd, London, 1918.
Cramp, KR, *Australian Winners of the Victoria Cross*, McCarron, Stewart & Co. Ltd, Sydney, 1919.
Creagh, Sir O'Moore, VC & Humphris, EM (eds), *The Victoria Cross 1856–1920*, JB Hayward & Son, Great Britain, 1920.
Daley, Paul & Michael Bowers, *Armageddon: Two Men on an Anzac Trail*, Miegunyah Press, Melbourne, 2011.
Danisman, HB, *Day One Plus: Gallipoli 1915: 27th Ottoman Inf. Regt. vs Anzacs*, Denizler Kitabevi, Istanbul.
The Dardanelles: An Epic Told in Pictures, Polsur Limited, The Cornish Press, London, 1916.
Darley, TH (Major), *With the 9th Light Horse in the Great War*, Hassell Press, Adelaide, 1924.
Denton, Kit, *Gallipoli: One Long Grave*, Time Life Books, Sydney, 1986.
Downing, WH, *To the Last Ridge: the WWI Experiences of W.H. Downing*, Duffy & Snelgrove, New South Wales, 1998.

Drake-Brockman, H, *Australian Writers and Their Work: Katharine Susannah Prichard*, Oxford University Press, Melbourne, 1967.

Edgar, WJ, *Veldt to Vietnam (Haleians at War)*, Hale School, Western Australia, 1994.

Ekins, Ashley, *A Guide to the Battlefields, Cemeteries and Memorials of the Gallipoli Peninsula*, Australian War Memorial, Canberra, 2003.

—— (ed.), *1918 Year of Victory: The End of the Great War and the Shaping of History*, Exisle Publishing, Wollombi, NSW, 2010.

Ellis, Captain AD, MC, *The Story of the Fifth Australian Division*, Hodder & Stoughton, London, 1919.

Fasih, Mehmed (Lieutenant), *Gallipoli 1915 Bloody Ridge (Lone Pine) Diary*, Denizler Kitabevi Kaptan Yayinvilik, Turkey, 2003.

Fewster, Kevin, *Bean's Gallipoli*, Allen & Unwin, Sydney, 2007.

—— (ed.), *Frontline Gallipoli: C.E.W. Bean's Diary from the Trenches*, Allen & Unwin, Sydney, 1983.

—— with Vacihi & Hatice Hürmüz Başarin, *Gallipoli: The Turkish Story*, Allen & Unwin, Sydney, 1985.

Fitchett, Dr WH, *Deeds That Won the Empire*, Smith, Elder & Co., London, 1897.

Forrest, Kay, *The Challenge and the Chance: The Colonisation and Settlement of North West Australia, 1861–1914*, Hesperian Press, Western Australia, 1996.

From the Australian Front, Cassell & Company Ltd, London, 1917.

Gammage, Bill, *The Broken Years: Australian Soldiers in the Great War*, ANU Press, Canberra, 1974.

—— with David Williamson & Peter Weir, *The Story of Gallipoli: The Film about the Men Who Made the Legend*, Penguin, Melbourne, 1981.

Garden, Donald S, *Northam: An Avon Valley History*, Oxford University Press, Melbourne, 1979.

Gerardy, Trooper, *Australian Light Horse Ballads and Rhymes*, HH Champion, Melbourne, 1919.

Gibbs, RM, *A History of Prince Alfred College*, 2nd edn, Peacock Publications, South Australia, 2008.

Gilbert, PF, *Australia at War 1914–18*, Jacaranda Press, Brisbane, 1976.

Godley, General Sir Alexander, *Life of an Irish Soldier*, EP Dutton & Co. Inc., New York, 1939.

Goodacre, Janice M, *The Northam Post Telegraph Office 1872–1992*, Avon Valley Arts Society, Northam, 1992.

Grey, Jeffrey, *Australian Brass: The Career of Lieutenant-General Sir Horace Robertson*, Cambridge University Press, Melbourne, 1992.

Guldiz, Mehmet, *Atatürk: The Birth of a Nation*, Revas Publishing, Istanbul, 1998.

Gullett, HS, *Official History of Australia in the War of 1914–18*, vol. 7, *Sinai and Palestine*, Angus & Robertson, Sydney, 1940.

—— & Chas Barrett (eds), *Australia in Palestine*, Angus & Robertson, Sydney, 1919.

Hall, Rex, *The Desert Hath Pearls*, Hawthorn Press, Melbourne, 1975.

Hall, RJ, *The Australian Light Horse*, WD Joynt, Blackburn, 1968.

Hamilton, General Sir Ian, *Gallipoli Diary*, 2 vols, Edward Arnold, London, 1920.

—— *The Tragic Story of the Dardanelles: Ian Hamilton's Final Despatch*, George Newnes Ltd, London, 1916.

Hamilton, Jill, *From Gallipoli to Gaza: The Desert Poets of World War One*, Simon & Schuster, Sydney, 2003.

Hamilton, John, *Gallipoli Sniper: The Life of Billy Sing*, Macmillan, Sydney, 2008.

—— *Goodbye Cobber, God Bless You: The Fatal Charge of the Light Horse, Gallipoli, August 7th 1915*, Macmillan, Sydney, 2004.

Hammond, Ernest W, *History of the Eleventh Light Horse Regiment*, William Brookes, Brisbane, 1942.

Hart, Peter, *Gallipoli*, Profile Books, London, 2011.

Hay, Ian, *The Ship of Remembrance: Gallipoli–Salonica*, Hodder & Stoughton, London, 1926.

Hemingway, Ernest, *Hemingway on War*, Scribner, New York, 2004.

Hetherington, John, *Forty-Two Faces: Profiles of Living Australian Writers: Katharine Susannah Prichard*, FW Cheshire, Melbourne, 1962.

Hill, Anthony, *Soldier Boy: The True Story of Jim Martin, the Youngest Anzac*, Penguin, Melbourne, 2001.

Hochschild, Adam, *To End All Wars: A Story of Loyalty and Rebellion, 1914–1918*, Houghton Mifflin Harcourt, New York, 2011.

Hogue, Oliver, *Love Letters of an Anzac*, Andrew Melrose Ltd, London, 1916.

—— *Trooper Bluegum at the Dardanelles*, Andrew Melrose Ltd, London, 1916.

Holloway, David, *Endure and Fight: A Detailed History of the 4th Light Horse Regiment*, 4th Light Horse Memorial Association, Melbourne, 2011.

Hughes, WM, *'The Day' – and After: War Speeches of the Rt. Hon. W.M. Hughes, Prime Minister of Australia*, Cassell & Co. Ltd, London, 1916.

Hutchinson, Garrie, *Pilgrimage: A Traveller's Guide to Australia's Battlefields*, Black Inc., Melbourne, 2006.

Idriess, Ion L, *The Desert Column*, Angus & Robertson, Sydney, 1932.

Jalland, Pat, *Changing Ways of Death in Twentieth-Century Australia: War, Medicine and the Funeral Business*, UNSW Press, Sydney, 2006.

James, Robert Rhodes, *Gallipoli*, Pimlico, London, 1999.

Jones, Ian, *Australians at War: The Australian Light Horse*, Time Life Books, Sydney, 1987.

Keith Murdoch, Journalist, Herald and Weekly Times Ltd, Melbourne, 1952.

Kerr, Greg, *The Lost Anzacs: The Story of Two Brothers*, Oxford University Press, Melbourne, 1997.

—— *Private Wars: Personal Records of the Anzacs in the Great War*, Oxford University Press, Melbourne, 2000.

The Kiaora Cooee: The Magazine for the Anzacs in the Middle East 1918, facsimile collection, Cornstalk Publishing, Sydney, 1981.

King, Jonathan, *Gallipoli Diaries: The Anzacs' Own Story Day by Day*, Kangaroo Press, Sydney, 2003.

—— & Michael Bowers, *Gallipoli: Untold Stories from War Correspondent Charles Bean and Front-Line Anzacs*, Doubleday, Sydney, 2005.

Knyvett, Captain R Hugh, *Over There with The Australians*, Charles Scribner' Sons, New York, 1918.

Laffin, John, (ed.), *British Butchers & Bunglers of World War One*, Sutton Publishing, Great Britain, 1988.

—— *Damn the Dardanelles*, Osprey, Great Britain, 1980.

—— *Letters from the Front*, JM Dent, London, 1973.

Lawson, Henry, *My Army, O, My Army! And Other Songs*, Tyrrell's Ltd, Sydney, 1915.

Lee, John, *A Soldier's Life: General Sir Ian Hamilton 1853–1947*, Pan Macmillan, Great Britain, 2001.

Likeman, Lieutenant Colonel Robert, CSM, *Gallipoli Doctors*, Slouch Hat Publications, Melbourne, 2010.

Lloyd, Clem & Jacqui Rees, *The Last Shilling: A History of Repatriation in Australia*, Melbourne University Press, Melbourne, 1994.

Lock, Sydney, *To Hell and Back: The Banned Account of Gallipoli*, HarperCollins, Sydney, 2007 (originally *The Straits Impregnable*, Murray, London, 1917).

Macdonald, Donald, *The Bush Boy's Book*, Sydney J Andacott, Melbourne, 1911.

MacDonald, Lyn, *1915: The Death of Innocence*, Headline Book Publishing, London, 1991.

Macintyre, Stuart, *The Reds: The Communist Party of Australia from Origins to Illegality*, Allen & Unwin, Sydney, 1998.

Mackenzie, Compton, *Gallipoli Memories*, Cassell & Co. Ltd, London, 1929.

McKenzie, Donald, *Brave Deeds of the War*, Blackie & Son Ltd, Great Britain, c. 1919.

McKernan, Michael, *The Australian People and the Great War*, Thomas Nelson, Melbourne, 1980.

Macklin, Robert, *Jacka VC Australian Hero*, Allen & Unwin, Sydney, 2006.

McQueen, Humphrey, *Tom Roberts*, Macmillan, Sydney, 1996.

The Manual of Drill for the Mounted Troops of Australia, comp. Authority Intercolonial Committee, Victoria Barracks, Sydney, 1895.

Masefield, John, *Gallipoli*, William Heinemann, London, 1916.

Maxwell, Lieutenantt Joe, VC, *Hell's Bells and Mademoiselles*, Angus & Robertson, Sydney, 1928.

Moorehead, Alan, *Gallipoli*, Hamish Hamilton, London, 1956.

Murdoch, Keith, *The Gallipoli Letter*, Allen & Unwin, Sydney, 2010.

Nevinson, HW, *The Dardanelles Campaign*, Nisbet & Co., London, 1918.

Newman, Steve, *Gallipoli Then and Now*, Battle of Britain International Ltd, London, 2000.

Nicholson, Juliet, *The Great Silence 1918–1920: Living in the Shadow of the Great War*, John Murray, Great Britain, 2009.

Nicholson, Virginia, *Singled Out: How Two Million Women Survived without Men after the First World War*, Penguin, Great Britain, 2008.

North, John, *Gallipoli: The Fading Vision*, Faber & Faber Ltd, London, 1936.

Olden, Lieutenant Colonel ACN, DSO, *Westralian Cavalry in the War: The Story of the Tenth Light Horse Regiment, A.I.F., in the Great War, 1914–1918*, Alexander McCubbin, Melbourne, 1921 (with supplement compiled by Neville Browning & Ian Gill, reprint, Perth, 2001).

Oliver, Bobbie, *War and Peace in Western Australia: The Social and Political Impact of the Great War 1914–1926*, UWA Press, Perth, 1995.

Olson, Wes, *Gallipoli: The Western Australian Story*, UWA Press, Perth, 2006.

Oral, Haluk, *Gallipoli 1915 through Turkish Eyes*, Turkiye Is Kultur Bankasi Yayinlari, Istanbul, 2007.

Örnek, Tolga & Feza Toker, *Gallipoli*, companion to documentary, Ekip Film, Istanbul, 2005.

Otto, Kristin, *Capital: Melbourne When It Was the Capital City of Australia 1901–27*, Text Publishing Co., Melbourne, 2009.

Patriotic Poems: An Anthology, Jarrold Publishing, Great Britain, 1994.

Pearl, Cyril, *Anzac Newsreel: A Picture History of Gallipoli*, Ure Smith, Sydney, 1963.

Pederson, PA, *Images of Gallipoli: Photographs from the Collection of Ross J. Bastiaan*, Oxford University Press, Melbourne, 1988.

Perry, Roland, *The Australian Light Horse*, Hachette Australia, Sydney, 2009.

Portman, Pam & Sally Clarke, *Katharine Susannah Prichard: Her Place*, Gooseberry Hill Press, KSP Foundation, Western Australia, 2010.

Prichard, Katharine Susannah, *Black Opal*, William Heinemann, London, 1921.

—— *Child of the Hurricane: An Autobiography*, Angus & Robertson, Sydney, 1963.

—— *Coonardoo*, Jonathan Cape, London, 1929.

—— *The Earth Lover and Other Verses*, Sunnybrook Press, Sydney, 1932.

—— *Haxby's Circus: The Lightest, Brightest Little Show on Earth*, Jonathan Cape, London, 1930.

—— *Intimate Strangers*, Jonathan Cape, London, 1937.

—— *Kiss on the Lips: And Other Stories*, Jonathan Cape, London, 1932.

—— *The Pioneers*, Hodder & Stoughton, London, 1915.
—— *The Real Russia*, Modern Publishers, Sydney, 1934.
—— *Why I Am a Communist*, Current Book Distributors, Sydney, 1953.
—— *The Wild Oats of Han*, William Heinemann, Sydney, 1928.
—— *Working Bullocks*, Jonathan Cape, London, 1926.
Prior, Robin, *Gallipoli: The End of the Myth*, UNSW Press, Sydney, 2009.
Pugsley, Christopher, *Gallipoli: The New Zealand Story*, Penguin Group, New Zealand, 2008.
The Register of the Victoria Cross, This England Books, Great Britain, 1981.
Reid, Richard, *The Anzac Walk*, Department of Veterans' Affairs, Canberra, 2009.
—— *A 'Duty Clear before Us': North Beach and the Sari Bair Range, Gallipoli Peninsula 25 April–20 December 1915*, Department of Veterans' Affairs, Canberra, 2000.
—— *Gallipoli 1915*, ABC Books, Sydney, 2002.
Rhodes James, Sir Robert, *Gallipoli*, Pimlico, London, 1999.
Rice, John C, *Wyalkatchem: A History of the District*, Wyalkatchem Shire Council, Wyalkatchem, 1993.
Richardson, Lieutenant Colonel JD, DSO, *The History of the 7th Light Horse Regiment*, Radcliffe Press, Sydney, 1919.
Robertson, John, *Anzac and Empire*, Hamlyn Australia, Melbourne, 1990.
Robson, LL, *Australia and the Great War*, Macmillan, Sydney, 1969.
—— *The First A.I.F.: A Study of Its Recruitment 1914–1918*, Melbourne University Press, Melbourne, 1970.
Roland, Betty, *Caviar for Breakfast: A Russian Diary*, Quartet Books, Melbourne, 1979.
Scates, Bruce, *Return to Gallipoli*, Cambridge University Press, Melbourne, 2006.
Schuler, Phillip FE, *Australia in Arms*, T Fisher Unwin Ltd, London, 1916.

Smyth, Brigadier Sir John, *The Story of the Victoria Cross 1856–1963*, Frederick Muller Limited, London, 1963.

Snelling, Stephen, *VCs of the First World War: Gallipoli*, The History Press, Great Britain, 2010.

Sparrow, Jeff, *Communism: A Love Story*, Melbourne University Press, Melbourne, 2007.

Stanley, Peter, *Quinn's Post, Anzac, Gallipoli*, Allen & Unwin, Sydney, 2005.

Starr, Joan, *From the Saddlebags at War*, Australian Light Horse Association, Brisbane, 2000.

Steel, Nigel, *Gallipoli*, Pen & Sword Books, Great Britain, 2007 (originally published as *The Battlefields of Gallipoli Then and Now*, Leo Cooper, London, 1990).

—— & Peter Hart, *Defeat at Gallipoli*, Macmillan, London, 1994.

Stephens, Tony & Steven Siewert, *The Last Anzacs*, Allen & Kemsley, Sydney, 1996.

Stone, Norman, *World War One: A Short History*, Penguin, Great Britain, 2008.

The Story of the Anzacs: An Historical Account of the Part Taken by Australia and New Zealand in the Great War, James Ingram & Son, Melbourne, 1917.

Taylor, Phil and Pam Cupper, *Gallipoli: A Battlefield Guide*, Kangaroo Press, Sydney, 2000.

Throssell, Hugo, '*For Valour: Lieut Hugo Throssell's Story of a Memorable Fight*', Westralia Gift Book to Aid Y.M.C.A. Military Work & Returned Nurses Fund by Writers and Artists of Western Australia, VK Jones & Co., Perth, 1916.

Throssell, Karen, *The Pursuit of Happiness: Australia, 'The Empire', Anzus, Nuclear Disarmament and Neutrality*, documentary accompaniment to film, Hyland House, Melbourne, 1988.

Throssell, Ric, *For Valour*, Currency Methuen Drama Pty Ltd, Sydney, 1976.

—— *My Father's Son*, William Heinemann Australia, Melbourne, 1989.

—— *Wild Weeds and Wind Flowers: The Life And Letters of Katharine Susannah Prichard*, Angus & Robertson, Sydney, 1975.

Travers, Tim, *Gallipoli 1915*, Tempus, Great Britain, 2001.

Trudgeon, EM & GA Johnston, *For King and Country 1914–1918*, Longman, Cheshire, 1980.

Tyquin, Michael B, *Gallipoli: The Medical War*, UNSW Press, Sydney, 1993.

Von Sanders, General of Cavalry Limon, *Five Years in Turkey*, Naval & Military Press Ltd, Great Britain, (1919).

Walter, George (ed.), *The Penguin Book of First Word War Poetry*, Penguin, Great Britain, 2006.

Welborn, Suzanne, *Lords of Death*, Fremantle Arts Centre Press, Freemantle, 1982.

Wigmore, Lionel, *They Dared Mightily*, Australian War Memorial, Canberra, 1986.

Wilkinson, Norman, *The Dardanelles: Colour Sketches from Gallipoli*, Longman Green, London, 1915.

Wilson, LC, *History of the Fifth Light Horse Regiment from 1914 to October 1917*, Motor Press of Australia Ltd, Sydney, 1926.

Wood, James, *Chiefs of the Australian Army*, Australian Military History Publications, Loftus, NSW, 2006.

The Wordsworth Book of First World War Poetry, Wordsworth Editions Ltd, Great Britain, 1995.

Wright, Tony, *Walking the Gallipoli Peninsula*, Allen & Unwin, Sydney, 2010.

Wylie, Michael (ed.), *Patriotic Poems: An Anthology*, Jarrold, Great Britain, 1994.

Australian War Memorial Records

Australian Red Cross Wounded and Missing Enquiry Bureau files.

Embarkation Roll First World War, AWM 8.

Recommendation files for Honours and Awards, AWM 28.

Roll of Honour.

Charles EW Bean Collection
Diaries: AWM 38 3DRL 606.
Correspondence 1926–31: AWM 38 DRL 7953/27 Part 3; AWM 38 DRL 606 Item 32; AWM 38 3DRL 8043 Item 25; Series 5, 3DRL 8042 Item 21; AWM 41 1359.

Diaries and Papers
Lieutenant Colonel J Antill, AWM 3DRL 6458, AWM 419/3/14.
Lieutenant Colonel N Brazier, AWM 1DRL 0147.
Lieutenant WM Cameron, AWM 1DRL 0185.
Corporal H Foss, AWM 1DRL 0298.
Major T Kidd, AWM 3DRL 3525, AWM PR 82/137.
Captain JM McDonald, AWM 3DRL/6038.
Private M O'Reilly, AWM PR 02014.
Lieutenant Colonel C Reynell, PR 84/194.
Lieutenant H Throssell, AWM PR 85/361, 1DRL/0581.
Lieutenant E Worrall, AWM 1DRL/0607.

War Diaries
3rd Australian Light Horse Brigade, AWM 4 10/3.
8th Australian Light Horse Regiment, 10/13.
9th Australian Light Horse Regiment, 10/14.
10th Australian Light Horse Regiment, 10/15.
14th Infantry Battalion, 23/31.
15th Infantry Battalion, 23/32.
18th Infantry Battalion, 23/35.

JS Battye Library of West Australian History
Evelyn Bartlett Day, letter, 1928, PR4747.
JS Battye (ed.), The Cyclopaedia of Western Australia, 1913.
Swan Express, 1919, 1933.
HVH Throssell, Scrapbook, 1903–12, PR 5678–C/5.

BROTHERTON SPECIAL COLLECTIONS LIBRARY, LEEDS UNIVERSITY, LIDDLE COLLECTION, FIRST WORLD WAR

Troopers CH Williams and J Fitzmaurice, transcripts of interviews, 1974, Tape 254.

MITCHELL LIBRARY, SYDNEY

Captain Stanley Fox, diary, 1915, MSS 1170.

Corporal Oscar Rhodes, diary, 1915, MSS 1199.

Hugo Throssell, letter to Tom Roberts, 24 February 1916, MSA 2480/265.

NATIONAL ARCHIVES OF AUSTRALIA

First World War Service Records of Hugo Throssell and all other Australian soldiers mentioned in this book, Series B2455.

Hugo Throssell, Department of Veterans' Affairs case file, including evidence given at inquest held at Midland Junction, 11 December 1933, Series PP645/1, Control M5273.

Captain Hugo Throssell, VC, Intelligence reports, Series A6119, Control 42.

Hugo Throssell, WWI pay cards, Series K1143, Throssell H.

Katharine Susannah Throssell (nee Prichard), ASIO files, Series A6119.

NATIONAL LIBRARY OF AUSTRALIA

Papers of Katharine Susannah Prichard, MS 6201, Series 1, Folders 7–14; Series 7, Folder 1; Series 9, Folder 2; Series 12, Folders 2 & 3.

Ric Throssell, transcript of interview by Don Baker, 1992, Oral TRC 2794.

Newspapers: *Goomalling Dowerin Mail* and *Northam Advertiser*. Other newspapers including *Albany Advertiser*, *Kalgoorlie Western Argus*, the *Kalgoorlie Miner, Sunday Times*, *The West Australian*, *Western Mail* and *The Worker* accessed via Trove (www.trove.nla.gov.au).

ROYAL ARCHIVES, WINDSOR CASTLE

King George V, diary, December 1915.

STATE LIBRARY OF VICTORIA

Katharine Susannah Prichard, letters to Spencer Brodney, 25 May 1930 – 5 January 1962, MS Box 1286/6, MS 7859.

Newspapers from the State Library collection, *The Age*, *The Argus* and *The Herald*.

WESTERN AUSTRALIAN PARLIAMENTARY LIBRARY

Biographical details of Hon. George Throssell.

Debates congratulating Hugo Throssell on being awarded the VC.

Extracts of speeches made by George Throssell in the Legislative Assembly and the Legislative Council.

OTHER ARTICLES, PAPERS, REFERENCE SOURCES

Army Museum of Western Australia, Fremantle and 10th Light Horse Regimental Collection, Irwin Barracks, Karrakatta.

Bastiaan, Ross, historical plaques, Gallipoli.

Brazier, Noel M, 'Charge of the Third Light Horse Brigade, Gallipoli, August 7 1915', *Sunday Times*, 22 December 1929.

Campaspe Light Horse Association, incorporating the Australian Light Horse Training Manual of 1910, comp. Lindsay Gunston.

'Colonel Todd, DSO, CMG: A Great Soldier Goes West', *Swan Express*, 31 January 1919.

Cunneen, Tony, 'Massacre of the Innocents: The Destruction of the 18th Battalion at Hill 60, Gallipoli, 1915', *Australian Army Journal*, summer 2010, reprinted in *Digger*, June 2011.

Dare, CMM, 'Hill 60 Attack: Snipers' Toll', *Reveille*, 1 March 1931.

—— 'No Gains: Many Casualties', *Revielle*, 1 August 1932.

Ellis, Cath, 'Socialist realism in the Australian literary context: with specific reference to the writing of Katharine Susannah Prichard', *Battlers and Stirrers: Journal of Australian Studies*, vol. 21, issue 54–55, Routledge, Great Britain, 1997.

Emerald in Focus and other local history papers, Emerald Museum, Victoria.

Fitzpatrick, Sheila & Carolyn Rasmussen (eds), *Political Tourists: Travellers from Australia to the Soviet Union in the 1920s–1940s*, MUP Academic Monographs, Melbourne University Press, Melbourne, 2008.

Gallipoli Peninsula Historical National Park Guide, Republic of Turkey.

The Gallipolian: The Journal of the Gallipoli Association, Great Britain.

Jeffery, Michael, AC, MC, 'The Official Unveiling of the Hugo Throssell VC Memorial', Northam, 28 August 1999.

Kidd, TA, 'The Struggle at the Nek', *Reveille*, 1 August 1932.

Livesey, Trooper Syd, 'With the Light Horse on Gallipoli: An Albany Boy's Experiences', *Albany Advertiser*, 21, 28 June and 5 July 1916, contributed by Sandra Playle and reprinted from *Digger*: *The Magazine of the Families and Friends of the First AIF Inc.*, December 2009.

McDonald, Greg, 'Glory and Tragedy of Throssell, VC: The War Medal That Was Sold for Peace', *Australian Coin Review*, January 1985.

McKernan, Michael, 'Shell-Shocked: Australia after Armistice', *Momento*, National Archives of Australia, 2009.

McNair, John, *'Comrade Katya': Katharine Susannah Prichard and the Soviet Union*, MUP Academic Monographs, Melbourne University Press, Melbourne.

Macnee, HM, MC, DCM, 'Hand to Hand Heavy Bomb Fight', *Reveille*, 1 August 1932.

Manera, Brad, 'Hill 60: The Last Battle 29 August 1915', paper presented at Australian War Memorial symposium on the August Offensive, 2000.

Prince Alfred Chronicle, Prince Alfred College magazine.

Robertson, HCH, DSO, 'Hill 60: 10th Light Horse Attack', *Reveille*, 1 August 1932.

—— 'Hugo Throssell, VC', *Reveille*, 1 March 1934.

The Swan, Guildford Grammar School magazine.

Wartime: Official Magazine of the Australian War Memorial, Canberra.

Private Papers

James Bentley, Noel Brazier, John Brown, Colin Cameron, William Coonan, Harry Corker, Charles Dare, Amos 'Ned' Doust, Sutton 'Sid' Ferrier, Henry 'Phil' Fry, Hubert Gillam, Sydney Gillam, Gresley Harper, Wilfred Harper, Oscar Hassell, Tom Kidd, Syd Livesey, Colin MacBean, John 'Jack' Macmillan, Harry Macnee, Thomas 'Tommy' Renton, William Sanderson, Thomas 'Brooke' Stanley, Frank 'Ric' Throssell, Hugo 'Jim' Throssell, Alexander White.

Websites

Anzac Centenary: anzaccentenary.gov.au
Australian Army History Unit: army.gov.au/ahu
Australian Dictionary of Biography: adb.anu.edu.au
Australian Light Horse Association Forum: lighthorse.org.au/forum
Australian War Memorial: awm.gov.au
Axis History Forum: axishistory.com
Commonwealth War Graves Commission: cwgc.org
Department of Veterans' Affairs: dva.gov.au
Families and Friends of the First AIF Inc.: fffaif.org.au
Gallipoli and the Anzacs: anzacsite.gov.au
The Gallipoli Association: gallipoli-association.org
Great War Forum: 1914-1918.invasion.com/forums
Imperial War Museum: iwm.org.uk
Lost Leaders of Anzacs: anzacs.org
Military Historical Society of Australia: mhsa.org.au
National Archives of Australia: naa.gov.au
National Library of Australia: nla.gov.au
The Ships List: theshipslist.com
Shrine of Remembrance, Melbourne: shrine.org.au
The Spirits of Gallipoli Project: spirits-of-gallipoli.com

Index

MORE BESTSELLING TITLES FROM JOHN HAMILTON

Goodbye Cobber, God Bless You

On August 7th, 1915, men of the 3rd Light Horse Brigade staged one of the most tragic, brave and futile charges of the First World War. As part of the wider offensive to break out of the Anzac trenches at Gallipoli they attempted to storm a Turkish position called The Nek. It was a heavily fortified network of trenches, defended by artillery, machine-guns and thousands of men. To attack it the Light Horse, dismounted and acting as infantry, used nothing but fixed bayonets and raw courage. The first wave of troopers were killed within seconds, yet over the course of the next hour, three more lines went over the top, across the bodies of their dead and dying comrades, only to be cut down themselves. All of them knew they were about to die. None held back.

Just before the order was given to send the third line, Trooper Harold Rush turned to his mate standing next to him and said, 'Goodbye cobber, God bless you'. These words appear on the headstone, in the little cemetery near the scene of the charge.

John Hamilton's book is a brilliant recreation of the charge and the events that led up to it. Using their letters and diaries, he follows the soldiers who fought and died in this action from the recruiting frenzy of August 1914, to their training camps, to Egypt, to the peninsula itself, and finally to that fatal morning. It is a work of meticulous research and detail, which puts flesh on the bones of long dead men and boys. *Goodbye Cobber, God Bless You* is compelling, personal and painfully moving.

Praise for *Goodbye Cobber, God Bless You:*

'Hamilton has brought the story to life with great care and compassion ... a wonderful and accessible insight into one of the darkest chapters of Australian military history.' – Herald Sun

'... brilliant ... this book perfectly captures the ambiguity of war.' – Sydney Morning Herald

'a vividly personal and moving narrative ... compelling.' – Weekend Australian

'A sharp insight into the horror of war ... this is a book that is history from the trenches.' – Age

'It is hard to read Hamilton's account, accurate and measured, without deep sorrow and anger.' – Canberra Times

Gallipoli Sniper: The Life of Billy Sing

The Anzac battlefield on Gallipoli was made for snipers. Scrub, cliffs, spurs and hills meant that both Anzac and Turkish positions often overlooked one another. The unwary or unlucky were prey to snipers on both sides, and the sudden crack of a gunshot and instant death were an ever-present menace.

The most successful and most feared sniper of the Gallipoli campaign, with over 200 credited 'kills', was Billy Sing, a Light Horseman from Queensland.

John Hamilton has written an extraordinary account of a hidden side of the Gallipoli campaign – the snipers' war. Following Sing from his recruitment onwards, Hamilton takes us on a journey into the squalor, dust, blood and heroism of Gallipoli, seen from the unique viewpoint of the sniper. It is also a moving exploration of the aftermath of war, as Billy Sing returned home, a celebrated killer trying to adapt to a peacetime world.

Gallipoli Sniper is a powerful and very different account of World War One and its effect on those who fought in it.

Praise for *Gallipoli Sniper:*

'Read [*Gallipoli Sniper*] if you want to know what war is really like.' – Canberra Times

'Woven into the tragic tapestry of the Gallipoli campaign are some wonderful tales of skill, heroism and mateship, and *Gallipoli Sniper* is right up there with the best of them.' – Herald Sun

MORE BESTSELLING TITLES FROM PAN MACMILLAN

LES CARLYON

THE GREAT WAR

The Great War is Les Carlyon's extraordinary account of the Anzacs on the Western Front from 1916 to 1918. It combines a brilliant overview of this immense conflict with telling detail, stories, letters and diaries that breathe life into those terrible battles of 90 years ago.

In *The Great War* Carlyon has produced a masterpiece that takes the reader from the generals formulating strategy to the troops fighting cold, filth and the terror of sudden death in their trenches. Written with the same narrative skill, humanity, vivid recreation and meticulous research that made *Gallipoli* a number one bestseller, Les Carlyon's astonishing new book is an epic that will stand as the lasting and definitive history of Australia's involvement in the Great War.

Praise for *The Great War*:

'The writing is lucid, spare, wholly engrossing, thrilling.' – Bulletin

'Destined to become an Australian classic... *The Great War* is a deeply moving monument to a generation and what they endured. Read this book and weep.' – West Australian

'A remarkably lucid and powerful narrative... This is a seasoned writer at the height of his powers.' – Courier Mail

'Monumental... An emotional journey back to the Western Front that is at times almost unbearably poignant... In *The Great War* Carlyon has succeeded triumphantly in bringing back to life the essential character of the men of the First AIF in France. The Australians who fought long ago at Mouquet Farm, Messines, Polygon Wood and Passchendaele have gone, but, thanks to Carlyon, they are still with us. – Australian

Les Carlyon
Gallipoli

Les Carlyon's *Gallipoli* is one of the most successful, and critically acclaimed, works of Australian non-fiction published in the last decade. Carlyon's book brilliantly captures the tragedy of the Gallipoli campaign, and grippingly tells the story of what was to become our national myth. It is the product of meticulous scholarship and research, it is writing of the highest quality, but above all else it is a work of extraordinary storytelling that has the reader gripped from the very first page until the last. As one review pointed out, *Gallipoli* is the definitive history for whole new generation of readers.

Praise for *Gallipoli*:

'Beautifully written ... definitive.' – Sydney Morning Herald

'Anzac is no myth. It is history with a capital H, and in this magnificent book, Les Carlyon has made himself its historian ... a great big rich magic pudding of a book.' – Peter Ryan, Quadrant

'An absorbing, sometimes pungent but always incisive review of a triumph of the human spirit.' – Lieutenant General Peter Cosgrove, AC MC

'A new historical tour de force ... Les Carlyon's massive new book on this emotional subject is a deeply felt, compassionate work, beautifully written.' – John Hamilton

Cameron Forbes

The Korean War

The Korean War has never really ended. Although a ceasefire agreement was declared in 1953 after three years of savage fighting, the divided peninsula remains one of the world's most dangerous flashpoints.

It was a war that shaped the Cold War, the great ideological conflict of the twentieth century, and where Australia won its key strategic alliance with America. Diggers paid a blood price for it. The pattern was set for our involvement in Vietnam, Iraq and Afghanistan.

Cameron Forbes, acclaimed author of *Hellfire*, tells the story in a riveting narrative. Researced in China and Korea, and drawing on extensive interviews with Australian, American, Korean, Chinese and Turkish veterans, *The Korean War* reveals the conflict on all its levels – human, military and geopolitical. It will serve as the definitive history of Australia and the Korean War.

Praise for *The Korean War*:

'... intelligent, elegiac, cool and fair ... This us a big canvas: history written from above and below, from foxholes and political salons. It is a splendid piece of storytelling.' – Les Carlyon, Weekend Australian

'*The Korean War*, precisely because of its breadth and range, is what military history seldom is: wise, thoughtful, and graceful ... I profoundly enjoyed this book.' – Canberra Times

'Wonderful; anecdotally rich, authoritative, this book does belated justice to a brutal, complex war.' – Harry Gordon, Korean War correspondent

'... a masterful piece of research and storytelling ...' – Courier Mail